11. **Materials**

What materials need to be uniquely considered or rejected?
References throughout.

12. **Acoustic control**

What special acoustical considerations affect the design?
255–64

13. **Lighting design**

What special lighting (day and artificial) considerations affect the design?
265–78

14. **Interiors issues**

What special considerations (scale, color, texture, finishes, furnishings, special features)
affect the planning of interiors?
279–98

15. **Wayfinding**

What special factors determine signing systems?
287

16. **Preservation/modernization**

What special considerations (historical authenticity, infrastructure retrofit) arise when
renovating a facility of this type?
299–306

17. **International challenges**

On international projects, what special considerations influence marketing, design,
presentations, document production, and field presence?
307–24

18. **Operation and maintenance**

How will design decisions influence the operation and maintenance of the completed facility?
325–34

19. **Key cost factors**

What are the principal determinants of the total construction cost?
335–42

20. **Finances, fees, feasibility**

What are the typical techniques for financing this facility?
343–50

BUILDING TYPE BASICS FOR

senior living

BUILDING TYPE BASICS

Books are available for each of the following:

BANKS AND FINANCIAL INSTITUTIONS
Homer Williams

COLLEGE AND UNIVERSITY FACILITIES, Second Edition
David J. Neuman

ELEMENTARY AND SECONDARY SCHOOLS, Second Edition
Bradford Perkins

HEALTHCARE FACILITIES, Second Edition
Richard L. Kobus, Ronald L. Skaggs, Michael Bobrow, Julia Thomas, Thomas M. Payette, Stephen A. Kliment

HOUSING, SECOND EDITION
Joan Goody, Robert Chandler, John Clancy, David Dixon, and Geoffrey Wooding

PLACES OF WORSHIP
Nicholas W. Roberts

RECREATIONAL FACILITIES
Richard J. Diedrich

RESEARCH LABORATORIES, Second Edition
Daniel D. Watch, Stephen A. Kliment, Perkins & Will

TRANSIT FACILITIES
Kenneth W. Griffin

BUILDING TYPE BASICS FOR

senior living

Second Edition

PERKINS EASTMAN

WILEY

Cover image:
Building: Hebrew Senior Life, New Bridge on the Charles
Architect: Perkins Eastman Photograph: © Chris Cooper
Cover design: Mike Rutkowski

This book is printed on acid-free paper.

Published by John Wiley & Sons, Inc., Hoboken, New Jersey
Published simultaneously in Canada

For general information about our other products and services, please contact our Customer Care Department within the United States at (800) 762-2974, outside the United States at (317) 572-3993 or fax (317) 572-4002.

Wiley publishes in a variety of print and electronic formats and by print-on-demand. Some material included with standard print versions of this book may not be included in e-books or in print-on-demand. If this book refers to media such as a CD or DVD that is not included in the version you purchased, you may download this material at http://booksupport.wiley.com. For more information about Wiley products, visit www.wiley.com.

Library of Congress Cataloging-in-Publication Data:

Building type basics for senior living / Bradford Perkins, David J. Hoglund, Douglas King, Eric Cohen. — Second Edition.
    pages cm
Includes bibliographical references and index.
   ISBN 978-1-118-00745-7 (cloth); 978-1-118-33018-0 (ebk.); 978-1-118-33290-0 (ebk.); 978-1-118-49443-1 (ebk.); 978-1-118-49449-3 (ebk.)
   1. Older people—Dwellings—United States—Planning.   2. Old age homes—United States—Design and construction.   3. Adult day care centers—United States—Design and construction.   4. Nursing homes—United States—Design and construction.   5. Congregate housing—United States—Design and construction.   6. Life care communities—United States—Design and construction.   7. Retirement communities—United States— Design and construction.   I. Perkins, L. Bradford.
   NA7195.A4B85 2013
   725'.560973--dc23
                                                                                         2012027156

Printed in the United States of America
10 9 8 7 6 5 4 3 2 1

CONTENTS

Preface   xvii
Acknowledgments   xix

1. Senior Living Today   **1**
State of the Industry   1
   Demographics   2
   Accessibility   3
   Solutions   4
Design and the Aging Process   5
   Biological Aging   6
   Social Passage   10

2. Programming & Planning Guidelines   **13**
Understanding the Marketplace   13
Programming Space Guidelines   14
Community Based Options   14
   Typical users   14
   Sponsors, Settings, Payments, and Reimbursements   17
   Geriatric Outpatient Clinic   17
   Adult Day Care   24
Long-Term Care   33
   Typical Users and Care   33
   Sponsors and Owners   34
   Settings   34
   Program and Design   37
   Housing Models   38
   Long-Term Care Programs   44
   Program and Design   47
Hospice   60
   Users and Services   60
   History of Hospice   61
   Sponsors and Owners   61
   Purpose-Built Hospice Care Settings   61
   Program and Design   62
   Payment, Reimbursement, and Regulation   64
Assisted Living Residences   64
   Typical Users   64
   Sponsors and Owners   66
   Settings   66
   Program and Design   66

CONTENTS

Resident Unit	66
Unit Features	70
Unit Amenities	75
Planning Approaches	75
Payment, Reimbursement, and Regulation	79
Regulation	79
Trends and Innovations	80
Residences for Persons with Alzheimer's and Dementia	82
Typical Users	82
Sponsors and Owners	83
Settings	83
Program and Design	83
Design Considerations	90
Payment, Reimbursement, and Regulation	95
Trends and Innovations	95
Independent Living with Services	96
Typical Users	96
Sponsors and Owners	98
Settings	98
Program and Design	98
Unit Features	100
Key Planning Issues	105
Payment, Reimbursement and Regulation	105
Trends and Innovations	107
Continuing Care Retirement Communities	107
Typical Users	107
Sponsors and Owners	108
Settings	108
Organization	108
Program and Design	108
Market Considerations	110
Program Components	111
Assisted Living Residences	115
Long-Term Care	115
Payment, Reimbursement, and Regulation	117
Trends and Innovations	117
Active Adult Communities	119
Typical Users	119
Sponsors	119
Settings	119
Program and Design	120
Payment, Reimbursement, and Regulation	122
Marketing	123
Ownership	123
Summary	123

3. The Future of Senior Living — 125

Demographics — 125
  Population — 125
  Health and Services — 125
  Ethnic and Cultural Diversity — 126
Consumers' Expectations — 126
  Privacy — 126
  Choice — 127
  Value — 127
  Non-Institutional Environments — 127
  Security — 129
  Integration into Existing Communities — 129
Lifestyle Changes — 129
  Future Consumers — 129
  Fitness and Wellness — 133
  Lifelong Learning — 134
  Lifestyle Apartments — 135
Service Partnerships — 135
  Economic Pressures — 135
  Existing Housing and Care Facilities — 136
  Evolving Staffing Patterns — 137
  Sustainable Design — 137
  Leveraging Assets and Brand — 137
New Housing and Care Concepts — 139
  Green Houses and Small Houses — 139
  Culture Change — 139
Affordability — 141
  Reducing the Cost of Housing for Seniors — 142

4. Project Process and Management — 149

Planning, Design, and Implementation Process — 149
  Strategic Planning and Preliminary Definition of Need — 149
  Feasibility Analysis — 150
  Selection and Organization of Project Team — 150
  Programming and Predesign — 153
  Schematic Design — 155
  Obtaining Approval and/or Financing — 158
  Design Development — 159
  Construction Documentation — 159
  Selection of the Construction and FF&E
    Installation Teams and Purchasing — 160
  Construction and Installation — 162
  Occupancy — 162
Common Problems and Cautions — 162
  Failure to Plan — 163

CONTENTS

Unclear, Timid, or Unrealistic Goals 163
Inadequate Client Leadership 163
Selecting the Wrong Project Team for
the Wrong Reasons 163
Ineffective Project Management 164
Tackling Issues Sequentially, not Concurrently 165
Poor Management of the Public Approval Process 165
Not Prioritizing Quality 165
Failure to Plan for Maximal Staffing Efficiency 166
Poor Cost Management 166
Failure to Plan for Maintenance 166
Conclusion 167

**5. Site Planning, Parking, and
Landscape Design** **169**
Site Size 169
Relationship to Adjacent Land Uses 171
Vehicular Circulation 171
Parking 173
Landscape Design 173

6. Building Codes **183**
Codes and Regulations 184
Federal 184
State 185
Local 186
Reference Standards 186
Energy Codes and Sustainable Design Standards 186
Regulatory Issues 186
Life Safety 187
Space Standards 188
Building Systems and Construction Practices 188
Public Policy 188
Accessibility 189
Enforcement 190
Fiscal and Bidding Controls 190
Land Use Policy 190
Waivers 191
Conclusion 192

7. Sustainability **193**
Market Expectations 193
Calculating Cost Benefit 195
Years to Payback 196
Life Cycle Cost 196

Strategies for Sustainability 196
  Create Sustainable Sites 197
  Save Water 198
  Reduce Use of Fossil Fuels 200
  Heating, Ventilation, and Air-Conditioning 200
  Lighting and Daylighting 202
  Alternative Energy Sources 203
  Smart Use of Materials and Resources 203
  Adaptive Reuse 204
  Indoor Environmental Quality 204

8. Structural Systems **205**
Considerations 205
  Program and Concept 205
  Applicable Codes 205
  Potential Code Changes 206
  Flexibility 206
  Soil Conditions 207
  Lateral Forces 207
  Impact on Finished Ceiling and Building Height 207
  Material Delivery and Construction Timing 208
  Local Construction Industry Preferences and Capabilities 208
  Ease of Construction and Schedule 208
  Life Cycle Cost 208
  Cost Impact on Other Systems 208
  Appearance and Aesthetics 209
Structural System Types 209
  Wood Frame 209
  Structural Metal Studs 209
  Masonry Bearing Wall 210
  Steel Frame and Concrete Plank 211
  Composite Steel 211
  Precast Concrete 211
  Concrete Frame 211
  Long-Span Structures 212
  Pre-Engineered Structures 212
  Combined Systems 213

9. Mechanical, Plumbing, Fire-Protection,
And Electrical Systems **215**
The Interior Environment and Comfort for an Aging Population 215
  Mechanical/Hvac 215
  Plumbing 215
  Fire Protection 216
  Electrical 216

CONTENTS

Program and Concept 216
Applicable Codes 216
    Mechanical and Hvac 216
    Plumbing 217
    Fire Protection 217
    Electrical 217
Program Impact on System Selection 217
    Mechanical and Hvac 218
    Plumbing 218
    Fire Protection 219
    Electrical 219
Finished Ceilings and Building Height 219
    Mechanical and Hvac 219
    Plumbing 219
    Fire Protection 220
    Electrical 220
    Flexibility 220
Construction 220
    Materials Delivery and Timing 220
    Local Construction Capabilities and Preferences 220
    Ease of Construction and Schedule 220
    First Cost and Life Cycle Cost 221
    Cost Impact on Other Systems 221
    Appearance and Aesthetics 221
    Noise and Vibration 221
    Controls 221
Mechanical and Hvac System Options 222
    Packaged Terminal Air-Conditioning Units 222
    Packaged Rooftop Units 223
    Air-To-Air Heat Pumps 224
    Water Source Heat Pumps 224
    Variable Refrigerant Volume Systems 226
    Fan Coil Systems 226
    Dehumidification Systems 226
Ventilation 227
    Fresh Air Requirements 227
    Filtration 227
    General Exhaust 228
    Kitchen Exhaust/Grease Ducts 228
    Laundry and Lint Traps 228
Plumbing 229
    Fixtures and Fittings 229
    Hot Water Distribution 229
    Metering 229
    Rainwater 230

Fire Protection   230
   Fire Alarm   230
   Fire Pumps and Backflow Preventers   230
   Wet Systems   231
   Dry Systems   231
Electrical Distribution   231
   Transformers   231
   Switchgear   232
   Metering   232
Emergency Power   232
Lighting   233

10. Communications and Low-Voltage Electrical Systems   235
Systems Proliferation   235
   Emergency Response/Nurse Call   236
   Movement Alarms   236
   Access Control   237
   Visual Monitoring   237
   Telecommunications   237
   Television   238
   Internet Access   238
   Networks and Intranets   238
   Wireless Technology   238
   Audiovisual   239
   Point-Of-Sale Systems   239
   Operations Systems   239
Trends   240

11. Special Technologies   241
Remote Biometric Monitoring Systems   241
   Personal Locator Systems   241
   Fall Detection   242
   Telemedicine   242
   Web Portals   243
   Virtual Reality Therapy   243
   Remote Learning   243
   Circadian Lighting   244

12. Products And Equipment   245
Medical Equipment   245
Universal Design   245
Mobility Devices   246
Food Service   246
   Adult Day Care   246
   Long-Term Care   246

CONTENTS

Assisted Living   248
Independent Living   248
Special Care and Dementia   248
Kosher Preparation   248
Bathing Equipment   249
Tubs   249
Showers   251

13. Acoustics   255
Key Acoustical Considerations   255
Noise Reduction Coefficients   257
Sound Transmission Class Values   257
Design Guidelines for Specialized Spaces   258
Lobbies   258
Dining Areas   258
Multipurpose Spaces, Spiritual Areas, Auditoriums,
   and Media Theaters   260
Bathing Areas and Other Hard-Surfaced Spaces   260
Indoor Pool Spaces   261
Mechanical and Electrical Systems
   and Mechanical Rooms   261
Hearing-Impairment Guidelines and
   Code Requirements   262

14. Lighting Design   265
Light Levels, Reflectance Values, and Glare   267
Lamping Options   268
Linear Fluorescent Lamps   268
Compact Fluorescent Lamps   268
Halogen Lamps   269
Other Lamp Types   269
Windows and Daylighting   269
Design Guidelines for Specialized Spaces   269
General Guidelines   269
Common Areas   270
Corridors   271
Resident Living Spaces   273
Conclusion   276

15. Interior Design   279
The Design Process   279
Trends   280
Color Theory   286
Wayfinding   287
Materiality   287

Interior Design Guidelines   289
    Flooring   290
    Other Floor Coverings   292
    Wall Coverings   292
    Windows and Window Coverings   295
Furniture and Furnishings   295
    Definition   295
    Trends   295
    Specifications   296
    Sustainability   297
Process   298

16. **Renovation, Restoration,**
    and Adaptive Reuse   **299**
Long-Term Care Facilities   299
Assisted Living Facilities   300
Independent Living Facilities   300
Cosmetic Renovation   301
Moderate Renovation   301
Major Renovation   301
    Key Questions   304
    Integrated Scenario Planning   304
Adaptive Reuse   305
    Key Questions   305

17. **International Challenges**   **307**
Service Development   309
Programming and Design   310
Service and Socialization   313
Process   313
Aging at Home   314
Country-Specific Issues   315
    China   315
    Japan   318
    India   318
    Thailand   323
    The Americas   323
    Europe   324
Conclusion   324

18. **Operation and Maintenance**   **325**
Introduction   325
Operations Costs   326
Ongoing Operating and Maintenance Costs   327
Durability, Useful Life, and Replacement Costs   329

Operational Efficiency	329
Cleanliness, Operations Quality, and Design	333

19. Cost Management **335**
Cost Management Program	335
Relative Costs	336
Value Engineering and Life Cycle Cost Analysis	336

20. Finances and Feasibility **343**
Ten Steps to Financing	343
Preliminary Feasibility Planning and Analysis	344
Potential Capital Structures and Sources of Financing and Equity	344
Financing Team and Method	345
Government Approvals	346
Financial and Market Feasibility Study	346
Underwriting	346
Preparing for Closing	348
Closing	348
Project Costs and Covenants	348
Ongoing Reporting of Performance and Covenant Compliance	348
Financing Variations for Senior Settings	349
Assisted Living	349
Skilled Nursing Facilities	349
Independent Living	349
Continuing Care Retirement Communities	350

Appendix A: Unit Types and Sizes for Senior Living	**351**
Appendix B: Building Net-to-Gross Factors for Senior Living	**352**
Appendix C: Geriatric Clinic: Typical Program Components	**353**
Appendix D: Sample Large Outpatient Clinic Program	**354**
Appendix E: Sample Enhanced Retirement Community Clinic Program	**355**
Appendix F: Adult Day Care: Sample Program for 50 Participants	**356**
Appendix G: Long-Term Care Gross Area per Bed Guidelines	**358**

Appendix H: Typical Long-Term Care Program Components   359

Appendix I: Sample Program: Long-Term Care, 126 Bed, 4-Story (and Basement) Neighborhood/Household Model   360

Appendix J: Freestanding 75-Unit, 3-Story Assisted Living Facility with 20-Bed Memory-Support Neighborhood   366

Appendix K: Sample Program for 40-person Memory-Care Residence   369

Appendix L: Sample Program for Independent Living with Services Building—150 Units, 4 Stories, 2 Wings   371

Appendix M: CCRC Program   375

Appendix N: Enhanced CCRC Therapy Program   383

Glossary   385

Bibliography and References   395

Index   399

PREFACE

This is the second edition of *Building Type Basics for Senior Living*. Since the first edition was published in 2003, the planning and design of facilities for the aging have continued to evolve. Many members of the baby boom generation have had to learn about the available services and facilities as they assisted their aging parents. What they have found in many communities across North America has left them unsatisfied and concerned. Too many of the existing options for their parents, and eventually for them as well, do not provide an attractive, supportive, and affordable lifestyle.

Over the last three decades, new and improved models for senior living and care have emerged to supplement the increasingly obsolete existing stock of nursing homes and "old age homes." The public has become aware that there are now alternatives, but the supply of well-planned and designed facilities has not kept up with the rapid increase in the number of frail and/or cognitively impaired elderly needing housing and care. In 2012, there were 40 million Americans over 65. Thanks to the baby boom, demographers predict that number will increase to 63 million by 2025. Moreover, 8 million will be over 85—an age at which most people need a supportive environment.

In the decade since the first edition of this book was published, there have been many creative responses to the specialized needs of the aging that have dramatically changed what sponsors and their design teams need to know about this specialized building type. Among the major new trends described in this edition are the "small house" and Green House movements, which have rapidly gained popularity across the United States; the widespread repositioning of existing facilities to respond to the many changes in the market—including the growing number of people moving into senior living facilities when older and frailer; new technologies, such as tele-health monitoring, that address specific senior living issues; the growing number of senior living options being developed in urban areas; and the explosive growth in interest in senior living facilities outside the United States.

This second edition not only includes another decade of experience in the field but also has incorporated contributions and experience from all 13 of Perkins Eastman's offices, as well as our national senior living leadership group. Moreover, it includes material from a number of other leading specialists in this field. As with the first edition, this book has been written and illustrated to provide sponsors, their design teams, and other interested readers with an introduction to the major issues and choices facing any organization planning a senior living building program.

The need for well planned and designed senior living facilities is not limited to North America, Western Europe, Japan, and other highly developed countries. China and India are facing even more rapid increases in their older age populations. In China, for example, the over-60 age group is projected to reach 436 million by 2050. China's one-child policy has seriously weakened one of the traditional pillars of its senior care system, and little else exists to provide an appropriate environment for those older Chinese who need specialized housing and care. Both the public and the national leadership are aware of this problem and are scrambling to develop appropriate responses. They see the United States as the only country that has tried to respond to the specialized needs of an aging population on a large scale. They recognize some of the weaknesses of the U.S. model, and they are adapting it to their needs. India and many other rapidly developing countries are also beginning to address the needs of their older citizens.

Ten years from now it is likely that the United States designers will be learning from their experiences overseas. Given the size of the worldwide need for attractive, affordable supportive senior living, the demand for informed interest and action will only increase. The many people who worked on the development of this book hope that it will be a useful contribution to future senior living building programs both in North America and abroad.

Bradford Perkins FAIA, MRAIC, AICP

Perkins Eastman

ACKNOWLEDGMENTS

This is the second edition of *Building Type Basics for Senior Living.* The first edition was authored by the senior living principals and staff of Perkins Eastman Architects.

This edition's lead editors were Bradford Perkins, FAIA, and David Hoglund, FAIA. Most of the first drafts of the revised chapters in this edition were written by the following senior living leaders of Perkins Eastman, including:

Laurie Butler

Dan Cinelli, FAIA

Stefani Danes, AIA

Susan DiMotta, AAHID, IIDA

David Hance, AIA

Joseph Hassel

Lori Miller

Leslie Moldow, FAIA

Richard Rosen, AIA

Martin Siefering, AIA

Gary Steiner, AIA

In addition, the chapter on site design has a significant contribution from David Kamp, FASLA, of LF Dirtworks, PC Landscape Architecture. The chapter on finance, fees, and feasibility has contributions from Plante Moran.

Sarah Mechling did her usual excellent job coordinating the photographs, drawings, and graphics. Thanks go to Katarzyna Dabrowska for her help with the plans and July Chan for her help with the graphics. Rachael Perkins Arenstein efficiently acted as research assistant, assistant editor, and sheepdog for this herd of cats.

CHAPTER 1

SENIOR LIVING TODAY

STATE OF THE INDUSTRY

Since the first edition of *Building Type Basics for Senior Living* in 2004, the senior living industry has expanded and diversified in order to address demographic change. Recent U.S. census numbers reveal a variety of societal transformations. The industry has responded by shifting its focus from the World War II generation to the "silent generation" (some would argue they are not so silent) that matured and raised families in the burgeoning suburbs and witnessed the increase in product branding, the expansion of consumerism, and the invention of fast food. Baby boomers are altering the equation once again, as they seek options for their parents' care and envision themselves growing old. Products of postwar consumerism, they have expectations about services—and their quality and delivery—that do not mesh with the way healthcare and aging services have traditionally been provided.

The economic realignment that began in 2008 has also forced consumers (and sponsors) to reexamine available retirement options and plan for the kind of financial security they will need for services and settings as they approach 80 years of age. For the past decade, there has been a rise of community-based options with retirement living facilitated by technology. Remaining at home is not only a preference but for many is the only financially viable option. *Choice, variety,* and *control* are now embedded in the industry's lexicon; paging through retirement living sales brochures and websites affirms this evolution. No longer is it the facility or organization dictating products, services, and rules. Today, consumers are challenging that prescription, and facilities are responding to these new expectations.

Retirement living providers continue to expand wellness, dining, and recreation options in response to demands for more choices and a healthier lifestyle. Options that emerged at the beginning of the century continue to develop, with urban (sometimes high-rise), university- and college-affiliated, and co-housing solutions gaining traction in many markets. Traditional life-care models of retirement living are being challenged by more flexible entry criteria, and the transition to such communities is being handled in new and novel ways. Long-term care has evolved: a wide range of paradigms, including the "Green House" and "small house," are replacing the traditional neighborhoods and households. The demand for sustainable and green design is growing to meet the new market's expectations of lower operating costs, healthy surroundings, and a concern for the environment.

Research metrics have also begun to shape the industry because quantifiable outcomes are expected. It is not enough to tell consumers their quality of life will improve. They want specifics: Will they fall less? Will their stress and blood pressure decrease? Will they have more friends and less depression? Government policies for reimbursing healthcare costs have set the stage for outcome-based measures, and these policies are trickling into long-term care. The Internet has made it possible to share consumer opinions—good and bad—of everything from washing machines to hotel rooms. Are senior living environments far behind?

Demographics

According to the 2010 U.S. Census, 13 percent of the population—over 40 million people—is 65 or older. That represents an increase of more than 5 million since the 2000 Census and makes this the fastest-growing age group: 15 percent per decade. Demographic projections for 2025 show the influence of the baby boom, with the population of those over 65 growing to over 63 million and that of those over 85 to over 8 million. By 2030, approximately 19 percent of the population in the United States, or 71 million people, will be over 65 (fig. 1-1). More people are living longer, and the growth of the over-100 age group is even more startling. The leading edge of the boomers, who are now 65, is almost 80 million strong.[1] Meeting the housing and care needs of this rapidly growing segment of the population has become a major challenge for those setting public policy, sponsors, operators of facilities for aging adults—and those in the design professions.

These demographic trends are not unique to the United States. The world's population aged 65 and over is expected to increase

▶ *Figure 1-1 Total number of persons age 65 or older in the United States, by age group, 1900 to 2050 (in millions).* U.S. Census Bureau, Decennial Census Data and Population Projections

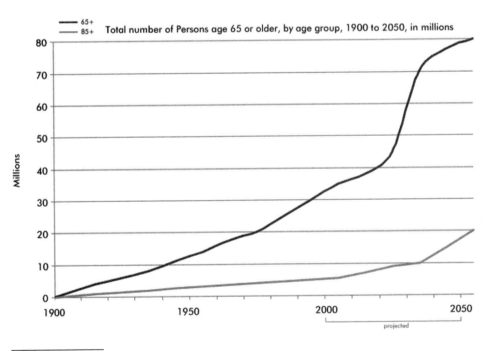

[1] Statistics have been drawn from the following U.S. Census Bureau publications: Grayson K. Vincent and Victoria A. Velkoff, *The Next Four Decades: The Older Population in the United States: 2010 to 2050, Population Estimates and Projections* (May 2010), http://www.census.gov/prod/2010pubs/p25-1138.pdf; Lindsay M. Howden and Julie A. Meyer, *Age and Sex Composition: 2010* (May 2011), http://www.census.gov/prod/cen2010/briefs/c2010br-03.pdf; and Carrie A. Werner, (November 2011) The Older Population: 2010, 2010 Census Briefs, http://www.census.gov/prod/cen2010/briefs/c2010br-09.pdf.

from 6.9 to 16.4 percent, or approximately 1.53 billion people, by 2050.[2] European countries are also dealing with a rapidly aging population and low birth rates. The rising cost of care, services, and housing for the aging has led to public policy changes in many countries. Asia is preparing for what many are referring to as the "aging tsunami." In Japan, for example, there are already more people over the age of 60 than under the age of 29. By 2050, people 65 and over will have increased to 33–35 percent of the population[3]. China currently has approximately 169 million individuals over 60 years of age (12.5 percent), but by 2050 this number is expected to increase to 31 percent of the population.

In many countries, these demographic changes are coupled with transformations in the traditional multigenerational family. Older adults are living alone, using informal means of meeting their needs for services or relying on primary-care health services that offer inadequate support for their special requirements.

The United States is also facing the demographics of a more diverse population. Minority ethnic groups, particularly Hispanics and Asians, will present unique

> The huge baby boom generation, which transformed public and private institutions… is poised to change our communities once again.
>
> American Society on Aging 2009

cultural requirements, and new affinity groups will appear as communities develop around religion, lifestyle, and even sexual orientation.

The increasing number of older people, combined with changes in the way they want to live out their later years and their expectations of a high-quality life, is creating the need for new care and housing options. New models of senior care and housing conceive of these environments not simply as healthcare facilities, but as seniors' homes. In addition, the search is on for new care models that support people at home longer and maintain them in the least restrictive (and least costly) conditions possible.

Accessibility

Such changes demand a flexible system that combines services with living arrangements. The aging in all countries have unique needs that must be recognized by those who provide them with care and housing. Most older adults will never occupy a residence designed specifically for older adults; most will stay at home and rely on family or community-based services. The built environment as a whole—including airports, shopping malls, and urban centers—must be planned and designed to respond to the large and growing segment of the population who will, over time, move a little more slowly, grasp a little less tightly, react a little less quickly, and process information differently. The environment has a greater impact on the quality of life of those who require a

---

[2] United Nations Department of Economic and Social Affairs, Population Division, World Population Ageing 1950–2050 (March 23, 2010), ch. 2, "Magnitude and Speed of Population Ageing," http://www.un.org/esa/population/publications/worldageing19502050/pdf/80chapterii.pdf, and ch. 4, "Demographic Profile of the Older Population," http://www.un.org/esa/population/publications/worldageing19502050/pdf/90chapteriv.pdf.

[3] National Institute of Population and Social Security Research, Japan, Population Projections for Japan: 2001–2050 (n.d.), ch. 1, "Summary of the Japanese Population Projection," http://www.ipss.go.jp/pp-newest/e/ppfj02/suikei_g_e.html.

more supportive setting than it does on any other major demographic group. If properly designed, a senior living facility can contribute positively to an older person's independence, dignity, health, and enjoyment of life. If poorly planned and detailed, it can imprison, confuse, and depress.

In recent decades, the direct impact of design on the aging has been more widely recognized by both the general public and design professionals. Previously, the frail elderly who could no longer live in their own homes had few, if any, good alternatives. Most of the very old saw a shared room at an "old folks' home" as the only option. For the majority, it was a dreaded inevitability. Tens of thousands of families can tell stories of the trauma of having to place Mom or Dad in an institution. By 1980, there was a growing demand for more attractive options that would meet health- and support-service needs in a more agreeable residential setting. Lifestyle options for retirement have had to adapt to a changing clientele who are older, with more needs, but who expect higher-quality housing and activities than even a decade ago.

Solutions

Older adults are looking for more options. Today's 70-year-olds are better educated, generally have more money than their predecessors, and expect to be motivated physically and stimulated intellectually. The great recession of 2008–2010, and continued slow economic growth, will certainly change available financial resources for future seniors. Young boomers born in the late 1950s and early 1960s may have enough time to rebuild a portion of their financial portfolio, but their older siblings may need to delay retirement and alter their lifestyle expectations. Portions of the "silent generation" with higher-risk investments and facing declining real estate

values have already decided to sit on the sidelines and look for less costly options. Affordability has always been a challenge for this industry, and it may be redefined to include a much broader swath of the older demographic who have assets that exceed the threshold for traditional subsidized housing but are insufficient for proper preventive healthcare and services.

This book provides an overview of the major issues involved in the planning, design, and development of specialized environments for this new group of aging Americans. Specifically, the book describes the issues associated with each of the 10 major building types within the general framework of design for aging. Chapter 2 has also been expanded to include specialized hospice programs and to review community-based options, some of which are driving new models of services and settings. The following are general definitions of these 10 types. Please see the following sections for more detailed descriptions, as well as the distinctions among the types.

1. *Community-based options.* Historically, the delivery of services to people in their homes through a visiting nurse or companion service. Beacon Hill Village—and the Villages Movement itself—has expanded this philosophy to one of keeping seniors in their neighborhoods by connecting them to service providers in the community.
2. *Geriatric outpatient clinic.* A specialized medical clinic that focuses on the physical, psychological, social, and medical needs related primarily to aging.
3. *Adult day care/adult day health.* A daily program that provides a blend of social and medical support during the day for those still residing in their own homes or with their families.

4. *Nursing home/long-term care.* A medically oriented residence for very frail seniors requiring 24-hour care.

5. *Hospice.* A specialized program to care for and support individuals and their families at the end of life.

6. *Assisted-living residence.* A catchall name for a wide variety of programs that balance housing with the support of activities of daily living (ADLs) such as bathing and dressing.

7. *Dementia/Alzheimer's care.* A specialized program and setting crafted to meet the special needs of people with impairment of abilities related to thought, perception, and memory.

8. *Independent/residential living apartments.* Housing with services designed for the elderly, such as the provision of meals, housekeeping, and activities.

9. *Continuing-care retirement community (CCRC).* Retirement living that provides a full spectrum of services and living accommodations, from independent living through assisted living and nursing services.

10. *Active adult community.* A lifestyle model that provides an appropriately designed residence linked to active recreation, entertainment, and continuing education options, as well as proximity to healthcare, fitness, and other community services.

> It is often said that the value and meaning of a civilization can be documented from the record it leaves in the form of architecture, and that the true measure of the compassion and civility of a society lies in how well it treats its frail older people.
>
> Regnier 1994, p. vii

DESIGN AND THE AGING PROCESS

Housing for the elderly has not historically attracted the level of design inquiry required to transform it from the traditional boilerplate solutions based on old or inappropriate models. Unfortunately, many of the existing design criteria are prescriptive, often contained in codes in the form of minimum square-footage requirements and other governmental standards. Some of the dread of those contemplating a nursing home is directly attributable to the acute-care hospital model governing the codes for virtually all nursing home design. Fortunately, new models are challenging such requirements, but progress is slow and many innovative concepts get affected only through exception or variance. In some cases, a partnership between the regulatory agency and the provider results in solutions that are equivalent to and/or meet the intent of the code requirements. A new generation of designers has been successful in transforming the physical environment into one that is responsive to the needs of older adults yet maintains their safety and improves operations.

Older models rarely prioritized privacy, independence, and personalization. A new generation is redefining what kinds of shared accommodations are acceptable; small studio apartments no longer match lifestyle expectations. Accessibility has also been poorly understood: there has been a narrow focus on the requirements of younger, partially paralyzed veterans in wheelchairs. Accessibility must be reexamined as it applies to the frailest portion of the population, who can no longer use a wheelchair by themselves. A turning radius, for example, becomes less relevant as staff support becomes more important and two-sided transfer-and-lift systems are needed. For many older adults, the changes attributed to aging are subtle, often invisible to the observer, and shift with time.

Understanding the necessity for, and inevitability of, the proliferation of senior housing begins with the basics of the aging process, the barriers and limitations it presents, and how they impact environmental design. Certain social and psychological issues may affect an individual's dignity, impeding participation in a full life the way physical disabilities do.

Life expectancy is near 76 years for men and 80 for women, and the elderly population is therefore becoming a larger and larger percentage of the overall population. According to the 2010 U.S. Census, women outnumber men in the older age groups, but the number of older men per 100 older women has increased as differences in the causes of male mortality narrow. Although statistical data creates a distinctive group called "the elderly," there is no average or typical older person. Like the rest of us, they have different expectations of life shaped by divergent ethnic and racial backgrounds, role models, lifestyles, personal experiences, health histories, and family settings.

Aging is often viewed from two related perspectives: the study of the biological process (geriatrics) and the study of the social passage that occurs over time (gerontology). Biological aging is measured as the decline in the body's ability to maintain a balanced interaction of the organs, muscles, bones, and endocrine systems. The gradual pace of this process, unlike that of a traumatic event, can fill individuals with doubts about their physical and mental capabilities. Social changes, just like physical changes, require people to adapt, as family and work-related roles are redefined.

Biological Aging

The body is composed of interactive systems that maintain its operation. As the individual ages, these systems begin to deteriorate in a somewhat predictable way. To design a facility that suits the needs of the aging, these physical changes must be accounted for. Well-designed facilities not only accommodate the physical and psychological changes that come with aging but also permit residents to exercise their remaining abilities as much as possible.

Communicating systems

Changes in the endocrine system, which controls hormones, can alter the maintenance of body temperature or decrease the body's ability to correctly identify and react suitably to stimuli, thereby increasing the individual's vulnerability. Sunburns, scalding, and bedsores can all be by-products of the body's inability to perceive the need for shade or cold water, or to roll over (also see "Detection senses," below). In addition, the nervous system becomes less efficient at coordinating movement: reflexes degrade, and reaction time slows. The nervous system's ability to store and recall information also diminishes with age; memory loss can be subtle and a part of the normal aging process, or more pronounced if related to Alzheimer's or other kinds of dementia.

Design implications

There are many ways for a designer to make the aging individual's environment better suited to the physical disabilities caused by the diminished function of the endocrine and nervous systems. They include

- extending time-operated devices (elevator doors, automatic entrances) to allow more time to complete activities;
- distinguishing repetitive/symmetrical spaces by providing landmarks (objects, views to the outside) and increasing the salience of important directional information, referred to in this book as "wayfinding";

- providing electrical appliances with lights to remind people they are on, or automating them to turn off after a preprogrammed time;
- designing mechanical systems that allow flexible temperature control and avoid drafts and moving air;
- providing covered and/or screened outdoor areas that protect from sun, wind, and insects;
- using sensors and technology to accommodate an individual's need for more time to perform a task or to warn the individual or staff of impending risks.

Mechanical systems

The muscular system loses strength and bulk after age 30. Lack of movement can lead to muscular atrophy that affects posture, endurance, and joint positions. Exercise and fitness programs can slow this decline or even restore function so independence in many daily activities can be maintained. The skeletal system loses calcium, making bones brittle and increasingly vulnerable to accidents. It also loses elasticity, affecting bending, kneeling, turning, and rising. Declining physical capacity can also impact an individual's gait, leading to shuffling or awkward steps and increasing the risk of falls.

Design implications

In response to these physical changes, the designer should

- avoid devices that require twisting, pinching, or other precise manipulation;
- minimize walking distances to key daily activities such as dining and create frequent places to rest in hallways and near elevators;
- provide chairs with appropriate seat height and arms that assist in rising, permitting some upper-body strength to compensate for weaker knees and legs (see chapter 15);

- meet accessibility requirements, focusing on how the physical needs of older adults differ from those of younger disabled users, upon which many standards are based (for instance, placing grab bars closer to a toilet to function like the arms of a chair);
- avoid loose rugs, raised thresholds, or slippery surfaces that may affect balance or gait changes;
- minimize sharp edges or corners that could cause injury if falls occur;
- provide opportunities for physical fitness, particularly water activities, which can strengthen muscles without impacting joints.

Control systems

The control systems of aging individuals often function less effectively than those of younger people. This can affect the digestive system in many ways, including reduced bladder control, difficulty with digestion, and (without proper diet) malnutrition. Declining efficiency in the respiratory system and in oxygenating blood can lead to curtailed movement and diminished energy reserves. Curtailed physical activity can also impact the body's ability to properly utilize (and eliminate) food, which can, in turn, curtail physical activity, a cycle that can exacerbate poor health. The efficiency of the cardiovascular system declines with age. It is subject to disease (often hereditary) that can reduce blood supply to the brain, causing dizziness, blackouts, and blurred vision.

> Today we look back at the 1960s and find it hard to believe that residents were regularly institutionalized because they were incontinent—a muscle-control problem, not a health-care problem.
>
> Regnier 2002, p. ix

Design implications

To create an environment that supports better health for older individuals, the designer should provide

- frequent and easily accessible bathrooms;
- residential kitchens (eat-in or open), preferably with light and view, that encourage cooking and good eating habits;
- walking paths (inside and outside) that encourage physical activity;
- fitness and aerobic spaces to encourage cardiovascular exercise;
- healthier food choices and flexible dining options that stimulate appetite and encourage dining as a social opportunity.

Detection senses

All five senses are affected by aging, especially those on which we are most dependent: sight and hearing. Most individuals experience hearing problems as they get older. The ability to hear higher frequencies is lost first. In addition, inner-ear changes affect balance, which can lead to falls. Impaired vision significantly affects how people perceive and use the environment (figs. 1-2 through 1-5). While some issues are correctable with surgery, others require different means of support.

The following sight-related issues need to be taken into account:

- Aging eyes take longer to adjust their focus between near and far objects.
- Glare can cause momentary blindness.
- Higher light levels are needed to compensate for failing eyesight.
- The lens of the eye yellows and thickens, changing the perception of color.
- Depth perception is altered.

The senses of taste, smell, and touch also change over time, and there is a diminished ability to detect pain or pressure. Because taste is approximately 90 percent dependent on aroma, some aging persons experience a decreased ability to enjoy food.

Design implications

The designer can adapt the environment to compensate for diminished vision and hearing. He or she can also limit the senior's

▶ *Figure 1-2 Normal vision.*
Understanding the
deteriorating vision of the
aging helps inform design.
Courtesy of National Eye
Institute, National Institutes of
Health.

◀ *Figure 1-3 Cataract vision.* Courtesy of National Eye Institute, National Institutes of Health.

◀ *Figure 1-4 Glaucoma vision.* Courtesy of National Eye Institute, National Institutes of Health.

◀ *Figure 1-5 Macular degeneration.* Courtesy of National Eye Institute, National Institutes of Health.

dependence on certain senses by substituting others. The designer may

- provide information by using more than one sense, such as visual and auditory alarms;
- encourage dining settings that increase visual and olfactory connections with food;
- avoid shiny surfaces, which reflect light sources and cause glare;
- prevent excessive background noises that limit reception of information (see chapter 13);
- increase light levels to provide sufficient lighting for both general and task-specific activities (see chapter 14);
- use tactile information for orientation, such as handrails, floor and wall textures, and the warmth of the sun (see chapter 15);
- select mechanical equipment that does not create drafts or contribute to background noise.

All aspects of biological aging should impact designs for senior living and care, as the physical environment has a profound effect on an older person's quality of life.

Social Passage

The literature on aging has commonly focused on the physical changes related to advancing age. However, the way older people are viewed by society and find purpose in life is affected by the subtle, often invisible transformation of aging. Four main theories attempt to explain the changes in the way adults interact with others and their environment as they age. Any or all of these theories may apply, as no one has a static personality, and factors such as health, finances, and social involvement affect people differently at different times. These theories can aid the designer in understanding the mindset of the aging adult.

Disengagement theory

As they age, some individuals disengage, withdrawing from certain roles and responsibilities. Of course, healthy disengagement can occur only when the individual determines its pace. For example, an aging woman might determine that meal preparation is no longer central to her societal role and therefore disengage from it willingly. But forcing her disengagement by designing apartments without kitchens may inhibit successful aging.

Design implications

To respond to those seniors seeking to alter their roles and disengage successfully,

- provide options for staying at home or in a familiar neighborhood, connected to the services that already support them;
- enhance communication with technology to aid in maintaining social and business connections;
- permit control in decision making (locked doors, set dining hours, and inflexible rules may force unsuccessful disengagement);
- consider intergenerational programs for those who want to be actively engaged with children or other age groups;
- create opportunities to participate in a larger community via easy access to community facilities (living room, dining room, library, community center) and services (such as stores), so lifestyle patterns can be continued. Facilities that are too far away or inaccessible may force disengagement.

Activity theory

Some individuals, rather than simply disengaging from previous roles, will seek to replace roles from which they have been displaced. For example, upon retirement, a corporate executive might become a volunteer board president. Others may elect to channel their time into long-lost passions, such as relearning a musical instrument or completing their education (fig. 1-6).

Design implications

In response to seniors' desire for activity, they should be provided with opportunities to take on new roles and responsibilities. They should be encouraged, for example, to host community events and to engage in meaningful volunteer work. Designers and operators may assist by

- creating access to lifelong learning either through distance learning or classroom spaces;
- creating a business center with access to computers, photocopiers, and similar technologies to facilitate volunteer leadership;
- Creating spaces and programs, such as performance venues, that engage the broader community.

Continuity theory

Aging adults often surround themselves with familiar objects and continue routines that reinforce their self-image. For example, couples who have traditionally hosted family holiday gatherings may select apartments with full kitchens even if they do not continue to prepare meals, or a widower may desire a large bed that he no longer needs. As these individuals adapt to changing physical capabilities, new situations, and different life experiences, they also develop a strong need to preserve continuity between their old and new lives.

◀ *Figure 1-6 A central role for most facilities for aging adults is to encourage continued social interaction.*

Design implications
To support maintaining a consistent self-image, designers may

- accommodate residents' desires to keep their own furniture through flexible layouts;
- create adaptable spaces that support interests such as art, music, woodworking, and performance arts;
- design units that can be customized for individual preferences and priorities that reflect lifestyle.

Environmental competence
There has to be a balance between the demands of an environment and the physical, mental, and emotional capabilities of those living in it if they are to adapt to it successfully. If older people can negotiate the tasks of daily living comfortably, their experience of their surroundings will likely be positive; it can be negative if those surroundings are more demanding than the individual can cope with. A designer cannot expect people to do all the adapting; spaces must be designed to adapt to their users. For example, walkers or electric carts allow an individual with impaired mobility to move around various settings. Spacious elevators and widened hallways adapt the environment to the individual, resulting in harmony between abilities and demands.

Because the competence of individuals utilizing senior living facilities will vary greatly, the setting should be flexible to allow them to adapt to it. In addition, the environment should provide choice and variety so that they can select the settings or services that appropriately conform the environment to their needs.

Design implications
Designers must maximize both residents' potential and the facility's accessibility by

- providing redundant information for wayfinding, allowing individuals to rely on their own abilities as well as environmental cues such as signage, color, and landmarks (examples of cues include the smell of bread baking, a grandfather clock in the hall, and artwork with a familiar regional scene);
- encouraging continued physical activity through well-designed stairs (while also providing an elevator as an accessible and adaptive option);
- encouraging walking by keeping distances to daily activities like dining as short as possible.

Addressing these physical and psychological aspects of aging is an evolving architectural trend responsive to the interests and passions of a new generation of seniors. The next chapter describes the operational and programmatic concepts influencing and creating new models of senior living.

PROGRAMMING AND PLANNING GUIDELINES

UNDERSTANDING THE MARKETPLACE

This chapter provides program and planning guidelines for each of the ten building types enumerated in chapter 1. These guidelines are only a starting point for the project planning or programming effort; there are a variety of successful models for each building type. Market research is a key first step in understanding the needs and preferences of a particular market. Successful market research will identify both the need (or demand) for particular products and services as well as consumer preferences for everything from unit size to amenities to common spaces. To make an analogy to the fashion industry, an increase in population predicts a demand for more clothes, but choices about style, color, design, and price point are decisions that can determine success or failure.

Assessing trends is important. To continue the analogy, simply asking men "Do you buy ties?" will not elicit critical information: Are men dressing for business more casually than a decade ago? Is tie-wearing in decline? Might making ties, then, not be the best business choice? Or might it be prudent to merely make ties a smaller part of the overall product line?

Good market research will combine the answers to such questions with a knowledge of current trends to determine programmatic and operational approaches that are both flexible and sustainable. After all, buildings take a lot longer to build (five to seven years from concept to move-in is not unusual) than ties take to make—and they are far less disposable.

Understanding the local market is essential: the local culture may beget behaviors and trends that differ from those elsewhere. For example, in some markets, an unusually large number of people have purchased long-term care insurance products; that will influence everything from whether healthcare services are bundled or unbundled to the number of nursing beds required. Preferences for dining times (early or late?), dining style (casual or formal?), and price point (all-inclusive meals or pay as you go?) may be influenced by national generational trends as well as by local lifestyle; all three will impact the size, character, and staffing of the dining program. Manhattan, Kansas, and Manhattan, New York, may both have older people in need of housing and services, but the products offered will likely be very different, in order to address local expectations. Even within those markets, the population is not homogeneous. This is why providing choices is so important for addressing individual expectations.

> The senior living industry needs to learn from the fashion industry. They know that people will need clothing. The key is to anticipate changing preferences and trends, and to understand what people want and how that meets their real—and perceived—needs.
>
> *Stephen Proctor, president and CEO, Presbyterian Senior Living (personal communication)*

> Offer the market what it wants instead of trying to sell it what you have.
>
> *Maria Dwight, Gerontological Services, Inc. (personal communication)*

PROGRAMMING SPACE GUIDELINES

Space standards vary. They are a reflection of market preferences and the income level of the target market. Typical unit areas for the senior living building types in this chapter are identified in appendix A, but these guidelines are not absolute. The appendices also provide sample space programs for these same building types, and describes the variety of resident common areas, staff support areas, and building services needed for a complete building.

When preparing a total program, a grossing factor (see appendix B) will account for wall thickness (which is not included in the net square footage), corridors, stairs, elevators, shafts, mechanical and electrical areas, and the like. Different programmatic goals may also impact these factors. For example, standard double-loaded corridors (i.e., those with rooms on both sides) would have a lower factor than single-loaded corridors. Because of the need for wider corridors for maneuvering, and, in some senior environment types, the mandate of 8 ft corridors, the grossing factor is typically larger than that of other building types.

Design choices may affect programmed and/or grossing factors included in the space program. The choice of a mechanical system may also impact the space needed for central equipment and terminal units (baseboard radiators, heat pumps, fan coil units) in the living space; this may, in turn, affect room sizes, clearances, and furnishability. Licensure codes and accessibility requirements will impact design and programs (see chapter 5 and associated appendixes). Financial ownership structures like condominiums may dictate specific ways that areas be measured to meet local legal requirements. And contractors may calculate areas differently; they see balconies, covered terraces, porches, and covered entrances/drop-offs as areas that will be built—and priced—separately (fig. 2-1).

The following divides the continuum of services and settings into ten building types. These divisions have historical meanings related to licensure codes and reimbursement or building code definitions. For international readers, these divisions may not be appropriate—or even necessary—as different countries have created their own models that respond to their own history and culture, as well as the typical lack of any public subsidy. New models blend these building types in unique and different ways.

COMMUNITY-BASED OPTIONS
Typical Users

Community-based options are an emerging set of service networks and facilities that enable older people to live at home. The majority of this book focuses on the purpose-built setting in which services and care are delivered. But the majority of seniors will never reside in such settings. A smaller number may live in them only for short periods. Most older adults want to remain at home, and they look for services that will help them maintain an independent lifestyle. Remaining at home may also be the only option for the (significant) population sandwiched between too much income for subsidized housing and not enough of a financial reserve to pay for retirement housing.

"Age-friendly communities" is the catchphrase that encompasses a range of ways municipalities are responding to the

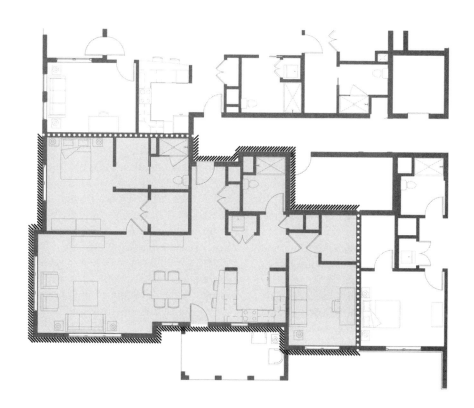

◀ *Figure 2-1 Unit area is calculated using the gross method in* Building Owners and Management Association Multi-Unit Residential Buildings: Standard Methods of Measurement (2010). *This includes the full thickness of exterior enclosing walls, the full thickness of walls between a unit and adjacent common areas, and half the thickness of demising walls between a unit and adjacent units.* Perkins Eastman.

demographics of aging, which will impact everything from their housing stock to their transportation network to public health issues such as obesity and diabetes. Organizations like AARP and publications like *U.S. News & World Report* rate the best cities for retirees and profile the best retirement communities. Suburban communities are struggling with land use policies that isolate residential areas from commercial zones,

> The biggest competition to senior housing is people staying at home. In the coming decade, technology will continue to facilitate this possibility even for the older, frailer population.
>
> *Victor Regnier, FAIA, University of Southern California (personal communication)*

making cars the only way to travel between the two. Cities are dealing with aging infrastructure and environments typically built well before accessibility was required by legislation. Cities like Portland, Oregon, and New York City have begun to embrace the inherent sustainability of urban planning that keeps and supports their aging residents in their homes, in order to avoid costly publicly funded healthcare and housing options.

Naturally occurring retirement communities (NORCs) are typically found in apartment buildings where a majority of residents moved in around the same time and are now aging in place. But municipalities are now discovering NORCs spread out across entire neighborhoods—and, therefore, without the benefits inherent in the density of a single apartment building. Homecare agencies are offering a range of services, from sophisticated in-home medical treatments to companions who provide intermittent or round-the-clock assistance. Technology has moved former hospital-based treatments into the home via portable equipment that can be monitored remotely.

The Villages Movement, pioneered by Boston's Beacon Hill Village, enables seniors to age at home. Beacon Hill Village was founded in 1998, and by 2010 there were 45 similar villages underway and over 100 in development across the country. Although still in its infancy, the movement has demonstrated that remaining at home, coupled with access to community-based services, can foster healthy aging and obviate a move to a traditional retirement community. The residents of such neighborhoods access coordinated services through volunteers or preapproved vendors. For a monthly service fee, member service coordinators can arrange for everything from dog walking and home repairs to grocery shopping and traditional homecare services by individuals or agencies like the local Visiting Nurse Service.

Facilities run under the Program for All-Inclusive Care for the Elderly (PACE) are another up-and-coming alternative to nursing homes; at a lower level of government reimbursement theyprovide essential healthcare services on a limited basis during the day. By integrating social and healthcare services in a day program, members can remain in their own homes as they age. (See "Adult Day Care," below). Mather LifeWays, based outside of Chicago, has created Mather Cafés to attract older, active seniors by offering educational, social, and wellness programs along with appealing, nutritional meals (fig. 2-2). Mather LifeWays is currently serving over 40,000 customers in three locations and is expanding its reach by partnering with two Villages under development in the greater Chicago area. Capitol Hill Village in Washington, DC, is in discussions with Volunteers of America to partner on new PACE programs that would serve Medicaid populations as well as private-pay individuals. The synergy of these groups is creating exciting models that challenge traditional thinking about how and where seniors want to live, and how services are delivered to them.

▶ Figure 2-2 This café offers meals as well as education, wellness, and social programs. It is targeted to those over 55 and provides strong community-based resources and support for healthy lifestyles. Mather's: More than a Café, Chicago, Illinois. Photograph by Mather LifeWays.

Sponsors, Settings, Payments, and Reimbursements

Community-based options encompass a variety of programs, sponsors, and funding sources, and fall into the following categories:

- *Homecare services.* Nonprofit and for-profit agencies that provide fee-for-service assistance at home. These are usually private-pay, although some private long-term care insurance programs do offer a service benefit. Some states have subsidized programs, and providers may subsidize services as part of an overall community-based mission.
- *Program for All-Inclusive Care for the Elderly (PACE).* Nonprofit community-based sponsors generally serving those eligible for Medicaid and Medicare. Typically government-reimbursed, private-pay PACE programs are being studied. Look-alike programs are establishing large networks of individuals who can access existing clinics, as well as rehabilitation and day programs.
- *Villages Movement.* Membership-based organizations typically founded by philanthropic organizations until they are financially self-sufficient. A fee-for-service structure is the norm; those fees may be included in the annual membership fee. Trading services among members is a core concept, and volunteers further community-building.
- *Naturally occurring retirement community (NORC).* Rental and condominium communities that evolve by attracting and maintaining older adults in their residences. Some sponsors and agencies are looking at ways to provide services and benefits coordination for older individuals in these buildings.
- *Continuing care at home (CCAH).* A growing number of states now permit CCAH programs, which offer the services of a continuing care retirement community (CCRC) to residents in their own homes. Participants pay the CCAH a one-time entrance fee as well as monthly charges to receive care coordination, routine home maintenance, in-home assisted living and nursing services, transportation, meals, and social and wellness programs. CCAHs are typically much less expensive than a traditional CCRC, since they involve no real estate.

An outgrowth of these community-based options in built-out urban areas may be the need for new accessible housing serving multiple age groups and economic strata, mirroring the larger community ("universal housing").

Geriatric Outpatient Clinic

Typical users

Geriatric medicine provides healthcare for older adults with cognitive, emotional, and/or physical challenges. Specializations within geriatrics include psychology, internal medicine, psychiatry, neurology, social work, and physical, occupational, and speech therapy. A multidisciplinary team may include services such as assessment for Alzheimer's and dementia, preventive medicine, and clinical services that focus specifically on older patients.

Freestanding geriatric clinics can include family services, and clinics within a nursing home or CCRC often include examination and treatment spaces for general exams, as well as dentistry, ophthalmology, podiatry, and other specialties. These are generally linked to areas for physical, occupational, and speech therapy. Other services that may be provided under the umbrella of geriatric medicine include mobile care (a van equipped to provide medical exams and minor treatments), in-home psychiatric assessment and treatment, agencies that coordinate community services for the elderly, and education for caregivers.

Sponsors and settings

The sponsors of geriatric clinical services fall into two categories: healthcare providers such as hospitals, clinics, primary care centers, and skilled nursing centers, and senior housing and community-based service providers. These sponsors can provide services in a number of settings—formal or informal, small or large:

- Private, community-based practice
- Component of a retirement community
- Part-time presence or affiliation with other sponsors
- Home health service network

Clinic and outpatient settings range from private family practices that are small and personal to major hospital outpatient programs comprising dozens of exam rooms and a home healthcare staff for in-home care visits. A suite of exam rooms that can be used flexibly by community medical practitioners is common in senior living clinical settings (figs. 2-3 and 2-4).

▶ *Figure 2-3 Larger exam rooms can meet the needs of aging adults who may want to bring family members with them. Electric exam tables lower closer to the floor or recline from a seated position. Laurel Park Medical Center, Hendersonville, North Carolina. Perkins Eastman. Photograph by Tim Buchman.*

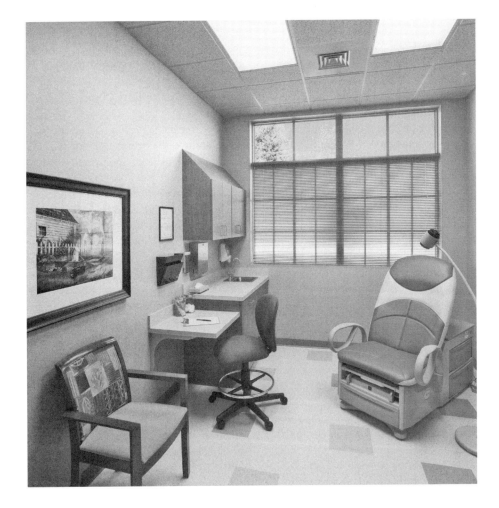

Program and design

Most licensed clinics must follow minimum area requirements for those parts of the building devoted to programs and services. These requirements are set by local and/or state agencies, such as the state department of health, and must be met when reimbursement for services comes from state- or federal-funded programs. City or county health departments may also establish minimum standards for outpatient clinic facilities. Regardless of the source, few standards have been developed to support older patient populations, and in some cases, existing standards may even be counterproductive to such end users if they do not deal with the need for greater accessibility, such as making toilets easier to use or addressing other special limitations of the frail elderly.

Licensing and other regulatory requirements may also stem from the clinic's occupancy classification—healthcare or business. The healthcare classification for facilities affiliated with licensed hospital programs or

Figure 2-4 This nurses' station is designed to permit chair-bound patients to converse directly with the nursing staff. University of Arkansas, Donald W. Reynolds Institute on Aging, Little Rock, Arkansas. Perkins Eastman. Photograph by Timothy Hursley.

providing overnight care comes with the strictest standards and requirements for monitoring. The business classification, which covers medical office buildings, typically permits most outpatient services and minor procedures without significant code restrictions. The classification will impact program, services offered, operations, and building costs. (Appendices C, D, and E provide a summary of the typical requirements for a variety of different clinic programs.)

Program and organizational alternatives
There are three commonly used models for clinic design (figs. 2-5 through 2-7):

Patient/escort-centered model
- There is lower staff efficiency.
- The circulation overlaps for staff and patient access to exam areas.
- There is shorter circulation for patients.
- Public/staff interface functions and private medical staff service functions are located remotely.
- The patient waiting and staff areas are positioned for access to natural light.

Staff/administration-centered model
- There is higher staff efficiency.
- The circulation overlaps for staff and patient access to exam areas.
- There is longer circulation for patients.

▶ *Figure 2-5 Patient-centered clinic design model. University of Arkansas, Donald W. Reynolds Institute on Aging, Little Rock, Arkansas. Perkins Eastman.*

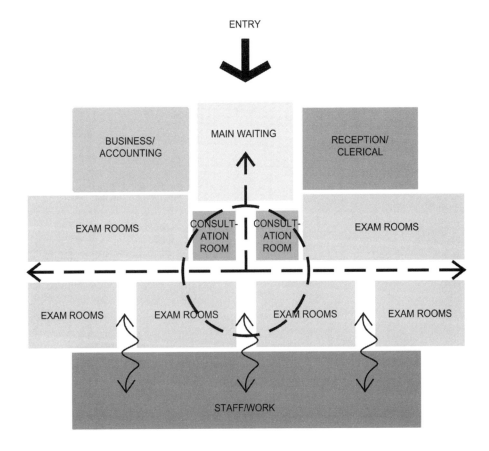

ENTRY

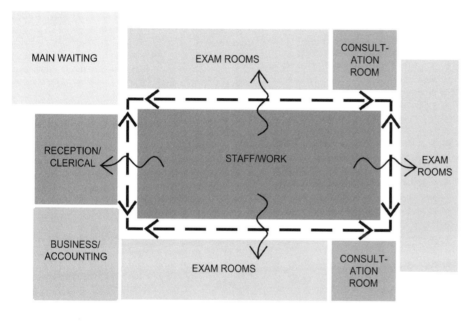

MAIN WAITING

EXAM ROOMS

CONSULT-ATION ROOM

RECEPTION/ CLERICAL

STAFF/WORK

EXAM ROOMS

BUSINESS/ ACCOUNTING

EXAM ROOMS

CONSULT-ATION ROOM

◀ *Figure 2-6 Staff-centered clinic design model. University of Arkansas, Donald W. Reynolds Institute on Aging, Little Rock, Arkansas. Perkins Eastman.*

- Exam rooms and patient waiting areas are positioned for access to natural light.
- The circulation is likely to form a ring, complicating patients' wayfinding.

Hybrid cluster model

- The waiting, check-in/out and consult areas are decentralized and repeated.
- There is moderate to high staff efficiency.
- There is moderate to low circulation for patients, with public and semiprivate zones formed by small service clusters creating a clear hierarchy.
- Staff and patient waiting areas are positioned for access to natural light.

Special design considerations

Regardless of type or sponsor, there are other considerations in designing a geriatric facility.

Frailty and limited mobility

Geriatric clinics require environments supportive of frail users. Patients require more time, and in some cases assistance, to move from one area of the clinic to another, to read and prepare needed paperwork, to dress and undress, and to use the toilet. Because of this, as well as the complexity of examinations, testing, and assessments, patients tend to spend between two and four hours in the clinic.

Because patient turnover is lower than in conventional clinics, more exam rooms must be provided. The most supportive clinics attempt to limit the number of transitions and relocations patients must make during their visit; nonetheless, there should be handrails on at least one side of all patient corridors to

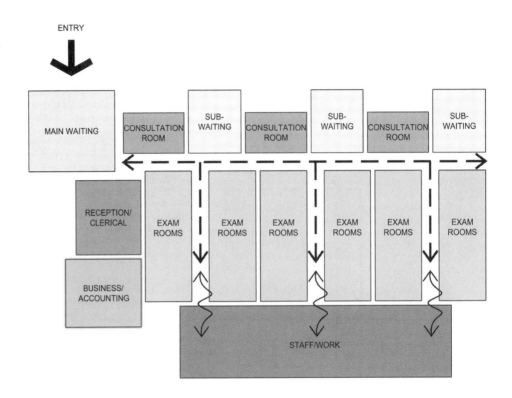

▶ *Figure 2-7 Hybrid cluster model. University of Arkansas, Donald W. Reynolds Institute on Aging, Little Rock, Arkansas. Perkins Eastman.*

assist with mobility. A widened circulation space to allow for wheelchairs and power-operated vehicles (POVs) as well as other staff/service equipment is recommended. Corridor widths of 6–8 ft are not uncommon, and doors should not swing into corridors, because many patients will be moving along the edges rather than the middle of circulation spaces.

Impact of escorts

Family and friends—sometimes two or three—often accompany a patient to the outpatient clinic. This places a strain on clinic waiting areas and exam and consult rooms, which must accommodate more people than the clinic is intended to serve directly. Therefore, educational diversionary activities, such as reading materials, video

seminars, and computers whose browsers have preset links to senior resource sites, can be helpful. Snacks, beverages, and outdoor spaces make lengthy waits more comfortable.

Access to toilet facilities

Single-occupancy, wheelchair-accessible public restrooms equipped with wall grab bars or seat-mounted sheltering-arm grab bars should be located near all clinic waiting areas. Special breakaway doors with emergency release hardware allow reverse operation of the door, in case a patient becomes ill or injured and falls to the floor, blocking it from swinging inward.

At a minimum, each large exam or procedure room should have a connecting accessible toilet room (fig. 2.8). Having toilet rooms connected to all exam rooms is

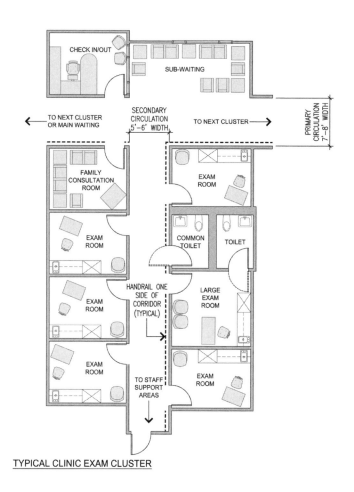

CHECK IN/OUT

SUB-WAITING

TO NEXT CLUSTER OR MAIN WAITING

SECONDARY CIRCULATION 5'-6' WIDTH

TO NEXT CLUSTER

PRIMARY CIRCULATION 7'-8' WIDTH

FAMILY CONSULTATION ROOM

EXAM ROOM

EXAM ROOM

COMMON TOILET

TOILET

EXAM ROOM

HANDRAIL ONE SIDE OF CORRIDOR (TYPICAL)

LARGE EXAM ROOM

EXAM ROOM

TO STAFF SUPPORT AREAS

EXAM ROOM

TYPICAL CLINIC EXAM CLUSTER

◀ *Figure 2-8 Larger healthcare centers serving the elderly can divide exam/ consult areas into smaller clusters. University of Arkansas, Donald W. Reynolds Institute on Aging, Little Rock, Arkansas. Perkins Eastman.*

preferable but often financially infeasible. A few such rooms will allow patients to avoid repeatedly dressing and undressing during a long examination or procedure in order to use a common toilet. This will, however, require staff to manage exam room assignments to match appropriate spaces with patient needs and intended services.

Group patient consults

It becomes impractical to discuss assessments and treatments in exam rooms when the patient as well as several family members and physicians are all in attendance. Informal areas, such as closed lounges, are more appropriate for such consultations and provide needed privacy for difficult diagnoses.

Multiple medical disciplines

A visit to the doctor can be a formidable experience for an anxious, slightly confused, or unsteady older adult with complex medical, social, and financial needs. A clinic must often be a comprehensive health service center that allows physicians and staff to surround the individual with all required disciplines and services. This allows physicians to assess, treat, and develop a long-term care plan that includes extended family members all in one place. Staff members from different academic and medical specializations can then meet to discuss patient assessments and care plans. Such interdisciplinary sessions are facilitated by bullpens isolated from patient areas but convenient to offices and work cubicles, soiled and clean utility areas, and medication rooms. They should provide for the review of charts, x-rays, and other medical records. The bullpen should be capable of accommodateing any teleconferencing technologies used, for discussions with off-site specialists or colleagues.

Wayfinding

Many older adults' vision, memory, and/or hearing is impaired, making orientation difficult for them, especially in larger facilities. Clustering functions reduces walking distances. Color, finishes, or lighting that differentiates clinic areas is helpful. There is no better support system than locating highly visible staff areas throughout the clinic so staffers can provide directions. However, the staff's need for privacy must be balanced with the patients' need for human contact.

Confidentiality and privacy

The clinic should be zoned to create clear hierarchies between visitor/escort, patient, and staff areas. Confidential information such as records, patient consults, and physician discussions must always be properly isolated.

Exam room turnover

At typical clinic facilities, each physician can manage a patient load of 30–40 per day by rotating two to three exam rooms among several physicians. Because geriatric patients require longer preparation and more time to dress and undress, and have more complex medical histories to refresh, a single physician may use four to five exam rooms to support a patient load of only 20–30 per day. Grouping exam and support areas will reduce time spent shuttling between patient exams and help clinic staff work more effectively.

Environmental comfort

As in other facilities housing and serving older populations, their increased sensitivity to temperature, drafts, direct sunlight, glare, and artificial illumination levels must be addressed. Heating, ventilating, and air-conditioning (HVAC) systems should have independent temperature controls for exam rooms, procedure rooms, toilet rooms, and areas where patients undress. Plan for a heat source for both summer and winter, as many older adults are cold year-round. Systems should deliver air at the lowest velocity possible to limit drafts.

In some settings, the program may be limited to serving the needs of the population of a CCRC or a nursing home. The space program for smaller clinics often ranges from 2,000–3,000 net sq ft (NSF). Facilities with a comprehensive rehabilitation program may have rehab suites that range from 2,500 to 3,500 NSF for occupational, physical, and related therapy programs.

Payment, reimbursement, and regulation

The variety of sponsors make it hard to generalize about payment structures. Typically, users will either have private insurance or Medicare for most services. If the clinic is part of a life-care retirement community, services may be provided at no additional charge as part of a monthly fee or entry fee. In most states, licensure to receive such reimbursements is typically through the department of health.

Adult Day Care

Adult day care is a group program that provides health and social services during a limited daily time frame to physically or cognitively impaired persons over 65. Features can include medical care, preventive and rehabilitative services, and Alzheimer's care. Typical hours of operation are 8 AM to 5 PM, but some facilities offer extended hours. Adult day care facilities have evolved as alternatives to assisted living and long-term care for those still living at home or with their families. For example, they allow family caregivers to go to work knowing that their aging parent is in a safe, active program; for care-giver spouses, it can provide much-needed respite.

Typical users

Day care participants are often cognitively impaired and cannot be left home alone. Other programs, sometimes referred to as adult day health programs, can meet the needs of very frail or medically compromised individuals who would otherwise be placed in long-term care or nursing homes. While social activities are a significant component of a day program, these are not drop-in senior social centers.

Sponsors and owners

It is common for the same sponsors to own both adult day care and other senior care services, as both provide a community-based network of social and medical services. According to the National Council on the Aging (NCOA), of the more than 4,000 programs nationwide in 2000, the majority were operated on a nonprofit or public basis, and many were affiliated with larger organizations such as homecare, skilled nursing facilities, medical centers, and multipurpose senior organizations.

Settings

Such programs can be found within another senior environment (such as a nursing home or retirement community) or as a standalone program located in the community. A PACE may be located in or adjacent to subsidized housing to provide a continuum of services for frail, low-income elderly.

Freestanding models

Community-based programs are typically run as business enterprises and can be found in a variety of locations, including storefront retail-type spaces, the education wings of churches and synagogues, and freestanding buildings. Day care programs are financially fragile operations, particularly in states where there is little or no public reimbursement. Adult day care providers are typically networked with other community-based organizations, social workers, physicians, and hospitals for their client referrals.

Integrated models

Adult day care centers are frequently developed within other residences, such as long-term care, assisted living, or retirement

---

Adult day care is a community-based group program designed to meet the needs of functionally impaired adults through an individual plan of care. It is a structured, comprehensive program that provides a variety of health, social, and related support services in a protective setting during any part of a day but less than 24-hour care. Individuals who participate in adult day care attend on a planned basis during specified hours. Adult day care assists its participants to remain in the community, enabling families and other caregivers to continue caring for an impaired member at home.

Standards for Adult Day Care, National Institute on Adult Daycare (NIAD), p. 20

communities. The ability to utilize the resources of a larger parent facility with trained staff increases management, staffing, and purchasing efficiencies—particularly for meals—and may also produce more creative programming. Many senior living providers see adult day care as a community service, an expansion of their continuum of services, and a natural referral/marketing opportunity for their other residential and care environments. There is a new demand for day programming for residents with

dementia whose spouse is the primary caregiver and needs respite. Such programs can be an adjunct to an existing dementia facility, integrated with such a program, or a separate "club" program (fig. 2-9).

Program and design

Considerations include what services the participants need and how many attend per day. Clients often attend part time, so that the number of registrants is higher than the actual number of participants on any given

▶ Figure 2-9 Plan for a 50-registrant freestanding urban adult day care program. Village Center for Care, New York City. Perkins Eastman.

day. The type and number of staff will depend on the facility model: social, medical, or dementia care.

Typical program components include the following (fig. 2-10):

Supportive services
Supportive services typically include the following:

Transportation. The provision of transportation helps guarantee attendance.

Whether public or provided by the facility, it must be reliable, accessible, and attentive to seniors' needs. If the program has a shuttle service, large groups of people will arrive at one time; the drop-off area, lobby, and coat storage must accommodate them. Protected drop-off areas are critical in many climates (fig. 2-11).

Food service. Nutritious meals are important. Partnership with a food-service provider such as a nursing home, or with a

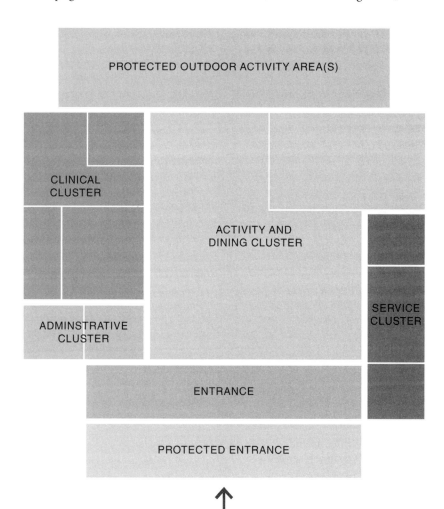

◀ *Figure 2-10 Day care clients often arrive in large groups from accessible vans, and the flow from a protected entrance directly into program areas must be easy. Day programming may include meals and social activities in the central area, with more specialized physical therapy and medical services in a clinical area. Perkins Eastman.*

▶ *Figure 2-11 Adult day care programs can inhabit existing buildings. Some new facilities are specifically designed to accommodate a client eligible for long-term care and provide intensive social, medical, and therapeutic services. Total Longterm Care Cody Day Center, Lakewood, Colorado. Boulder Associates Inc. Photograph by Ed LaCasse.*

nutritionist who plans a meal program that accommodates special dietary needs, is common (fig. 2-12).

Medical service. The medical model of adult day care provides for the medical assessment of clients. Some sponsors may include other standard checkups. Dental care and podiatry are often provided.

Rehabilitation services

Rehab services may include the following:

1. *Occupational therapy.* Helping with the activities of daily living (ADLs)
   - Small-group activities such as cooking; simple handicraft work; and sewing, knitting, painting, and ceramics in an arts-and-crafts room
   - One-on-one activities such as teaching the patient how to get in and out of a

bathtub or shower, or how to position his or her body for toileting
2. *Physical therapy.*
   - *Ambulation.* Teaching participants how to walk using handrails and/or aids
   - *Simple modality.* Upper- and lower-body exercise, if there is a physical therapy program. (There should be a hand-wash sink in the room, and a single-service toilet room nearby.)
3. *Speech therapy.* Easily provided in a private office or small meeting room
4. *Personal hygiene.* Facilities and staff for bathing clients. (Many frail seniors do not have the appropriate facilities or assistance at home.)

Adjunct services

These complementary programs expand the scope of wellness programs. They can be provided in an adult day care setting or be

◀ *Figure 2-12 Adult day care typically involves both activities and at least one meal. Village Center for Care, New York City.* Perkins Eastman. Photograph by Chuck Choi.

part of a service network affiliated with it. They may include medical services (such as audiology, ophthalmology, gynecology) and psychological counseling, exercise programs (such as tai chi, yoga, and dance therapy), a learning center (to teach computers or languages), and so on (fig. 2-13).

Sample program

As a rule of thumb, allow 100–150 gross sq ft (GSF) per client if the facility is all on one level. A program on two contiguous levels requires a larger allowance of GSF per person to account for stairs, elevators, and corridors.

The program outlined in appendix F is typical for highly regulated states that offer significant reimbursement. Space programs,

however, vary widely from state to state because of the many differences in codes and regulations, as well as other variables. Some states permit such a program to operate in less than half the space outlined in appendix F.

While it may be permitted, it is not recommended. Licensed programs integrated with another use, such as an assisted living building, may be required to have separate, defined areas for the day care participants, even if areas are functionally shared.

There are additional requirements for discrete program areas at facilities serving Alzheimer's or dementia patients. Such clients need separate activities and dining spaces, a quiet room, and space to walk and exercise for working through periods of agitation.

▶ Figure 2-13 Newer day care programs create a variety of smaller program areas. North Shore Senior Center, Arthur C. Nielsen, Jr. Campus, Northfield, Illinois. O'Donnell Wicklund Pigozzi & Peterson. Photograph by Steve Hall at Hedrich Blessing.

HISTORY OF ADULT DAY CARE

The concept of adult day care started in 1933 in Moscow as a day hospital program to solve the huge psychiatric bed shortage. Subsequently, in 1943 Great Britain adopted the same idea as a measure to maximize the limited health-care resources for medical and rehabilitation services to war-afflicted veterans. This program became so well received that in the 1950s day hospitals (adult daycare centers) were set up throughout the United Kingdom to attend to the needs of frail and physically disabled senior citizens. This system of community-based care-giving had built a direct linkage between the delivery of health-care resources and the national health-care system. Canada and South Africa were the next countries to follow.

The first adult daycare programs in the United States started in the 1960s. The Older Americans Act of 1965 gave support to the development of programs that would provide socialization and recreational services dedicated to seniors.

In 1977, 200 programs were listed in the first directory of adult daycare programs published by the National Council on Aging. There were 600 programs listed in 1980, and 1,200 in 1986 under the National Institute of Adult Day Care Centers. The rapid growth rate demonstrated the need for an alternative to nursing homes for frail seniors who choose to remain in their homes and communities as long as possible.

National Institute on Adult Daycare 1984

Payment, reimbursement, and regulation

Because day care keeps people at home—and out of more expensive publicly supported housing or nursing homes—some states have encouraged the provision of day care with Medicaid waiver programs and other forms of public reimbursement. Such reimbursement is usually accompanied by regulations with larger space requirements.

Most states require licensure of adult day care if services are provided to three or more people. The licensure agencies vary by state and may be part of the department of health, the social services department (public welfare), or a specialized department on aging. Facilities integrated into a long-term care building may have to follow institutional building code standards. There are likely less restrictive standards for freestanding locations. Code requirements focus on basic administration, safety, and sanitation standards, except in states providing reimbursement, where stringent space and programmatic standards are typically specified.

Expanding services

As the United States' over-85 population grows, the demand for healthcare resources will continue to increase. Advances in medicine have resulted in an increase in the number of "old-old" Americans. A community-based healthcare system that promotes and supports wellness for seniors is the future of geriatric care.

By pooling medical and social services, a healthcare provider can develop a network for coordinating and supplying various complex care packages. These services can include home healthcare, adult day care, geriatric medicine, and respite care. Although most states only reimburse day care programs through Medicaid, some are beginning to offer Medicare Part B reimbursement if the programs are medically oriented.

Program for All-Inclusive Care for the Elderly

PACE, started by the On Lok senior care group in San Francisco, is a successful model for a comprehensive care system. PACE provides adult day care and primary care, rehabilitation therapy, and home healthcare services. Its innovation is services brought to the client, rather than the other way around (fig. 2-14).

Integrated dementia care

Over the past decade there has been a significant increase in the number of specialized assisted living residences for people with dementia. New models are being developed that provide an integrated day care program with dedicated program areas in which they spend the day in activities with other persons with dementia. These smaller-scale

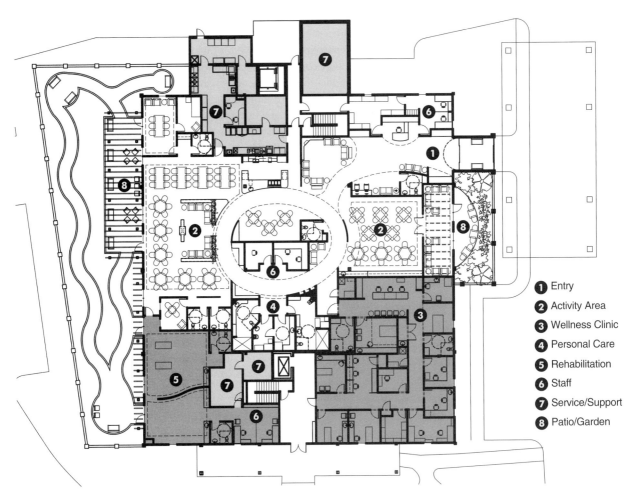

1 Entry
2 Activity Area
3 Wellness Clinic
4 Personal Care
5 Rehabilitation
6 Staff
7 Service/Support
8 Patio/Garden

Figure 2-14 Concept plan for PACE. JSR Associates, Inc.

day care programs (usually 10–15 people per day) allow for cost-effective utilization of space and staff resources. Such facilities are typically developed with a small social space (sized to meet state licensure requirements) that can be secured during arrivals and departures and also be used for dining.

LONG-TERM CARE
Typical Users and Care

Known variously as nursing homes, convalescent care, nursing centers, chronic-care centers, skilled-nursing facilities, skilled-care facilities, comprehensive-care facilities, and intermediate-care facilities, such places provide long-term care and specialized services that fall into the following categories:

- *Long-term care.* Typically for the very frail and elderly, who often have multiple chronic or cyclical illnesses or have disabilities requiring 24-hour care.
- *Alzheimer's/dementia care.* For individuals with significant memory impairment, often with other compounding conditions, the combination of which requires extensive daily care and treatment.
- *Short-term, subacute rehabilitation.* For individuals recovering after a hospital stay and not yet able to return home
- *Hospice and palliative care.* For residents in the last stage of life. (See page 60 on Hospice.)

Other areas of dedicated programming include respite care, temporary care, and care for younger adults with brain trauma.

Long-term care provides a combination of medical (skilled-care) and nonmedical (custodial-care) services for people incapable of caring for themselves but who do not require the services of an acute-care hospital. Their care is often provided by an interdisciplinary team of medical professionals

> We need bold thinking that questions the status quo and calls for more humane environments. Each year, millions of people will enter environments for the frail. Let us hope that these places will be more like the homes they left and less like the institutional environments they fear.
>
> *Regnier 2002*

(physicians, nurses, and specialists), social workers, spiritual counselors, community organizations, friends, and family.

The decision to move into long-term care is based on need rather than choice. Many residents enter long-term care through a subacute program after hospitalization, where placement in a facility is often dependent on a referral from a physician or discharge planner at the hospital. Other residents come directly from their homes. In the majority of cases, it is the family of the person requiring care that is making decisions about his or her future. Spouses or adult children are faced with the responsibility of selecting a facility, interacting with staff, and understanding the care plan. This requires a different marketing effort—one aimed at referral sources and adult caregivers.

Many nursing homes now provide for short-term rehabilitative stays (through a subacute program with Medicare-licensed beds) for those recovering from an injury, operation, or illness. Others offer hospice and programs for residents with dementia. Long-term care residents have complex medical conditions that routinely require skilled nursing services and other highly intensive care, which is provided by licensed nursing staff under the supervision of a family physician or the facility's part- or full-time medical staff.

2004 Data on Nursing Homes

Proprietary: 1,045,500 beds

Voluntary nonprofit: 523,600 beds

Government and other: 130,900 beds

(Centers for Disease Control and Prevention 2004)

Characteristics of a typical long-term care resident have changed drastically over the last 30 years, and the trend is continuing. The average age, level of frailty, and limitations in mobility have soared. In most facilities the average age of residents is over 85 years of age, close to 70 percent utilize a

EVOLUTION OF LONG-TERM CARE

Since they were originally thought of as health facilities—not housing with 24-hour healthcare supervision and support—early models were patterned on acute-care hospitals. As more and more residents relied on Medicaid to pay for their stay, states tried to contain this rapidly growing part of their budgets. By restricting reimbursement for construction that exceeded (often unrealistic) limits on maximum allowable costs, they compelled most sponsors to build facilities as small as the code would permit.

The codes in many states did not recognize how old, ill, and cognitively impaired the average resident would become. So many older buildings are not fully wheelchair accessible, nor do they meet resident needs or expectations for privacy, comfort, and other basic quality-of-life issues. As new centers are being developed and old ones renovated, such older homes are becoming obsolete.

wheelchair during at least part of their daily routine, and over half suffer from some level of dementia or memory impairment.

Historically residents have typically shared a room with one to three others, and those who are able to leave their rooms have been served meals in a central dining area on the nursing unit or in a central location. At most facilities, activities are also available during the day and evening.

Sponsors and Owners

For-profit

For-profit providers account for the majority of nursing home beds. Large national chains such as HCR ManorCare, Genesis Health-Care, and Golden Living are the largest providers of long-term care. Smaller, privately owned nursing homes still exist in many communities, but they are no longer the norm for new facilities.

Nonprofit

Many nonprofit, often faith-based organizations sponsor long-term care services. Such nursing homes may be a part of regional organizations or even national networks.

Public

Occasionally, local governments, usually at the county level, own and operate nursing home beds for underserved and low-income populations. The Veterans Administration also has a network of long-term care facilities.

Settings

While most long-term care facilities are freestanding, some are specialized units in hospitals or in continuing care retirement communities or other forms of senior housing. Much of the existing stock is organized into nursing units of 40–60 beds each. Current long-term care design trends break the scale of the freestanding facility down even further into buildings, "houses," or clusters, each with enough program spaces to support a small group of 10–20 residents independently.

Deinstitutionalization

Historically, the characteristics of the physical environment of long-term facilities were determined by the most efficient system of delivering care; the primary concern was residents' medical and basic custodial needs. Residents were usually ambulatory and less frail at the time of admission and able to access centralized common spaces that were often distant from their own quarters. This impacted the program of a typical nursing floor, where, typically, a central nurses station was surrounded by corridors of residents' rooms. Very little, if any, shared resident space was nearby. The residents' experience was not a priority. There were rigid schedules, privacy and dignity were sacrificed for shared sleeping rooms and common bathing facilities, and residents had very few choices about their daily routine or activities. As a result, many suffered from loneliness, boredom, anxiety, depression, disassociation, and withdrawal.

Size

Most states have codes that establish the minimum square footage of the major spaces, but these minimums are often far too small. There are older facilities where the gross square footage of the entire facility is less than 500 GSF per resident. Today, the minimum size for a modern facility is over 700 GSF, and the best facilities often exceed 850–900 GSF per resident.

For facilities to remain competitive, that size is likely to grow, since most sponsors now recognize that their facilities are the residents' homes, not just healthcare centers. Extended-stay hotels such as Marriott's

The Pioneer Network was formed in 1997 by a small group of prominent long-term care professionals to advocate for person-directed care. This group called for a radical change in the culture of aging so that when our grandparents, parents—and ultimately, ourselves—go to a nursing home or other community-based setting, it is to thrive, not to decline. This movement away from institutional provider–driven models to more humane, consumer-driven models that embrace flexibility and self-determination has come to be known as the long-term care culture change movement.

Culture change is the name given to the national movement for the transformation of older adult services based on person-directed values and practices, where the voices of elders and those working with them are considered and respected. Core person-directed values are choice, dignity, respect, self-determination, and purposeful living. Culture-change transformation supports the creation of both long- and short-term living environments as well as community-based settings where both older adults and their caregivers are able to express their choices and practice self-determination in meaningful ways at every level of daily life. Culture-change transformation may require changes in organization practices, physical environments, relationships at all levels, and workforce models, leading to better outcomes for consumers and direct-care workers without being costly for providers.

Pioneer Network

Residence Inns or Executive Apartments provide at least 700 GSF per guest. Is it any wonder that traditional nursing homes are widely disliked for their cramped living spaces and lack of privacy? Nevertheless, they are still a necessity for almost 2 million frail aged. An understanding of the history of long-term care (see sidebar) facilitates a discussion of current standards for the major components of a nursing home program. And a movement toward person-directed care that will deinstitutionalize long-term care is well underway.

This change is evidenced by the transformation of the traditional nursing unit—typically 40–60 resident beds with a central nurses station—to a variety of smaller-scale environments (fig. 2-15).

There are five organizing concepts for long-term care:

1. *Nursing units* centralize resident and staff spaces for groups of 40–60. This is no longer the preferred model for new facilities.
2. *Clusters* break down a nursing unit into smaller staff groupings that can respond to different staffing patterns over different shifts.
3. *Neighborhoods* centralize staffing resources and spaces for 20–40 residents while creating smaller-scale living experiences for 10–20 residents.
4. *Households* create self-contained living and staffing environments for 10–16 residents who share some central services and social spaces.

▶ *Figure 2-15 The plan for a 40-bed nursing unit.* Perkins Eastman.
1. Resident room
3. Dining
4. Kitchen
5. Activity meeting room
6. Staff workroom
7. Staff workspace
8. Service
9. General support
10. Bathing

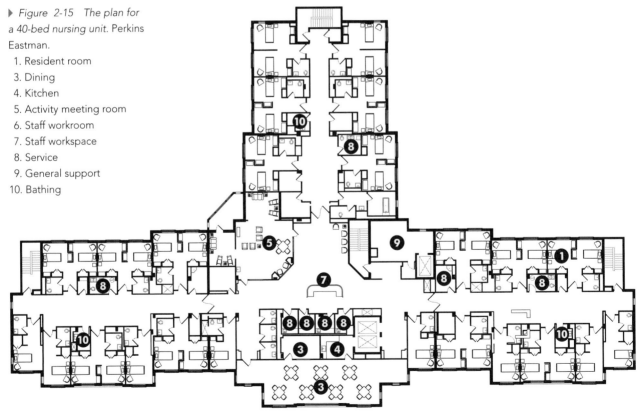

5. *Houses* are entirely freestanding both operationally and physically. Green Houses and small houses are two common models and typically serve 10–12 residents.

Appendix G provides gross area-per-bed guidelines for each of these models and illustrates the subtle shift in program areas between resident living areas, shared common areas, administration, and back-of-house (service) areas. Appendix H provides typical code minimums for spaces in the resident living area, as well as recommended minimum areas in keeping with new philosophies of care delivery and resident experience. Appendix I provides a sample program that combines features of household and neighborhood models.

Program and Design

Traditionally, long-term care facilities made the nursing unit the key organizational element and the nurses station the key planning focus. Most older nursing units were organized in the shape of an *L, T, X, V,* or *Y.* These designs emerged from an operations philosophy that placed the nurses station in the center for control, surrounding it with all the support spaces (utility, bathing, dining, etc.) and locating lounges at the ends of corridors. These plans also derived from code requirements mandating a maximum distance (commonly 120 ft) from the nurses station or utility space to any resident room.

Over the last 20 years, the primacy of the nursing unit has been greatly reduced. In some new facilities, call systems and computer-based medical records have made sight lines and centralized paperwork obsolete. In addition, the paradigm of the nurse as the central controlling figure is being replaced by one of an autonomous, self-directed team of caregivers in a small group of residents (called a "small house" or "household") supported by a team of nurses, social workers, therapists, and physicians who essentially make house calls to the households (fig. 2-16).

The household has become key to the organization of long-term care facilities. But the definition of *household* is still contested. Some believe that a household can only be successful if it is truly autonomous, the gold standard for which is cooking. All of the Green Houses and most of the small houses do most if not all of the cooking in the house kitchens. Others, seeking efficiency, compromise by placing a kitchen between two households, which maintain separate living, dining, and support spaces. Others are going further by utilizing a centralized kitchen to do the bulk preparation of the food.

The use of trademarked Green Houses and generic small houses skyrocketed between 2000 and 2010. Autonomous freestanding houses or apartments for 10–12 residents are supported by a team of caregivers. There is no nursing unit, nor are nurses stationed in each house. The houses are typically grouped into a community of at least four adjacent houses. This grouping offers some staffing efficiency to those professionals who make house calls.

This new organizational scheme is at the center of a debate about staffing and physical space standards in new long-term care facilities. Critics are concerned about increased operating costs and about residents feeling confined or isolated by day-to-day exposure to a fixed, small group of residents and staff. This is of special concern where harsh winters make travel from one house to another challenging. As an alternative to the freestanding house, some sponsors are developing neighborhoods of connected households, a solution that offers residents more choices about what they do and whom they spend their time with. These models typically share staff across households, which some sponsors believe is more cost-effective and operationally more flexible.

Housing Models

Nursing units

The oldest and most common model in long-term care is a nursing unit in which residents' rooms are organized around a central nurses station, clean and soiled utility rooms, and bathing, dining, and lounge spaces. This model results in the letter-shaped floor plans. Wings of resident rooms radiate out from the central nurse's station, from which there are sight lines to the hallways.

The number of residents varies from less than 30 in smaller specialized units to a maximum of 60 in most states. Some states have permitted nursing units exceeding 60 beds, but there is agreement among experienced nurses that even 60 beds are too many. There are more typically 40 beds per unit, but there is no universal standard. As more and more nursing units are organized around a series of nursing substations and decentralized support spaces, the size of each unit has become less and less important.

Dining and lounge areas

While some older facilities still have only central dining and lounge areas, most now distribute these functions to each nursing unit.

Dining options and dining spaces are changing dramatically. Facilities are moving away from large dining rooms for 40–60 residents (or more) and meals served on trays in favor of smaller rooms, country kitchens, and family-style meals served in courses. High-quality food and pleasant dining experiences are features of a well-run facility. Key design parameters include:

- adequate space for residents in wheelchairs and geriatric chairs: 30–35 sq ft/

The biggest cost in operating a long-term care facility is the staff, so designing a unit that maximizes staff efficiency is important to the bottom line. A variety of staff, from nurses to dieticians to housekeepers, maintains the residents' quality of life and environment (fig. 2-16).

Most nursing units are planned around licensed nursing and direct-care staff—care attendants and certified nursing assistants (CNAs). Staffing is typically organized in traditional medical-model nursing shifts: 7 AM to 3 PM (day), 3 PM to 11 PM (evening), and 11 PM to 7 AM (night). Staff requirements are based on residents' care needs and mandated codes: one CNA for every 10 residents, and a registered nurse (RN) or licensed practical nurse (LPN) for every 40–60 residents is common. Due to the frailty of some residents, CNA ratios of 1:7 or 1:8 on day and evening shifts and 1:15 to 1:21 on night shifts are typical. The typical ratios of RNs and LPNs to residents are 1:20 to 1:30 on day and evening shifts and 1:30 to 1:40 at night. Some nursing units are therefore designed to operate as smaller units during the day and then be combined into a larger unit supervised by a central nurses' station or work area at night.

person (state codes often mandate at least 28 sq ft/person);
- multiple dining rooms serving 15–20 residents each;
- large-scale dining rooms broken into smaller environments for better acoustic control, visual privacy, and more comfortable dining;
- an open country kitchen (if permitted by the local department of health) that

◀ Figure 2-16 The relationship between the caregiver and the resident is still the most important aspect of any senior care setting. Woodside Place, Oakmont, Pennsylvania. Perkins Eastman. Photograph by Martha Rial.

supports the food-service program, allows for baking activities, and has pantries that allow aromas to stimulate residents' appetites;

- space for refrigeration (commercial and/or residential), steam tables, ice machines, microwaves, and other food-service support; and
- a "private" dining room seating 8–10 for family visits, birthday parties, and other special meals. It can double as a conference room as well as space for supportive feeding programs and recreational activities.

Social activity spaces—lounges, activity rooms, or living rooms—within or near nursing units provide:

- private places for residents and their families or guests;
- activity areas for games, cards, or organized activities;
- comfortable places for discussion groups, watching TV, and so on; and
- space for small parties or shared meals.

Cluster model

The cluster model is a staffing model that utilizes the day, evening, and night shifts to create a "neighborhood"-based nursing unit. Some facilities also decentralize support areas to minimize walking distances for residents and staff; this also distributes the direct-care staff across clusters. Nurses' workstations are often integrated into lounges or living rooms. Clusters are arranged so that they can be converted from 7–10 rooms or residents on the day shifts to 14–21 on evening and night shifts in response to changing staff needs (fig. 2-17).

There is one nurse unit manager to supervise and manage the staff for each shift. The number of residents in a cluster varies

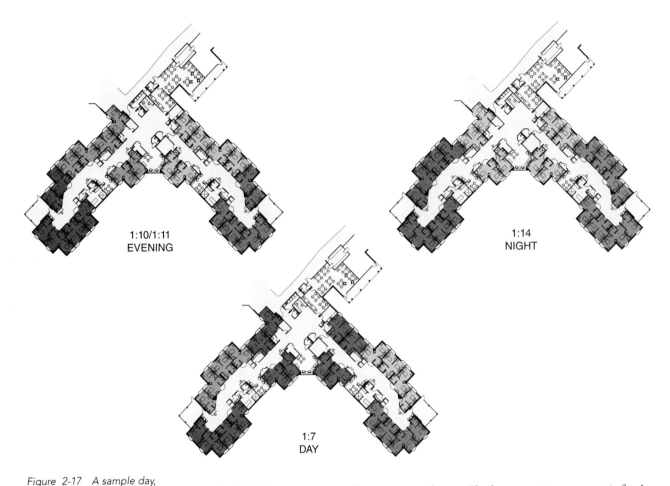

1:10/1:11
EVENING

1:14
NIGHT

1:7
DAY

Figure 2-17 A sample day, evening, and night shift staffing plan for a 42-bed nursing unit.
Day shift: 1 CNA per 7 residents, 1 RN or LPN per 21 residents Evening shift: 1 CNA per 14 residents, 1 RN or LPN per 21–42 residents Night shift: 1 CNA per 21 residents, 1 RN or LPN per 42 residents Perkins Eastman.

with the shift. The maximum staffing ratio occurs during the morning shift, when residents require more assistance for meals, bathing, dressing, therapy, and recreation, in addition to medical care.

Neighborhood model

The neighborhood model takes the cluster model one step further. Not only is the staff decentralized into smaller groups with support areas, but resident spaces like dining and living rooms are, as well (fig. 2-18). A neighborhood is typically a group of 10–20 residents. Nearby social spaces are more accessible because the travel distances are

shorter. The key organizing concept is food service and dining: smaller dining rooms for 10–20 residents are serviced from a kitchen that also services another, adjacent neighborhood's dining room. This approach holds down initial costs. The smaller scale means a full-time food-service worker in the household—rather than a CNA—can handle meal prep and cleanup (fig. 2-19).

Some models aggregate several households on a floor with other shared spaces rather than combining them in a central location. Likely program elements for this approach include rehab and fitness, a spa or salon, and a bistro or coffee shop.

◀ *Figure 2-18* The
*decentralized stations bring
the staff closer to the people
they serve. Presbyterian
Village at Hollidaysburg,
Hollidaysburg, Pennsylvania.*
Perkins Eastman. Photograph
by Sarah Mechling.

◀ *Figure 2-19 A shared
open kitchen services two
neighborhood dining rooms.
Presbyterian Village, Austell,
Georgia.* Perkins Eastman.
Photograph by Creative
Sources Photography.

In some settings, the number of households in a neighborhood is large enough for the neighborhood to function as if it were a stand-alone facility with a dedicated team of management and administrative staff. For instance, at NewBridge on the Charles in Dedham, Massachusetts, there are 88 residents in 6 households. The administrative team is housed in a suite of offices and support spaces that allows it to function autonomously from those in other neighborhoods.

Household model

Households create smaller, family-size social groupings with shorter walking distances to common living spaces, giving residents a greater level of independence and access to more social experiences.

Households differ in size from traditional nursing units; the model also restructures the hierarchical staff system and redirects how decisions are made around residents' care. Staff are often given permanent assignments so they can develop relationships with a small group of residents. Flexibility is crucial: residents must be able to choose when and what to eat, when to bathe, the types of household activities, and whether to participate in them. The result is a community in which residents and staff all have choices and can make meaningful contributions to their environment. Initial studies note that most household residents become more engaged and enlivened, and have a better quality of life than their counterparts in more institutional facilities.

Each approach to household programming must address two variables: the number of residents in each household and the degree of the household's self-governance. A household is intended to be operationally autonomous from other households and from the common spaces. Household staff, typically CNAs, have clear care responsibility and can then develop personal relationships with household residents. This model encourages cross-training the staff, who then become "universal workers." Care, housekeeping, recreation, and dining needs can then be met by a team of individuals without narrowly defined roles or responsibilities.

Staffing within these households is typically provided at a ratio of one cross-trained CNA per five residents. This is a significantly higher staffing ratio than in traditional long-term care facilities. But these CNAs are doing several tasks that were previously done by central staff, such as food-service workers and housekeepers; their training means they require less direct supervision. It is therefore possible to provide higher levels of frontline caregiving without additional staffing costs.

Residence areas will vary between 600 and 750 sq ft per resident. The ideal number of residents in a household is 10–16: 10 is the smallest that can be efficiently staffed; 16 is the largest number of residents that can fit into a dining room with a residential ambience and appropriate staffing. Freestanding houses range 670–880 sq ft per resident.

Households include the following:

- *Private resident rooms.* There are 10–16, each with a bathroom that has a shower.
- *Living room.* The living room is typically the first room one encounters on entering, contributing to the household's residential character. It is used for activities and socializing between residents, staff, and family.
- *Den.* The den offers a quiet space away from the other household common spaces. It is generally acoustically and visually separate from the living room and dining room and houses the only common television—an arrangement that is regularly

debated. Some think the common TV creates distraction that prevents social interaction and that it is unnecessary because residents have TVs in their rooms. Some sponsors equip the den with a sleeper sofa so visitors can stay overnight; others utilize the den for quiet activities. It is an important household element for those who prefer a quiet environment or enjoy socializing in small groups.

- *Dining room.* High-quality food and comfortable dining are fundamental to everyone's lifestyle. Key design parameters include the following:
  - Providing 30–35 sq ft/person ensures adequate space for the large numbers of residents in wheelchairs and geriatric chairs as well as the staff to assist them.
  - Considering using one large harvest-style table to accommodate everyone in houses and households with only 10–12 residents. This allows meals to be served

family-style rather than individually. Some providers question this approach, as it doesn't give residents freedom to choose their meal times and assumes that all residents are comfortable with each other socially (fig. 2-20).

- Offering an alternative to dining at the main table or in the dining room provides flexibility for those who need additional assistance, or who like to eat at times other than when meals are being served.
- Using the dining room for crafts and activities when not in use for meals.
- Making the dining room large enough to accommodate two extra chairs, enabling visitors to enjoy meals in the households.

House model
The house model turns the household into an entirely separate living environment; no

◀ *Figure 2-20 Household kitchens become the center of life for residents and staff. Hebrew SeniorLife: NewBridge on the Charles, Dedham, Massachusetts. Perkins Eastman. Photograph by Sarah Mechling.*

spaces are shared between houses by residents or staff. Direct-care staff are entirely house-based, with central nursing, medical, and therapy services provided by visits to the house. Most house models are for 10–12 residents, all with private rooms surrounding an open living room and kitchen. Staff areas are typically integrated into the living and kitchen spaces, but most houses have a small office for private calls, record-keeping, and reference materials. Most house models are set in freestanding houses in rural or suburban locations (fig. 2-21), or in apartments in multistory buildings in urban locations.

The model owes much to the Green House Project started by Dr. Bill Thomas, who also started the Eden Alternative, an international nonprofitorganization dedicated to transforming care environments into habitats for human beings that promote quality of life for all involved (see chapter 3). The Green House is a philosophy for providing

long-term care that maintains the dignity of elders by creating a home for them. This branded concept has clearly delineated operational guidelines and building requirements. Joining the Green House Project comes with access to assistance and oversight in developing and operating these homes (fig. 2-22).

The small house movement is a response to the philosophy of the Green House but does not follow all of its prescribed operational and physical design requirements. While most small houses are also freestanding, the term has come to embrace models that may also share common areas and staff, and may be physically linked.

Long-Term Care Programs
Short-term rehabilitation
For long-term care providers who also operate home health agencies, short-term rehab is a natural extension of their service

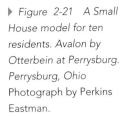

▶ *Figure 2-21 A Small House model for ten residents. Avalon by Otterbein at Perrysburg. Perrysburg, Ohio* Photograph by Perkins Eastman.

offerings. Such services are an important selling point for long-term care facilities because some short-term rehab patients will never be able to return home and must therefore find long-term care. And it is not unusual for those who *can* live at home, even with the support of family and/or visiting nurse services, to require ongoing outpatient rehab.

Short-term rehabilitation (or subacute care) is a cost-effective way to enable patients with injuries, acute illnesses, or postoperative care needs to recover outside a hospital environment. It has emerged as a critical component of the senior living continuum—one that is tightly bound to the healthcare industry. The high cost of hospital stays has driven insurance providers to move patients out of the hospital as quickly as possible, creating a demand for short-term rehab and spurring its growth (fig. 2-23).

Short-term rehab is usually reimbursed through Medicare for a maximum of 28–31 days. When first developed, average stays of 30 days or more were not unusual. But as pressure from insurance providers mounted, and as home health agencies' service offerings broadened, the length of stay has fallen as low as 7–10 days in some regions. Facilities offering short-term rehab must be certified by Medicare, and many facilities carry dual Medicaid and Medicare licensure.

Typical short-term rehab patients are elderly, but not as old as those in long-term care; some are even in their 50s or 60s. But the majority of patients are in their 70s and 80s.

Short-term rehab patients typically fall into one of three categories:

1. orthopedic (bone fractures and joint replacements);
2. cardiovascular (heart surgery); and
3. neurological (strokes).

▶ *Figure 2-23 A neighborhood-based short-term rehabilitation model of care. MorseLife Short-Term Rehab Center, West Palm Beach, Florida.*

1 Resident room
2 Living room
3 Dining
4 Kitchen
5 Activity meeting room
6 Staff workroom
7 Staff workspace
8 Service
9 General support

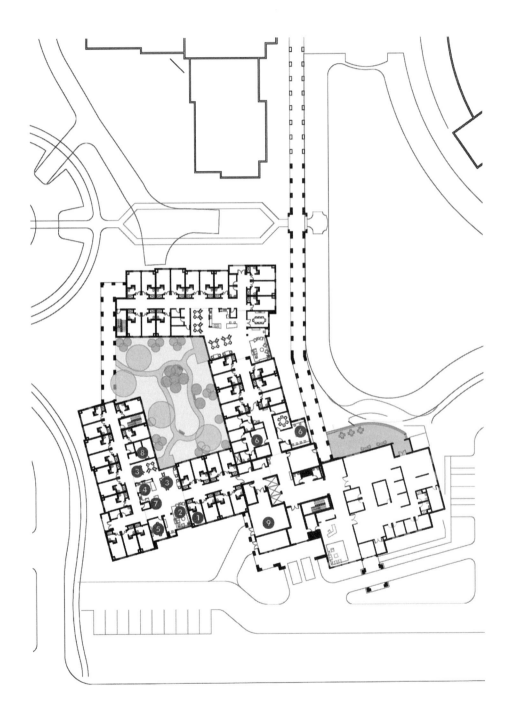

In most locations, Medicare reimbursement rates are much higher than those for long-term care; many providers use the higher profits from short-term rehab to cover their operating losses in long-term care. But the average length of stay is growing shorter and the market for short-term rehab patients is becoming more competitive. In response, built-in flexibility in new short-term rehabs allows them to shift between short-term rehab and long-term care.

Short-term vs. long-term facilities
In some states, short- and long-term care operate in dual-licensed facilities, and short-term residents are integrated into the long-term care population. However, some states require a separate certificate of need (CON) and license for short-term rehabs.

Those that integrate short-term rehab patients with their long-term care residents enjoy the flexibility to fill empty beds with either type of customer. But integration with residents who are older, frailer, and will never return to their homes can impact marketing appeal significantly. As a result, many providers are creating discrete short-term rehabilitation facilities.

Residents' quality of life is the focus of a long-term care facility, while short-term rehab facilities center on the patients' rehabilitation. Thus the length of stay, the differences in care needs, and expectations about returning home are the key distinctions between the short-term patient and the long-term resident. These distinctions drive the program and service differences between the two facilities:

- Short-term rehab has a dramatically higher turnover rate. The average length of stay is approximately 10 days, compared with approximately 12 months at

long-term care facilities. As a result, there is less need for social space.
- Because varying rehab schedules make serving meals at a specific time difficult, patients often eat in their rooms.
- Staffing requirements for therapists, nurses, and physicians are higher at short-term rehabs. A larger staff is also needed to transport patients, who attend rehab daily or even more frequently.

Facilities for patients with dementia
There is ongoing debate about whether it is best to develop separate households or neighborhoods for those short-term rehab patients with dementia or for them to live side by side with other patients. Many sponsors believe that dementia care can be best provided in a specialized setting providing a continuum of specialized services, from adult day care through assisted living and long-term care. Other sponsors believe that integration in a long-term care facility is easier to manage for staff, creates less disruptive moves for residents with advancing dementia, and encourages better socialization. However, the behavior of some dementia patients is disruptive or potentially hazardous to both themselves and to other residents, so specialized households or units may be appropriate for them.

Program and Design
Resident rooms
The basic building block of a long-term care facility is the resident room. Most long-term care beds are configured as small shared rooms. Such rooms are permissible by code in all states, but as users and decision makers demand more privacy and dignity for the aging population in long-term care homes, sponsors are responding. The most thoughtful sponsors of new beds want to build

private rooms. However, when the cost of increased square footage and additional private bathrooms becomes prohibitive, semiprivate room configurations that provide some degree of separation between residents, such as the "toe-to-toe," or biaxial, configuration, are used. Many older facilities are being renovated to increase residents' privacy, in some instances by reducing the number of licensed beds.

Most codes establish 100 or 120 sq ft as the minimum room size for a single person and 80–90 sq ft per person in a multi-bed room. This minimum does not include resident storage, toilet space, or entry vestibule. Other codes establish minimum accessibility and furnishing requirements, which then determine the minimum room size. Codes also regulate certain components of the resident room. They typically include

- a hospital bed, which come in several sizes but are wider and longer than a normal bed,
- a wardrobe or closet for the resident's storage needs,
- a nightstand,
- a bedside chair,
- an over-bed table, and
- minimum floor clearances around all sides of the bed to provide easy access for the resident and staff.

Other considerations not addressed in the code minimums include

- furniture or built-in cabinets for additional storage;
- a television, located so it can be viewed with minimal glare from the place the resident usually sits;
- additional floor clearances to accommodate mobility issues regarding wheelchairs and walkers;

- an area for medical equipment;
- a small table and chair for visitors; and
- individually controlled mechanical systems, which often require a heat pump or fan coil be located in the room.

To realistically accommodate residents' needs, the size of a resident room's living space should be 140–150 sq ft. Pragmatically, a wheelchair-accessible room with a bed, side table, dresser, chair, and closet or wardrobe cannot be much smaller than 12 × 12 ft, or 144 sq ft.

Sharing a room with a stranger, with nothing but a curtain for privacy, is the single most disliked aspect of nursing homes. In response to the expectations of residents and their families, a growing number of sponsors have therefore experimented with room designs providing more privacy, and some are now offering private rooms exclusively. Newer semiprivate room designs are typically toe-to-toe, or biaxial (with or without a partial dividing wall); L-shaped; or private but with a shared toilet. While these room types add square footage, and therefore cost, they are popular with residents, family, and staff (figs. 2-24 through 2-28).

Other resident room features in current designs include the following:

1. Large windows for sunlight, with low sills that make looking outside easier
2. Multiple light sources for reading in bed or a chair, observation by staff (especially for skin conditions), and night lighting (through floor lighting) that makes getting to and from the bathroom easier
3. Cable TV, high-speed Internet access, and a conveniently located telephone
4. A "nurse server" or storage cabinet, within or immediately outside the

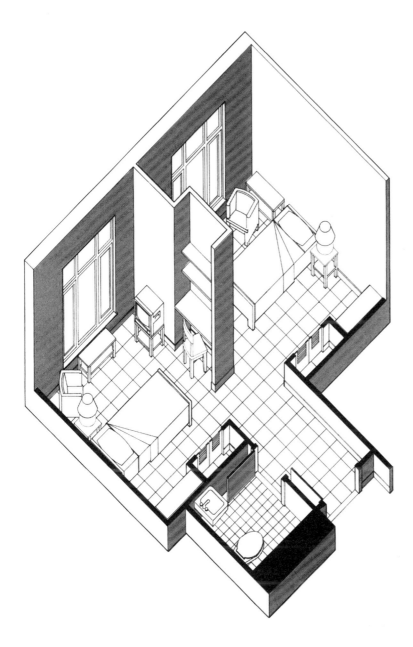

◀ *Figure 2-24 One approach to creating more privacy is to move the beds into a toe-to-toe configuration, now commonly referred to as a biaxial room.* Perkins Eastman.

resident room for storing clean linen, wound care and incontinence products, and other supplies used by staff

5. A lockable medicine cabinet (in addition to the resident's in the bathroom), so nurses can store and document medication

6. A lift system to assist with resident transfer and prevent back injuries among staff (fig. 2-29).

▶ *Figure 2-25 Greater resident privacy can be created by building a wall or a storage unit between the two beds. Hebrew SeniorLife: NewBridge on the Charles, Dedham, Massachusetts. Perkins Eastman. Photograph by Sarah Mechling.*

▶ *Figure 2-26 The ability to personalize room décor is an important cueing aid for residents with Alzheimer's. Copper Ridge, Sykesville, Maryland. Perkins Eastman. Photograph by Curtis Martin Photography Inc.*

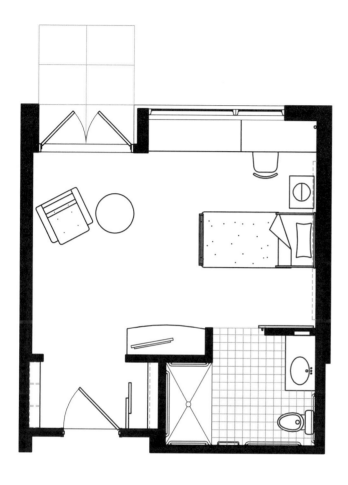

◀ *Figure 2-27 Large private resident room (340–425 sq ft).* Perkins Eastman.

Resident bathrooms

Historically, resident rooms have been designed with a shared bathroom with two fixtures: a toilet and sink; a shower was only included if required by code for an isolation room. But the majority of new resident rooms built by leading owners have a three-fixture private bathroom (fig. 2-30).

The typical features and detailing of the bathroom include the following:

- A roll-in shower (approximately 3' × 5') that accommodates a wheeled shower chair

and provides space for a caregiver to assist in bathing. The bathroom flooring is often extended into the shower to provide a continuous surface. (Proper drainage is of particular concern in this configuration.)

- A vanity countertop rather than a wall-mounted sink, giving residents space to set grooming devices while using them.

- An open area below the vanity countertop so it can be used in a seated position. This also provides space for a walker or wheelchair.

▶ Figure 2-28 Due to growing resistance to the typical semiprivate room, sponsors are creating rooms that are more homelike and offer more privacy and dignity. The Mary E. Bivins Foundation: Childers Place, Amarillo, Texas. Perkins Eastman. Photograph by Chris Cooper.

- A small wall-recessed cabinet or wall-mounted shelf (with rounded corners) for toiletries. It should be hung such that residents with poor sight or limited physical abilities do not have to reach over a sink to get to it.
- Towel bars (in shared accommodations).
- A nonslip floor.
- A large surface-sliding bathroom door with a wide opening (32–42 in.), which requires less accessibility clearance than a swinging door. Although this door configuration often requires a variance from code requirements, it is easier for residents with mobility assistance devices to use.

- Bedpan washers in each toilet, depending on the nursing staff's requirements and state regulations. (Disposable bedpans are now obviating the need for institutional plumbing.)
- A handicapped toilet or a standard toilet with a raised seat, making it easier for older people to rise.
- A supplemental heat source if there is a shower in the bathroom.
- Toilet grab bars. Side (42 in.) and rear (36 in.) bars are required by many codes. With a code variance, flip-down grab bars can be mounted on both sides of the toilet. Some manufacturers make toilets with chairlike "sheltering" arms

◀ *Figure 2-29 Overhead lift system in resident room. Hebrew SeniorLife: NewBridge on the Charles, Dedham, Massachusetts. Perkins Eastman. Photograph by Sarah Mechling.*

mounted on both sides for residents unable to use fixed grab bars, which can also get in the way when staff must help a resident move from a wheelchair to the toilet. (See chapters 12 and 15 for further discussion of finishes and other details.)

The bathroom should appear residential but be accessible. Residential lighting products, paint-finished grab bars, and conventional tank toilets create a familiar, comfortable atmosphere (fig. 2-31). Because most accidents occur in the bathroom, easy, well-lit access to the toilet room is essential: residents use the bathroom frequently at night, when the elderly are likelier to lose their balance or become disoriented.

Open kitchen

In most new nursing homes there is a dining room for each nursing unit, with at least 28 sq ft per resident (30–35 sq ft per resident is recommended). Most also have

- a separate dining space for family parties and small group meals;
- a serving pantry designed to support the food delivered from a central kitchen (on trays, in bulk for steam tables or warming carts) and located near a service elevator; and
- a bathroom.

In the household model, the dining room often is an extension of an open kitchen.

Kitchens that support the house model food-service program can enable residents to decide what they want to eat right at

▶ *Figure 2-30 Private resident room with full bathroom (290–320 sq ft). Perkins Eastman.*

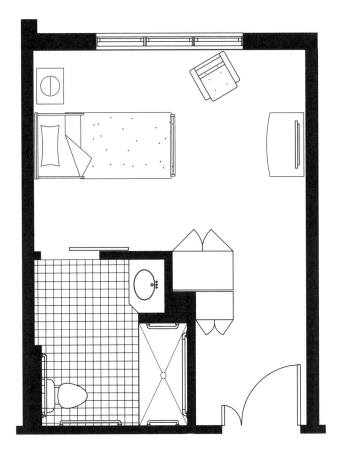

mealtime; aromas from baking and food preparation can stimulate residents' appetites. The open kitchen also makes it easier to see and interact with the relatively small staff and allows the staff to observe household activity. Kitchen equipment should support the desired degree of autonomy.

Houses and households typically have fully functioning kitchens that typically contain the following:

- Two residential refrigerators (one located in the pantry).
- An electric conduction range. Because regulations in some states prohibit a range in an open kitchen, it is fitted with electronic controls that make it operable only when staff is present. A commercial exhaust system and a fire-protection system may also be required.
- A double wall oven, with one oven doubling as a microwave.
- Separate sinks: one for food preparation, and a second, equipped with a garbage disposal, for washing dishes. In some jurisdictions, a third, small handwash sink is required.
- A commercial or robust residential under-counter dishwasher. Automatically dispensed detergent and very hot water are required in many jurisdictions.
- A separate ice maker.
- Countertop appliances such as toasters, coffee makers, and food processors.
- Trash and recyclables containers.

◀ *Figure 2-31 A bathroom with a roll-in shower, flexible grab bars, a vanity countertop with space below it, and storage for personal items. Multiple lighting sources, nonslip floors, and supplemental heat are becoming standard features. Danville Community Living Center, Danville, Illinois. Perkins Eastman. Photograph by Sarah Mechling.*

There should be separate areas in the kitchen for food preparation and dish washing. Most regulators are demanding a National Sanitation Foundation rating for equipment used to prepare daily meals.

Some providers want residents to be able to enter the kitchen; others, as well as some regulators, want barriers to prohibit residents from entering the kitchen at certain times, such as when food is being prepared.

If prepared hot food is served from a central kitchen, a set of steam-table wells are required. If cold food items are served from a central kitchen, one of the refrigerators must be capable of handling racks of food-service trays of salads, desserts, and so on.

Support spaces

The following are the support spaces typically for in a cluster, household, or nursing unit:

- *Pantry.* A walk-in space that contains one of the refrigerators, the coffee maker, a handwash sink, and ample storage for food and dry goods.
- *Public toilet.* Near common areas and accessible to visitors and residents.
- *Staff toilet.* Some regulatory agencies permit only one toilet in small households with few staffers.
- *Laundry.* Primarily for residents' laundry; some houses use the laundry room for napkins and tablecloths, as well.
- *Clean utility room.* Used for storing clean supplies such as IV racks, monitors, incontinence products, and medical supplies. Storage cabinets and a handwash sink are typically required.
- *Soiled utility room.* Used for the temporary storage of soiled linen and clothing. As the number of incontinent residents in long-term care facilities has increased,

these spaces have gotten larger and more complex. It is not unusual to find one or two multiple-compartment carts or bins (2' × 4') for sorting bed linens, infectious linens, and personal clothing. Limited cabinetry, a handwash sink, and a bed-pan-washing device are typical features.

- *Clean linen.* Most facilities use a cart-exchange system: fully stocked carts are rolled into a closet or room, and empty carts are taken away for restocking. There can be two or three carts (approximately 24" × 60" each) and some limited fixed shelving for extra pillows and blankets, depending on the number of beds the room serves. This space is sometimes combined with a clean utility room.
- *Housekeeping closet.* Some states dictate a minimum size; it should be a minimum of 40 sq ft.
- *Medication room or alcove.* A locked room with lockable cabinets, a small refrigerator, and a sink for the storage and preparation of medications.
- *Charting room or alcove.* This can be a desk in the living room or a separate office. Some providers combine it with the medication room.
- *Support spaces.* For mechanical, electrical, telecommunications, and data equipment and/or distribution panels.

Bathing areas

Bathing areas have evolved from centralized "hygiene machines" to more spa-like experiences that afford greater privacy and a more pleasant environment. Most states are agnostic about whether they are to be equipped with a shower or a tub. In either case, a bathing suite is comprised of a private room with a changing area, access to toilets, and adequate space for bathing. Roll-in showers must be large enough to maneuver residents in shower chairs comfortably (a minimum of 48" × 48"). There must be adequate maneuvering space around three sides of specialized tubs for staff and specialized lifts or transfers.

Items to consider include the following:

- Nonslip floor services with appropriate drainage
- Storage space for soaps, shampoos, and cleaning products
- Storage space for bathing tub manufacturer's product requirements for size, power, water, and access (see chapter 12)
- Vanity counter for grooming
- Handwash sink for staff
- Additional heat source for comfort
- Shower curtains and cubicle curtains to maintain privacy
- External controls for showers so staff do not have to reach into the shower
- Places to put towels, clothes, robes, and so on
- Private, easily accessed toileting facilities

Nurses station

The term *nurses station* is something of a misnomer because there may be up to a dozen different staff, only one or two of whom are nurses, using the records, computer, telephones, and supplies in this location. A reception zone for visitors, family, and residents is important; equally imperative is a work zone for charting, staff meetings, care conferences, and confidential phone calls about resident care. In many states, active medical records must still be kept in hard-copy form, but the use of computers for ordering, communicating with other departments, and record keeping will change as policies catch up with technology. The need for the nurses station to function as an emergency-call hub has largely been supplanted by pagers and cell phones that route emergency calls to staff wherever they may be.

Central common areas

There are additional common areas at a skilled-nursing facility that serve all of the nursing units (figs. 2-32 through 2-35):

- *Multipurpose room.* Suitable for large group activities, holiday celebrations, religious services, and performances
- *Coffee shop/snack bar.* An alternative visiting area for residents and guests
- *Gift shop.*
- *Living room.*
- *Library.* Often includes computers for residents' use as well as a growing choice of reading materials and other media developed specifically for the aging
- *Gym.*
- *Outdoor terraces and recreation areas.*
- *Art/activity space.* Large central space for specialized activities inappropriate for the nursing unit

- *Clinic.* Space for specialized exams (e.g., dental, ophthalmology) and treatments
- *Rehabilitation facility.* For restorative therapies and rehabilitation, including physical, occupational, and speech therapy
- *Family areas.* For informal meetings or private dining for meals and celebrations
- *Support space.* For community-based administrative tasks
- *Volunteer area.* A home base for any outside volunteers

There are a significant number of administrative tasks at a long-term care facility performed by human resources, marketing/admissions, accounting, and management staff; in larger facilities, there can be well over 20 such personnel. These functions are generally accommodated on a facility's ground floor, near the entry or common

◀ *Figure 2-32 Living rooms and libraries beyond the resident areas are important destinations for residents and their families. Mary E. Bivins Foundation: Childers Place, Amarillo, Texas. Perkins Eastman. Photograph by Chris Cooper.*

▶ *Figure 2-33 Well-designed outdoor areas include sitting areas protected from the wind and sun, level paths, and colorful seasonal plantings. Hebrew Home of Greater Washington, Rockville, Maryland.* Perkins Eastman. Photograph by Edward Massery.

▶ *Figure 2-34 New long-term care models include small gyms near resident living areas so residents can exercise daily and maintain their strength. Hebrew SeniorLife: NewBridge on the Charles, Dedham, Massachusetts.* Photograph by Perkins Eastman.

◀ Figure 2-35 Many facilities have renovated or added attractive common areas, including a coffee shop or snack bar, for resident and family interaction. Council for Jewish Elderly. Lieberman Center for Health and Rehabilitation, Skokie, Illinois. Perkins Eastman. Photograph by Sarah Mechling.

spaces, so that they are easily accessible to residents and family members alike.

Support infrastructure spaces

Away from areas for residents, family, and visitors is a large support infrastructure:

- Commercial kitchen
- Laundry
- Central receiving and storage
- Resident storage
- Housekeeping
- Facility maintenance
- Mechanical rooms
- Administrative offices
- Staff break, dining, and training rooms

The program in appendix G includes typical (i.e., neither minimum nor generous) net space allocations for the most frequently found common and support spaces in a 120–200 bed facility. The specific allocations differ widely for a variety of reasons:

- The frequency of deliveries
- Whether flat linen laundry is done in-house or outsourced
- The type of mechanical system
- Whether the facility also supports assisted living or independent living
- Whether the kitchen is used to prepare food for residents with special dietary requirements (e.g., kosher food) or other food programs (e.g., meals on wheels, day care); and the type of food service (tray or bulk delivery to the dining rooms, cook/chill) (see also chapter 10)
- Whether the administrative services and management is handled on-site or centralized

Payment, reimbursement, and regulation

Nursing homes are the most regulated form of senior living due to concern for protecting the well-being of frail seniors, their historical connection to hospitals, and the desire to control the quality and cost of nursing-home care. Long-term care facilities' space and construction are licensed and regulated by the state department of health (DOH). The local DOH may also cite federal or national standards, such as the American Institute of Architects (AIA) Guidelines for the Design and Construction of Hospitals and Health Care Facilities, the American National Standards Institute (ANSI) standards, and the life-safety codes of the National Fire Protection Association (NFPA) and the Americans with Disabilities Act (ADA).

The cost of nursing-home care (which exceeded $80,000 per year on average in 2011) is typically covered by the resident and his or her family through private financial resources, health insurance, and long-term care insurance, or, for financially qualified individuals, by Medicaid. Because of the increasing need for and explosive growth of publicly funded reimbursement, local and federal governments have been working to contain costs by reducing reimbursement and changing the services and eligibility for reimbursement. Many states have a certificate of need (CON) process, which regulates the construction, replacement, and renovation of facilities. Some states, such as Pennsylvania, have made it difficult to build or replace existing facilities by declining applications and providing minimal reimbursement for the capital costs; other states provide no reimbursement for capital costs at all.

HOSPICE
Users and Services
What is hospice? Hospice care provides support and palliative care to patients and their families when a fatal illness no longer responds to treatment. These services are not intended to either prolong life or hasten death. Hospice can be provided in a variety of settings.

Who uses hospice? Hospice patients have incurable illnesses. Some come to hospice in the last days of their lives; others, with chronic diseases, leave the facility once their symptoms and pain level are manageable. Hospice patients can be of any age, though the majority are elderly: more than 80 percent are over 65, and more than 35 percent are over 85 (National Hospice and Palliative Care Organization 2010). Families and friends of hospice patients are supported throughout the illness and the bereavement process.

The number of providers and the patients whom they serve has increased steadily since the beginning of the hospice movement. There are approximately 5,000 hospice programs nationwide, which serve approximately 1.5 million patients each year; over a million of them die in hospice care. This represents more than 40 percent of all deaths in the United States (National Hospice and Palliative Care Organization 2010).

Typical hospice patients have received hospice care at home and come to an inpatient hospice facility only when their medical needs are so acute they cannot be managed at home. The patients are highly dependent on intravenous medication and respiratory support, are not physically active, and are likely to stay only 4–7 days.

Hospice care is provided by a team of specially trained professionals, volunteers, and family members who provide medical care, pain management, and emotional and spiritual support. The goal of hospice care is to improve the quality of a patient's final days by maintaining his or her comfort and dignity. Hospice addresses all symptoms of a disease, with a special emphasis on pain control. It also deals with the emotional, social, and spiritual impact of the disease on the patient and the patient's family and friends and offers a variety of bereavement and counseling services to families before and after a patient's death. The median length of service for hospices is 21 days (National Hospice and Palliative Care Organization 2010).

Hospice services are provided in a variety of locations—at senior living settings, at homes, and in hospitals. Approximately 50 percent of hospice services are provided in the patient's home or apartment, 20 percent in long-term care settings, 20 percent at inpatient hospice facilities built specifically to provide such services, and 10 percent in acute-care hospitals.

This chapter focuses on hospices built expressly for the 300,000 patients who need inpatient hospice services every year—those who require medical attention that cannot be effectively provided at home, those who prefer not to die at home, and those who do not have family support structures to assist in their care at home.

History of Hospice

Hospices have been created by many civilizations for thousands of years. In modern times, they began as small-scale accommodations, but as society institutionalized the care of the ill, hospice accommodations became larger—and, by today's standards, inhumane. The modern hospice movement that led to the evolution of the services and facilities in use today began in London in 1967. It was founded by Dame Cicely Saunders, a nurse and, subsequently, a physician. It began as a movement to return the care of the terminally ill to small-scale residential environments where "people could find relief from pain, where they could meet with encouragement for self-awareness and socialization, and where the setting would be uplifting, not depressing" (Worpole 2009). The hospice movement took off in the United

States in 1982, the year Congress passed the Tax Equity and Fiscal Responsibility Act, which created the Medicaid hospice benefit. This meant providers could be reimbursed by Medicare (as well as by private insurance) for the services hospices provide.

Sponsors and Owners

In 2009, 49 percent of hospice providers were nonprofit, 47 percent were for-profit, and 4 percent were governmental (National Hospice and Palliative Care Organization 2010). For-profit hospice groups are often associated with for-profit hospitals or for-profit long-term care providers. Nonprofit groups, often faith-based organizations are the typical sponsors of hospice services. Nonprofit long-term care providers are common hospice providers. A number of facilities are part of regional organizations or, occasionally, national networks.

In many locations, the services are provided by an organization that focuses on home healthcare services (including hospice), while the physical facilities are provided by a hospital or long-term care provider.

Purpose-Built Hospice Care Settings

Freestanding purpose-built settings tailor their environment to patient care and distance themselves from institutional associations. These freestanding buildings are often single-story structures with a residential character sited in a natural landscaped setting. They therefore provide a quiet, serene, and more private atmosphere (fig. 2-36). Hospice settings integrated into hospitals or long-term care facilities often struggle to provide this kind of environment within a larger institutional setting.

In dense urban settings, it is usually not possible to build freestanding hospice facilities. A facility built specifically as a hospice will usually be more successful at creating

▶ *Figure 2-36 A growing number of specialized facilities for hospice and palliative care are being built for those in the last days of life and their families. Hospice settings range from small, homelike structures to larger specialized facilities. Hospice of Lancaster County: Mount Joy Care Center, Mount Joy, Pennsylvania. Reese, Lower, Patrick & Scott, Ltd. Photograph by Larry Lefever Photography.*

the appropriate atmosphere than a renovated institutional building: physical autonomy, separate entries, and separate circulation systems are more easily accommodated in new construction.

Program and Design

Hospice programs are typically licensed based on either skilled nursing facility or hospital regulations, with whose minimum standards for many programmatic elements they must comply. Hospice facilities are typically distributed throughout larger communities so that travel distances for families are minimized. Hospice programs are often small, with as few as 8 patients and rarely more than 24 patients. As a result, they are well suited to the household and neighborhood models described in the section of skilled nursing in this chapter.

Program elements and design considerations for hospice are similar to those for skilled nursing. The differences arise from the acuity of hospice patients' illness, their relatively short stay, and the larger nursing staff required to care for them, as well as the large number of visitors and the trauma associated with their visits. These differences result in the need for the following additional program elements and design considerations.

Resident room

While similar to the programming and design criteria for those in skilled-nursing facilities, resident rooms must include space for families. They must therefore be larger to accommodate additional furniture for a large number of simultaneous visitors as well as the amount of medical requirement—

usually on the headwall of the room—required by patients who are very ill. A sleeper chair or sofa is often provided to accommodate family members who prefer that someone remain with their loved one at all times during the final days of his or her life.

Some providers supply a small café table and chairs so the patient and guests can eat comfortably; many install large windows and a door with direct access to a patio or garden. While it may be unlikely for patients to use them, even an open door can connect patients to nature and pleasant memories. The need for a shower in the bathroom is debatable, as most patients will be too frail to use it; however, a shower may be appreciated by visitors who stay overnight (fig. 2-37).

Household

While the household spaces described in the skilled nursing section create a comfortable residential character for hospices, they will not be as highly utilized by hospice patients. They are, however, highly prized by families, who are much more involved throughout the day in hospice than in skilled-nursing facilities. The extended families of multiple patients are often present at a hospice simultaneously; the household common spaces provide comfortable places for them outside the patient's room.

In the skilled-nursing households, meals are at the center of daily life. In hospice, very few patients eat their meals in the common spaces. Many providers keep soups, sandwiches, and snacks on hand for families. Some provide a flexible space for family members to sleep outside the patient's room, often in a den-like setting with a sleeper sofa and adjacent bathroom.

Meals

In most hospices, patient meal service is not handled on-site. Patients, who often have no appetite or can only drink liquids, generally

◀ Figure 2-37 The resident room in a hospice must provide privacy, visual access to the outdoors, and accommodate family and visitors as overnight guests. Hospice of Lancaster County: Mount Joy Care Center, Mount Joy, Pennsylvania. Reese, Lower, Patrick & Scott, Ltd. Photograph by Larry Lefever Photography.

eat very little. The patient meals that *are* provided are typically delivered prepackaged. A residential kitchen in the common spaces enables family members to eat; occasionally, a patient or family member might cook or bake cookies or a cake for a special event.

Support

Support spaces for hospices are the same as those in long-term care facilities or hospitals. Their size and functionality is often dictated by long-term care or hospital regulations. Because of the intensity of the medical care provided by hospice, staffing levels are significantly higher than those in long-term care. The staff can be accommodated in one central multidisciplinary space or decentralized so they can be readily available to patients and their families.

Neighborhood

Some larger hospices divide their programs into multiple "households" similar to those described in the section on skilled-nursing facilities, above. In addition to the household spaces, they provide common space for the families of patients in more than one household; this space includes a residential kitchen, television, fireplace, and children's play area. These spaces are often used less during the workday but become crowded in the evenings and on weekends. A room for families to meet privately to discuss stressful end-of-life issues and receive counseling is always appreciated (fig. 2-38).

Payment, Reimbursement, and Regulation

In the United States, hospice care is covered by Medicare for patients with a prognosis of six months or less. A patient can remain in hospice care beyond six months if a physician recertifies that the patient is terminally ill. Regulatory requirements are typically the same as those for long-term care, but some states do have specific regulations for hospice.

ASSISTED LIVING RESIDENCES
Typical Users

Also known as assisted-care communities, assistive living, adult homes, domiciliary care, personal-care homes, sheltered care, board and care, and catered living, assisted living residences are designed for seniors who are no longer able to live on their own safely but who do not require the high level of healthcare provided in a nursing home. Assistance with medications, activities of daily living, meals, and housekeeping are routinely provided. Three meals per day are often served waiter-style in a common dining room. Residents live in their own apartments, which frequently have a small pantry or "tea kitchen" with a sink, small refrigerator, and microwave.

Staff is usually available 24 hours a day for added safety. Some assisted living residences provide licensed nursing services, but hours vary from community to community. In fact, the extent to which residents require assistance with activities of daily living (dressing, bathing, etc.) can vary greatly. The typical resident is in his or her mid-eighties; three out of four are women. Over 40 percent of residents in assisted living have some form of cognitive impairment, ranging from the mildly confused to the profoundly debilitated. Children often move their mothers to assisted living when "Mom can't live alone anymore."

Social activities and scheduled transportation are available in most communities. A special unit for men and women with Alzheimer's is sometimes available, and there are many assisted living residences especially for them, as well. The assisted living industry has seen a period of phenomenal growth, comparable to that of the nursing home

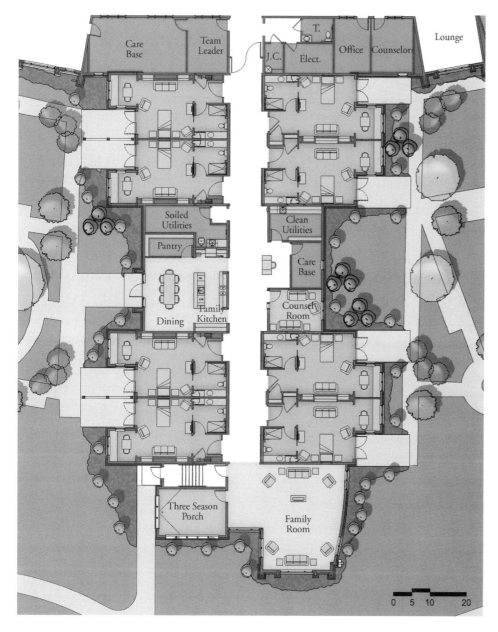

Labels on plan:
Care Base · Team Leader · T. · J.C. · Elect. · Office · Counselors · Lounge · Soiled Utilities · Clean Utilities · Pantry · Care Base · Dining · Family Kitchen · Counsel Room · Three Season Porch · Family Room

0 5 10   20

◄ *Figure 2-38 Many hospice programs create smaller neighborhoods or clusters to provide nearby medical and staff support as well as places for families and visitors. Hospice of Lancaster County: Mount Joy Care Center, Mount Joy, Pennsylvania. Reese, Lower, Patrick & Scott, Ltd. Photography by Larry Lefever Photography.*

industry in the 1960s and 1970s. From the late 1980s to the late 1990s, the number of assisted living beds more than doubled. Recently, development has slowed, as upscale markets have become saturated and expanded community-based services have effectively replaced or delayed the need for assisted living.

The industry is responding with innovative service models that allow residents to age in place and bring services into their apartment. "Apartments for life" are blending traditional senior apartment design criteria with the expanded services typically offered in an assisted living building and are dually licensed. The National Center for Assisted Living (NCAL) estimates that there are at least 28,000 facilities that provide assisted living services for over one million Americans. This number is projected to double as baby boomers need this form of senior living. The assisted living model has become a common alternative to nursing-home care for all but the most medically dependent and for low-income residents.

Sponsors and Owners

For-profit

Assisted living, in its broadest definition, has existed for many decades in the form of small family-care homes with less than six residents, or small board-and-care facilities. For-profit developers have been the most aggressive sponsors of assisted living, having created the industry and defined its products. Sponsors like Sunrise, Emeritus, Atria, and Brookdale have combined traditional real estate housing development with services and, at times, a hospitality philosophy. These types of companies have focused on upper-income residents in wealthy communities.

Nonprofit

Nonprofit sponsors have also focused on providing housing and services to frail older adults in an assisted living setting. Like for-profit sponsors, they have typically focused on upper-income seniors who can afford to pay without public assistance. Nonprofit sponsors have also developed a number of models that offer affordable housing and services through external and internal reimbursement, subsidies, and other programs.

Public

In a limited number of cases, public entities have subsidized assisted living—usually in order to offer a lower cost alternative for the frail elderly in their communities.

Settings

Beginning in the 1980s and up until recently, most new assisted living developed was freestanding and separate from other senior housing. These models have evolved considerably to keep pace with the increased frailty of new residents and the shorter lengths of stay. (Two years is not uncommon today, compared with three to five years in early communities.) Many of these new models include specially designed settings and programs for people with dementia.

In a growing effort to provide an environment that allows for aging in place with a spectrum of services that respond to the changing needs of aging residents, assisted living programs are now frequently added to existing senior living communities or designed as a part of continuing care retirement communities. (See the section on CCRCs, below.)

Program and Design

Assisted living facilities have four major program components:

1. Resident unit
2. Common facilities serving each floor, wing, or cluster of residents (often called a house or neighborhood)
3. Common facilities serving all residents
4. Support spaces

Resident Unit

Sponsors, operators, and developers of assisted living bring their own interpretation to the specific program and project. As a result, there is a wide variety of unit types, unit mixes, and design features being incorporated into projects in North America. Some of the variety stems from differences in market expectations, cost, code, and program issues, but much of it is the result of each sponsor's or developer's ideas.

Unit size and mix

The most apparent conceptual difference is in unit size. Some early for-profit developers believed that a high proportion of their potential residents would find a small studio acceptable, so attractive communal spaces were emphasized. Many early units were studios 325–375 sq ft in size. Later sponsors, including the research group that developed LeadingAge (formerly the American Association of Homes and Services for the Aging, AAHSA) prototype and some for-profit sponsors, believed the typical unit should be larger, with the basic features of an apartment. The recommended basic LeadingAge prototype unit, for example, was a 435–550 sq ft one-bedroom.

Many successful projects have been based on these program concepts, and it may be some time before there is definitive data on user preferences and the long term success of facility operations to support any one approach. As more projects are completed and the field becomes more competitive, however, sponsors and developers are moving toward larger units. Even those that still build a high proportion of studio units are building them larger and with more private sleeping areas.

Differences in program concept also show up in the unit mix. Today, most programs include various unit types and sizes. A typical resident mix might be 70–80 percent single women, 10–15 percent single men, and 5–10 percent couples. Most sponsors prefer to offer a mix that appeals to as wide a variety of resident preferences and budgets as possible. Thus, it is not unusual for a project to include both smaller and larger studios, smaller and larger one-bedrooms, and a few two-bedrooms or shared units. Most experienced sponsors also include a wing or "neighborhood" with special units for residents with behavioral issues related to dementia. Other sponsors, particularly many nonprofits, use size differences to justify pricing. It is not uncommon to disguise an internal subsidy for lower-income residents by creating an artificially large spread between the larger and smaller units. The real debt-service and operating-cost difference between a small studio and a one-bedroom (where the size difference is often less than 100 sq ft) is nominal, since the most expensive rooms—the bathroom and tea kitchen—are the same.

Ten typical unit types have evolved. There are many differences within each unit type, but the following examples illustrate the most common program options.

Semiprivate

This option is likely to become less common for the reasons noted above, but it is still being included in some projects. It is an expanded version of semiprivate nursing-home accommodations, and it assumes that its lower cost will make it acceptable as supportive housing for some residents. It is also an appropriate unit type for a specialized facility or wing for residents with dementia, who sometimes bond with another resident, thereby requiring a shared living arrangement.

Small studio

This unit type—typically about 250 sq ft—is popular and has many of the features of a hotel room. It has the cost advantage of limited floor area and minimum building perimeter, but lacks a private sleeping area.

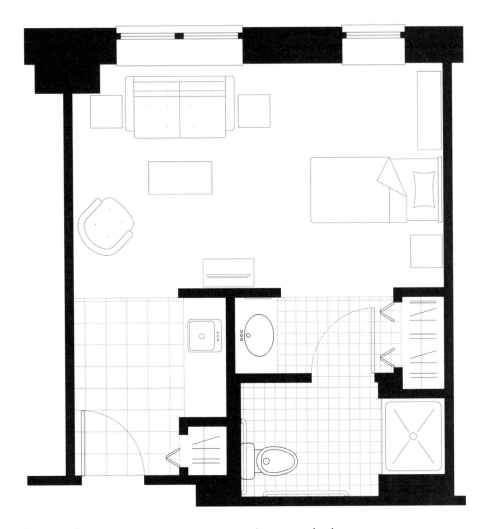

▶ *Figure 2-39 The alcove studio (350–375 sq ft). Perkins Eastman.*

Alcove studio
The alcove studio—typically 350–375 sq ft—is a well-liked option because it provides a more private sleeping area. It requires 16–18 ft of perimeter—often an issue when keeping the building size to a minimum (fig. 2-39).

Small one-bedroom
The smallest fully accessible one-bedroom is about 450 sq ft and requires 22–24 ft of perimeter. It has all the features of an apartment, but they are reduced to minimum dimensions (fig. 2-40).

Large one-bedroom
LeadingAge prototype research settled on a unit with approximately 550 sq ft as its full one-bedroom. The living and sleeping rooms are both more generously sized, and there is typically a walk-in-closet (fig. 2-41).

Two bedroom/double master
This model has two equal bedrooms and baths. It is increasingly popular with couples (especially those who no longer sleep together), siblings, friends, and even individuals who did not know each other previously.

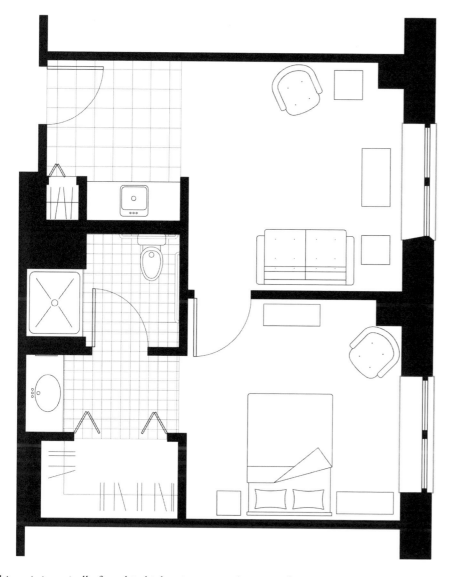

◀ Figure 2-40 *The small
one-bedroom (450–480 sq ft).
The bathroom door is fitted
with double-swing hardware
so it can open out in an
emergency.* Perkins Eastman.

This unit is typically found in higher-income markets and in the assisted living wings of retirement communities (fig. 2-42).

Suite hotel unit
This unit is modeled after the suite hotel, with two rooms on either side of a bathroom. Arranged like a dumbbell, the suite contains one room with no natural light

that typically opens onto a corridor. These suites can be occupied by one person or, in some markets, by two (fig. 2-43).

Bedroom unit
This unit has historically been utilized in room-and-board–type settings where residents share common areas. Newer models have used this unit type in special

▶ *Figure 2-41 The large one-bedroom (500–600 sq ft). Perkins Eastman.*

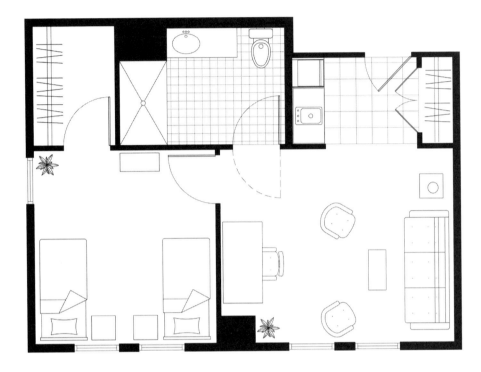

programs for residents with dementia. These specially designed dementia programs have combined this unit type with a family-size house or cluster where the common areas are shared by a group of 8–12 residents (fig. 2-44).

Unit Features

Bedroom

The sleeping area must accommodate a bed as well as dressing area and clothes storage. Most residents furnish their own units with items of varying size. The transition from independent to assisted living can be difficult, particularly if related to a dramatic change in physical health and/or the loss of a spouse. Possessions take on enhanced meaning, and a full-size (or larger) bed may bring a significant sense of security. For couples no longer sharing a bed, space for two twin beds is essential.

In units without a separate bedroom, the view of the bed should be screened from the unit entrance. This will maintain the appearance of apartment-style living and distinguish the unit from more institutional settings where the bed is (inappropriately) the focus of the room. An alcove to distinguish the living and sleeping areas can be an important part of the unit design (fig. 2-45).

Bathroom

The bathroom requires significant planning to allow its intended users to remain functionally independent and to distinguish it from the traditional institutional product. It should be residential in appearance and detail, but its design should acknowledge that staff may be providing assistance with grooming and toileting functions. Accessibility standards are a good beginning for planning adequate space, but many

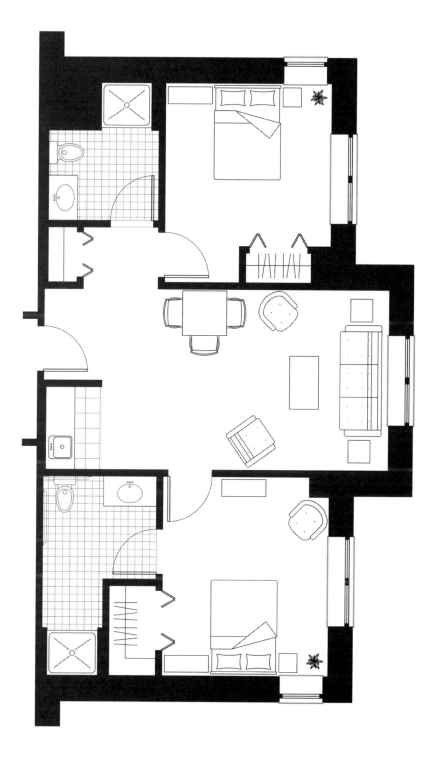

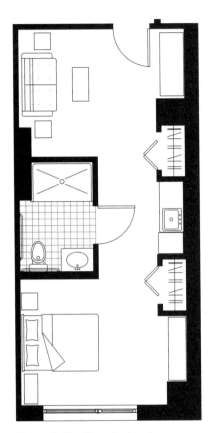

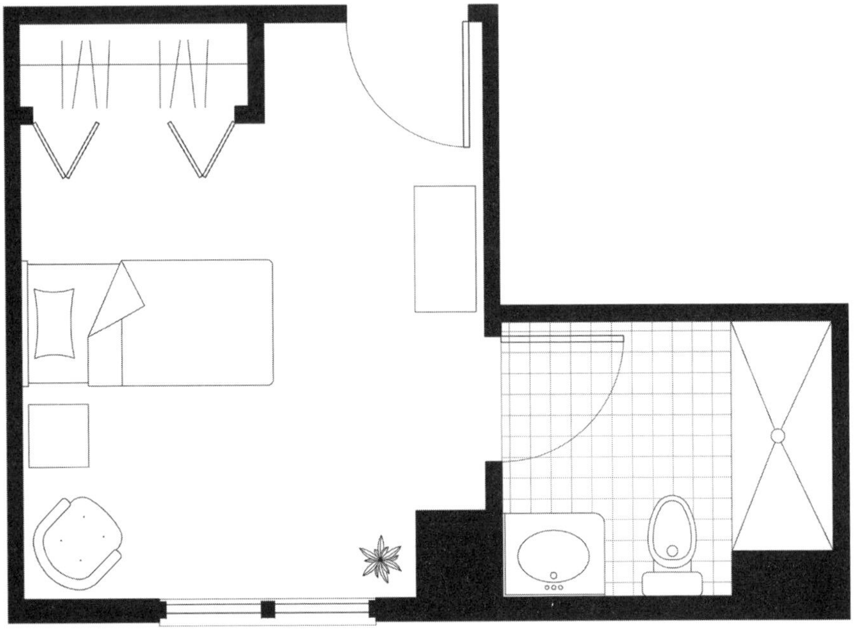

Figure 2-44 *The bedroom unit (230–250 sq ft). The bathroom door is fitted with double-swing hardware so it can open out in an emergency.* Perkins Eastman.

Figure 2-43 *The suite hotel unit (450–550 sq ft).* Perkins Eastman.

physical limitations are not covered by those standards:

- A shower big enough to accommodate the use of a portable shower chair (36" × 42" minimum; 30" × 60" recommended)
- Shower controls and a shower wand that can be reached from a seated position
- A shower threshold that minimizes height, or a neoprene threshold adapter, which is flexible yet creates a partial water dam
- An additional heating source to make bathing more comfortable
- An additional vertical grab bar at the entrance to the shower to help the resident enter and exit easily

Most of the features enumerated for the skilled-nursing resident bathroom design are relevant here as well.

Living room

The unit living space should relate to what the resident previously liked to do at home—watch television, do puzzles or crafts, use a computer, and so on. These activities are important for maintaining self-esteem and engaging with the world. Residents who bring their own furniture often attempt to crowd in more objects—and memories—than is practical. Favorite furnishings include china cupboards, kitchen tables (or drop-leaf dining tables), lounge chairs and recliners, and bulky sofas with several side chairs.

◀ Figure 2-45 Most assisted living units have all of the components of an apartment but are very compact. Cloverwood Senior Living, Pittsford, New York. Perkins Eastman. Photograph by Woodruff/Brown.

Kitchen

In assisted living, the kitchen defines the unit and distinguishes it from being simply a bedroom. While some sponsors provide a full kitchen, a Pullman kitchen is more typical. It has a sink, small refrigerator, microwave, and cabinets above a 5–6 ft-long counter. This "tea kitchen" arrangement originated in Europe. Assisted living sponsors typically provide three meals a day, so the tea kitchen is not used to prepare full meals but rather for snacks, affording residents some autonomy around food. The kitchen also maintains continuity with previous lifestyles, allowing residents to keep their dishes and to entertain. Tea kitchens are not provided in units specifically planned for people with dementia; their use

of the house or neighborhood kitchen decreases the risk of injury (fig. 2-46).

The tea kitchen can be built of component parts, which must be coordinated with the cabinetry and ventilation, as well as with the senior's special needs. The kitchen should include the following:

- Refrigerator with a separate freezer compartment large and cold enough for ice cream, not merely ice trays, and raised 10–12 in. off the floor so the user does not have to bend down or stoop
- Easy-to-reach pantry with eye-level storage
- Under-cabinet shelf for the microwave, with convenient counter space below it for setting down hot food
- Under-cabinet task lighting for countertops

▶ *Figure 2-46 New housing options for the aging have encouraged manufacturers to work with architects and interior designers to create new, specialized products, such as this assisted-living tea kitchen.* Perkins Eastman. Photograph courtesy of Dwyer Kitchen.

- Removable base cabinet below the sink for accessibility if the resident uses a wheelchair.

Unit Amenities

Emergency call systems

Emergency call systems have made great strides since the hard-wired nurse call systems developed for nursing homes and hospitals. These systems can now be integrated with phone systems and wireless technologies. Systems integration consolidates most communication systems, such as telephone, emergency call, fire alarm, passive notification, security, and staff paging/communication (see also chapter 10).

Heating, ventilating, and air-conditioning

In assisted living units, sponsors and their design teams generally employ relatively simple heating, ventilating, and cooling systems, with individual controls in the units.

The typical assisted living resident is often more susceptible to chills than younger adults, so units are often kept warmer than in a normal apartment. Virtually all new units are air-conditioned (see also chapter 8).

Unit personalization

Continuity with the past is of major importance to many residents in assisted living. As their new home, an assisted living unit must have features they associate with home. The most important concerns are

- bringing favorite pieces of furniture;
- wall space, shelves, or windowsills that accommodate photographs, memorabilia, and other personal items;
- multiple telephone and cable TV outlets so that furniture can be rearranged to suit the resident without extension cords (which are tripping hazards);
- window-treatment hardware that enables the installation of decorative drapes over

building-supplied window blinds or shears to control light levels and provide privacy; and
- neutral carpet and paint selections that work flexibly with various styles and color schemes.

Sponsors who install "package" shelves at unit entrances find that these shelves are also often used for the display of silk flowers, pictures, or memorabilia that individualize the unit. Providing ways to personalize the unit door and entry hallway is important. Residents appreciate things like a simple door hook for hanging a wreath or a flexible signage system that identifies more than just the unit number, including a name and perhaps a photograph as well.

Storage

Storage is typically very limited and is always an issue. Most assisted living units come with only one or two closets. Operational issues affect storage needs. For example, if sheets and towels are provided along with housekeeping, then they do not need to be stored in the unit. However, if there is no central storage, then suitcases and other bulky items must be stored within the unit.

Storing medical supplies is a major issue if the occupants use oxygen concentrators or other large items. The increased reliance on power-operated vehicles is affecting the way senior housing is designed, as they take up a lot of space when not in use and must also be recharged.

Planning Approaches

While there are a variety of organizational approaches for these facilities, in concept there are two common approaches. The first is illustrated in the diagram developed for the LeadingAge prototype (fig. 2-47).

▶ *Figure 2-47 This diagram was created for LeadingAge. It represents to its members the typical planning diagram for an assisted living residence. Perkins Eastman.*

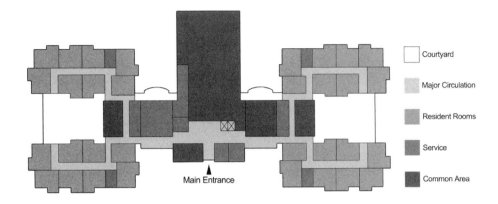

Courtyard

Major Circulation

Resident Rooms

Service

Common Area

Main Entrance

It utilizes a series of neighborhoods linked to the shared common facilities. Another approach, pioneered by Sunrise Senior Living, creates a densely packed cluster of rooms around a central core and activity area on each floor. Both models shorten walking distances to elevators and common areas.

Neighborhood areas

A neighborhood (or cluster) commons serving 12–20 resident units supports the neighborhood and allows for informal gatherings. Among the spaces that can be included in this neighborhood commons are the following:

Sitting area. This small gathering space for informal activities is sometimes associated with the elevator lobby. These areas may also be developed as libraries, living rooms, dens, or TV rooms. They may also include a desk area for staff use.

Resident kitchen/pantry. In some cases, the resident or "country" kitchen is provided within a resident cluster. It is suitable for informal breakfast buffets, small group activities, and resident/family meetings.

Laundry. While many facilities contract with an outside service for general and

even personal resident laundry, a laundry room on each floor gives residents or their families the option of doing their own. The laundry room should have pleasant views or adjacent activities, such as access to the Internet, cards, or a snack bar, any of which can be located in the dining area adjacent to the country kitchen.

Support spaces. All facilities offering meals, as well as a variety of staff support, require a number of support areas. The most common are listed in the sample program in appendix J.

Common facilities

The center of the facility typically contains a number of common areas serving all the residents:

Connecting corridors. As a general guideline, there should be no more than 150 ft of corridor travel from the farthest resident unit to an elevator and to the main common spaces, such as the dining room. Most corridors are 6 ft wide to permit two people with walkers to pass. A lean rail or handrail is needed on at least one side, but rails on both sides are recommended.

Dining. Dining is one of the most important daily resident activities, and the ambience surrounding it is an important marketing tool aimed at prospective residents and families. Many facilities opt for two seatings per meal. Some sponsors are creating open kitchens so the chef, aromas, and cooking activity all become part of the dining experience. Dividing the dining area into more intimate settings minimizes background noise. Allowing at least 25–30 sq ft per resident is desirable.

Private dining. This is a residentially scaled and furnished space that seats up to 15 people, accommodating family gatherings or smaller groups of residents. The private dining room is usually situated adjacent to the main area, and can be separated from it with French doors to allow the space to function as an extension of the main dining

room. These rooms also typically double as meeting spaces for staff and/or residents (fig. 2-48).

Multipurpose/large group activity area. This space accommodates most of the building's population for movies, religious services, musical entertainment, exercise, or parties. These spaces can vary widely, depending upon the culture and/or religious affiliation of the particular residence. The space's acoustics and lighting should be designed with their impact on an aging population in mind. (See chapter 13 for acoustics, chapter 14 for lighting, and chapter 15 for design issues.)

Living room/library. Most facilities have a smaller, more formal space that can double as a library. In addition to being an information center, a library can be used for small group activities. Wireless Internet access here and in all common areas provides

◀ *Figure 2-48 Dining is probably the most important common activity in senior housing. Private dining rooms for family dinners, birthday parties, and other special meals are a typical feature of newer facilities. Atria Hacienda Assisted Living, Palm Desert, California. Perkins Eastman. Photograph by Anthony Gamboa.*

an opportunity to socialize while maintaining business or family contacts. Providing computers for those who do not own one is becoming more common as basic computer literacy in older age cohorts increases. In some designs, this space is replacing a formal lobby to create a comfortable residential feeling at the front door (fig. 2-49).

Café. Space for a café can become a bistro where alcoholic drinks are served, an ice cream parlor, or even a small gift shop or convenience store. The goal is to provide street-life-like ambience and an informal opportunity for socializing. When coupled with the living room/library and mailroom, this space can become a well-trafficked destination.

Specialized activity areas. The traditional crafts room includes pottery, woodworking, and jewelry design. Once messy activities are moved to a crafts space, the pantries within resident clusters can be used for baking and tidier projects for small groups. Aromas from baking will enhance the residential quality of these neighborhoods.

Wellness center. Most facilities have a nurse's office and an exam room. These can be combined with other spaces used for health-, nutrition-, and exercise-related purposes. Like the general population, older adults have recently shown an increased interest in health maintenance and wellness, rather than simply seeking treatment for the diseases and challenges

▶ *Figure 2-49 Attractive common spaces are an essential element of a successful assisted living residence. Asbury Villas, Pittsburgh, Pennsylvania. Perkins Eastman. Photograph by Edward Massery.*

that plague them. Spaces for exercise and nutrition education are now supplementing or even replacing the traditional institutional models of occupational and physical therapy and clinics.

Spa/assisted bathing. While there is a full bathroom with a shower in each unit, some residents prefer the occasional bath and may require some assistance with bathing. The current accent on wellness has led some facilities to create bathing areas that also offer massage, aromatherapy, and beauty and hairdressing services in a spa-like atmosphere. Special tubs (see chapter 12) with doors or pull-up sides make bathing more accessible. Privacy and the ability to control temperature should be addressed in the design of these spaces.

Mail. Adequate space for sending and receiving mail should be located conveniently; it is often near or on the way to the dining room. Mail arrives in two ways: via U.S. Postal Service front- or rear-loading mailboxes controlled by the local post office, and a separate set of mail slots for facility-delivered notices, express service deliveries newspapers, and the like. Mailboxes and slots should be no lower than 30" and no higher than 54" from the floor to minimize the need for residents to bend down and reach up. Shelves to set mail on, good lighting, waste containers, and comfortable seating nearby are important features.

Outdoor space. An outdoor area adjacent to program spaces frequented by residents will get more use and benefit nearby staff, as well. Breezes, sunlight, glare, and insects are all concerns to address. Provide a variety of outdoor spaces:

- Terraces and patios off dining rooms for picnics and barbecues
- Screened porches
- Open porches
- Shady areas
- Gardening opportunities (e.g., raised planters)
- Formal gardens
- Walking paths

Parking. Parking will need to meet any local zoning requirements. Typically, less than 10 percent of residents keep a car, so parking needs are largely determined by visitor and staff requirements (see chapter 5).

Sample program

The total building area for typical facilities ranges from 600 to 1,000 GSF per resident and must meet local codes. Typically, 45 to 50 percent of total space is dedicated to circulation, support, and common areas, with the remaining 50–55 percent to the resident units. Unit sizes tend to be smaller than for independent living facilities because the common spaces replace or enhance what would otherwise be living space within the unit (appendix J).

Payment, Reimbursement, and Regulation

The residents or their families typically pay the full cost of rent and services at assisted living facilities. Some states have programs that help Medicaid-eligible individuals pay their monthly charges.

Regulation

All states regulate assisted living, but it is licensed differently and by different agencies (department of health, social services, aging, etc.). In some states, such as Massachusetts, the *services* are licensed and regulated, but the buildings and facilities follow state building codes for multifamily housing.

Assisted living regulation varies more than most senior living building types. Some states, such as Massachusetts, license the services and treat the building as multifamily, "R" construction. Other states, such as New Jersey and Pennsylvania, require construction to meet the same I-2 standards as nursing homes. Regulations have evolved as the frailty and cognitive impairment of residents in assisted living has become more apparent to regulators and fire marshals.

Because of residents' frailty and cognitive impairments, local building officials will be concerned with their ability to evacuate the building unassisted. Some states require an institutional construction standards equivalent to those of a nursing home to house frail and even mildly confused residents. This will likely limit multistory wood-frame construction and increase development costs. A shift in building codes in recent years suggests a trend of building at a standard higher than current codes mandate.

Trends and Innovations

Assisted living now serves a population that in the 1980s would have been institutionalized. Its services and environment reinforce the capabilities of residents, ensure their safety and allow them to age in place successfully. The building boom of the 1990s through the early 2000s focused on a particular set of assisted living products, but there are many others as well.

Assisted living services

Some retirement community sponsors are exploring the provision of assisted living services to clients in their own homes. Distance— and, therefore, cost—make serving those who

live in sprawling suburban communities more challenging than those who live in a dense, urban environment. New models will maximize the opportunity for residents to age in *one* place.

Urban models

Most of the products built over the past decade have focused on the suburbs. There have been few options for city dwellers. Using their own financial resources, urbanites have networked the services of public, private, and home health agencies with pharmacies, grocery stores, and restaurants that deliver.

Sponsors of urban models have found that urban assisted living or residential communities are typically older and frailer than their suburban counterparts. The availability of services, coupled with personal financial resources, often delay their need to move until a crisis occurs.

New urban models must address an ethnically diverse population. Affordable options in urban centers are few because of the high cost of land and development in cities. Options for lower-income seniors are typically publicly subsidized and address only the need for housing, not services. New models will undoubtedly utilize generic community-based services rather than facility-based programs (fig. 2-50).

Affordable models

The level of services (and, therefore, the staff size) accounts for 60–70 percent of the daily fees in assisted living. (The debt service on the physical building is typically 20–30 percent.) Few affordable models have been built; those that exist are subsidized either internally by an organization or through public subsidy from a local or federal government. Reimbursement and the need for more Medicaid waiver programs are crucial. Assisted living is a

◀ Figure 2-50 The high cost of land and construction has slowed the introduction of assisted living in many urban areas, but new models are now being developed. Willow Towers, New Rochelle, New York. Perkins Eastman. Photograph by Chuck Choi.

proven effective alternative to the nursing home for a large sector of the population, but most people who could make use of it cannot afford it.

Consumer expectations

There is increasing demand for larger units. Over the past decade, the retirement living industry has seen a significant shift in product expectations, as the generation of postwar homeowners has entered the marketplace. Assisted living is now serving those with the personal resources to select a product that meets their expectations. The first assisted living units were largely studios with limited amenities, but new facilities offer one-bedroom units exceeding 500 sq ft, and there is a demand for two-bedroom units. Because the units are the hardest to change, designing models with the flexibility to meet consumer expectations is essential.

Niche products

Most assisted living products are freestanding suburban buildings with 60–100 units, a service component in a CCRC model, or specialized care programs for people with dementia (see next section). New models will emerge that meet specific demographics. The aging in rural areas have been largely ignored and are not really covered by any existing model. Specialized programs for the younger physically disabled, for people who are blind or deaf, and for gay men and lesbians must address their specific needs, expectations, and resources.

RESIDENCES FOR PERSONS WITH ALZHEIMER'S AND DEMENTIA
Typical Users

One of the most important innovations in senior living has been the development of successful models for special units serving persons with Alzheimer's and other forms of dementia.

There is perhaps no more diverse a population among the aging than those with Alzheimer's and dementia. Alzheimer's

> Memory loss alone is not a good enough reason to institutionalize an older person in a healthcare setting.
>
> *Regnier 2002*

disease is one of the most common causes of the loss of mental function known broadly as dementia. Today, 5.1 million Americans over the age of 65 suffer from Alzheimer's disease, and that number is expected to increase by approximately 50 percent—to 7.7 million—in the next 20 years (Alzheimer's Association 2010, pp. 9–14). This type of dementia proceeds in stages, gradually destroying memory, reason, judgment, language, and eventually the ability to carry out even the simplest tasks. The effects of the disease can vary greatly with the individual, or even from day to day. The goal of specialized housing is to maximize what residents with Alzheimer's can do so they can live in a dignified residential (rather than institutional) environment.

The design of a residence for those with Alzheimer's moves away from conventional skilled-care models by avoiding traditional institutional symbols, objects, spaces, and configurations, such as nursing stations and institutional finishes. Following the example of Woodside Place in Oakmont, Pennsylvania, one of the first national models of a specialized residence for those with Alzheimer's, nursing homes and other assisted living residences have begun to address the unique needs of those with the disease. First appearing in the 1980s, special care units (SCUs) can be found in a growing number of U.S. nursing homes, where approximately 60 percent of the residents are afflicted with dementia.

SCUs—also known as dementia care facilities, memory care units, and residential Alzheimer's facilities—vary widely. Some are housed in skilled care facilities, others in assisted living settings. Some offer only one special feature, such as a sheltered area for wandering, a typical symptom of Alzheimer's. Most have several special features, such as family counseling, support groups, and therapeutic activities for residents.

With two decades of research on special memory care settings, we can now firmly say that a carefully designed program and environment can support a higher quality of life and maintain, even extend, higher functioning with activities of daily living.

Jane Rohde, Principal, JSR Associates, Inc. (personal correspondence)

This section focuses primarily on programs licensed for assisted living, but the program and design parameters are similar to those for a long-term care model.

Seniors with cognitive impairment reside in, and use the services of, many kinds of facilities, from geriatric clinics to congregate living. Retirement communities struggle to support couples, one of whom has dementia and the other has become the caregiver, without separating them. Assisted living facilities may have a special-care wing for those with profound confusion, but much of the rest of the population will also have cognitive difficulties that vary in expression (benign confusion to aggressive elopement) and change over time.

Sponsors and Owners

These facilities are being developed by many of the same nonprofit and for-profit organizations responsible for other facilities for the aging. Most of the initial innovative projects were accomplished by nonprofits. For-profit sponsors have learned from these projects and have developed their own models, at times creating prototypes that can be built in almost any community.

Settings

Freestanding

Most of the early examples and many of the new models are entirely freestanding.

Because the residents are unlikely to be involved in the activities of a larger community, separate buildings that provide a balance between security and independence are appropriate (fig. 2-51).

Special wing or neighborhood

Many programs are developed as a section of a larger assisted living or nursing building to care for those who need specialized attention and to maximize their abilities while keeping them safe. These facilities, sometimes called "a house within a house," usually have a full complement of program areas (such as dining, activities, bathing, etc.) that are separate from the larger population's.

Integrated models

Some sponsors believe strongly in keeping people with dementia integrated in the larger community. These buildings may have special programs and activities for those residents who require a more structured day or evening.

The following section focuses on the first two models.

Program and Design

While program elements and design consideration are geared more or less toward the same services found in household-type long-term care facilities, there are some significant differences in the way the following program elements are organized:

- The house
- The neighborhood
- The garden
- Service support

The house

Most models replicate the elements of a house, with an area of bedrooms, a kitchen and dining area, and a living room or activity space. Households with private rooms for 8–12

▶ *Figure 2-51 One of the first specialized residences for people with dementia, Woodside Place set a new standard for integrating program, operations, environmental design, and creating households. Woodside Place, Oakmont, Pennsylvania. Perkins Eastman.*

residents are typical. The division of the program into smaller spaces is key to such facilities. Research and experience have shown that residents are able to function better, with less agitation and stress, in smaller group settings. In one type of household, rooms open off a private bedroom hallway; in another, they surround dining and living areas. Facilities based on the latter model must screen the private bedrooms from the public areas. In both types, the building blocks of the house are as follows (see appendix K for a sample program):

Resident room. Residents occupy a bedroom rather than an apartment. Most sponsors provide private rooms with private bathrooms but may reserve 10–15 percent of the rooms to be shared by couples or roommates. Several room features have proven beneficial (fig. 2-52):

- *Dutch door.* A door whose bottom half can be closed to discourage entry while its top half is open for visual connection and orientation into the room.
- *Closet.* A two-door clothes closet, one side of which can be locked to secure seasonal and additional clothing while the other door leaf remains operable for residents to use, restricting clothing choices. This concept has been extended to an open-wire dresser drawer unit so that socks, undergarments, and the like remain visible.
- *Plate shelf.* The shelf encourages personalization with artwork, objects, and items hanging from pegs. It is mounted 5–6 ft above the floor and located on a wall visible from the hallway.
- *Window seat.* A built-in seat with a hinged, locked top that provides additional storage,

Figure 2-52 This well-known early example of a specialized assisted living facility for residents with Alzheimer's incorporates many of the most widely used details: Dutch door, plate shelf for personalization of the room, and specialized signage. Woodside Place, Oakmont, Pennsylvania. Perkins Eastman. Photograph by Robert Ruschak.

a place for visitors to sit, and an additional opportunity to personalize the room.

Resident bathroom. Private bathrooms are among the greatest improvements in quality of life for both residents and staff. Concerns for safety or affordability have limited bathrooms to two fixtures, with separate bathing facilities elsewhere in the household; newer facilities tend to include a full three-fixture bathroom with shower. Sponsor experience indicates that the three-fixture arrangement provides the most familiar and comfortable bathing experience. The bathroom is typically designed with a direct visual connection from the bed to the toilet. Research has demonstrated that this visual reminder reduces incontinence and minimizes nighttime accidents. Other features include

- a vanity countertop for toiletries;
- contrasting toilet-seat colors to distinguish them visually;
- mirrors, sometimes with shutters for those who have fearful responses to mirrored images;
- a high shelf or storage cabinet for toiletries;
- a low-threshold or roll-in shower of at least 36" × 42" used with staff assistance (a separate water shutoff valve limits inappropriate use); and
- a supplemental heat source, especially if a shower is provided.

Kitchen/dining room. The typical model is a larger version of a residential kitchen and family room. It should encourage use through a sensory connection to food. A household kitchen enables staff to more easily accommodate residents whether they choose to eat during conventional meal hours (when food may come from a central source) or at times that suit their personal rhythm. The use of the kitchen may decrease over time as the residents age. Controlled access will help maintain sanitary conditions and keep residents safe. These residential-style kitchens can serve one or two houses, depending on their design. They provide a nearby work space for direct-care staff (fig. 2-53).

Other key features include:

- Residential appliances to support food service, snacks and nourishment, and programs like baking. In many jurisdictions, codes require separate certified commercial refrigeration and freezers for the food-service program.
- Keyed switches for all major appliances and outlets for residents' safety.

- A large table for cooking programs, informal activities, and proximity to staff.
- Separate handwash sinks for staff and food-service personnel (a typical code requirement).
- Dishwashing capabilities with an under-counter unit that meets temperature requirements (typically 180°F).
- Staff work space in the kitchen or its vicinity for maintaining records, making calls, and so on.
- Some type of visual connection to the outside, with protected or shaded places to sit.

Living/activity room. A living room or informal activity space, like a den or TV room, if the program permits. In some facilities, it is a distinct space at the entrance to the household. Other designs connect it with the kitchen as a dining/living room, a

▶ *Figure 2-53 A typical dining arrangement in a memory care residence is illustrated by this country kitchen serving the dining program for two ten-unit houses. The Mary E. Bivins Foundation: Childers Place, Amarillo, Texas. Perkins Eastman. Photograph by Chris Cooper.*

familiar, homelike arrangement that also enables residents to be near staff in the kitchen.

Spa/bathing. The quantity and location of spa/bathing spaces will depend largely on decisions about the resident bathrooms. If there are showers in all private rooms, then one central room will suffice for hygiene and therapeutic whirlpools for skin care, and those who prefer a tub for bathing over showering.

Programs without private showers will typically have a central spa/bathing room with a tub, as well as a residential bathroom with shower in each house. Many of the planning criteria for bathing in long-term care facilities (see chapter 11) are the same here, but ensure that the appearance and movement of the mechanized bathtub is not frightening. (Familiar-looking tubs will be most successful.) Designing them within a niche, like a residential tub, adds some sense of security but forfeits flexibility in staff access.

Neighborhood and facility organization

The programming models for Alzheimer's residences have continued to evolve. Most programs have 30–50 residents in 3–5 houses. There is usually an area that programmatically joins all of the houses to a common area (figs. 2-54 and 2-55).

The common area contains a variety of program elements for both large- and small-group activities:

Entry. The entry sequence for a specialized dementia program is different from that in other facility types. Because the residents do not come and go frequently (if at all), entrance identification is primarily for visitors, families, and staff. It should be welcoming, reassuring, and comfortable while providing direct access to administrative areas. Entry, from the resident perspective, should not be featured and should be screened from the most active resident areas.

Great-room. An assembly space that can be used for large group activities (such as music, dancing, special dinners with families, exercise, etc.). This room is sometimes used for staff training and caregiver support-group meetings, as well.

Crafts room. Many programs provide a room for messy or unstructured activities or projects that can be left out and completed over a long period of time.

Hair care. This use can be incorporated into a spa/bathing area.

Private dining/activity. A place for families to be alone, share a meal or coffee, and spend time together. This space is also useful for family conferences, staff meetings, and the like.

Living room/den. The living room is a familiar setting that contains comfortable seating and becomes the heart of the house or neighborhood. The scale of this space should be residential: it is intended for use by a small group, not by the full facility population all at once.

Staff workroom. While direct-care activities occur in the houses and neighborhoods, there is still a need for a private workroom for care staff, healthcare professionals, and supervisors for discussions and collaborative work, with ancillary spaces for record keeping, medical supplies, resident medications (e.g., a locked cart), and private phone calls. It should be located strategically within the resident environment for easy access by staff, or near administrative areas and backup services like photocopying.

▶ *Figure 2-54 This is one of the best-known plans of the house concept for Alzheimer's residences. Woodside Place, Oakmont, Pennsylvania. Photograph by Perkins Eastman.*

1. Resident room
2. Living room
3. Dining
4. Kitchen
5. Activity meeting room
6. Staff workroom
7. Staff workspace
8. Service
9. General support
10. Bathing

The garden

A central feature in the planning of almost all special-care programs is easy access to a secure outside garden (see chapter 5). Giving residents free access to the outdoors reduces agitation and frustration, and improves overall physical fitness simply by providing walking space. The area must be safe and secure so that staff and families are comfortable with the residents' unaccompanied access. Important design features are as follows:

- A secure perimeter with fencing at least 6 ft high. Camouflage the fence so it does not feel prisonlike or attract the residents'

attention. The fence design cannot include any horizontal elements that could be used for climbing, and the plan should discourage residents from using site furniture to climb over the fence.
- Planting materials that are not toxic or thorny.
- Walking paths that are continuous and lead back to building entry points. Paths should be wide enough for two to walk side by side and built of a stable material that will not create tripping hazards.
- Shaded areas with porches or trees for sunny days and protected areas for spring, fall, and pleasant winter days.

◄ Figure 2-55 The common areas in this dementia-care facility evoke the local main street. Waveny Care Center, New Canaan, Connecticut. Reese, Lower, Patrick & Scott, Ltd. Photograph by Larry Lefever.

- Perimeter lighting for security in case someone leaves the facility at night.
- Direct egress into the garden from all exit doors (except the front entry door) for safety. If there are errant fire alarms, egress doors will open into a familiar area. An exit from the area will be required for evacuation in an emergency.
- Comfortable areas to sit.
- Passive and active recreation opportunities, from bird and squirrel feeders to patios for cookouts to places to putt golf or throw a basketball.

Support services

As with other senior housing facilities, additional areas are required to support the residential care program. These are the key planning issues:

- These facilities are usually small, so their infrastructure needs to be carefully planned to minimize cost.
- Professional development for staff is ongoing. It can be accommodated in a separate space or shared with other program elements throughout the building.
- Staff retreat space is essential for private time away from the demands and stresses of the job. This is distinct from professional development space.
- Administrative areas may need to be separate from resident areas to minimize disruptions from visitors, salespeople, mail deliveries, and so on.
- Staff entries should be visually separate so that coats and bags at shift changes do not trigger reactions among residents.

Design Considerations

Research and several postoccupancy studies have yielded important information about designing for people with dementia (Schwartz and Brent 1999). The following is offered as an overview:

Privacy and community

Postoccupancy studies at some of the early Alzheimer's facilities revealed that a strong sense of community developed in those facilities where residents socialized freely among houses. They were observed enjoying the common areas as if they were a front porch or even a town square. The hierarchy of public-to-private spaces within a building helps the cognitively impaired feel comfortable in gatherings. Inappropriate adjacencies, such as bedrooms opening directly to living rooms, must be avoided; they can confuse residents, causing them to act inappropriately or become frustrated.

- Provide private bedrooms with bathrooms that contain at least a toilet and a sink and access to a shower. (Some accommodation for shared rooms should be made for couples or others who choose to share.)

Research-Based Planning Considerations in Designing for Residents with Dementia
- Acknowledging privacy and community
- Flexible rhythms and patterns
- Small group size
- Caregiver and family relationships
- Engaged wandering
- Alternative wayfinding systems
- Independence with security/safety
- Focused and appropriate stimulation
- Residential qualities

Hoglund 1985

- Create a private residential zone, preferably a private bedroom, where residents can be alone and keep important personal items that help them feel secure.
- Maintain privacy and dignity by locating public circulation away from private residential hallways, and by locating and designing private rooms and bathrooms to reduce obtrusive visual observation. (Residents with Alzheimer's may behave immodestly; for example, residents may undress or use the toilet without closing the door.)
- Provide appropriate bathing facilities within the private zone of the house or room. Residents do not like to leave the privacy of a bedroom, go through common spaces, and into a public zone to find a bathing room. Many facilities now provide showers within the resident room bathroom.

Flexible rhythms and patterns

Eliminating rigidly enforced schedules by substituting small, informal group activities and allowing flexible meal times contributes to a noninstitutional environment. Because people with Alzheimer's and related dementias often have trouble adapting to changes and transitions, settings should conform to their needs and preferences, rather than demand conformity. An individual resident's routine provides continuity over time and a reliably fixed feature in a confusing world. People with Alzheimer's cannot be expected to follow an institutional schedule or adapt well to the disruption of their daily patterns.

- Make a kitchen available between meals or leave a warming cart in the household kitchen so that staff can meet residents' requests to eat meals at different times or for alternatives to the meals being served.

- Separate activity areas from resident rooms so residents can sleep or nap without interruption.
- Create a variety of settings of different room sizes, orientations, characters, and degrees of stimulation.
- Reinforce seasonal and daily rhythms by providing views to the outside, so it is clear whether it is day or night, summer or winter. Traditional institutions typically have few windows and depend on artificial light, contributing to disorientation.

Small group size

In a traditional nursing-care facility, people with dementia are sometimes overwhelmed or distracted by large groups of people or large spaces, especially at meal times. Staff report that people with dementia can cope better with smaller activity groups not larger than 10–12 persons. Smaller groups at meals or in programmed activities can be held in smaller spaces that are less noisy and less distracting.

- Arrange clusters or houses to accommodate no more than 10–14 persons.
- Provide small group spaces in each unit and some visual separation from other spaces so that residents vulnerable to distraction can be comfortable.
- Create spaces for small groups that offer distinctive attractions, such as a large window, a fireplace, or special seating. Some spaces should be less enclosed than others, offering a place from which to watch other activity.
- Multipurpose spaces are confusing to residents with dementia because they do not know how to alter their behavior to respond to changing uses. It is better to provide several different rooms that residents can associate with different experiences, such as games, dining, cooking, sleeping, and watching television.

- However, a space should not be designed so specifically for one activity that it cannot be adapted to other uses, since how rooms are used will change over time in response to changing resident needs or as the management style of the facility evolves.

Caregiver and family relationships

The primary caregiver in a residential facility, a trained member of the staff, plays a key role in the quality of a resident's life. The quality of care is, of course, a function of the facility's philosophy and management, but these are intertwined with the design of the physical space. If the primary responsibility of the direct-care staff is to attend to residents, then the facility should be designed to minimize time spent at other tasks. Protecting the privacy of residents' records tends to interfere with contact and accessibility but must also be accommodated.

- Integrate a staff workstation into each house as part of the residential furnishings (desk) or equipment (kitchen counter). Locate the workstation near the unit's main circulation path, where the residents and caregivers can enjoy casual meetings and participate in everyday activities. Provide a lockable file drawer at the workstation for information other than residents' records, which should be kept in a secure room nearby.
- Design the workstation as a social seating area where residents can interact comfortably with the caregivers. Provide a table or counter for residents to share.
- Furnish storage for the supplies caregivers use regularly in order to minimize trips out of the unit.
- Include laundry machines and a well-equipped janitor's closet.
- Create homelike settings where residents can enjoy time with family members.

- Provide an exit sequence from the facility so that residents are less aware of staff or family leaving and then are not frustrated if they try to follow.

Engaged wandering

Wandering—movement without apparent purpose—is common among people with Alzheimer's disease, though little is known about the physiological reasons for it. Rummaging, another common behavior, involves the apparent search for personal items.

An indoor wandering path is a major opportunity for innovation. Although some facilities strongly endorse loop-shaped paths to eliminate dead ends (which can lead to frustration), they can also lead to repetitive behaviors without engagement in activities.

Do not assume there is only one way to walk through the facility, or even that wandering will be limited to corridors. Rooms woven creatively into the circulation path can orient residents and provide spaces for socializing while they wander. A path must be easy to follow. Transitional changes in texture, lighting, and acoustics along the way will make different segments memorable and the activity of walking more enjoyable.

- Create circulation loops to provide walking circuits. Multiple intersecting loops are preferable to a single one.
- Keep the scale of circulation paths small and residential, and leave room for seating, especially near intersections and entrances.
- Avoid dead ends and locked doors at the ends of corridors. Seating at the end of a corridor, preferably with a good view, provides a destination and cues the resident to turn around.
- Incorporate both interior and exterior wandering areas. Temperature, sunlight, and breezes all reinforce daily rhythms and will orient residents to place and time.
- Minimize the number of changes to the flooring, particularly a change from carpet to vinyl. People who shuffle or have trouble walking are a fall risk.
- Avoid sharp color and light value contrasts in the flooring. Residents tend to watch the floor as they walk; such contrasts may look like steps, changes in depth, or objects.
- Provide cues such as artwork or furnishings that lead disoriented residents back to a secure, familiar area.
- Minimize the choices a resident must make, and mark predetermined choices clearly.
- Vary the length and location of walking places to provide different experiences and accommodate those who are more impaired (see also chapter 5).
- Provide unobtrusive ways for the staff to observe residents along the paths. Security systems can prevent residents from wandering outside or into staff areas. Avoid devices with auditory signals, which can confuse or agitate those with Alzheimer's.
- Make sure plants are nontoxic (see chapter 5).

Alternative wayfinding systems

Wayfinding (see chapter 15) relies on one's ability to associate objects and sensory stimulation with particular places. Cognitive impairment reduces common wayfinding ability. Residents will be unable to form a mental map of their surroundings; some subtle cues, such as color changes, are lost even on staff and families. According to environmental sociologist John Zeisel, president, Hearthstone Alzheimer Care Ltd.:

For people with dementia, the concept of wayfinding should be thought of as 'place knowing.' People with dementia know where they are when they're there; they only know where they are going if they see the destination; and they realize where they were going when they arrive. The in-betweens—the connections between destinations—are lost on them.

Conventional signage, color coding, and differentiation in finishes alone (flooring, hardware, and lighting), are not perceptible cues for most people with dementia.

• Reinforce visual connection between the path (or hallway or corridor) and important destinations (fig. 2-56). Residents who do not know what they

are searching for may choose to join in an activity if they can see into a room.

• Prepare for flexibility so visual connections can be controlled. For example, Dutch doors and curtains on interior windows can be open, closed, or half open.

• Provide visual stimulation for residents as they move through the building—clustered sitting arrangements, pets such as fish or birds, and the opportunity to view a programmed activity without actually engaging in it.

• While still maintaining code standards for emergency exit, the traditional corridor design should be more residential in character. Low partitions and interior

◀ *Figure 2-56 The shelf above the bed allows residents and families to display personal items as visual cues for room recognition. Air Force Village, San Antonio, Texas. Perkins Eastman. Photograph by Casey Dunn.*

windows may help to increase visibility and enhance the feeling of openness.

- Use landmarks and objects that will attract a resident's attention.
- Supply visual cues for important activities. For example, design the bedroom so the toilet can be seen from the bed while maintaining the resident's privacy.
- Mark the entrance to residents' rooms with objects of importance to them—photographs, a piece of clothing, and so on. Personalized spaces, such as a plate shelf, deep windowsill, or window seat, make residents' rooms familiar and easier to find.

Independence with security/safety

The aging process can mean having to adapt to maintain independence. For those with Alzheimer's disease, independence becomes steadily and increasingly elusive. Making the environment accessible and safe from injury is only a partial solution. Choice is important in maintaining independence. But for those with dementia, choices may need to be restricted to limit confusion and distress. The environment should support an individual's abilities and enhance his or her remaining skills safely and securely.

Complicated procedures and an abundance of options to choose from can lead to confusion and diminish a person's ability to independently complete an activity or navigate a building.

- Allow residents independent access to resident kitchens by locking cabinet drawers containing potentially harmful products, but allowing access to other cabinets and installing staff-controlled power switches and keyed electric outlets.
- Create a secure outdoor area with 6 ft fences to which residents have unrestricted access. Select nontoxic garden

plants without abrasive or sharp-edged leaves.

- Provide adequate lighting levels and supply night lighting for resident bathrooms (see chapter 14).
- Restrict windows from opening more than 8 in.
- Install handrails on at least one side of major indoor walking paths.

Focused and appropriate stimulation

Mental health professionals continue to debate the degree to which sensory stimulation is therapeutic for persons with Alzheimer's. The goal of designing for people with dementia should be an interesting environment that piques their curiosity without becoming distracting or stressful. It should also account for "sundowning," a decreased ability for physical activity in the late afternoon experienced by many Alzheimer's patients.

There is no easy formula for striking this balance, and the design implications are numerous. They range from the size and location of rooms to the color of walls, the lighting sources, and the design of the wallpaper (see chapter 15).

- Construct multiple smaller-scale rooms that comfortably accommodate groups of 6–14.
- Dampen sound so noise from one room does not distract those in another. Carpeting will reduce unwanted noise. (It will also eliminate glare from floor surfaces.)
- Be aware that a single room used for multiple activities—dining, exercising, and dancing, for example—can confuse residents as to what behavior is appropriate.
- Provide a staff exit hidden from residents; staff members' departure can engender feelings of despair and abandonment.

- Orient some rooms to the west to capture light from sunsets.
- Screen the public entrance with a vestibule or lobby to keep deliveries and visitors from intruding on the residents' domain.

Residential qualities

There is near-universal support for a "residential" environment but little agreement on what the term means. Many dementia facilities are much larger than a single-family home. And whether the housing is in a rural, suburban, or urban setting affects how it is perceived. Creating a homelike environment involves many variables: size, appearance, interior and exterior materials and finishes, lighting, furniture, and the purpose, scale, and detailing of rooms. Here are some suggestions:

- Break up the building volume so the exterior does not appear monolithic or institutional.
- Organize spaces from public to private as they would be in houses and hotels.
- Name rooms as you would in a house: living rooms (not dayrooms), bedrooms (not private or semiprivate rooms), family rooms or dens (not lounges), and bathrooms (not toilets).
- Limit the use of hard finishes typically found only in institutional settings, such as vinyl tile, ceramic tile, sheet vinyl, plastic laminate, and metal for doors.
- Hide operational equipment, such as carts, fire-alarm panels, and nurse call stations, from view.
- Select comfortable furniture. While specially designed geriatric furniture meets hygienic and physical comfort requirements, it is generally unattractive. In addition to other ergonomic criteria, check tables and chairs for stability, as residents will use them for physical support.

- Treat surfaces as you would in a home setting. For example, soften windows with fabric curtains or valances.
- Install residential light sources; fluorescent lights with acrylic lenses do not look residential and their glare makes them poor sources of light.

Payment, Reimbursement, and Regulation

Payment and reimbursement models are the same as those described in the sections on assisted living and long-term care. Some states and local building officials have begun to require higher construction standards for dementia facilities because of their population's inherent inability to evacuate without assistance.

Trends and Innovations

Because of the many forms and sources of dementia, it is unlikely to be eradicated in the near future. New models must support interventions that manage and control the condition. But they must also foster residents' remaining capabilities through a setting that remains appropriate throughout the disease's progress. These models will explore the following:

Integration throughout the continuum. Dementia is a disease that can unfold over years; it is not only an end-of-life issue for long-term care. Over the past decade, specially designed assisted living settings have begun offering new opportunities in less restrictive settings. Adult day care provides services for those who wish to remain at home. Senior living environments must manage cognitive deficits while embracing remaining capabilities. Family and spouses will need programs that enhance their caregiving abilities and also provide respite services to meet their own needs.

Montessori methods. Maria Montessori's methods, well-known for transforming the lives of "unteachable" street children in post–World War I Rome, are now used to improve the quality of life of people with dementia. Caregivers are encouraged to construct scenarios in which residents can succeed and to provide praise for even small accomplishments. In place of insisting on "correct" behaviors, they invite residents to take whatever small steps they can toward such behavior, reinforcing their dignity and sense of self-worth. The Montessori approach sees dignity not only in the ability to care for oneself, but in caring for others, and residents are also encouraged to do things for other residents.

Affordable options. Dementia care is intrinsically expensive because of the need for—and high cost of—round-the-clock staff. Cost-effective buildings are only a small portion of the solution. New home-based models allow spouses and family to remain caregivers without jeopardizing their own health. Unfortunately, some home settings are inappropriate, unsafe, or not easily altered to meet the needs of the patient or his or her caregiver. In a few experimental "caregiver

cottages," the spouse or family member remains the primary caregiver while on-site staff and respite resources provide backup. (See chapter 3 for further discussion of affordable senior housing.)

Cottages. Some sponsors are developing group home–type models in which 6–10 residents share a large house in a conventional residential neighborhood or apartment building. These models can be integrated easily into an existing neighborhood, provide options for rural and smaller communities, and meet smaller-scale expectations.

"House for Betty." Pioneered by a planning and design team from Perkins Eastman and Asbury Communities, House for Betty is a single-family cottage that supports aging in place as well as cognitive changes that take place over time. It is targeted to at-risk older adults who acknowledge early cognitive changes but want to remain with a spouse or family member in their own home. Physical design features coupled with universal design and technology make the environment adaptable to the individual (fig. 2-57 and fig. 2-58).

INDEPENDENT LIVING WITH SERVICES
Typical Users

There are several residential living options available to people without significant healthcare support needs. Residents are usually in their late seventies or early eighties. Though specific concerns have arisen through a change in their health or lifestyle expectations, they want to remain in control of their quality of life. Some also want to plan for their futures while they are still able. Still others want to downsize and reduce their expenses. Independent living

> "People with Alzheimer's live in the moment, and our job is to give them as many good moments as we can. We need to think about these people in a new way. Instead of focusing on their problems and deficits, we need to ask what strengths and abilities remain."
>
> *Dr. Cameron Camp Center for Applied Research in Dementia*

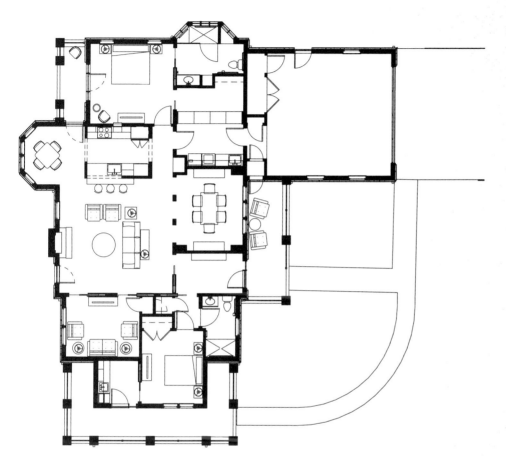

◀ Figures 2-57 and 2-58 The House for Betty is a cottage residence that incorporates the best of universal design as well as features that support those with memory deterioration over time. House for Betty, Asbury Methodist Village, Gaithersburg, Maryland. Photograph by Perkins Eastman.

◀ Figure 2-58

with services typically combines apartment-style living with services like meals, activities, and some limited personal care services such as housekeeping and transportation.

These facilities—also known as catered living, adult congregate living facilities (ACLFs), and senior service apartments—differ widely in size, staffing, and in the services and organized social activities they offer. Services can include one or two meals per day (versus three in assisted living and skilled nursing), housekeeping, transportation, and security, including on-site emergency call systems. Additional services are sometimes available for a fee. Independent-living sponsors do not usually provide healthcare, as doing so invites regulation. Healthcare services are sometimes offered à la carte and provided by a separate, licensed healthcare provider (such as a home health service). Personal care assistance, including companion services, may be provided by the sponsor or an outside vendor.

Independent living is offered in apartments, duplexes, and cottages in an array of facility types. Some developments are similar to assisted living facilities; others mimic the independent living components of continuing care retirement communities.

Sponsors and Owners

An independent living developer may be a nonprofit, a proprietary corporation, a partnership, an individual, a syndicate, or an association of residents. Not-for-profit sponsors are generally faith-based, fraternal, or community organizations.

The sponsor's priorities will have a significant impact on design. If the sponsor is dedicated to building community—through shared interests or shared beliefs, for example—the design will reflect those priorities. The design of a facility run by a religious organization will differ from that of one centered around golf or one for veterans of the armed services.

Settings

Independent living is found in three major models:

1. *Freestanding.* A conventional apartment building—of any size—with services
2. *Blended service/living options.* Apartment- or cottage-style living physically associated with another level of care, such as assisted living
3. *Continuing care retirement community (CCRC).* A continuum of care that includes independent apartment/cottage living with assisted living and long-term care.

This section focuses on the first two models. The CCRC model is covered in the following section.

Program and Design

Independent living typically resembles an apartment building with enhanced public areas for dining, activities, and socializing. Some independent living facilities are age-restricted apartment buildings located in neighborhoods with restaurants, doctors' offices, public transit, and other services.

The most significant program elements are the residential living units and the public spaces, as well as the services that support them. (See appendix L for a sample program.)

Residential-living units

Independent-living apartments have grown larger to meet the desires of postwar-generation retirees, whose expectations and standards are higher than those of previous generations. Few new projects, including those built with government subsidies, are being developed with studio apartments; in many places it is even difficult to market standard-size one-bedroom apartments. Most consumers want room for guests or an office; a one-bedroom with a den is usually the smallest unit configuration offered.

These are the typical unit configurations and the design criteria for each:

One-bedroom. A conventionally laid out apartment (650–900 sq ft) with a living room, bedroom, bathroom, and full kitchen. New models are typically arranged with the bathroom directly off the bedroom.

One-bedroom with den. A one-bedroom apartment (750–1,100 sq ft) with an added den (90–120 sq ft). Some models include an extra half-bath or powder room (fig. 2-59).

Two-bedroom. A two-bedroom unit (1,100–1,400 sq ft) with all the features of a one-bedroom plus a second bedroom that can be used as a sleeping room (for couples who sleep in separate bedrooms or for guests), an office, or a studio. Most models include a full bathroom and a powder room, or two full baths (fig. 2-60).

Two-bedroom/double master. A unit (1250–1500 sq ft) with two bedroom suites (i.e., a bedroom with full bathroom), which are usually located on either side of the living room.

Two-bedroom with den. A unit (1,200–1,800 sq ft) with all the features of a two-bedroom plus a 90–100 sq ft den.

Deluxe unit. Variations of these models with special spatial features such as a dining alcove/area, an eat-in kitchen, a dining room, or a larger living room.

Cottage/duplex. See section on CCRCs.

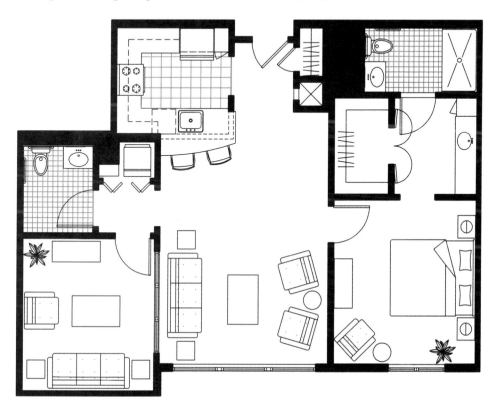

◀ *Figure 2-59 There has been an increased market demand for one-bedroom with den units with an additional powder room (950–1,100 sq ft). Perkins Eastman.*

▶ *Figure 2-60 Two-bedroom/two-bath unit in a typical butterfly plan, with bedrooms on either side of the living areas (1,100–1,400 sq ft). Perkins Eastman.*

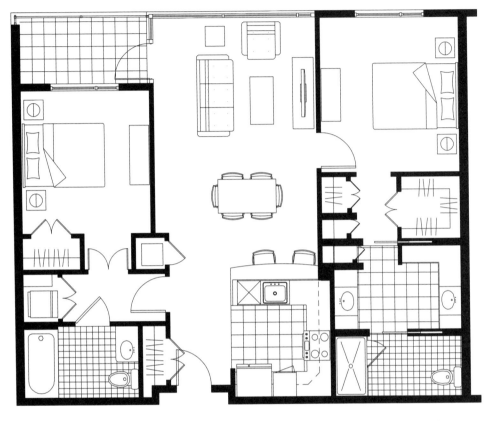

Unit Features

Bedroom/sleeping area

In addition to conventional bedroom planning features, senior residents can expect amenities such as

- additional space and clearances around furniture, making it easier to maneuver a mobility device;
- space for two twin beds, for couples who sleep separately or when one spouse requires a hospital bed;
- ample storage space, including walk-in closets in the master bedroom of larger units;
- hardwired or flexibly installed wireless emergency-response systems;
- sufficient power, telephone, and computer connections for TVs and computers that are not located in the bedroom; and

- small utility closet for wi-fi, sound system, and cable TV equipment.

Bathrooms

Bathrooms in independent living apartments have more or less the same features as those in assisted living apartments; some have an additional sink. In new projects, both bathrooms are sometimes full baths, although the shower in the second bathroom may be smaller (36" × 42").

Living room

Living rooms in independent living units have all the standard features of a residential living room, with a variety of furniture. Most are laid out flexibly enough to create a small office or dining area within them (fig. 2-63).

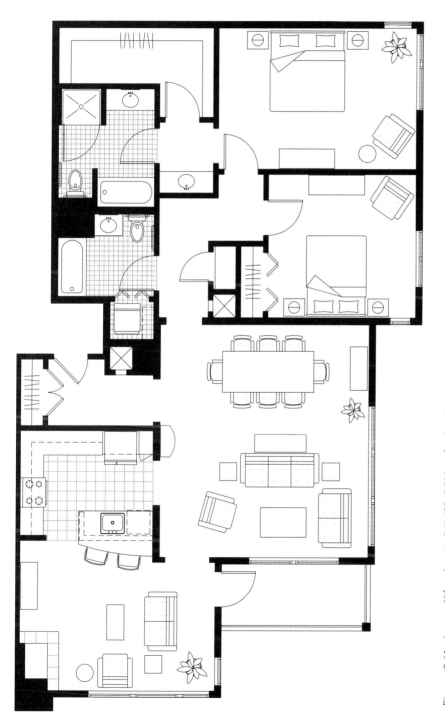

Figure 2-61 In new "lifestyle units" (1,600–2,000 sq ft), the den is now a great-room—part dining room, part office, part entertainment center—attached to the kitchen. Perkins Eastman.

Figure 2-62 Cottages (1,200–2,500 sq ft, excluding garage) are popular in many markets, regardless of weather. They are larger than apartments, and have a two-car garage. Perkins Eastman.

◀ *Figure 2-63 Independent living units resemble a typical apartment but have special features: wider doorways, accessible hardware, emergency call systems, towel bars that double as grab bars, and many other details that facilitate aging in place. The Karmel, Deerfield, Illinois. Perkins Eastman. Photograph by Sarah Mechling.*

Kitchen

Today, residential kitchens are designed with more features and amenities than they were previously. Solid surface/stone countertops, upgraded appliances like dual-door refrigerators or those with the freezer on the bottom, and cabinets with sliding shelves are now standard in many markets. There are few senior markets where the following amenities would be questioned:

- Full-size, self-defrosting refrigerator with ice maker
- Four stovetop burners (usually electric so there is no open flame) and a self-cleaning oven with front-end controls (for safety) and recirculating exhaust hood
- An under-counter microwave with a slide-out cooking drawer or cabinet and convenient counter space
- Dishwasher
- Single- or double-bowl sink with garbage disposable (and safety cover operation)

Designers of senior living units should also consider incorporating the following special features:

- Pantry cabinet for eye-level, easily reached storage
- Space for a small table or extended counter for both dining and preparing food while seated
- Cabinet accessories that slide out and turn, for easily reached storage space that doesn't require bending, twisting, or reaching
- Wall ovens, garbage drawers, or wine refrigerators (for upscale units)

Washer/dryer

Most developments are meeting consumer expectations for in-home laundry facilities with a stacked washer/dryer, although there is a growing demand for conventional side-by-side units and front-loading machines with pedestals.

Common areas

Public areas vary greatly from project to project and market to market. The basic common areas—dining room, living room, library—will be similar to those found in assisted living. In most cases these common areas are located on the first or second floor, with the upper floors organized like a typical apartment building. The larger size of these communities calls for a wider variety of common spaces, as well as more activity options, to respond to the varied interests of the residents. Game rooms (with billiards), card rooms, and greenhouses are not unusual (fig. 2-64).

In new urban models, some common areas, such as those for dining and fitness equipment, are open to seniors (and others) who live in nearby neighborhoods. Others are located near fitness clubs and restaurants and do not offer these services in the building itself.

Lifelong learning

Today's seniors are actively engaged in the world around them and want lifelong learning opportunities. New independent living sponsors provide Internet connectivity, have expanded their libraries, and are including classrooms for lectures and academic-style classes (fig. 2-65). Many new models borrow concepts from bookstores: casual sitting and reading areas complement open, accessible shelves and space for informal discussions and presentations. Auditoriums are used as both movie theaters and lecture halls.

Fitness

Exercise equipment rooms and swimming pools were not formerly among the amenities at retirement living communities, but

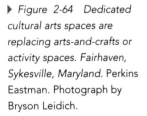
▶ *Figure 2-64 Dedicated cultural arts spaces are replacing arts-and-crafts or activity spaces. Fairhaven, Sykesville, Maryland. Perkins Eastman. Photograph by Bryson Leidich.*

◀ *Figure 2-65 Libraries are for more than just books: they are used for research, lectures, book clubs, and other lifelong learning activites. Hebrew SeniorLife: NewBridge on the Charles, Dedham, Massachusetts. Perkins Eastman. Photograph by Chris Cooper.*

they are now a significant part of the common area programs of many buildings. Swimming pools with level or slightly sloped bottoms 3–4 ft deep accommodate 10–20 participants and are used for aquatic aerobic exercise. Space for exercise and weight-training equipment, separate from aerobic exercise rooms, may also be included (figs. 2-66 and 2-67).

Support areas

The programs for service and support vary with the size of the community, the range of programs offered, and the presence of other services and settings, such as assisted living.

Key Planning Issues

Over time, residents will become older and frailer and will need more services and mobility aids. These buildings must therefore be fully accessible and accommodate services and programs that facilitate aging in place.

Payment, Reimbursement and Regulation

Units in independent living facilities may be rented or purchased. There may also be an entry fee in addition to the monthly rent or maintenance. The entry fee is sometimes partially or fully refundable when a resident leaves the facility or dies, or is refunded over time. The amount of the entry fee is related to unit size and the range and quality of the common spaces.

Rents and sales prices vary with the market. Those with limited income and assets may qualify for government-subsidized housing or services. (See chapter 3 for a discussion of affordable senior living.)

Independent or congregate living is not typically licensed, but a facility may need to meet consumer protection laws imposed by a state department of aging. Building standards in most states follow traditional multifamily building codes.

▶ *Figure 2-66 Fitness facilities, such as swimming pools and exercise equipment, are increasingly popular program elements in residential communities. Williamsburg Landing, Williamsburg, Virginia.* Cochran, Stephenson & Donkervoet.

▶ *Figure 2-67 Fitness programs now provide excellent gym programs, with sophisticated, age-calibrated equipment and personal trainers. Hebrew SeniorLife: NewBridge on the Charles, Dedham, Massachusetts.* Perkins Eastman. Photograph by Sarah Mechling.

Trends and Innovations

Naturally occurring retirement communities

Sometimes older apartment buildings *evolve* into senior housing as their residents age. Sponsors, particularly nonprofit organizations, are looking into ways to provide an array of services—meals, home healthcare, housekeeping, senior centers, scheduled transportation, and so on—to the elderly who have chosen to age in place in their own community.

Service house model

Several European countries have developed neighborhood-based residential independent living facilities with supportive programs that provide meals, activities, and health services to age-qualified seniors who live in their own homes in that neighborhood. The service house model meets several needs:

- Provides neighborhood-based services to maintain seniors in their own homes
- Increases the use of services and spaces provided by the independent/congregate-living program
- Develops additional revenue sources (membership fee or fee-for-services) to support staff and operating costs
- Integrates the building and residents into the larger community
- Functions as an organic marketing tool for seniors who may need to move into the housing in the future

Co-housing

Co-housing, also referred to as elder co-housing, is a neighborhood of individual houses for seniors, an idea that was reinvented in Denmark in the 1970s and has since given rise to hundreds of communities in Europe and America. A co-housing community is a group of independent housing units with a shared common house—essentially a clubhouse for neighborhood or family activities. The houses are typically owned individually, and residents form a homeowner association that manages the common areas. Because each household has its own home, residents can choose the degree of their community involvement. Co-housing has been most successful when there are 20–30 units.

Apartments for life

The concept of apartments for life also originated in Europe. In such buildings, seniors remain in their home and the services provided to them increase gradually as their need for them increases. This allows residents to remain in the same apartment for the rest of their lives, rather than having to relocate each time they need an additional level of care.

The apartments incorporate universal design features for accessibility. With minor changes, they can be adapted to meet a wide variety of healthcare and service needs, such as emergency power for healthcare equipment and a technology infrastructure for telemedicine. A second bedroom can be converted to a caregiver den. The design of the independent living building itself should accommodate a variety of delivered services (e.g., meals and medications) as well as homecare workers. An additional elevator in staff support areas, supply storage, and staff parking are all helpful. The design of public areas should support both those residents who can live independently as well as those who require a lot of care. For example, discreet sitting and dining areas that do not force residents to interact with one another will be appreciated.

CONTINUING CARE RETIREMENT COMMUNITIES
Typical Users

Continuing care retirement communities (CCRCs) offer older adults housing, health-related services, and other supportive services that allow residents to live in their own home within the community for the rest of their lives. CCRCs are sometimes referred to as life-care retirement communities; the specific financial and contractual implications of the term *life care* are outlined in the coming sections.

In addition to the residential units, CCRCs typically provide

- coordinated social activities;
- dining services;
- housekeeping;
- scheduled transportation;
- emergency call monitoring;
- healthcare;
- assisted living, dementia care, and long-term care; and
- a fully accessible or adaptable environment.

Residents' are usually between their mid-70s and early 80s upon entry. Those who choose cottage- and villa-type products are, on average, slightly younger. As the community matures, the average age across the CCRC may rise into the mid-80s.

Sponsors and Owners
Historically, CCRC sponsors have been nonprofit, faith-based organizations with the desire to provide supportive settings for their aging constituents. Such groups continue to play a major role in developing and operating CCRCs, though most also serve people unaffiliated with the organization. During recent decades, a number of for-profit and proprietary businesses have entered this field. Many of these emphasize the social and hospitality qualities of CCRCs while limiting the range of healthcare services.

Settings
Typically, CCRCs are set in park-like suburban or rural locations, on campuses with

low-rise buildings. They offer a mix of independent living apartments and cottages, with a complement of assisted living units and long-term care beds, together with common facilities. As land has become more costly and development approvals more difficult to secure, CCRCs, especially those near large cities, have been built on smaller properties with mid- to high-rise structures offering only apartments, with assisted living units and long-term care nursing units stacked in a single building. As both urban and non-urban dwellers have recognized the convenience and benefits of urban living, urban CCRCs have been developed.

Because they were community-based and often supported by volunteers through their religious affiliations, many older CCRCs are small, with fewer than 100 independent living units. As residents demanded a greater number and variety of common facilities, a range of dining options, and conveniently located healthcare facilities, communities had to grow bigger and add staff to remain financially viable. As a result, few CCRCs under development have fewer than 100 independent living units; most have 200–300, and some CCRCs—usually developed in phases—have more than 1,000.

Organization
In early CCRCs, cottages and independent living buildings were linked to a central common building with housing for frailer residents, dining facilities, and healthcare services. Today's CCRCs are more often single structures, although some add housing and services over time (fig. 2-68).

Program and Design
The major program components of CCRCs are independent living, assisted living, assisted-living for dementia patients, short-term rehab, and long-term care. Each has a

◀ Figure 2-68 In this CCRC, skilled nursing, assisted living, and independent living units, along with common activity, dining, and support areas, are housed in a centrally located building surrounded by 130 independent-living cottages. Buckingham's Choice, Adamstown, Maryland. Perkins Eastman. Photograph by Tom Lesser.

residential living environment and shared common areas similar to those described in the previous building type sections of this chapter. CCRCs, however, develop a layer of community programs used by all residents. The design of these areas depends on the size and configuration of the community.

Large CCRCs

Communities of over 500 residents have multiple dining options dispersed throughout the site to minimize walking distances, to create the feel of a small neighborhood, and to provide choice and variety. Large communities may also duplicate living rooms and gathering spaces, activity areas, and staff support

spaces throughout the site. The various program components of the care continuum typically each have their own dining and gathering spaces. As the community grows, activity spaces, multipurpose rooms, wellness centers, and more service and support staff areas can be added. Even large communities may have only one fitness center, swimming pool, auditorium, or chapel space, so they are typically proximate to the assisted living and long-term care elements (fig. 2-69).

Medium-size CCRCs

Communities with 250–500 residents typically have an array of program and activity areas but only one service support chassis housing the

▶ *Figure 2-69 This CCRC has skilled nursing, assisted living, and independent living units, along with common activity, dining, and support areas, in a centrally located main building surrounded by almost 250 independent living apartments and cottages. Hebrew SeniorLife: NewBridge on the Charles, Dedham, Massachusetts. Perkins Eastman.*

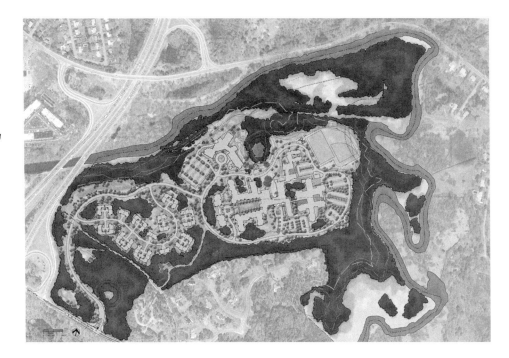

kitchen, laundry, loading area, and space for the administrative staff. The planning and design of these spaces must minimize staff required, maximize product and service quality (especially food), and obviate cross-traffic between residents and service functions. While the assisted living and long-term care programs may be smaller, they usually have their own dining and living spaces; however, they will share some activity, gathering, and wellness spaces with independent living residents. Appendix M is a sample program for a 260-unit CCRC with an additional 30 assisted living units, 20 memory support/dementia rooms, and 40 skilled nursing beds.

Small CCRCs

Sponsors of CCRCs with fewer than 250 residents may find it difficult to afford the type and variety of spaces the marketplace expects. If their core components are too small to meet residents' requirements, they some-

times affiliate with other organizations and facilities to provide the full range of fitness, activity, and social opportunities desired by their residents. Smaller communities may also partner with off-site long-term care providers or offer assisted living services to residents in the independent living apartments.

Market Considerations

A number of market considerations impact the design of a CCRC:

- The unit size, level of service, and number of common and support areas are dependent on how much the target residents are able to pay in entry fees, rents, and monthly fees.
- Most CCRCs have some unique program areas and services that reflect the sponsor's understanding of the target market.
- Typical mature CCRCs are occupied by single women. Facilities with larger units

and cottage or duplex housing options attract more couples, and they should offer male-oriented common space for woodworking, billiards, Monday-night football, playing cards, golf—even a barber shop. In a facility with smaller units and one-bedroom apartments the majority of single residents are likely to be female.

- CCRCs often design common spaces and facilities related to the surrounding community—a college or university, local history (like Williamsburg, Virginia), nearby cultural institutions, or even retail destinations (fig 2-70).
- Some CCRCs market themselves to a particular population, such as a branch of the military or a religious or fraternal organization.

Program Components

CCRCs offer more variety in independent living and common areas. The following program elements are either different from or not found among those in independent/congregate living, assisted living, Alzheimer's and dementia residences, and long-term care. (Appendix M tabulates a typical program for a CCRC with 260 independent living units [200 apartments and 60 cottages], 30 assisted living units, 20 dementia/memory-care beds, and 40 long-term care beds.)

Residential living apartments

The unit types, design features, and amenities are similar to those previously discussed in this chapter's section on independent living with services, but CCRCs offer more variety in their housing products. Rural and suburban models are typically developed with both apartments and cottages. These units come in a variety of styles:

- Detached, single-story, single-family unit with garage

◀ Figure 2-70 Kendal Corporation has pioneered retirement communities built near college campuses. Kendal at Oberlin residents ride bicycles on the Oberlin College Campus, Oberlin, Ohio. The Kendal Corporation

- Duplex or clustered single-story unit with garage
- Freestanding multistory buildings with 4–6 units per floor and enclosed parking
- Large apartment building linking units to common areas

Cottages are usually larger than their counterparts in independent living communities; it is not unusual to find 2,000 sq ft units with three bedrooms, two-car garages, and eat-in kitchens. Units with walk-out basements and additional loft space can increase their size to 3,000 sq ft. The majority of these units are occupied by couples who neither want to live in an apartment nor require the added safety and proximity to common areas apartment living provides. Many CCRCs with cottage units develop pedestrian circulation paths that are sometimes covered or partially enclosed for weather-protected access to common areas. Communities on large sites will often allow residents to use motorized golf carts. Some communities need additional parking spaces for carts or cars near common areas for those who drive from the farthest units (figs. 2-71, 2-72, and 2-73).

Common areas
These are some distinctive characteristics of common areas in CCRCs:

- *Dining areas.* Dining programs in new CCRCs are changing to meet a range of consumer expectations. In addition to smaller formal dining venues with waiter service, informal dining options—a casual bistro, grill room, or café—are often included. New dining options are developed to respond to residents' desires to dress casually, to eat in informal settings, and to have meals at flexible times, as well as for evolving menu preferences—for smaller portions and more options, for example. Other popular alternatives include snack shops, pubs and bars, chef's tables, wine-tasting rooms, buffets—even take-out.
- *Living rooms and activity spaces.* In addition to the communal living rooms and informal meeting places found in most senior living settings, residents expect spaces for new or lifelong interests. Crafts rooms are evolving into studios for painting, drawing, ceramics, and weaving. Traditional spaces like libraries, auditoriums, and fitness programs are being expanded and reinvented as greenhouses, woodworking shops, music rooms, and photography labs (fig. 2-74).
- *Libraries.* No longer merely locations for donated books, libraries are becoming active resource centers with wi-fi, study spaces, reference books, travel guides, and comfortable reading areas stocked with a wide variety of publications. They are also meeting places for discussion groups and book clubs.
- *Multipurpose rooms/auditoriums.* These spaces are evolving from simple large gathering spaces into rooms for lectures and the performing arts with well-planned acoustics, theater lighting, and sound systems. There are even some with back-of-house spaces for staging shows with sets, props, and costumes (fig. 2-75).
- *Fitness areas.* Exercise is important for healthy aging; it boosts endurance, enhances mobility, and helps seniors remain independent longer. Fitness programs range from tai chi and aerobics classes (in chairs or on floor mats) to strength training on stationary bicycles, rowing machines, and other equipment specially designed for older people.

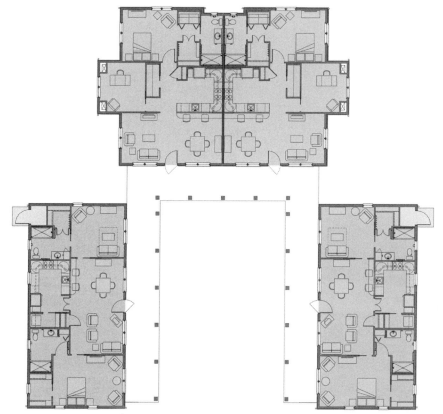

◀ Figure 2-71 Some cottage communities cluster units around small courtyards linked by covered walkways to shared parking areas. The Houses on Bayberry at Arbor Acres United Methodist Retirement Community, Winston-Salem, North Carolina. Reese, Lower, Patrick & Scott.

◀ Figures 2-72 and 2-73 (following page) Clustering cottages around common car courts can create small neighborhoods, increase density, minimize the length of driveways, and eliminate garage doors facing the road. Hebrew SeniorLife: NewBridge on the Charles, Dedham, Massachusetts. Perkins Eastman. Photograph by Sarah Mechling.

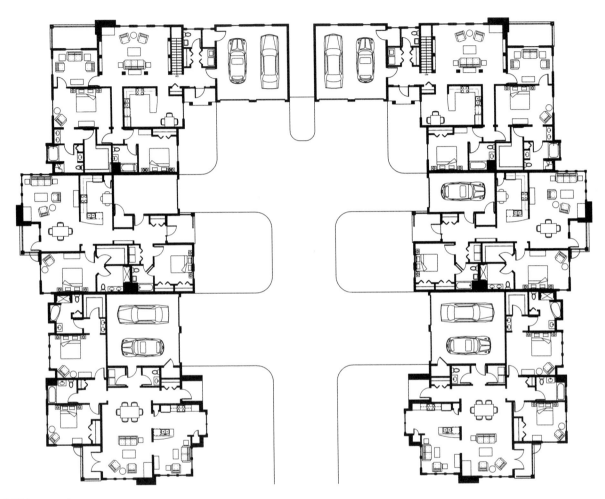

Figure 2-73 (see previous page)

The most expensive space to build and operate is a swimming pool, which should be a minimum of 20' × 42', with a level or slightly sloping bottom and a water depth 3–4 ft—large enough to swim laps in and for aquatic aerobics.

Pools have very specific requirements:

- A variety of means of access, including ladders, graduated steps, ramps, and chair lifts.
- Water temperature of 88–95°F and air temperatures a few degrees higher.
- Environmental controls to maintain air temperature, minimize humidity, and prevent drafts.
- Aprons large enough for safe walking areas, with places to sit and for instructors to conduct classes.
- Space for storing kickboards, floats, and other equipment.
- Lifeguard stations from which the entire pool and the entrance can be seen.
- Locker-rooms with multiple showers and changing areas to accommodate residents who need more time to

◀ *Figure 2-74 Art programs can accommodate performances by guest artists, juried resident art shows, and more. Hebrew SeniorLife: NewBridge on the Charles, Dedham, Massachusetts. Perkins Eastman. Photograph by Sarah Mechling.*

change and groups who arrive all at once.

- A showerhead on the pool apron so swimmers can rinse off before and after using the pool.
- A one-person locker room with room for an assistant, so a user can be assisted with showering or dressing.
- Privacy in pool areas, since residents may prefer not to be seen in swimming attire.
- Bathrooms immediately adjacent to the pool if locker rooms are farther away.
- *Outdoor space.* In addition to passive activity areas such as porches, terraces, patios, and covered outdoor areas, there should be recreational opportunities for walking, gardening—even fishing, tennis, and putting.

Assisted Living Residences

Assisted living services are usually provided in a wing or floor of the CCRC dedicated to the care needs of those residents who need a supported environment—including residential and common spaces—tailored to their needs. If the CCRC is large enough, it may have a separate cluster of units dedicated to residents with Alzheimer's disease and dementia; the spouses of such residents may live in this area as well. In general, the design guidelines for assisted living and Alzheimer's facilities set forth earlier in this chapter apply here as well. Ten to twenty percent of the units in a CCRC are usually devoted to assisted living. However, as sponsors offer more homecare services in the independent living apartments, the demand for assisted living in a CCRC has decreased.

Long-Term Care

The health center for short- and long-term care is typically comprised of single-occupancy bedrooms with a roll-in shower that are adjacent to the rehab clinic. Short-term

▶ *Figure 2-75 More sophisticated spaces for movies, lectures, and other presentations are now becoming a popular element in some retirement communities. UPMC Senior Communities: Cumberland Woods Village, McCandless, Pennsylvania. Perkins Eastman. Photograph by Sarah Mechling.*

care (lasting 10–32 days) is for rehabilitation after a hospital stay or for acute illness requiring 24-hour care. Long-term care is for residents who require assistance with most activities of daily living, including eating and walking. Both short- and long-term care are provided with round-the-clock nursing services similar to those in a nursing home.

Payment, Reimbursement, and Regulation

CCRCs are regulated in many states, though these regulations vary greatly. Typical regulations protect future residents through a review of proposed resident contracts and agreements, an assessment of the financial feasibility of the proposed community and its long-term viability, and other financial matters.

States also have varying provisions for long-term care beds within CCRCs. Some states have no restrictions; others permit a fixed ratio of long-term beds to independent living units. In those states where skilled nursing is permitted without a certificate of need, the direct admission of nonresidents to long-term care beds is usually limited to the first few years of operation. Physical and environmental standards and requirements for long-term care and assisted living facilities within CCRCs are controlled by state regulations for these uses.

Contracts

CCRCs usually offer residents one or more of four types of agreements or contracts:

- *Extensive or life-care contracts.* These provide independent living and healthcare-related services for a fee—usually both an entrance fee and a monthly fee. Entry fees may be fully refundable or partially refundable when the resident dies or moves out; the value of the refund may also diminish over time. Monthly fees remain the same regardless of which of the continuum of services the resident uses. Some in the industry refer to this as an insurance product because it guarantees healthcare services.
- *Modified contracts.* These provide independent living and a specified amount of health-related services for an entrance fee plus monthly fees. Some health services, such as a stay in the health center, are covered, but the cost, number of days covered, and other terms vary. Assisted living and long-term care generally cost more per month, and in some cases the sponsor may require residents to purchase long-term care insurance to cover this cost.
- *Monthly rental contracts.* These cover housing, utilities, and a specified service package, such as the provision of 20 meals per month.
- *Equity contracts.* These involve a purchase that transfers ownership of the unit. Health-related service arrangements vary but usually require an additional monthly fee.

Trends and Innovations

CCRCs are an evolving senior living option. Some of the current trends include common areas that reflect current retail concepts. Some of the new program areas have been inspired by commonly used community retail and services.

Common area

- *Copy/mail center.* Lifelong learning, second careers, and ongoing involvement in outside organizations create a need for photocopying, color printing, express mail delivery, and computer access. FedEx-style business centers adjacent to or affiliated with the administration area are becoming more popular.
- *Theaters.* Internet-based video on demand, DVDs, and other electronic media such as wii or other gaming products, have led some communities to provide small home theaters with fixed theater-style seating. These rooms can also be used for lectures and distance learning (fig. 2-76).

▶ *Figure 2-76   Home theaters for 20-75 people can create comfortable settings for movies, lectures, and distance learning. The Osborn, Rye, New York. Perkins Eastman. Photograph by David Lamb.*

- *Display cooking.* Dining options follow restaurant trends. Display cooking provides both entertainment and the opportunity to customize food orders to meet specific dietary needs and preferences.
- *Take-out/grab-and-go.* Expectations of flexible eating opportunities have led to take-out menus and prepackaged chilled or frozen meals sold in the CCRC's store or café.

Unit size, amenities, and features
Retirement living unit design continues to emulate the features found in the private

homes from which residents relocate, and residential design trends inform retirement living unit design. Current concepts include

- great-rooms that combine the den, kitchen, and dining room into one large, informal area;
- bathrooms that feature multiple (his-and-hers) sink and counter areas, more storage, more space, and body jet sprayers;
- remote-controlled lights, temperature, and security systems; and
- multiple telephone lines for separate voice, fax, and data, as well as pre-wired units for community-wide computer networks.

Community integration

Intergenerational independent living permits older adults to meet their retirement needs without removing themselves from the larger community. European "new towns" have planned senior living options integrated into the community—often at its center—with direct connections to the town library, retail core, and civic center. American interest in traditional neighborhood design and New Urbanism will yield similar products that reinforce access to community-based services such as schools, libraries, and recreational centers.

Urban models

The graying of the urban population is giving rise to new CCRC models in cities that allow residents to remain connected to cultural institutions and their own communities. These models are inherently more flexible and build on existing urban resources such as restaurants, groceries, pharmacies, laundries, dry cleaners, and the like; all offer delivery services that minimize the costs and infrastructure for CCRCs.

ACTIVE ADULT COMMUNITIES
Typical Users

Active adult communities (AACs), also known as empty-nester developments, are marketed as a lifestyle choice rather than simply a place to live. Potential buyers are looking to trade in the responsibilities and maintenance that comes with owning a large home for convenience and readily available activities and entertainment. Many residents have become lonely in neighborhoods where they have lived for decades as their neighbors and friends are replaced by younger—and sometimes less compatible—neighbors.

Sponsors

Sponsors for active adult communities have typically been for-profit, proprietary developers. Not-for-profit sponsors of CCRCs are now entering this market as a way to build brand loyalty among future residents of their own CCRCs, as well as to expand the customer pool for CCRCs services such as housekeeping, yard maintenance, and home healthcare.

AAC sponsors market to people 55–74 years of age. Buyers are typically in their mid-sixties to mid-seventies and wealthy; most no longer have children who live with them, although not all are retired. Baby boomers will swell this market in the coming decades.

Settings

Active adult communities have traditionally been large with over 1,000 units, but the high cost of land is driving down their size. AACs with more than 1,500 units are considered large, those with 300–1,500 units as moderately sized, and those with fewer than 300 units as small; new communities may have as few as 50–100 units.

Large communities feature a range of site plans, amenity packages, and housing types, and attract buyers from a wide geographic area. Many are organized around golf or other recreational amenities. Moderately sized communities typically offer a clubhouse but may not have a golf course within the development. If they do not, they will likely be affiliated with a golf course or country club. There will be fewer home choices and fewer amenities in a small AAC. All communities may be age-restricted to people 55 and older.

In 1999, over 60 percent of AACs were located in Florida, Arizona, California, South Carolina, and North Carolina (National Directory of Lifestyle Communities n.d.). Because baby boomers often want to remain near their jobs and their children, AACs are now being built near major metropolitan areas.

Program and Design

Active adult communities are either *age-restricted* or *age-targeted*. Either way, many municipalities court their development because AACs increase their tax base without adding children to the school system. There are marketing advantages and disadvantages to both. Age-restricted communities appeal to those who want to live among people with similar interests and the leisure time to enjoy them. And all the facilities and programs in an age-restricted community will be directed toward them. But there are many prospective buyers who may balk at age restrictions, either because they prefer to live among a more diverse group of residents or because they, or a younger spouse, think of retirement communities as places for old people. There is a larger market for age-targeted communities, but developers cannot prohibit children and teenagers from living there. Other products that compete for the 55–74-year-old market include country club communities, second

home and preretirement communities, and resort/empty-nester communities. Such communities often evolve over time from second homes into age-targeted communities for active adults as the average age of residents rises.

Lifestyle

Lifestyle is determined by the community's design. Incorporating natural features such as open space, landscaping, and water into the project's design will yield the relaxing resort or country club atmosphere characteristic of many active adult communities.

Wellness and fitness have become key components of AACs, and residents often want an outdoor environment conducive to golfing, fishing, boating, hiking, and walking (fig. 2-77). In fact, walking trails are the most sought-after outdoor amenity among prospective buyers.

Site design

Many seniors are drawn to the controlled environment of an AAC. The following will promote a sense of security:

- A dramatic entrance that creates a distinctive transition from the surroundings, with signage, a guard booth, gates, well-defined boundaries, and extensive landscaping
- A hierarchy of spaces from public—a prominently located community center or clubhouse, for example—to private
- Separate vehicular and pedestrian circulation

The plan should encourage socializing among residents. Homes can be clustered in neighborhoods; small parks, mail centers, shopping areas, and the clubhouse will become natural gathering places.

A community's homes and common facilities often adopt the architectural style and

material of the region of the country in which they are located. The architectural character of the entrance communicates the architectural style—and quality—of the community.

Whatever the design, the site should be phased such that the community looks complete at each stage of the build-out.

Unit sizes and amenities depend on the income level of the target market. Single-story residential units are popular in AACs, reflecting the preferences of a population anticipating age-related difficulties like stairs. Even in two-story residences, all the main living spaces, including the master bedroom, will likely be on the ground floor. Unfinished attics or basements provide the flexibility to enlarge the living spaces.

In addition to one-story villas, many communities offer attached townhouses (which may have finished second floors) and midrise apartment buildings, often built over a level of structured parking. The increasing appeal of urban living has prompted the construction of high-rise AACs located near cultural and retail centers, as well as restaurants.

The average size of residential units, excluding the garage, are as follows:

Detached home	1,800–2,400 sq ft
Attached home	1,690–2,000 sq ft
Manufactured home	1,500 sq ft
Condominium	1,300–1,500 sq ft

Characteristics of AAC homes
- Open space rather than defined, formal rooms
- Up-to-date kitchens and appliances for gourmet cooking and entertaining
- Clear connection from kitchen to living room
- High-speed Internet connectivity so residents can continue to work full- or part-time
- One- or two-car garage for cars, boats, storage, or hobbies
- Generous master bedroom suite with copious closet space and multifixture bathroom, including separate walk-in shower
- Second (or third) bedroom for guests, home office, or hobbies
- Private outdoor space like a patio or yard

Program standards
AAC programs for common space usually fall within the following ranges (National Directory of Lifestyle Communities n.d.).

ACC of 100 units or fewer: 1,200–1,500 sq ft meeting/social building with a meeting room, efficiency kitchen, and restrooms.

ACC with 250–300 units: 5,000–7,000 sq ft recreational building with social activity spaces, small library, exercise room, meeting area, small kitchen, and restrooms.

ACC with 300–1,500 units: 16–18 sq ft per residential unit.

ACC with 1,500 units or more: 3–15 sq ft per residential unit.

Characteristics of AAC community centers
- Focal point of community
- Main lobby
- Fireplace
- Gathering room
- Multipurpose rooms
- Party room with kitchen to be used by residents and caterers
- Bar, coffee shop, or grill
- Business center, including small meeting rooms and computers
- Card and billiard rooms
- Indoor fitness area, including exercise equipment, aerobics area, and a lap pool
- Men's and women's locker rooms with sauna
- Pro shop (if the community has a golf course)

The following reports the percentage of 353 communities surveyed that offered each amenity (National Directory of Lifestyle Communities n.d.):

- Clubhouse: 88.7
- Outdoor swimming pool: 87.0
- Fitness center/spa: 69.8
- Arts-and-crafts room: 62.6
- Walking trails: 62.6
- Tennis courts: 55.3
- Recreational vehicle storage: 50.0
- Shuffleboard: 48.8
- Ballroom with stage: 45.3
- Computer center: 40.9
- Golf course: 39.7
- Bocce court: 38.2
- Restaurant: 34.6
- Community gardens: 29.8
- Indoor swimming pool: 22.7

Payment, Reimbursement, and Regulation
Active adult communities must conform to local zoning regulations, which impact decisions about land use, building density, setbacks, roadway standards, open spaces, building height, parking requirements, and

the like. AACs are often regulated as multifamily dwellings. A state agency may require condominiums to disclose certain information in the development's prospectus.

Marketing

Marketing an ACC successfully means showing prospective residents how their lives will improve by moving there. Some developers, attracted by an easier public approval process for age-restricted communities, have built projects that are little more than subdivisions—without the features the target market expects. Marketing small communities without significant amenities is usually not a pathway to a profitable enterprise.

Ownership

The properties at some AACs are for rent; at others, they are for sale. Rents are usually market rate. Those for sale are either fee-simples or condominiums. A monthly fee is usually charged for the use of the development's amenities and services such as yard care and housekeeping.

SUMMARY

The ten building types discussed here are a snapshot of the most common facilities built for seniors. As the population of older people in North America, and around the world, continues to grow—and grow more demanding—new building types, services, and programs will emerge to respond to their requirements.

INDEPENDENT LIVING

▶ *Figure C-1 Downtown high-rise senior living has even come to smaller cities like Milwaukee. Saint Johns on the Lake, Milwaukee, Wisconsin. Perkins Eastman. Photograph by Chris Barrett.*

◀ *Figure C-2 Many campuses that now offer a full continuum of care began as nursing homes. With the addition of The Tradition, the Morse Geriatric Center became Morse Life, offering the services of a continuing care retirement community. The Tradition, West Palm Beach, Florida. Perkins Eastman. Photograph by Edward Massery.*

Figure C-3 Independent living developments in town centers near public transportation, dining, and services are popular with many seniors. Christie Place, Scarsdale, New York. Perkins Eastman. Photograph by Sarah Mechling.

▶ Figure C-4 Affordable senior living in urban environments offers community amenities like Mission Creek's adult day care, public library, public meeting facility, offices, and retail. Mission Creek Community, San Francisco, California. HKIT Architects. Photograph by Alan Karchmer.

CONTINUING CARE RETIREMENT COMMUNITIES

▶ Figure C-5 This Portland, Oregon, CCRC is located on the city's south waterfront. Mirabella, Portland, Oregon. Ankrom Moisan. Courtesy of Ankrom Moisan.

Figure C-6 Tokyo's first CCRC is located on a one-acre site overlooking the harbor. Sun City Ginza East, Tokyo, Japan. Perkins Eastman. Photograph by Milroy and McAleer Photography.

Figure C-7 Set within an existing park-like setting, the Garlands of Barrington is a campus of buildings and gardens designed as an intergenerational neighborhood. A hierarchy of public, semi-public, and private spaces exists throughout the site. The Garlands of Barrington, Barrington, Illinois. Torti Gallas and Partners. Photograph by Steve Hall for Hedrich Blessing Photographers.

◀ Figure C-8 Marsh's Edge evokes the southern lowland architectural vernacular of historic Charleston and Savannah to create a strong sense of place for the retirement community. Marsh's Edge, St. Simon's Island, Georgia. Cochran, Stephenson & Donkervoet Inc. Architects. Courtesy of Cochran, Stephenson & Donkervoet Inc. Architects.

Figure C-9 This large suburban intergenerational campus includes a day school and a CCRC; in addition, a large number of beds were relocated from an existing long-term care facility in Boston. Hebrew SeniorLife: NewBridge on the Charles, Dedham, Massachusetts. Perkins Eastman.

▶ Figure C-10 This CCRC occupies the upper floors of a downtown mixed-use tower, while the base is occupied by Loyola University's Water Tower campus. The Clare at Water Tower, Chicago, Illinois. Perkins + Will. Photograph by James Steinkamp.

Figure C-11 This CCRC, located along the Hudson River, is founded on the Quaker ideals of inclusion and respect for all people. Sloping riverfront topography allowed for the creation of dramatic views from units and common areas. Kendal on Hudson, Sleepy Hollow, New York. Perkins Eastman. Photograph by Chuck Choi.

◀ Figure C-12 Most upscale CCRCs feature an indoor pool as part of their wellness and fitness programs. Kendal on Hudson, Sleepy Hollow, New York. Perkins Eastman. Photograph by Chuck Choi.

Figure C-13 This upscale CCRC was originally developed by Classic Residence by Hyatt, Palo Alto, California. Steinberg Architects. Photography by Benny Chan/Fotoworks.

▶ Figure C-14 Attractive dining options are important to the success of CCRCs, such as this one near Osaka, Japan. Sun City Takatsuki, Takatsuki, Japan. Perkins Eastman. Photograph by Chuck Choi.

Figure C-15 Some freestanding assisted living residences use prototype designs and then adapt them to their regional context. Sunrise of Bellevue, Bellevue, Washington. Mithun. Photograph by Robert Pisano.

▶ Figure C-16 Some assisted living residences are built to fit into existing low-rise urban neighborhoods. Weinberg Terrace, Squirrel Hill, Pennsylvania. Perkins Eastman and Urban Design Associates. Photograph courtesy Perkins Eastman.

Figure C-17 Market shifts have prompted senior living sponsors to provide smaller, less formal and more intimate lounge and dining areas instead of large, formal common areas and central dining rooms. Westminster Village, Scottsdale, Arizona. Perkins Eastman. Photograph by Chris Cooper.

◀ Figure C-18 Most assisted living units have all the features of a full apartment, but the kitchen is usually a limited tea kitchen. Hebrew SeniorLife: NewBridge on the Charles, Dedham, Massachusetts. Perkins Eastman. Photograph by Chris Cooper.

SKILLED NURSING

▶ *Figure C-19 A long-term care "center of excellence" that sets the standard of nursing and memory care for the next generation offers extensive outdoor spaces with easy resident access. Ground-floor terraces enable beds to be wheeled outdoors; others feature bay windows with expansive views. Childers Place, Amarillo, Texas Perkins Eastman. Photograph by Chris Cooper.*

Figure C-20 The design captures an extraordinary amount of daylight and offers immediate connections to nature while reflecting regional character throughout the interiors. Childers Place, Amarillo, Texas. Perkins Eastman. Photograph by Chris Cooper.

Figure C-21 A new skilled care/rehabilitation residence, designed in a "small house" connected model, offers a central kitchen, dining, and living room space. Air Force Villages, San Antonio, Texas. Perkins Eastman. Photograph by Casey Dunn.

▶ Figure C-22 Many new and renovated skilled nursing facilities have moved far away from the hospital room model. Air Force Villages, San Antonio, Texas. Perkins Eastman. Photograph by Casey Dunn.

Figures C-23 and C-24 The U.S. Veterans Administration is one of the rapidly growing number of sponsors that have adopted the small house model for many of their new long-term care facilities. Danville Community Living Centers, Danville, Illinois. Perkins Eastman. Photographs by Sarah Mechling.

▶ Figure C-24

Figure C-25 A growing number of residents are finding long-term care residences in mid- and high-rise buildings in vibrant city neighborhoods that support their urban lifestyle. Jewish Home Lifecare: Bronx Campus, Bronx, New York. Perkins Eastman. Photograph by Chuck Choi.

Figure C-26 This leading long-term care provider was one of the first to recognize the importance of—and then implement—an all-private-room program for long-term care. Montefiore Home, Beachwood, Ohio. Perkins Eastman. Photograph courtesy Perkins Eastman.

ALZHEIMER'S CARE

▶ *Figure C-27 Some specialized facilities for residents with Alzheimer's and dementia are designed to create a familiar setting, such as this re-creation of the town's main street. The Village at Waveny Care Center, New Canaan, Connecticut. Reese, Lower, Patrick & Scott Ltd. Photograph by Larry Lefever Photography.*

Figure C-28 Many of the planning, design, and operations concepts for specialized residences for those with Alzheimer's were first demonstrated and tested at Woodside Place. Woodside Place, Oakmont, Pennsylvania. Perkins Eastman. Photograph by Robert Ruschak.

SPECIALTY CARE

◀ *Figure C-29 Some large senior living campuses have built facilities that engage and can be shared with the surrounding community, such as The Point on the C. C. Young Campus in Dallas. C. C. Young: The Point, Dallas, Texas. Perkins Eastman. Photograph by Chris Cooper.*

▶ *Figure C-30 A growing number of major medical centers are creating specialized facilities focused on geriatric medicine, education, research, and clinical services. Donald W. Reynolds Center on Aging, University of Arkansas, Little Rock, Arkansas. Perkins Eastman with Polk Stanley Yeary Architects. Photograph by Dero Sanford.*

Figure C-31 Day care facilities can be developed within larger senior living campuses, commercial storefronts, or freestanding buildings. Total Long-Term Care Cody Day Center, Lakewood, Colorado. Boulder Associates. Photograph by Ed LaCasse.

▶ Figure C-32 Some hospices are built as special nursing units within large hospitals and nursing homes, while others, such as Mt. Joy Hospice, operate in small, home-like structures. Hospice of Lancaster County: Mount Joy Care Center, Mount Joy, Pennsylvania. RLPS Architects. Photograph by Larry Lefever Photography.

CHAPTER 3

THE FUTURE OF SENIOR LIVING

Since the 1980s, the senior living industry's response to a variety of trends and challenges has yielded new models for housing and care. This chapter summarizes some of the catalysts for that change as well as those that will accelerate the rate at which the industry continues to evolve. At the end of this chapter there is an extended discussion of the biggest challenge for the senior living: affordability.

The following six issues have been particularly challenging in recent years:

1. Demographics
2. Consumer expectations
3. Lifestyle changes
4. Economic pressures on owners and sponsors
5. New housing and care concepts
6. Affordability

DEMOGRAPHICS

There are three demographic trends driving change:

1. The elderly population is growing larger.
2. Older people are staying healthy longer.
3. American society is growing more diverse.

Population

Demographic projections point to rapid growth of the number of elderly in the United States and most other countries. Particularly striking are the projections for the number of "old-old"—those over 85—for whom supportive housing and care is especially important (fig. 3-1). The growing

number of seniors will drive demand for products, services, and housing but will also drive new models that are more responsive to their cultural, lifestyle, and financial expectations.

Health and Services

Because people are remaining healthy longer, they are able to age in place, relying on community-based services and family to meet their needs for healthcare and services. They are therefore accessing senior housing and care options later—often after they are very old and frail. This has reduced the demand for assisted living apartments in some markets, as they cater to healthier individuals who now choose to stay at home and access care services brought to them. Also the average length of stay in long-term care facilities is actually growing

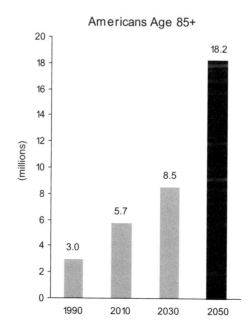

Americans Age 85+

(millions)

1990	2010	2030	2050
3.0	5.7	8.5	18.2

◀ *Figure 3-1 Projections for the number of Americans 85 and older. The aged are the fastest-growing segment of the U.S. population.* U.S. Department of Commerce, Census Bureau.

shorter because residents' healthcare needs are more acute when they arrive and the demands on staff and services in such facilities are increasing. Because residents remain in these facilities for a shorter amount of time, marketing efforts must be more aggressive to ensure a steady admission of new residents (fig. 3-2).

Ethnic and Cultural Diversity
The United States and Canada are continuing to grow more ethnically and culturally diverse—rapidly. The influx of immigrants from Latin America is particularly large, bringing with it different attitudes about family care responsibilities, housing options, and food/language/activity choices. Moreover, senior housing choices are increasingly made based on shared interests, quality, and location—factors other than religion and ethnicity. In fact, some faith-based organizations are finding that their resident population is more diverse due to intermarriage, multicultural families, and less adherence to traditional religious doctrine.

Cultural diversity is also reflected in new choices responding to seniors' search for communities of "like-minded" individuals. Universities like Penn State are building

affiliated retirement housing options for their alumni and retired faculty. Businesses such as Rainbow Vision have developed senior living facilities for lesbians, gay men, and bisexual and transgender men and women. Organizations like Generations of Hope in Urbana, Illinois, have coupled retirement living with volunteer opportunities for housing and caring for orphaned children.

CONSUMERS' EXPECTATIONS
Identifying and responding to consumer expectations in a country as diverse as the United States is a challenge. While it is difficult to generalize about what seniors want, some preferences are clear.

Privacy
The desire for privacy is changing the design of senior living and care facilities. A study of assisted living commissioned by the American Association of Retired Persons (AARP) found that only 4 percent of respondents over 50 preferred a shared room. In fact, an overwhelming majority preferred a smaller private room to a larger double room. While quality of care ranked

▶ *Figure 3-2 The aged are staying healthy longer, but once they get ill, their health declines rapidly.*
Fries 1980; Rowe and Kahn 1998

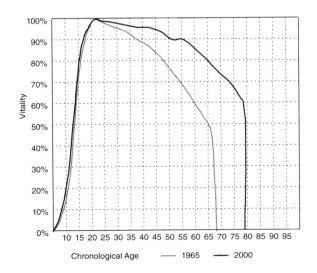

as the top concern, sharing a bedroom with a stranger was the next greatest concern for women and third highest among men.

Shared rooms, group bathing, and a lack of privacy in public areas are all being rejected by the coming generation of seniors, and the expectation of privacy is making much of the country's stock of care settings (long-term care and assisted living) obsolete.

Choice

A desire for more autonomy is changing unit mix, food service options and activities offered—almost every amenity in senior living care facilities. Consumers are no longer satisfied with a single unit type, dining option, or dinner entrée, or a limited range of activities. Contract types are changing, too, as seniors demand payment and ownership models that are responsive to their financial situations and preferences.

Like anyone else, seniors want to shape their environment and choose how their needs are met. Aging in place requires a complex interface between the individual and the environment. Progressive facilities provide features that residents can use as they need to. For example, bathrooms that are fully accessible and include supportive features allow a resident to choose the amount of support they need, and at what point they need it.

Value

The next generation of seniors will be far more value-conscious. They will want to clearly understand and endorse the "value" of the senior living and service options they select. Continuing care retirement communities (CCRCs) cannot be the only housing available to couples over 75, who want options like active adult communities and age-targeted senior condominiums and rental apartments. And they may reject the old Lifecare Type A Contract that requires

them to turn over a majority of their assets and retirement savings to a CCRC sponsor in exchange for a lifetime of care.

The World War II generation was unable to shop around for unbundled service options. Thanks to the Internet, today's seniors can choose from many different types of products—and from competitors offering those products—and devise their own housing strategies. For example, an independent living apartment might be paired with a home healthcare agency, allowing someone to age in place longer before moving to an assisted living or long-term care facility.

Non-Institutional Environments

A major argument against large facilities is that they feel institutional no matter how focused on hospitality they are. Sponsors today realize that seniors and their families prefer a residential (or at least a small hotel-like) environment. In the last two decades, many existing facilities have been renovated with this in mind; virtually all new environments are designed as residences (figs. 3-3 and 3-4). (See also chapters 15 and 16.)

Figures 3-3 and 3-4 (following page) Sponsors have responded to consumer preferences by reimagining their dining programs and offering more menu selections at different price points, longer dining hours, and a choice of dining venues. The large formal dining room, pictured above, is converted to cafés, bistros, and other dining venues. Westminster Village, Scottsdale, Arizona. Photograph by Perkins Eastman.

▶ *Figure 3-4 (see previous page)*
Perkins Eastman. Photograph by Chris Cooper.

Security

The aged feel vulnerable. To satisfy their—and their family's—concerns, a facility must not only be safe and secure but also create the perception of safety and security. And this sense of security must be evident from the first time a senior or his or her family enters the lobby to visit the marketing office.

The following are some ways to secure a senior living facility:

- Manned gatehouse or video cameras at the main entrance
- Perimeter fences and/or visual surveillance
- Exterior lighting
- Controlled-access parking garage
- Elevators with keycard access
- Security cameras
- Monitored doors and windows

In newer mixed-use CCRCs, residents can enjoy open-to-the-neighborhood restaurants and wellness clubs and then, with a security swipe card, reenter the private residential area.

Integration into Existing Communities

One of the myths about older adults is that they want to be segregated with people their own age, enjoying views of the countryside. In fact, most would prefer to stay in their own community and remain near their children, grandchildren, and friends. The majority of potential residents for a new assisted living facility usually live, or have children who live, within 5 miles of the facility (fig. 3-5).

For the last 30–50 years, the majority of CCRCs were planned and built in the outer suburbs of major cities. These CCRCs catered to local, affluent men and women

over 75. As "silent generation" consumers approached retirement, there was an increased demand for independent living facilities nearer cities. Such facilities often include ground-floor businesses such as "partner" restaurants, dry cleaners, wellness centers, and medical offices. Proximity to a city's cultural and social amenities allows the independent living resident to remain active in the wider community, a short cab ride or walk away from museums, symphonies, retail shops, and theaters.

One such urban CCRC is constructing a new high-rise independent living tower for silent generation consumers ten blocks from the heart of downtown. Its residents are attracted back from suburban communities, where they moved years ago to raise their children. This CCRC has partnered with a local college to provide access to the fine arts and to world-class wellness programs. It is integrated into the fabric of the city, and its residents live among people of all ages (figs. 3-6 and 3-7).

LIFESTYLE CHANGES

While a lifestyle change is not sought by all seniors, the expectations of those who do want one must be met by future senior living and care building programs.

Future Consumers

In the twentieth century, residents in senior living communities were from the World War II generation. Born between 1901 and 1924, they were children of the Great Depression and managed their wealth very carefully. Most nonetheless accepted the limited senior living options available.

The following generation, born between 1925 and 1945, is what demographers call the "silent generation." This generation, which began reaching retirement age in

▶ *Figure 3-5 The aged do not want to be segregated from the larger community. Integration with the surrounding neighborhood and intergenerational programming are now common goals for both new and existing senior communities.*

1990, is very different than the World War II generation. It is much more likely to demand quality alternatives to existing senior living choices. They want to be involved in creating the service packages offered, from dinner menus to wellness and fitness programs. And they want to examine a sponsor's financial statements before making deposits or signing agreements. They know they will live longer than their parents and want facilities to help them maintain their physical and mental health. Because they are Internet savvy, they are able to compare offerings and costs among competitors, and they discuss their expectations in public forums—especially those expectations that they feel are not being met. In short, the silent generation is not so silent and demands both choice and value.

This generation is also heavily influenced by their adult baby boomer children, born between 1946 and 1964. This influence extends to everything from fashion, appliances, and home décor to an interest in green furnishings and building materials. They may even subscribe to the same magazines and cable TV channels.

As a result, they are leaving their suburban, single-family homes for urban centers with a "sense of place." They want to live among all age groups in an economically and racially diverse environment, and they want to live near public transportation systems. They are concerned about sustainability, and,

◀ *Figure 3-6 Urban, green, and a part of city life. Mirabella, Portland, Oregon.* Ankrom Moison.

▶ *Figure 3-7 Urban high-rise housing offers seniors the ability to stay "in town," with easy access to public transportation as well as educational resources, cultural amenities, sports, and shopping. Saint John's on the Lake, Milwaukee, Wisconsin. Perkins Eastman. Photograph by Chris Barrett.*

therefore, "green" construction and operations. And they want retirement communities that are associated with a university or college offering opportunities for lifelong learning.

Fitness and Wellness

A major fear of the silent generation is becoming mentally impaired and physically frail before having the opportunity to enjoy retired life. A senior's ongoing wellness is directly tied to his or her environment. And wellness means more than just taking an aerobics or spin class, or swimming laps in a heated pool. Today's seniors are looking for a range of wellness-related features, including a choice of dining venues, access to nature, designs and colors that enliven the senses, mind and body exercises that promote healthy aging, and the freedom to socialize with whom they choose. A design team must address these desires—whether through a cosmetic makeover, a small remodeling or addition, or a brand new building—to ensure the ongoing financial viability of their products in this market.

There has been—and will continue to be—a shift away from a focus on supporting and caring for aging adults and toward empowering seniors through an increased emphasis on wellness. Indeed, retirement communities of the future will be "wellness communities" devoted to lengthening and improving the quality of residents' lives. And their programming and environments—informed by the seven dimensions of wellness (see sidebar)—will align with this purpose.

Programs directly related to wellness have begun to move beyond a lone fitness room with a few treadmills and exercise bicycles. More and more communities are embracing well-rounded exercise programs that include spa-like services such as a beauty shop, massage room, along with a pool, hot tub, aerobics studio, and yoga room. While this type of wellness center is a big improvement, it still falls short: wellness is not just a room; it is a holistic attitude that should pervade an entire community's environment and programs (fig. 3-8).

SEVEN DIMENSIONS OF WELLNESS

1. *Physical.* Using your knowledge, behavior, and skills to achieve your personal fitness and health goals by eating well, exercising, and making healthy lifestyle choices.
2. *Vocational.* Matching your core values to your interests, hobbies, employment, and volunteer work.
3. *Environmental.* Living in harmony with the earth and becoming aware of the impact your interactions with the environment have.
4. *Social.* Being aware of, participating in, and feeling connected to your community.
5. *Intellectual.* Maintaining an active mind through mental stimulation, lifelong learning, and remaining curious and creative.
6. *Spiritual.* Seeking a meaning to your life and integrating your spiritual beliefs and values with your actions.
7. *Emotional.* Handling issues and emotions constructively and maintaining a positive mindset.

▶ *Figure 3-8 Communities struggle with balancing the expectations of future consumers with those of existing residents who feel everything is fine the way it is. Brandon Oaks reinvented its fitness programs and added an aquatics program; resident participation increased to over 70 percent. Brandon Oaks, Roanoke, Virginia. Perkins Eastman. Photograph by Amy Nance-Pearman.*

Lifelong Learning

Accompanying the trend toward healthier lifestyles is a growing interest in lifelong learning. Many people in their 80s and 90s continue to seek intellectual and even vocational opportunities that they were previously unable to attain. This interest has changed the activities and programming offered at senior living facilities and created a market for retirement communities adjacent to colleges and universities. Such communities provide cultural and intellectual stimulation in addition to any needed medical care, often in an area with a relatively low cost of living. The Kendal Corporation has pioneered this concept with five continuing care retirement communities adjacent to college campuses, including Dartmouth College (Hanover, New Hampshire), Cornell University (Ithaca, New York), and Oberlin College (Oberlin, Ohio).

College campuses, once the source of baby boomers' zeal for political change, could be the place where the silent generation embraces both learning and giving. Over a hundred colleges and universities have completed or are involved in the planning of a hybrid CCRC on or near their campuses for alumni, retired faculty, and staff, as well as nearby seniors. Such CCRCs permit the elderly to audit classes, host study sessions in the library, and become involved with intergenerational student think tanks (where boomers facilitate discussions about major social needs). Attending plays, musicals, recitals, poetry readings, sporting events and, in some cases, performing in their own ensembles, adds vibrancy to seniors' lives. And undergraduates integrated into these lifelong learning programs have formed strong connections with their "senior" classmates, and through computer

◀ *Figure 3-9 Lifelong learning is a priority for many retirees.*

and technology swap-training, gain a deeper understanding of ageism (fig. 3-9).

Lifestyle Apartments

Carl Jung once said that "one's home is a symbolic mirror of one's inner self, of unconscious wishes and emotions." How many CCRC apartments reflect the essence of that quote?

An emerging trend has the design team, together with residents, reinventing the "lifestyle apartment" of residents' dreams. In the past, communities took a one-size-fits-all approach, providing few options for carpet color, countertop design, and appliances. The past decade has seen an increase in available options for finishes, lighting, appliances, and bathroom fixtures—all at little or no additional cost to residents. Sponsors have also provided pre-priced upgrades for further customization. And these options only just begin to allow residents to "mirror" their interests—in cooking, entertainment, work, and so on—in the way their space is arranged and utilized.

SERVICE PARTNERSHIPS

The owners and sponsors of most well-established retirement communities believe they can supply all the services a retiree needs. But as they plan for the future, they should really look beyond in-house capabilities and collaborate with other providers.

Many older adults are already purchasing services from non-institutional providers such as restaurants, fitness facilities, and homecare/companion services. These providers are the perfect partners to assimilate into a community's programs. Many progressive nonprofit early adopters are looking to the operators and owners of restaurants, salons and spas, boutique food and gift stores, medical clinics, and commercial retailers to enhance the services for their residents and staff.

Economic Pressures

Forty years ago, senior living was straightforward. There were limited options in most communities, and the facilities stayed full. Income, whether private pay or reimbursed through Medicaid or other sources, was adequate and predictable. Design was governed by prescriptive codes and established models. And the senior residents had only modest expectations. All of that has changed.

Today, owners and operators are facing economic uncertainties. There is more competition, the number of private-pay residents has declined, reimbursement has become inadequate and unpredictable, facilities built in accordance with the old models are becoming obsolete, and the senior consumer has become far more demanding. The result is that many existing senior living communities are under tremendous financial pressure. Those that fail to change will eventually go out of business. But many are responding to these challenges.

The first step for many has been to reposition the physical environment and service offerings of their campuses. They have correctly judged that if they fail to adjust to the market, their occupancy will deteriorate and they will eventually have to shut their doors. Over the last 20 years, every experienced senior living designer has been engaged to find ways to make existing facilities more attractive and accessible, increase the amount of resident privacy, change the dining options, add new programs such as specialized Alzheimer's care and Medicare-eligible subacute care, and so on.

Existing Housing and Care Facilities

Many of the existing facilities serving the aged are obsolete. In some cases, superior service helps mask their deficiencies, but as the market becomes steadily more demanding and sophisticated, out-of-date facilities will suffer. Architects and interior designers are therefore being asked to mitigate the physical factors contributing to obsolescence. In some cases, this may mean a simple

interior facelift that makes the facility more homelike and attractive; in others, it may involve reconfiguring existing units as larger apartments or building additions to increase the number of private rooms in a skilled nursing facility.

However, no amount of renovation or interior design can revive some existing facilities. Too many were poorly planned, designed, constructed, and/or maintained. As newer, more appropriately designed facilities are built in the same markets, such facilities will have to be replaced in order to stay competitive on any basis other than price. (See chapter 16 for a more detailed discussion.)

Changing an existing campus can be difficult. How can a 30- to 50-year-old community be transfused with the vibrancy desired by the silent generation? Repositioning an older campus by using information from trade publications and conferences to inform the needed programming and architectural changes may have been acceptable to the World War II generation. But today's residents expect to collaborate in the planning process.

Public vs. private payor sources

Some of the largest new building programs have been on campuses that were once used predominantly for skilled nursing. Many of these sponsors have added housing, day care, and other programs to both respond to the market and to move away from an overdependence on increasingly unreliable Medicaid reimbursements. Residents are likely to move to the skilled nursing facility owned by the same sponsor when the time comes; it also gives residents seeking a retirement community more choices. Moreover, the rents and service fees for housing are minimally regulated, if at all, and can offset the risks of Medicaid reimbursement.

Evolving Staffing Patterns

Staff accounts for the largest part of a facility's operating budget, and there are many strategies for reducing its cost. In non-union areas, operators have embraced the "universal worker" concept: staff tasks are not tied to job descriptions. Some efficiencies are thereby achieved because the same person can be used for housekeeping, to assist with serving meals, and for a variety of other tasks that would otherwise each require a specialized staffer. This model is essential for operating a "small house" profitably.

Other facilities have been redesigned to make them both more responsive to residents and more efficient for staff. The "cluster concept" was one such change. Staff are positioned near clusters of resident rooms and adjacent to clean and soiled utility rooms, charting desks, and other features. This allows them to remain near the residents they are attending to rather than constantly returning to a central nurses station to fill out charts or pick up supplies.

Sustainable Design

Sustainable design concepts can lower long-term operating costs. The current generation of seniors are concerned about climate change and have likely incorporated recycling, fluorescent light bulbs, energy-efficient appliances, and the like into their homes. They will be impressed by buildings built and run sustainably, with features like low-voltage exterior lighting, solar hot water systems, occupancy sensors that automatically turn lights on and off, drought-tolerant plants and graywater irrigation for the campus's landscaping, wind generation (in locations where it is practical), and a communal car exchange program to reduce automobile emissions on campus.

Leveraging Assets and Brand

A growing number of operators are lowering costs—and improving quality—by outsourcing one or more departments (such as food service, laundry, and even physical and occupational therapies). Other operators have entered into partnerships to both enrich their programs and spread their costs over a more specialized and larger client base. Some CCRCs expand their services to other locales. Others offer programs and services beyond the needs of their residents.

Whatever it ultimately becomes, a community must respond to the demands of future consumers. One older CCRC was faced with an outdated long-term care facility on its campus. The obvious solution was to replace it with a brand new building. Instead, this CCRC decentralized those beds, building "small houses" in the zip codes where its residents used to live. The result: five 10-bedroom long-term care homes that are woven throughout the suburbs and adjacent to long-standing active adult communities or large medical center campuses. By constructing homelike, subacute-care products throughout a 5-acre community, this CCRC has changed long-held consumer perceptions of institutional care.

In another community, a new 25,000 sq ft community center on a 35-year-old campus provides space for 25 local nonprofit partners. They offer programs and services—including a café, aerobic and dance studios, theaters, and classrooms—to CCRC residents as well as older adults living in their own homes within a 15-mile radius. Community center staff make a special effort to reach out to isolated seniors nearby. This model is very different from that of a traditional CCRC (figs. 3-10 and 3-11).

▶ Figures 3-10 and 3-11
Twenty-five local community
organizations partnered with
C. C. Young, a retirement
community in Dallas, Texas, to
create a community resource
for all ages with a theater,
classroom, a café, and rooms
for art and meetings. C. C.
Young, The Point, Dallas,
Texas.
Perkins Eastman. Photograph
by Chris Cooper.

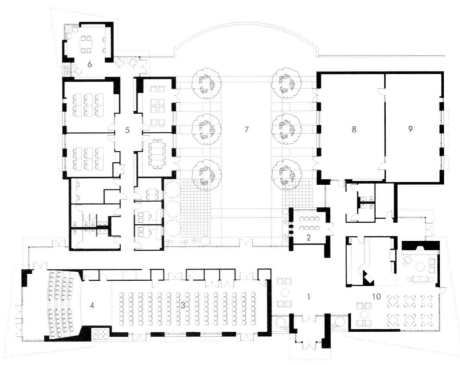

C.C. YOUNG: THE POINT first floor

1	Lobby	6	Resource/Library
2	Chapel	7	Courtyard
3	Multi-Purpose	8	Fitness
4	Stage/Auditorium	9	Exercise
5	Classrooms	10	Café

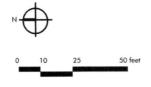

0   10   25   50 feet

▶ Figure 3-11

NEW HOUSING AND CARE CONCEPTS

Progressive facilities have implemented a variety of new concepts to respond to evolving market expectations and improve operating efficiency and quality of care. The most common are discussed below.

Green Houses and Small Houses

The Green House Project (www.thegreenhouseproject.org) transforms the traditional long-term care setting through specific design and operational criteria. Since the Green House Project is trademarked, similar programs are often referred to as the "small house movement." The Green House Project's senior housing facilities are small, 10–12 person houses (or apartments in urban settings), linked by a sophisticated care delivery network. Centralized management ensures quality, provides expertise, organizes backup staffing, and delivers accounting services.

Culture Change

Over the last 10 years, many Fortune 500 companies have undergone a culture change assessment and implementation process that, when successful, realigns their business

---

What is the Green House Project?

The Robert Wood Johnson Foundation awarded a five-year, $10 million grant to NCB Capital Impact (www.ncbcapitalimpact.org) in November 2005, to spur replication of the Green House concept, an innovative model for residential long-term care that completely reworks traditional architecture, organizational structure, and philosophy of care. The Green House Project provides predevelopment loans and advisement to organizations that want to establish Green House homes. NCB Capital Impact, the base of operations for the Green House Project's national replication center, has continued to administer the program beyond the term of the original grant.

The Green House model is the vision of Dr. William Thomas, a Harvard-educated geriatrician. The national Green House Project team, led by Robert Jenkens, is comprised of experienced leaders in the fields of culture change and long-term care.

What is a Green House home?

A Green House home is an independent, self-contained home for 10–12 people designed to look like the private houses or apartments in the surrounding community. Green House homes are typically licensed as skilled nursing facilities and meet all applicable federal and state regulatory requirements. Each person who lives in a Green House home has a private bedroom and full bathroom. The resident rooms open onto a central living area, which includes an open kitchen and a dining area. Residents eat meals at a common table. Family members, friends, and staff are encouraged to join the community at mealtimes and for other activities.

Each home is staffed by a team of cross-trained workers known as *shahbazim*. The staff has core training as certified nursing assistants (CNAs), plus extensive training in the Green House philosophy, the self-managed work team structure of the Green House home, culinary skills, and household management. Shahbazim provide personal care, prepare meals, and do light housekeeping and laundry, among other duties.

culture with the demands of their future customers. A similar process has taken place at organizations that own and operate senior living facilities, which have historically been healthcare-oriented, top-down businesses or nonprofits. Many publications by Leading-Age (formerly the American Association of Homes and Services for the Aging, or AAHSA) are aimed at leading its nonprofit members through this process of change.

In the senior living industry, culture change has resulted in four practice models, or philosophies of care, adopted to deinstitutionalize long-term facilities. Each practice model has its own advocates; all have the potential to change a facility's design and operations and improve staff morale and residents' quality of life.

These approaches are summarized by their advocates as follows:

1. *The Eden Alternative.* Developed by Judy and Bill Thomas of Sherburne, New York.
   - It creates a "human habitat" with plants, pets, and young children.
   - It combats residents' loneliness, boredom, and sense of helplessness.
   - Residents and staff have continuing contact characterized by variety and spontaneity.
   - Residents can provide care as well as receive it through their involvement in daily activities.
   - Caregivers and residents are decision makers.
2. *The Regenerative Community.* Developed by Debora and Barry Barkan of El Sobrante, California.
   - Staff members act as community developers in addition to their conventional work responsibilities.
   - Regular community meetings are opportunities for residents and staff to

socialize and discuss problems, with the aim of building a life of shared experience and concerns.
   - Residents are regarded as esteemed elders, regardless of physical or mental disability.
3. *Resident-free/individualized care.* Developed by Joanne Rader of Mt. Angel, Oregon.
   - Maintains the right of residents—particularly those with dementia—to direct their own care.
   - Staff must be creative and compassionate when addressing residents' behavior, considering the residents' perspective when making decisions.
   - No physical constraints or psychosocial medications are used.
   - Bathing is personalized based on residents' preferences and comfort level.
   - Staff learns to "speak the language of dementia."
4. *Resident-directed care.* Developed by Charlene Boyd and Robert Ogden of Seattle, Washington.
   - Nursing homes are made up of small "neighborhoods" instead of large units. Each community has its own budget for social work, activities, housekeeping, nursing, personal assistance, and management. Each also has its own laundry and family-style kitchen.
   - Residents choose their own daily routine: when to get up, when to eat, and so on.
   - There are fewer managers and more frontline staff.
   - Workers are cross-trained—everyone can make a sandwich or answer a phone call.
   - Nurse aides, called residents' assistants, are well paid and highly respected.

AFFORDABILITY

Affordability is the single biggest challenge facing the senior living industry—for consumers, sponsors, and their design teams. This chapter concludes with an extended discussion of this issue.

During the senior housing building boom of the last 30 years, much of the demand was for luxury options. Medicaid, various federal and state housing programs, and mission-driven nonprofits have paid for the care for lower-income individuals. But those who cannot afford high-priced facilities yet do not qualify for one of the subsidized options have been left to fend for themselves. Building design is only one part of the answer. Financing, creative reuse of existing land and facilities, containment of operating costs, and technology must all contribute to the solution.

Millions of people in the United States—from single heads of households to the very old struggling to stay independent—have difficulty paying for housing. The elderly are not the hardest hit by this problem; those older adults who own their house and have paid off the mortgage actually enjoy a good degree of financial stability. However, of the 5 million elderly renters, 2.7 million are hard-pressed to pay for housing.

Even the most spartan housing units cost more than many elderly households can afford. The median rent paid in 2008 by occupants 65 and older was $652 per month. But approximately half of that population earned

> Millions of elderly households continue to live in housing that costs too much, is in substandard condition, or fails to accommodate their physical capabilities or assistance needs.
>
> (U.S. Department of Housing and Urban Development 1999)

> Finding even modest housing at such a low cost is next to impossible. Nowhere in the country is the HUD fair market rent for even a one-bedroom apartment at or below $372. Without government subsidies, property owners find it difficult to operate and maintain housing at such rents, let alone service debt and earn a risk-adjusted rate of return.
>
> —Robert Schafer
> (Harvard University. Joint Center for Housing Studies 2010, p. 28)

less than $15,000 per year—approximately $1,250 per month—and, according to federal affordability guidelines, could pay no more than $372 per month without seriously compromising their quality of life. (The guideline defines affordability as spending no more than 30 percent of household income on housing costs, including utilities.)

How do these low-income seniors survive? Some live with younger family members, some share housing, and some are cared for in nursing homes. But most depend on subsidized housing. Of those 2.7 million low-income renters, 1.8 million live in federally subsidized rental housing, and others receive rent subsidies from municipalities and states.

But there is troubling evidence that homelessness is on the rise among the elderly. As baby boomers age, the elderly population will increase. There has also been an increase in the number of homeless adults between 50 and 64. These and other factors suggest a potential for a dramatic increase in the elderly homeless population between 2010 and 2020.

Among its other challenges, aging also increases housing costs by limiting housing options. If an older person can no longer drive, his or her housing must be near public transportation. The frail may find walking to neighborhood destinations frightening if the community is unsafe. Many elderly also prefer to be close to friends or family, who may live in more expensive areas. For older people who find negotiating stairs difficult and need a single-floor home, one on the first floor of an apartment building, or one that can accommodate a wheelchair, most of the existing housing stock is not even an option. The added cost of paying for maintenance chores they can no longer perform themselves exacerbates the problem.

Reducing the Cost of Housing for Seniors

When contemplating where to live, the elderly usually consider three well-known options: a retirement community, a nursing home, or living with their children. Of these, moving in with family is the only option most can afford. But it is not always possible to do so. This section discusses other affordable housing alternatives: assisted aging at home, adaptive reuse of obsolete buildings, single-room occupancy housing, shared housing, accessory units, and co-housing.

Assisted aging at home

It is not surprising that people want to remain at home for as long as they can. In addition to being comfortable and familiar, living at home is the least expensive option for most elderly, particularly for those whose homes are mortgage-free. It is the preference for the majority of older adults, provided the neighborhood remains socially and environmentally intact, although sometimes adaptations (like building a ground-floor bathroom) must be made to make it feasible.

In a survey conducted by AARP entitled "Home and Community Preferences of the 45+ Population" almost three-quarters of the respondents wanted to stay in their current residence for as long as possible, and over 60 percent wanted to remain in their community. Approximately 25 percent reported that they would stay in their community because they could not afford to move (Keenan 2010).

Manufactured housing

One way for people with limited means to live in their own home is to buy a mobile home, which can usually be purchased for less than $35,000. According to the U.S. Census, over two million older homeowners live in manufactured housing (the industry's term for mobile homes), making it an important source of affordable housing. More than half of all mobile homes are bought by middle-age and younger people who then age in place.

However, according to a 1999 AARP survey of mobile home owners, there are widespread deficiencies in their construction. The survey found that more than three-fourths of the owners reported problems with the construction or installation of their homes, and 57 percent reported multiple problems. Moreover, respondents said that only 35 percent of the deficiencies were repaired by the manufacturer, even though 95 percent of the homes were under warranty (AARP 1999). Although strict housing and safety standards have been in place since 1974, they have not been consistently enforced.

Adaptive reuse

In many American cities, the population of school-age children is decreasing as the population of elders grows larger. As schools—and commercial buildings like hotels, motels, and old office buildings—become obsolete, developers and nonprofit sponsors are converting some of them into affordable senior housing. For example, Eastern Village Cohousing in Silver Spring, Maryland, recycled a vacant 1950s office building and created 56 apartments. Such buildings provide an inexpensive "chassis" for housing as well as interesting architectural character. Sometimes, it is a building's location, rather than the building itself, that makes it appropriate senior housing—even though a creative design solution is required to convert it to apartments (figs. 3-12 and 3-13).

Single-room occupancy buildings

The single-room occupancy (SRO) facility is similar to the rooming or boarding house of old. Residents live in a single room and share a bathroom and kitchen. Unlike the rooming house, however, an SRO is a permanent residence. SROs are often the result of the adaptive reuse of old hotels or single-family houses. They may even be staffed and licensed as group homes for the care of the frail elderly or other populations with special needs.

Over 400,000 elderly people live in SROs nationwide. Such facilities serve people with very low incomes. The single elderly are far more likely to be poor and to live in rental housing than the elderly with families. Without a family or a job, they can become isolated, and they have no one to help them if they become impaired. These elderly are at risk for homelessness—a risk that has increased in recent years. Provided it is well-managed, an SRO can mitigate these concerns. Recognizing the valuable service the SRO can provide, some cities have enacted laws to prevent SROs from conversion or demolition.

An alternative for those with a slightly higher income is the retirement hotel, which, like the SRO, is run as a permanent residence. Some older hotels in central cities are converted to residences for seniors to improve their occupancy rate. They sometimes offer meals and organized activities such as card playing. The hotels are a good fit for self-reliant elderly who wish to live an independent, urban lifestyle without the responsibilities of housekeeping.

Shared housing

Home-sharing programs enable two (or more) unrelated people to occupy a house or apartment together, essentially becoming housemates. A homeowner is matched with someone seeking a residence, who then pays rent and shares the utility costs. The homeowner may also agree to accept services such as doing light household chores in lieu of rent.

Home-sharing arrangements can provide an elder homeowner with income; both people benefit from the companionship, security, and economic advantages. The arrangement also allows the homeowner to remain in his or her own home, and gives both the freedom of independent living.

Accessory units

Accessory units, also called granny flats or in-law houses, are small homes constructed or installed on the lot of an existing house. These units are designed around the physical needs of the elderly and allow them to live independently or semi-independently while remaining near family or friends. They are usually located on the property of an adult child of the senior. Accessory units are also developed by (typically nonprofit) sponsors in housing clusters on small tracts of land and then leased to elderly residents.

Elder cottage housing opportunities, or ECHOs, are trailer homes that can be attached to existing homes and removed when no longer needed. The concept originated in the state of Victoria, Australia, in 1972. It was adopted first by Scandinavian countries, then in Canada (in the 1980s). The U.S. Administration on Aging recognized them as

▶ *Figures 3-12 and 3-13*
*Creative adaptive reuse has
turned heritage buildings like
schools and churches into
affordable housing that keeps
seniors in their own
community. The housing is
networked with community-
based services. Buena Vista
Terrace, San Francisco,
California.*
HKIT Architects. Photograph
by Cesar Rubio.

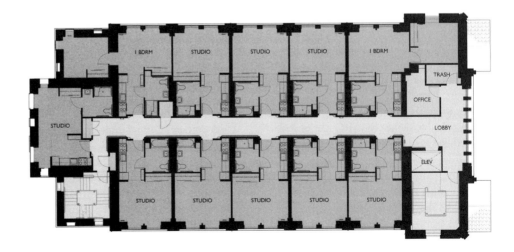

▶ *Figure 3-13*

accessory units in 1998. These units come with several advantages: there are minimal, if any, associated land costs; they are small; and they are easily connected to existing utilities. Prefabricated units are usually less expensive than site-built units, since they can be mass-produced. Building them off-site also reduces the logistical difficulties of construction behind or between existing houses. Unless the factory is nearby, however, those savings will be eroded by transportation costs.

ECHOs have been embraced in other countries but, despite positive attention from the media and housing professionals, not in the United States. The major barriers to their development in this country are rigid zoning laws and opposition from neighbors to increased density or anticipated decreases in property values.

Nevertheless, some companies now sell such units. FabCab, a Seattle-based manufacturer of timber-frame kit homes, builds accessory units ranging in size from 300 to 1,800 sq ft. A Salem, Virginia, firm called N2Care began manufacturing the MED Cottage, a portable accessory unit with options for high-tech medical monitoring and security equipment, in January 2011. And the Home Store, a well-established manufacturer of high-end modular homes in the Northeast, now offers freestanding, custom-designed "in-law units." All are built or prepared for assembly in a factory, trucked to a building site, and set on a foundation; depending on site work, this can cut construction costs and time from initiation to occupancy.

Housing choice vouchers

The federal Section 8 Housing Choice Voucher program was created to enable people with very low incomes, including the elderly, to secure decent, safe housing in the private rental market by paying a portion of the monthly rent. The program provides financial assistance to eligible households whose annual gross income does not exceed 50 percent of the Department of Housing and Urban Development (HUD) median income guidelines. Participants usually pay no more than 30 percent of their adjusted monthly income for rent. The program pays the balance of the rent to the landlord, provided the rent does not exceed HUD guidelines.

Due to the huge demand for affordable housing, there is a waiting list for Section 8 housing. According to HUD's Housing Choice Voucher fact sheet, "long waiting periods are common" before receiving Section 8 assistance.

Public housing

Public housing is the largest federal program providing housing assistance to low-income elders. These residents are not only poorer than the general senior population, but also older, disproportionately female and of an ethnic minority, and more likely to live alone. For many, it is their only housing option and provides their only security from homelessness or institutionalization (fig. 3-14).

Longer life expectancies and ongoing economic hardships are increasing this population. Yet public housing authorities are less able to provide appropriate facilities than ever before. Public housing, which was not originally intended for older Americans, was extended to seniors beginning in 1956; they were granted preference on waiting lists. In the 1960s and 1970s, a large number of developments were built specifically for low-income seniors. With few exceptions, these were traditional apartments in high-rise or mid-rise buildings.

Unfortunately, a significant portion of the public housing for seniors is rapidly

▶ Figure 3-14 High-quality subsidized housing is frequently supported by several different sources of financing. This project is a unique joint effort of a private developer, a nonprofit operator, and the City of Pittsburgh, and leveraged over 10 different funding sources. Silver Lake Commons, Pittsburgh, Pennsylvania.
Perkins Eastman. Photograph by Alexander Denmarsh.

becoming physically and functionally obsolete. While still adequate for most low-income older residents, it does not provide the flexibility to permit residents to age in place, nor can it serve the increasing share of frail or cognitively impaired seniors. Without these services, the only alternative is often costly and inhospitable nursing homes.

Some public housing authorities are, however, finding ways to address these problems. In Pittsburgh, the city teamed with a developer and a nonprofit sponsor to replace two high-rises with new assisted living–ready replacement housing. In Miami, Florida, Milwaukee, Wisconsin, and Cambridge, Massachusetts, public housing agencies have converted older independent living buildings into assisted living facilities.

Service-enriched housing

Both public and private sponsors of senior housing are looking for ways to provide the support that elderly residents require to age in place. Cathedral Square in South Burlington, Vermont, built in 1979 with HUD 202 funding (see below), recently converted independent living apartments into 28 assisted living units; daily meals, personal care activities, housekeeping, and social activities provide a continuum of care. Other solutions involve serving not only on-site residents but also the surrounding community. Allegheny County Housing Authority's Homestead Senior Apartments in Pittsburgh, Pennsylvania, used a HOPE VI grant to renovate the building and introduce an associated "life center" that serves both its own residents and seniors who live nearby.

It provides a community center, a community adult day care program, a wellness clinic, and a physical rehabilitation facility.

HUD 202 rental housing

The Section 202 program provides direct, low-interest loans to nonprofit sponsors to finance the construction or rehabilitation of residential projects and related facilities for those 62 and older and for the disabled. There are more than 300,000 Section 202 units serving very low-income seniors (fig. 3-15).

Over the last several years, however, the limited funding available for the construction of new Section 202 units has yielded fewer than 4,000 units each year—far fewer than are needed to meet the growing demand. An AARP study conducted in 2006 estimated that there are ten eligible residents for every unit that becomes available. A recent HUD study recommended that 10,000 Section 202 units be built annually for the next ten to fifteen years to keep up with the growing senior population and provide a cost-effective alternative to premature placement in institutional settings.

Low-income housing tax credits

While public housing is the largest public sector provider of senior affordable housing, the Low-Income Housing Tax Credit program is the largest production subsidy for privately sponsored affordable senior housing. In return for federal income tax credits,

◀ Figure 3-15 Many affordable senior housing projects are components of reinvented urban neighborhoods. This HUD 202 building is part of a much larger Hope 6 project that reused and rebuilt a former urban renewal project into an age- and income-integrated neighborhood. Pennley Supportive Housing, Pittsburgh, Pennsylvania. Perkins Eastman. Photograph by Alexander Denmarsh.

▶ *Figure 3-16 Cabrini First Hill Apartments provides 50 units of affordable senior housing with support services and, in a unique financing structure, combines HUD funds with low-income housing tax credits. Cabrini Senior Housing, Seattle, Washington.*
GGLO. Photograph by Steve Keating Photography.

a syndicate of investors provides the financing for rental projects that meet the criteria for low-income tenant eligibility. Tax credit programs are administered by state housing finance agencies, which select projects on a competitive basis. Tax credit financing is typically insufficient to fund an entire project, so it must be supplemented with other subsidy programs as well as with conventional financing. The program entails significant legal costs, so it is rare to see a project with less than 50 units (fig. 3-16).

CHAPTER 4

PROJECT PROCESS AND MANAGEMENT

This chapter focuses on two major issues in planning, design, and construction:

- The major steps and tasks involved in planning, designing, and implementing a building program
- The most common management problems that occur in senior housing and care building programs

PLANNING, DESIGN, AND IMPLEMENTATION PROCESS

The design of facilities for the aging typically involves many client representatives, outside agency and public reviews, complex functional issues, rapidly changing technology, restrictive codes, and other significant design influences. Even relatively small projects can take two to three years, and larger projects take from four to seven or more years from initial conception to completion. Successful design professionals understand both these issues and the implementation process during which they are resolved.

The implementation process for most facilities for the aging involves 11 steps:

1. Strategic planning
2. Feasibility analysis and scoping of market need
3. Selection and organization of the project team
4. Programming and pre-design work (defining scope of the proposed facility)
5. Schematic design
6. Obtaining approval and/or financing/premarketing and sales

7. Design development
8. Construction documentation
9. Selection of the construction and furniture, furnishings, and equipment (FF&E) installation teams
10. Construction and FF&E installation
11. Occupancy

The first part of this section discusses the design team's tasks for each of these steps. Understanding all the steps—as well as the design team's role in each—is an essential responsibility of any design professional. Figure 4-1 is a typical schedule for these eleven steps in a new continuing care retirement community (CCRC) building project.

Strategic Planning and Preliminary Definition of Need

Many projects are done within existing facilities or on existing campuses. Therefore, any project needs to be defined within the framework of a long-range plan. Even in new facilities, the initial design has to assume future growth and change.

An effective strategic plan will respond to more than site and facility issues; it will account for the way changes in technology, demography, and funding will impact the future need for and use of the facility. For example, experienced owners and architects recognize that many of a facility's initial occupants will age in place and that the facility must be designed to accommodate increased frailty over time.

Typically, design professionals evaluate existing conditions—mechanical systems, interior finishes, operational issues, code

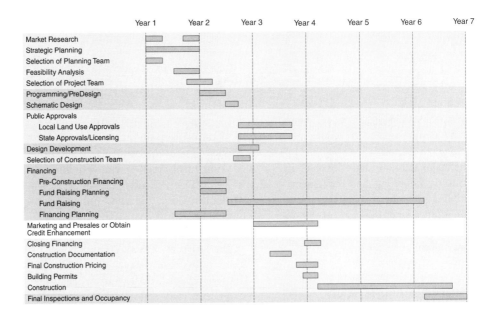

▶ *Figure 4-1 Typical minimum timeframe of major tasks for a CCRC or large senior housing project.* Perkins Eastman.

compliance, site conditions and constraints, and the ability of facilities to support their mission. Once these issues and any problems are defined, the design team can develop possible solutions as well as the cost and schedule for each potential development strategy. In most strategic plans, the options for the facility's expansion or modernization are then evaluated according to how well they achieve the institution's goals. Then the options are reduced to a preferred strategic direction.

Feasibility Analysis

Once the strategic-planning framework is set, the scope of the specific project is defined. The sponsor may do this, but it is often more efficient to include specialists in market or needs analysis and design professionals in this process.

The primary tasks of this step are establishing an outline program and statement of project objectives, setting a realistic schedule, outlining a preliminary project

budget, and defining the professional services that must be retained. In certain cases, this step also includes some preliminary feasibility testing of a specific site or building. Because projects always face market and financial constraints, clients need confirmation early on that their project is financially viable.

As discussed in chapter 20, the owner may now retain a market and/or financial consultant to provide an independent professional opinion of the market and financial feasibility—a basic requirement for the financing of most projects. All the project parameters—program, budget, schedule, and feasibility—must be reconfirmed and refined after the full team is selected, but it is important to have a realistic outline of the project before selecting the full team.

Selection and Organization of Project Team

The design of any facility is a team sport; it is not uncommon for 10 or more professional disciplines to be involved. Typically, the architect retains most of these professionals and forms a single cohesive team, thereby providing the owner with a single source of responsibility. The team may include the following specialists (fig. 4-2):

- Architects
- Gerontologists
- Food-service and laundry consultants
- Equipment specialists
- Interior designers
- Civil engineers
- Mechanical engineers
- Structural engineers
- Electrical engineers
- Plumbing and fire-protection engineers
- Cost consultants and/or construction managers
- Telecommunications and low voltage technology consultants
- Lighting designers

- Landscape architects
- Acoustical consultants

There is, in addition, a second group of consultants that often includes the following:

- Accountants
- Financial consultants
- Market analysts
- Sales and marketing professionals
- An advertising agency
- Certificate-of-need or other public-approval specialists
- Development-management consultants
- Investment bankers
- Attorneys
- Bond counsel
- Fundraising consultants
- Environmental and hazardous materials consultants
- Traffic analysts

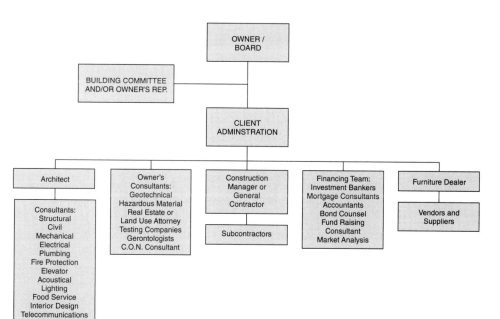

◀ Figure 4-2 The typical project organization for a large senior living project. Perkins Eastman.

- Parking consultants
- Zoning consultant

The client typically selects the lead professionals (usually the architect), who, in turn, chooses the remainder of the design team. Members of that team must possess all critical professional skills. The complexity of many projects demands that the team find a way to provide expertise in the disciplines listed above, even if the budget curtails the degree to which some of those specialists are involved.

The selection process for the lead professionals can vary, but a thorough process includes the following:

1. Research is done on firms with relevant experience.
2. A written request is sent to a "longlist" of firms asking them to submit letters of interest, references, and information about similar projects they have worked on. This request, sometimes known as a request for qualifications (RFQ), includes a statement of the project's objectives, an outline of the program, a schedule, and a budget.
3. After a review of these submittals, four to six firms are placed on a short list and asked to make a formal presentation.
4. The short-listed firms are sent a request for a written proposal, known as a request for proposal (RFP), summarizing

- the firm's understanding of the project,
- a proposed work program,
- a proposed schedule,
- key personnel and sub-consultant firms to be involved and their relevant experience, and
- proposed fees and expenses.

Following formal presentations and interviews, a contract is negotiated with the selected firm. A fee is finalized once the team is retained and there is a comprehensive discussion of scope, schedule, proposed specialist consultants, and other variables. No two projects are the same, so the appropriate fees should be carefully calculated on a case-by-case basis to reflect the full scope of the services to be provided. The form of contract is typically based upon one of the standard American Institute of Architects (AIA) contract forms, but the client may edit these.

Once the lead firm is selected, the entire team must be organized. This organization must begin with the client because only the client can

- select the team or the lead professionals who will assemble the full team,
- set the overall project goals and monitor whether they are being met,
- select the program and design solutions that best meet the objectives from among the options prepared by the design team,
- resolve differences and problems between team members (e.g., design team and builder)
- administer the contracts with the team members, and
- lead the relationship between the project team and the public.

Clients who create a clear decision-making structure and build a strong team relationship with all the firms involved in the process are much more likely to be successful. Some clients have even used one- to three-day "partnering sessions" at the beginning of a project to build such team relationships. Recognizing the importance of the client's role in this relationship, the renowned Finnish-born architect

Eero Saarinen would begin a project by saying to the design team, "Let's see if we can make this guy into a great client."[1]

In some large projects, a development manager provides overall project management expertise to the owner. While such firms can provide essential expertise and manpower for some projects, they should never become a filter between the owner and the rest of the team. Most owners benefit from direct communication with the experienced leaders of the other key team members.

Programming and Predesign

One of the most challenging steps for the design team is translating market data, owner objectives, state codes, and other input into an architectural program and initial concept. In the past, the client would often prepare a detailed statement of the project requirements or program during the scoping phase (see chapter 2). Today, the increased complexity of the average project means that its full detailed scope must be analyzed and defined with the assistance of the design team (fig. 4-3).

Program analysis has become a standard service provided by the architects, planners, and interior designers on most senior living projects. Among the additional issues the design team and specialists must define

- the number of each type of space;
- the detailed functional and equipment requirements (type of food service, number and type of physical and occupational therapy equipment, etc.);
- mechanical, electrical, plumbing, and other system choices and service needs;
- the dimensions of each space; and
- the relationships between spaces.

◀ *Figure 4-3 Conceptual diagram for the first floor of a typical suburban assisted living residence.*
Perkins Eastman.

---

[1] Saarinen to Larry Perkins, personal communication.

This important initial step is discussed in more detail in chapter 2. The project team also has several other tasks before design can begin, including

- a detailed assessment of existing conditions in the project area;
- preparation of base plans showing the conditions of the existing structures, a site survey, utility analyses, and subsoil analyses (if new construction is involved);
- an analysis of the zoning, building code, and public-approval issues that will influence the design;
- a review of the latest evidence-based design experience and research; and
- special analyses of any other issues (asbestos, structural capacity, and so on) that could affect the project's design, cost, schedule, or feasibility.

The results of the programming and related analyses are then combined into one or more preliminary concepts, an expanded statement of project goals, and an updated project schedule and budget.

Once these materials are available, two important parallel series of tasks begin: land use approvals (zoning, site plan approvals, wetland permits, etc.) and financing.

When required, the local land use approvals typically start with informal meetings with the municipal officials or planning department staff. The meetings help outline the steps in the process, identify whether any special approvals (such as zoning variances) are necessary, and define the information required at each step in the process. Most local approval processes for projects involving more than interior renovation require detailed site design and schematic building design for land use approval. On larger projects, this may also require detailed analyses of the environmental impact of increased traffic, noise, storm drainage, and similar issues before local officials grant their approval. It is not unusual for the land use approval process to take one year or more. In many cases, the design team must take the lead in this effort.

The second task that typically begins during pre-design is securing pre-construction and construction permanent financing for the project. Few major projects are paid for with the sponsor's cash reserves or endowment. Most involve borrowing and/or fundraising. Financing a project can also take more than a year. During this process, the design team is often asked to assist in the required documentation, public presentations, and other steps. This is covered further in chapter 20.

Once these pre-design tasks near completion, it is time to start the traditional design process.

Definition of Schematic Design

Schematic design documents shall establish the conceptual design of the project, illustrating the scale and relationship of the project components. The schematic design documents shall include a conceptual site plan, if appropriate, and preliminary building plans, sections, and elevations.
(American Institute of Architects 2007)

Schematic Design

Schematic design is the first phase of the traditional design process. On most senior housing and care projects, this phase does not begin until preliminary fundraising or additional feasibility studies confirm the project's viability. During this first design phase, the basic design concept is developed for all the major components of the project. The standard forms of agreement for design services provide brief definitions of schematic design as well as the subsequent phases.

The standard contractual definitions of design services are based on a process that would theoretically permit the design team to move in an orderly way through the most common steps in the design, documentation, and construction of a building. This theoretical process assumes that a clear definition of the client's program exists and that the design process can progress in a linear fashion from that definition through a series of steps—each of which results in a more complete definition of the design—until the project is sufficiently detailed to go into documentation for bidding (or negotiation) and construction.

The reality is not so orderly. Evolving program requirements, budget realities, increased knowledge of site considerations (such as subsoil problems), and many other factors make it necessary to go back and modify previous steps. Design moves forward, but rarely in the straightforward fashion implied by the standard two-phase description of design. In fact, most design professionals agree that design choices occur at every step of the process. In other words, building design neither starts with schematic design nor ends with the completion of the second phase, design development (fig. 4.4).

The process by which a design team and its consultants convert all of the design influences into a specific design solution varies from firm to firm. In schematic design, most firms begin with a period of analysis of the key issues (function, cost, codes, aesthetics, etc.) followed by a period of synthesis into a single concept.

It is common for the design team to consider several conceptual solutions to a design problem. For this reason, most have developed a process for narrowing down to a single concept. Selection may be based on the formal grading of a concept against the original project objectives, on an intuitive judgment based on experience, or, as is often the case, on a combination of both.

In the past formulaic design solutions were used for many senior living projects. Today most of these standard solutions are considered obsolete. Most current senior living projects require design solutions that respond to each project's unique mix of site, program, budget, owner goals, and other key variables (fig. 4-5).

Underlying this diversity of approaches are some common themes and design tasks. The first is an expansion of the original client's goals statement to include clear design goals. These will help in making the inevitable decisions on trade-offs between budget and quality, appearance and energy efficiency, as well as the thousands of other major decisions for which competing priorities must be reconciled.

The next basic task is the development of a parti, or basic conceptual diagram for the project concept. Sometimes this concept evolves from the site and program; other times, it starts with a strong formal concept. As architect Edward Larrabee Barnes, FAIA, put it, "It is not just a case of form following function. Sometimes function follows form."

Designers also choose a design vocabulary. The vocabulary includes the formal

▶ Figure 4-4 A concept plan for an assisted living facility.
Perkins Eastman

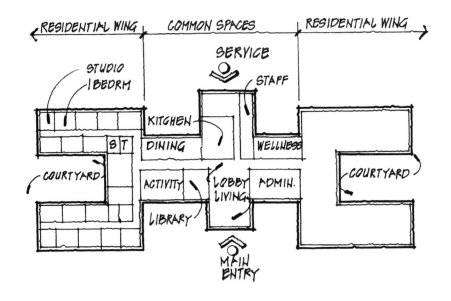

▶ Figure 4-5 Design options.
Perkins Eastman

Design Options					
	1	2	3	4	5
Program Fit	●	●	∅	●	●
Appropriate Adjacencies	●	∅	∅	∅	●
Clear Circulation	∅	∅	∅	o	●
Code Compliant	●	●	o	●	●
Impact on Staffing	∅	∅	●	∅	∅
Potential Disruption	∅	∅	×	∅	∅
First Cost	∅	∅	∅	∅	o
Life Cycle Cost	o	o	o	o	∅
Site Utilization	∅	∅	∅	o	∅
Conformance with Zoning	●	o	●	o	●

- ● Good
- ∅ Acceptable
- o Poor
- × Prohibitive

or aesthetic ideas that will govern the development of the design concept. Some designers develop a personal vocabulary of ideas, details, preferred materials, and so on, and refine it on each project. Others approach each project as a unique problem and select a vocabulary appropriate to that problem. In senior housing projects, there has been a debate for years on this subject. Most specialists in the field try to incorporate residential scale, materials, and detailing appropriate to the region. Others, however, argue for a break from what they see as overly traditional design vocabularies.

Beyond the first conceptual steps, the process becomes more complex. In all but the smallest and simplest projects, the steps that follow the original planning concepts involve a team of people. While it is true that significant projects are usually developed under the guidance of a single strong design leader, in most projects more than 10 people are involved in the decision-making process. Thus, design excellence is dependent upon the effective management of a complex team, all of whose members contribute to the quality of the final result.

The result of all these steps is a completed schematic design. While different projects, clients, and design teams have different definitions of the completion of this phase, there are certain commonly agreed upon objectives and delivered documents.

Objectives
The primary objective is to arrive at a clearly designed, feasible concept and to present it in a form that the client understands and accepts. The secondary objectives are to clarify the project program, explore the most promising alternative design solutions, and

provide a reliable basis for analyzing the cost of the project.

Products
Communicating design ideas and decisions usually involves a variety of media. Typical documentation at the end of this phase can include the following:

- A site plan
- Plans for each level, including conceptual reflected ceiling plans
- All elevations—exterior and conceptual interior elevations
- Two or more cross-sections
- An outline specification—a general description of the work indicating major systems and materials choices
- A statistical summary of the design area and other characteristics in comparison to the program
- A preliminary construction cost estimate (see chapter 19 for a more detailed discussion)
- Other illustrative materials—renderings, models, or drawings—needed to adequately present the concept

Other services
As part of the schematic design work, the design team may agree to provide the client with energy studies, life cycle cost analyses or other economic studies, or special renderings, models, brochures, or promotional materials.

Approvals
The final step in schematic design is to obtain formal client approval. The schematic design presentation must be clear enough for the client to understand and approve. To confirm this approval, each item in the presentation should be signed and dated by the client so that the design development phase can begin.

Obtaining Approval and/or Financing

At this stage, the design may also be subject to review by state, local, and sometimes federal agencies. A certificate of need (CON) may be required for nursing homes, medical-model adult day care, some assisted living facilities, and most other projects for which the care will be reimbursed by Medicaid, Medicare, or other public programs. Some clients will apply for a CON during conceptual design, but most approvals require plans and reliable cost estimates.

Most CON applications also require comprehensive demographic analyses, analyses of staffing and of care plans, protection plans for existing residents during construction, and many other studies. Other specialist consultants prepare most of these, but some require input from the design team.

Continuing care retirement communities and some active adult retirement communities also require state approval in most states. State approval usually requires a detailed offering plan for potential residents describing facilities, services, and costs, which cannot be defined without at least schematic design information.

Though less common, many nursing homes and assisted living projects use federal mortgage guarantee programs as part of their financing plan (see chapter 20). These typically require the review and approval of both the schematic drawings and cost, and later, the contract documents and final pricing.

At the same time they are undergoing state and/or federal review, most projects also proceed with local land use approvals. For reasons that are hard to understand, there has been widespread resistance to the development of senior care and housing options in many regions. As a result, the most complex task in many projects has become obtaining local land use approvals and permits (site plan approval, wetlands permits, approval for curb cuts, etc.).

Local land use approvals typically require detailed site engineering (public utility demand, sanitary waste disposal, etc.) and special impact studies (traffic, visual, etc.) that are far more detailed than the architectural design is at this stage. The local land use process must be carefully planned and executed. Failure to manage any of the public approvals is one of the most common reasons for projects to come to a halt.

In recent years, the local public approval process has become one of the hardest tasks to navigate. Indicative of this increasing opposition is a comment made during a public hearing for site plan approval of a nursing home in a small upper-income community:

A local resident: "How many people die in your facility each year?"

The proposed facility's executive director: "The average age is 88, and about one-third pass on each year."

The now irate local resident: "Do you realize that you will raise our village's death rate from 2 to over 60, an increase of 3,000 percent? Do you realize that you will make us the death capital of New Jersey?"

Design Development

The primary purpose of the design development phase is to define and describe important aspects of the project so that all that remains is the formal step of producing construction contract documents.

As schedule pressures and the amount of fast-track construction have increased, some clients and design firms have attempted to cut down or even eliminate this phase. However, there are strong arguments against doing this. Design development is the period during which all the issues left unresolved at the end of schematic design can be worked out. Eliminating this phase increases the possibility that major modifications will be required during the construction contract documents phase. Such changes are costly and more likely to lead to coordination problems during construction.

For CCRCs requiring formal state approval of their marketing materials and offering plans to prospective residents, most experienced clients ask for design development documentation. This minimizes the need for amendments after the marketing has begun.

Effective design development results in a clear, coordinated description of all aspects of the design. This typically includes fully developed floor plans, interior and exterior elevations, reflected ceiling plans, wall and building sections, and key details. This also includes the evaluation of alternative interior finishes and furnishings. In addition, the basic mechanical, electrical, plumbing, and fire-protection systems are accurately sized and defined, if not fully drawn. No major issues should be left unresolved that could require significant restudy during the construction contract documents phase.

The products of the design development phase are similar to those of schematic design drawings and specifications that fix and describe the size and character of the project, as well as any recommended adjustments to the preliminary estimate of construction cost. The design development phase should be brought to a close with a formal presentation to, and approval by, the client.

Construction Documentation

The design process does not really end with the completion of the design development phase, but the emphasis shifts to producing a complete coordinated set of documents to guide the purchasing, construction, installation, and initial operations steps that follow.

The construction documents typically include drawings, specifications, contract forms, and, if the project is being bid, bidding requirements. These four documents play an important role:

1. Drawings provide the graphic description of the work to be done.
2. Specifications outline the levels of quality and standards to be met.
3. Contract forms include the actual contract, bond and insurance requirements, and general conditions outlining the roles, rights, and responsibilities of all parties.
4. Bidding requirements set the procedures for this process.

The professional design organizations (such as the AIA and others) have model documents for the specifications, contract forms, and bidding requirements that can be adapted to incorporate each project's unique requirements.

The most complex part of this step is the production of a comprehensive set of drawings and technical specifications. This often takes four to six months. A new building or the large renovation of a nursing home or retirement community can involve over 100 sheets of architectural drawings and several hundred pages of technical specifications. Each sheet of the drawings may take 100–200 hours to complete because the drawings must provide a clear, accurately dimensioned graphic description of the work to be done. Moreover, each drawing must be coordinated with the many drawings of the other design professionals working on the same project (fig. 4-6).

Selection of the Construction and FF&E Installation Teams and Purchasing

Once part or all of the construction documents are available, the next critical step is the selection of the builders, FF&E manufacturers, and others who will provide the construction and other installed elements of the facility. Typically, the design team either manages the selection process or is an active participant with the client, as any experienced architect or owner will attest.

A number of selection strategies are available. For selection of the builder, there are five major alternatives:

1. The most common is for the construction documents to be completed and

▶ *Figure 4-6 A schematic plan for an assisted living facility. The greater detail required for design development and construction documentation is illustrated at lower left. Inn at Silver Lake, Kingston, Massachusetts. Perkins Eastman.*

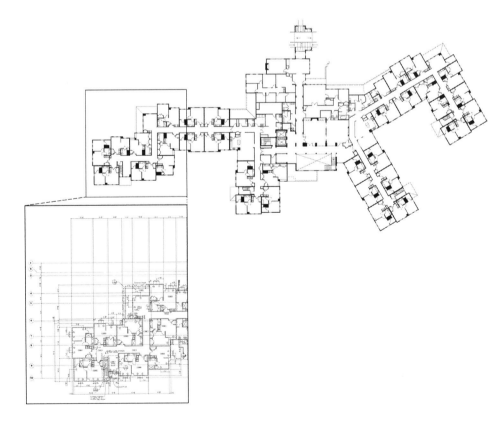

put out for a bid to companies attracted by public advertisement, solicited by the owner and design team, or selected from a list of prequalified general contractors.

2. For many projects, it is a good idea to hire a construction manager (CM) to work side by side with the design team. During design, the CM provides advice on cost, schedule, and constructability issues. When the construction documentation nears completion, there are two ways in which the CM may continue to be involved in the project. In the first scheme, the CM bids all of the various subtrades and then provides a guaranteed maximum price (GMP) and becomes the general contractor. Most senior living financing requires a GMP.

   In the second scheme, the CM is a consultant to the client during construction as well. The CM may replace the general contractor on a fee basis. The construction subcontracts may be bid, but the CM—in its professional service form—does not guarantee the price. If the price is guaranteed, too much power is placed in the hands of the CM, and he or she can no longer be expected to work solely in the client's interest—the risks are too great.

3. For projects whose scope is unclear or the construction must start long before the completion of design, some clients will retain a builder to work on a cost-plus basis. Most clients do not like the open-ended nature of this method, but there are times when it is necessary.

4. A variation sometimes occurs on projects for which common components such as sheetrock walls, electrical outlets, light fixtures, and doors can be identified. The client may negotiate unit prices for each component and can then choose to buy as many units as it needs or can afford. This works for projects such as window replacement programs, repaving of parking lots, replacement of light fixtures, and repetitive interior renovations.

5. An increasingly common option is design-build. In this alternative, the client typically retains a team that includes both a builder and a design team, or a design team that includes a "builder" component. Some clients like the simplicity and the assumed higher degree of cost control. The success of the design-build approach, however, depends upon the selection of a design-build team committed to the client's interests, since the normal quality-control check provided by an independent design team is compromised. Because the design team works for or with the builder, it often cannot communicate quality and value concerns directly to the client. For furnishings, the equivalent is the furniture procurement specialist, who bids furniture packages within the framework of a performance specification.

The selection of an approach, as well as the of appropriate companies, should be carried out in a systematic fashion. Advertising for bidders and hoping the right people show up to bid is rarely enough. Most experienced design teams will research the options, identify the most qualified firms, solicit their interest, confirm their qualifications, and then limit the final proposals to the four to six best candidate firms. As is the case for many of the other steps in the process, the AIA and other professional organizations have standard forms to facilitate this.

The purchasing of interior finishes, furnishings, and equipment involves some of the same options. Dealers, who may represent one or several manufacturers, will provide fixed-price bids for furniture and/or finishes. There are also many firms prepared to provide cost-plus services with or without a guaranteed maximum price, and there are a growing number of services offering the equivalent of a design-build approach. Finishes and furnishings are not typically purchased by the same team. Finishes are typically handled by the GC or CM through their subcontractors, but furniture is usually not included in their scope of work.

Construction and Installation

With the start of construction and the production and delivery of furnishings and equipment, many additional companies and individuals take on major roles. In most senior housing and care projects, the design team is expected to provide both quality control and management throughout this process. The management role typically includes administration of the various construction and supplier contracts; review of payment requests, change orders, claims, and related contract issues; and assistance in resolving problems in the field. It is not uncommon for 20–30 percent of the design team's total project effort to be spent during this phase.

Occupancy

Most clients need their buildings to be effectively complete one to two months prior to occupancy, during which time the staff learns to operate the new facility and prepares for resident occupancy. There are also several final inspections required for licensed facilities such as nursing homes.

The design team's work is not complete when the facility is ready for occupancy. Virtually all clients moving into new facilities require assistance during the first few months. The design team's tasks during the occupancy or "commissioning" phase fall into two categories: following up on incomplete or malfunctioning construction, furnishing, and equipment issues; and organizing and transferring the information necessary to occupy and maintain the facility.

Occupancy frequently reveals construction, furnishing, and/or equipment that do not perform as intended. Design teams should prepare their clients for the probability of some lingering issues and assure the clients that they will be there to help resolve them.

At the same time, clients should be weaned from dependence on the design team for routine operation and maintenance. This begins with the collection and transfer of operation and maintenance manuals, training information, and related materials to the client. This information should include a set of record drawings (in both electronic and hard-copy forms) describing what was actually built based on the contractors' marked-up working drawings. In addition, some design teams prepare a reference manual containing samples, supplier data, and other information on all furnishings and finishes.

COMMON PROBLEMS AND CAUTIONS

The design team and the facility's owner/sponsor are the threads that tie together the 11 steps outlined above into a unified planning, design, and construction process. Since most owner/sponsors are not very experienced with the process, one of the other team members—typically the architect but in some cases a development manager working as an extension of the sponsor—needs to guide the process and help the owner/sponsor avoid the problems that can jeopardize the project. Eleven of the most common and serious problems are summarized below.

COMMON PROBLEMS

1. Failure to plan
2. Unclear, timid, or unrealistic goals
3. Inadequate client leadership
4. Selecting the wrong project team for the wrong reasons
5. Ineffective project management
6. Tackling issues sequentially, not concurrently
7. Poor management of the public approval process
8. Not prioritizing quality
9. Failure to plan for maximal staffing efficiency
10. Poor cost management
11. Failure to plan for maintenance

Failure to Plan

Senior living is in a period of dramatic change. Many owner/sponsors have to build to address changes in market expectations, Medicaid and Medicare reimbursement, and many other variables. Owners, however, can no longer rely on simple financing and formulaic design solutions. Instead, each project and each development process must be carefully planned. This critical initial planning task should define why the building is required, why it is feasible, how it will be financed, and what building alternatives should be considered. Too many projects begin without careful market studies, financial feasibility analyses, or a realistic definition of the proposed building program. If the flaws in the initial planning assumptions are discovered late in the process, it can be very expensive and, in some cases, fatal for the proposed project.

Unclear, Timid, or Unrealistic Goals

Many project plans are built around unclear or unrealistic goals: an ambiguous business plan, a too timid program, overly optimistic budgets and schedules, and other flaws. For example, some projects start as "powder and paint" renovations when a more extensive renovation program is needed to make the facility more accessible, efficient, and appealing to the market in the future. Others veer away from solutions required by the market due to an aversion to challenging existing models and codes.

Overly optimistic budgets are a common problem. Owners and their teams routinely assume too small a space program, underestimate the costs associated with existing conditions, include unrealistically small contingency allowances, ignore an inflation adjustment tied to a realistic schedule, and fail to include appropriate budgets for such important items as furniture and equipment. In addition, many compound the problem by announcing this unrealistic budget to their boards and other constituents. This initial number takes on a life of its own and complicates all of the later phases until it is corrected.

Inadequate Client Leadership

Selecting a strong professional team does not relieve the owner from the role of team leader. Many inexperienced clients are overwhelmed by the complexity of their projects, climb into the backseat, and ask their professional advisers to drive. It is almost impossible to create a good building without a good client's decisive leadership.

Selecting the Wrong Project Team for the Wrong Reasons

Few clients can analyze their needs and develop a realistic and appropriate plan without help. Owners should always try to assemble a team comprised of firms and individuals that bring relevant experience, can work together, and are committed to achieving the project goals. Too often team members are selected for reasons that have little to do with these basic criteria. For example, many owners select their design team based on minor differences in proposed fees and fee payment schedules. Others are unduly influenced by a model or some renderings prepared for the interview. Most fee differences can be reduced or eliminated through negotiation, and work done up front for free is rarely of any value. A successful design comes from a careful, interactive process between the right design team and the client.

Some owners are seduced into selecting a construction manager or contractor because of an initial construction cost estimate that is often prepared as a sales tool rather than a thoughtful and accurate projection of the eventual cost. And still other owners select financial advisers because the overall reputation and size of the firm rather than the track record of the specialist group that will be guiding the financing process.

Many experienced people in the field quote the axiom, "If any member of the team is in trouble, we are all in trouble." The corollary is that project success is usually dependent on a mutually supportive team without any weak players.

Ineffective Project Management

A successful project is dependent on good client leadership. Unfortunately, some owners are not effective managers. Some fail to establish and maintain a clear decision-making process. Others micromanage. And still others fail to build a positive relationship with their professional teams. All of these can cause serious problems, and the owner must choose a decision-making structure that minimizes these common project management problems.

Multi-project owners have usually built an experienced team to run their projects. But the majority of owners, including most nonprofits, must create a project management structure from scratch. Among the more common models are the following:

- The client's executive or administrative staff provides the day-to-day leadership while their board reviews and approves the major policy issues (budget, project goals, team selection, major design choices, etc.).
- The administration and board assume joint leadership and are supplemented by a building committee and/or additional staff with the skills to help manage the project. If the supplemental capability comes from a building committee, it should include at least one design professional, an attorney with real estate and construction experience, and a builder that understands the building type. If the skills required are provided by temporary staff additions, they must have proven project management capabilities and relevant experience. Moreover, if additional staff are employed, they must have more authority than the traditional "clerk of the works," since they will provide management as well as administrative support.
- The owner retains a professional development or project management organization to strengthen its capabilities and guide the process. These companies must have relevant experience with the issues specific to senior living. Moreover, these firms should be carefully defined as team members rather than team managers. The owner must remain the team leader.

Regardless of which approach is used, the owner must give someone or some group the authority to make the many day-to-day decisions critical to the project's success. This individual or group should have the ability to build consensus and the authority to make decisions in the absence of consensus.

Tackling Issues Sequentially, not Concurrently

Effective project management requires commitment to attack the several tasks on the critical path (state approvals such as a certificate of need or approval for a CCRC, local approvals such as zoning and site plan approval, design and documentation, financing including fund raising and credit enhancement, initial marketing, etc.) in parallel rather than in sequence. Owners that try to play it safe by tackling each step in sequence often stretch the schedule out so far that the project loses momentum, is subject to continual cost inflation, and dies. Some sequential decision making can be prudent where there are major risks involved, but most projects require a team that can deal with every issue in a coordinated way that shortens the schedule as much as possible.

The importance of compressing the schedule and maintaining momentum should not be underestimated. A project that does not proceed in a steady, orderly fashion is often more expensive than one that does. And as its schedule stretches, the project risks changes in key leadership or project team members and a subsequent lack of continuity in decision making. In addition, team members can simply become exhausted by a drawn-out process. Once a building program is initiated, it should be completed as expeditiously as possible, while the understanding of the need is clear and the team is fresh.

Poor Management of the Public Approval Process

Even needed senior living projects often face resistance from the public. Some resistance is bureaucratic, but opposition from potential neighbors is common. Failure to navigate the bureaucratic and land use approval reefs successfully can imperil the project. Therefore, all steps in the public approval process should be carefully planned and managed.

For example, state processes, such as a CON or related approvals, should begin with a consultation with the relevant agencies. When the formal application is made, it should be prepared with the help of professionals who understand what can and cannot be approved. Often these advisers can help expedite approval of projects or specific project features that might otherwise be rejected. Many innovative projects require waivers of code mandates or adjustments in regulations, but in many states, properly presented innovation is encouraged and supported. For example, few of the early residential alternatives developed for persons with Alzheimer's fit existing codes and, thus, waivers were required and obtained.

For local land use approvals, experienced professionals can identify the issues (environmental impacts such as traffic, utility impacts, etc.), highlight the project's benefits, and minimize negative impacts. And meeting with the local land use authorities and the neighbors early in the project planning process can build understanding and support before starting the formal approval process.

Not Prioritizing Quality

No client sets out to build a low-quality building, but many end up doing so anyway. Among the common reasons are an overemphasis on minimizing construction costs, an initial budget that was too low and later requires cost cuts, short-term thinking that precludes normal growth and change over time, and overreliance on obsolete models. For example, many skilled nursing facilities continue to build traditional, hospital-like, semiprivate rooms, when every market study warns the market will likely reject them in the future.

The client and the team must work to find the right balance of cost and quality. Life cycle costs, staffing flexibility and efficiency, market trends, and changes in public policy should all be considered during the planning process. For example, in some states, owners will select lower-cost incremental heating and air-conditioning systems rather than more expensive but more efficient central systems because their states still reimburse energy costs. If that public policy changes, these facilities will face a significant operating cost increase.

As part of the cost vs. quality debate, the planning and design team owes it to their client to challenge traditional senior housing and care models with concepts and alternatives that more accurately reflect the owner/sponsor's current and future needs.

Failure to Plan for Maximal Staffing Efficiency

Too few sponsors look at the staffing implications of their proposed plans. In 2011, the salary of one registered nurse was greater than the debt service on $1 million of construction. Careful planning can save the need for more than one expensive professional. Therefore, such key building blocks as the nursing unit must not only optimize the delivery of care to the residents but also minimize the required staffing.

One common approach is to design the unit so it can be operated as a series of smaller subunits during the staff-intensive morning and afternoon shifts but combined under the supervision of just one nurse at night.

The same planning should be applied to every aspect of the operation. Keep the following in mind:

- Multiple entrances may require increases in security staff.
- Different approaches to food service, preparation, and delivery have different staffing requirements (as well as different levels of resident satisfaction).
- The selection of mechanical, electrical, and other systems should reflect the skills and numbers of the maintenance and operations staff that the facility can afford.
- The use of durable, easily cleaned finishes; long-life light fixtures; and other choices made during design can affect future maintenance and housekeeping staff requirements.

Poor Cost Management

Most building programs are heavily focused on containing first costs. This is usually due to a legitimate fear of unmanageable cost overruns. Construction costs—even life cycle costs—can be managed. There is no reason why most building programs should not finish within budget, but doing so can only be accomplished with the help of an effective cost-management process.

A common cost-management mistake by the project's leadership is allowing the team to change decisions and add scope late in the process. Many owner/sponsors cannot resist approving costly and disruptive changes even during construction. This temptation should be resisted. (This subject is covered in detail in chapter 19.)

Failure to Plan for Maintenance

No matter how well designed and built a facility is, it will not last unless it is maintained. An overemphasis on construction cost (vs. life cycle cost) or poor choices in the planning and design can accelerate the costs and scope of future maintenance. When owners fail to plan for maintenance or balance their operating budget by deferring essential repairs and preventive measures, they usually increase long-term liabilities and costs.

CONCLUSION

The development of a successful senior living project is a challenging endeavor. The owner/sponsor and their project team must understand the process and be able to deal with the inevitable issues and problems they will encounter. All senior living building programs—even the most successful—face some complications. A well-run program will surmount these challenges. The difference between a successful program and one damaged by the dilemmas it faces is usually due not to the financial strength of the owner or the natural qualities of the site but to the quality of the planning and the effectiveness of the management.

.

CHAPTER 5

SITE PLANNING, PARKING, AND LANDSCAPE DESIGN

Most site-planning issues for buildings for the aging are relatively straightforward and revolve around the following: the amount of land required; its relationship to adjacent land uses; resident, staff, vehicular, and service circulation; and appropriate parking ratios. There are additional, more precise strategies for those site areas used by residents. This chapter discusses and illustrates each of these issues.

SITE SIZE

The size of a site for a senior housing or care facility is impacted by differing zoning requirements for buffers or setbacks, height limits, parking, and other land use restrictions. The building design, resident unit mix and density, outdoor program areas, use of structured parking, and other variables can also have a major effect on size (figs. 5-1, 5-2, and 5-3).

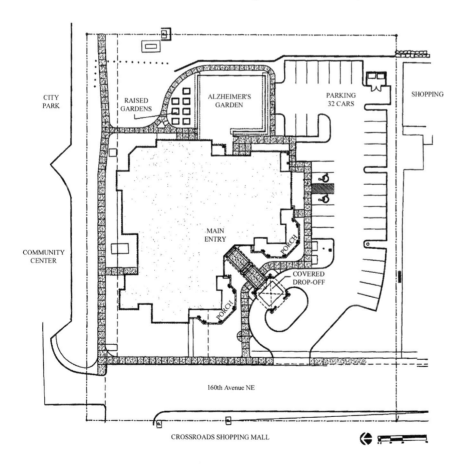

◀ Figure 5-1 This 70-unit Sunrise assisted living residence was designed to fit on a very compact half-acre site. Sunrise of Bellevue, Bellevue, Washington. Mithun Inc.

▶ *Figure 5-2 The buildings and parking of Kendal on Hudson's 288-unit and bed CCRC in Sleepy Hollow, New York, cover only 5 acres of the 20-acre site. Kendal on Hudson, Sleepy Hollow, New York. Perkins Eastman.*

Table 5-1 Typical Site Sizes by Facility Type*			
	Small	**Medium**	**Large**
Long-Term Care	120–160 beds	161–250 beds	251–400 beds
	4–10 acres	6–12 acres	10–20 acres
Assisted Living	Under 60 units	61–100 units	101–200 units
	3–5 acres	4–8 acres	6–20 acres
Active Adult	Under 300 units	301–1,500 units	1,501+ units
Communities	Median size: 181 units	Median size: 566 units	Median size: 2,999 units
	Median land: 43 acres	Median land: 282 acres	Median land: 1,600 acres
CCRCs	100–200 units	201–400 units	401+ units
	15–20 acres	20–50 acres	50+ acres

*These estimates are for suburban and rural locations. Many suburban, town center, and urban sites are one acre or less, even for large facilities.

RELATIONSHIP TO ADJACENT LAND USES

It is a myth that all seniors want to live in their own isolated campus or building. While true for some, it is untrue for the majority. Most experts in the field argue that the best place for many of these facilities is in the center of the community, convenient to public transit, shopping, services, healthcare providers, and family.

Despite the judiciousness of using central locations, various historical factors, including site availability, zoning, and development resistance, have forced many developments from the center of their communities. Yet hundreds of studies of existing facilities consistently demonstrate that these building types have minimal traffic impact, create no school demand, and are quiet

neighbors. They also generate positive tax revenues; even tax-exempt facilities usually contribute to community revenues through a payment in lieu of taxes, or PILOT. Moreover, they meet a growing need in virtually every community: appropriate, supportive housing for a growing number of aging adults.

VEHICULAR CIRCULATION

Because the staff is not typically large, shift changes do not coincide with rush-hour traffic, and staff often utilize public transit, it is rare for a new senior living facility to impact traffic significantly.

The majority of senior housing facilities have 24-hour staffing. CCRC and assisted living facility shift times vary and overlap, with a day, evening, and night shift. In

◀ *Figure 5-3 A covered drop-off creates the first impression of the community's character and design quality upon arrival. The Garlands of Barrington, Barrington, Illinois.* Torti Gallas and Partners, Inc. Photograph by Steve Hall for Hedrich Blessing Photographers.

long-term care, the shifts are typically 7 AM to 3 PM, 3 PM to 11 PM, and 11 PM to 7 AM. The first (morning shift) is the largest, since this staff has the most tasks (helping residents get up and dressed, preparing and serving breakfast and lunch, assisting with bathing, leading activities, etc.). Thus, most traffic studies focus on the two shift changes at each end of the morning shift.

During the morning, the facility's peak hour usually precedes the street peak hour, whereas in the afternoon the peaks do not overlap. The table below details the traffic generated by each facility based on surveys conducted by the American Association of Housing and Services for the Aging (AAHSA) and the Institute of Transportation Engineers (ITE).

Service vehicles are also not typically a major issue. There are a few truck visits (primarily food deliveries and garbage pickup) each day. Most facilities can schedule deliveries so that they do not aggravate rush-hour traffic or annoy neighbors. If the site allows, separate service and staff traffic from residents and visitors with different entrances.

Most facilities are planned with a service entrance and/or loading dock. This is typically also the location of the employee entrance, because it is operationally desirable to concentrate staff access and egress at a single location for control, security, and monitoring purposes. This is not an attractive area and should be hidden or screened.

Residents and visitors usually enter through the facility's front door; in CCRCs and independent living communities, they

Table 5-2 Weekday Peak-Hour Traffic Generation*							
	AM Peak Hour				**PM Peak Hour**		
	Street Peak		Facility Peak		Street Peak		Facility Peak	
Type of Facility**	in	out	in	out	in	out	in	out
Senior housing/ independent living units	0.08	0.09	0.15	0.14	0.15	0.12	0.19	0.15
Congregate care	0.04	0.02	0.08	0.08	0.10	0.07	0.13	0.08
Assisted care	0.12	0.08			0.11	0.10		

*Expressed in vehicle trips per bed.

** Peak-hour trip-generation rates for the assisted living facility are based on a survey of more than 100 facilities. Trip-generation data for the senior housing and congregate care facilities are based on samples of less than 10 facilities.

Sources: Institute of Transportation Engineers, *Trip Generation Manual*, 6th edition; American Association of Housing and Services for the Aging, *A Study of Traffic & Parking Implications*.

come in from an open or covered parking space convenient to their apartment. Almost none of the residents in assisted living or skilled nursing drive. All facilities for the aging should provide a covered drop-off area at the main entry to protect residents from the weather, ice, and other hazards.

PARKING

Parking demand varies by building type, as well as with the location of the facility (e.g., whether it is in an urban area close to services and public transportation or in an area with limited services). For the purpose of assessing parking demand, a distinction is made between (1) senior housing and independent living facilities that offer very few, if any, services; (2) assisted living facilities (i.e., a housing facility that includes additional staff to help with activities of daily living); and (3) continuing care facilities that contain a full spectrum of housing types, from independent living to nursing care. The following summarizes the results of parking surveys undertaken at the three types of facilities.

Based on a research paper prepared for the Institute of Transportation Engineers, a survey of CCRCs and assisted living and independent living facilities found an actual parking need of 0.3–0.5 cars per unit. Most zoning codes, however, mandate at least 0.3 spaces per bed for nursing homes, 0.5 spaces per unit for assisted living, and one or more spaces per unit for market-rate independent living. Active adult communities typically must comply with normal residential zoning. Since the parking required by zoning is often excessive, some local planning boards permit less, with a portion of the site land banked for additional parking should it be required.

The above parking ratios include residents, employees, and visitors, and they represent the peak parking ratio on a typical weekday. Do not segregate visitor parking demand from employee and resident parking; because the individual demands do not peak at the same times, they can share the same spaces. Peak parking demand on weekdays generally occurs during the early afternoon, when the number of visitors is relatively high and staff shifts overlap. The impact of the shift overlap can be minimized if a portion of the day shift leaves before the bulk of the evening shift arrives. The peak day of the year is generally Mother's Day. Temporary parking overflow possibilities should be provided for this annual event as well as other major holidays.

For all the above facility types, the proximity to public transportation and the provision of shuttle services affects parking demand. These services are important for employees as well as for residents. Access to public transportation or a shuttle service allows staff to get to work without driving, thereby decreasing the need for parking spaces, and allows residents to travel to nearby shopping areas and visit friends and relatives in the area.

LANDSCAPE DESIGN

Settings that stimulate the senses, both inside and outside a building, can add interest and support memory. In CCRCs and active adult communities, landscaped and natural areas should be developed for walking, contemplation, golf, lawn sports, shuffleboard, gardening activities, fishing, and other recreational activities (fig. 5-4).

Outdoor spaces should resemble their interior counterparts, responding to the site and to the cultural and activity needs of the specific residential setting. A hierarchy of spaces, from indoors to outdoors, might include the following:

- *Indoor-outdoor blend:* Spaces within the building that have an indoor-outdoor

173

▶ *Figure 5-4 Outdoor spaces well integrated with the natural landscape provide residents with both contemplative and active options for recreation. These spaces can also become resting points along larger community walking trails. Sun City Yokohama, Yokohama, Japan. Perkins Eastman. Photograph by Nacasa and Partners.*

character or porches that extend from the building to provide shelter, shade, security, vistas, and an experience for residents who do not want or are unable to venture from the building. For those with dementia, spaces that feel like rooms are more easily understood.

- *Paved program area:* Areas large enough to accommodate community activities, such as a concert or barbecue.
- *Meaningful walk:* Pathways with things of interest, including an area for butterflies, bird feeders, benches for resting, water fountains, and so on.
- *Landmark/destination:* An outdoor structure, such as a gazebo, that can serve as a small-group activity spot, an enticement to venture further outdoors, or as a landmark for those returning to the building from a walk.
- *A nature walk:* If site space permits, a natural walking path that allows for more exercise and a more natural experience.
- *Children's play areas:* Attractive places for grandchildren to play while their parents are visiting.
- *Outdoor exercise/therapy:* Areas, site details, and equipment to support exercise, stretching, and physical therapy.

If the residents are frail, cognitively impaired, or vulnerable, these outdoor areas must be carefully planned and landscaped. When designing these spaces, consider the following (note that most apply equally to designing for the general population):

- Flowering trees, shrubs, and perennials provide seasonal change to reinforce awareness of life's rhythms and cycles. Bird feeders attract wildlife, which stimulates the senses.
- Accessible outdoor areas are helpful for ambulatory residents with Alzheimer's or other forms of dementia; the ability to walk freely has been found to slow the physical deterioration that often comes with the disease, and it also reduces agitation.
- Gardens can be designed to provide an outdoor physical therapy area. Gardening is a popular activity and reinforces memories.
- The elderly are more vulnerable to the skin damage and vision problems caused by too much direct sunlight. A mix of umbrellas, vegetation, and building elements, such as porches and trellises, are all means of introducing shade.
- Seating with backs and arms near entrances encourages socializing. (See chapter 14 for furnishing guidelines.)
- Entrances to gardens and the width of pathways should accommodate walking side by side.

APPROPRIATE PLANT MATERIAL

- Select plants for fragrance, color, tactile qualities, and movement. Trees that flower or whose leaves change color provide cues about the seasons.
- Research which species might have special cultural meanings for the residents.
- Avoid vegetation that is poisonous or irritating to the touch, as well as plants that attract stinging insects. The part of a plant that is toxic can differ from plant to plant. For example, the flowers may be toxic and the leaves not, and vice versa.[1]

---

[1] Robin C. Moore, *Plants for Play: A Plant Selection Guide for Children's Outdoor Environments* (MIG Communication, 1993), is a good source for information about plants.

DESIGN CONSIDERATIONS FOR OUTDOOR SPACES FOR THE ELDERLY

David Kamp, FASLA, LF, NA, Dirtworks, PC Landscape Architecture

Overview

Most of us know, either intuitively or from experience, that contact with nature is essential for a balanced, healthy life. The time spent in a garden can play a critical role in the maintenance and restoration of health. This is true for the young and the old, for the healthy as well as the frail. Successfully incorporating nature in senior living and elder care settings is predicated on a collaborative approach to design, one that incorporates a working team of designers, healthcare professionals, and other advocates.

Understanding the Site

Assess the proposed garden site in order to effectively integrate the design's program and objectives with the site's particular opportunities and constraints. Consider the following:

- *Site history:* What was the site used for previously? Are there any interesting natural, historical, or cultural features that can be incorporated in the new design? Are there negative associations, such as abandoned underground structures or soil contamination, that should be addressed?
- *Site surrounds:* Should the site harmonize with or be distinct from its surroundings? If there is no surrounding landscape, how can a "space away" be created? Regardless of the setting, consider the proposed garden's access, security, and privacy.
- *Site topography:* Gradients have a physical and economic effect on site development. Their modification may be a constraint or an opportunity, such as creating

easily accessible raised beds. Flat sites might incorporate subtle grade changes for interest and a sense of enclosure.
- *Climate:* Local climate, prevailing breezes, and the site's microclimate will influence plant selection and growth and the garden's use. Surrounding buildings can modify the garden's microclimate, providing shelter from sun and wind; this can augment the garden's uses.
- *Orientation:* A garden's orientation influences how it will be used. When setting location and orientation, consider uses at different times of day and in different seasons. North-south orientations affect how the garden will be used during different seasons, while east-west orientations affect its use at different times of day.
- *Views:* Select and enhance a variety of active and passive views to vary interest and to highlight seasonal changes in evergreen and deciduous plant materials. For courtyard gardens, consider the views across the exterior space to and from resident rooms, activity rooms, and so on.
- *Existing site features:* Existing features can introduce both opportunities and constraints. Extant trees can provide essential shade as well as seasonal interest, but they also require careful protection during construction. In weighing the merits of existing trees, consider their proximity to construction and site disturbance, their age and health, and their species, as some trees weather surrounding disturbances better than others.
- *Soil conditions:* Soil and subsurface conditions are the growing medium for plants, provide a suitable base for pavements and foundations, and provide proper drainage. Poorly draining soils may require remediation to achieve proper drainage and may be particularly susceptible to compaction during building construction.
- *Site pollutants:* Consider the effects of on-site and off-site conditions and activities, including fumes and noise. Determine how prevailing winds might affect any mechanical system exhausts, and locate mechanical equipment away from the garden whenever possible.
- *Utility services:* Account for existing and proposed utilities to avoid conflicts with planting, garden uses, views, foundations, access, and maintenance. Carefully coordinate utility service layouts and water and power service for the garden early in the design process.

- *Access and phasing:* What are the construction needs for access, and the long-term needs for maintenance and security? The width and placement of access doors should account for anticipated maintenance needs.

Understanding the Users

The goals for the garden are the goals of the staff. The project team should explore opportunities for the garden to engage residents, offer a range of activities, and facilitate specific therapeutic outcomes. To better understand the opportunities the garden offers, discuss the following questions with the team:

- How can the garden address varying physical considerations and achieve individual goals, such as providing exercise and improved manual dexterity?
- How can the garden support psychological considerations such as independence and socialization?
- Contributing to the garden's upkeep will underscore that the garden belongs to them. How might the

garden engage residents in daily tasks such as checking bird feeders, tending to plants, and raising a flag? And how might those tasks further other goals, such as exercise, dexterity, and motor coordination?

- What programs are currently underway or planned?
- Should there be structured, casual, and spontaneous activities? What are the daily routines and how are special events handled? Who participates?
- How can families, friends, and visiting children enjoy the garden? Is there a garden or a separate area for staff, too?

Understanding the Concerns

Many elderly people face physical challenges inherent in the aging process. Consider these varying, incremental, and often progressive physical limitations when determining specific programs and design elements:

- *The aging process.* A range of physical abilities should be accommodated. Do the garden's users rely on

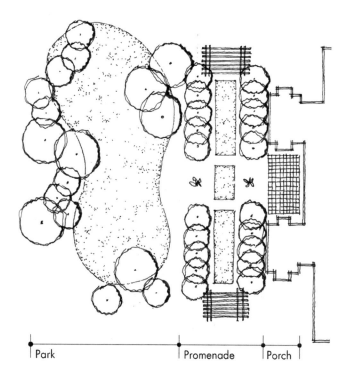

◀ *Figure 5-5 Garden concept plan. The concept plan establishes the basic structure of the open space, including important relationships, adjacencies, and scale. In this plan, there is a progression of spaces: a protected porch, a structured area for activities, and an open, park-like setting. Dirtworks, PC Landscape Architecture.*

| Park | Promenade | Porch |

motorized vehicles, walkers, or wheelchairs? Do they have difficulty stooping and bending? Will they need a place to rest? Will they need assistance with activities? Is their vision seriously impaired?

These concerns influence the design pathways; the placement of chairs and benches, features, and activity areas; and the design of architectural components, such as the width of a porch. For example, benches and chairs should be plentiful but carefully placed to encourage walking in the garden and to provide a choice of settings and destinations. Structured shade near the entry (porches, trellises, etc.) provide a progression of light levels and protective spaces when entering the garden so individuals can comfortably adjust to changing light levels and be sheltered from the elements.

- *Physical limitations.* Injuries from falls are a major concern, as are diminished strength, stamina, and visual acuity; sensitivity to sunlight; and impaired sensory abilities, awareness and sense of orientation.

Elderly adults with gait problems, Parkinson's disease, or severe arthritis, or those recovering from strokes are predictably vulnerable to falls. Falls can occur at times other than when people are walking. In a garden, people may fall getting in and out of wheelchairs, on and off benches and chairs, or near doors as they try to open them. Diminished sight adds to the problem. Some medications cause sun sensitivity, while others interfere with the ability to regulate body temperature.

- *Health and safety.* Regulations regarding health and safety vary with resident groups and care settings. While interior courtyards and atriums are regulated as interior spaces, regulations for exterior gardens are almost nonexistent. Landscape architects must discuss the potential for injury—including plant toxins and allergies—with healthcare professionals. Such discussions are invaluable in helping clients make informed decisions regarding the design of both the interior and exterior garden spaces.
- *Perception.* The garden must not only *be* safe, it must be *perceived* to be safe. The entire garden should be clearly visible from key interior and exterior places. For example, a porch with clear views of the garden or a greenhouse window in a kitchen or activity room allows

staff to monitor residents in the garden while attending to other residents. To ensure a sense of security and comfort, pathways should be firm and level, with clear circulation, obvious destinations, and frequent places to pause and rest (fig. 5-6).

- *Poisonous plants and insects.* Adults with dementia and visiting children must be protected from toxic plants. In addition to common allergies to poison ivy, poison oak,

Figure 5-6   Clear sightlines and modulated light levels at the garden's entrance create a comfortable transition between indoor and outdoor spaces. Deciduous vines provide dappled shade in the summer and allow sunlight indoors during the winter. *Dirtworks, PC Landscape Architecture. Photograph by Bruce Buck.*

and poison sumac, many plants—even common bulbs—can be irritants or allergens. Pollen allergies, or hay fever, are caused by a small number of plants (grasses, weeds, and specific tree species) that depend on wind for cross-pollination. The American Medical Association Guide[2] is a good source for information, and many poison control centers publish information on native poisonous and nonpoisonous plants. Insect bites, particularly bee stings, can cause allergic reactions. Designers must consult a medical practitioner to properly evaluate the danger of bee stings and flea, spider, tick, and mosquito bites. A *perceived* threat from insects can undermine the use of the garden and be as limiting as a real threat.

Identifying Design Considerations

Although general in nature, design considerations are a good starting point from which the design concept can evolve. This is often a new and valuable idea for staff and underscores that the site is unique and each resident is an individual with discrete needs, abilities, and perceptions. Design efforts should respond to both the site's inherent opportunities or constraints—as well as the residents' needs and desires—to create a fully engaging experience for them. The following is a general outline of design parameters.

Diversity in Site Design

Gardens should offer aesthetic and functional variety and accommodate a range of uses. Their overall organization should be easily identified and understood, to provide comfort and security, both real and perceived. Engaging outdoor spaces offer a variety of distinct settings with opportunities for observation or activity and varying levels of participation. For example, one area might provide a sunny and lively setting for group activities, with nearby seating for residents to observe without participating. Another area might provide a calm, intimate setting in dappled shade for private moments. If space permits, consider areas with varying levels of sensory stimulation. Some spaces might be filled with color and fragrance; others might be calming shades of green.

Accessibility, Ease of Use, and Safety

Gardens must be easily and safely accessible, accommodating individuals with varied and changing interests, abilities, and needs. Spaces should be easy to enter, move through, and exit. Such mobility facilitates the use and enjoyment of all features within the garden. Safety considerations include careful plant selection. Plants that create hazardous conditions, such as those that are poisonous, thorny, or scratchy; trigger allergies or itchiness; or produce messy or slippery droppings of sap, pods, fruit, or leaves must be avoided. Consider root structure in tree selections: avoid trees with surface roots that can cause unevenness in adjacent paths and paving (fig. 5-7).

Diversity of Plant Material

Plants should provide a variety of sensory interests, including seasonal changes in color and fragrance, form, and texture. Use plants to demarcate spaces and displays and provide screening and shelter. Plant selection and arrangement should maximize interest, allow gardening participation at a variety of levels, and require desired maintenance levels and security. Plant selections might emphasize familiar local landscapes, including farmland, woodlands, and

Figure 5-7   An active area might have several distinct spaces that allow several groups to use the garden simultaneously. Clear views across the garden permit staff to easily monitor users. *Dirtworks PC Landscape Architecture. Photograph by Bruce Buck.*

---

[2]Kenneth Lampe, *AMA Handbook Of Poisonous And Injurious Plants* (American Medical Association, 1985)

meadows. Trees and shrubs can frame seasonally interesting views of the garden from resident windows while also providing privacy from views within the garden.

Quality of Maintenance

Gardens will remain attractive, safe, and functional only if properly maintained. Determine the garden's ongoing maintenance needs and provide sufficient funds for staff, training, supplies, and equipment. A rich and diverse planting design need not require intensive maintenance. To plan a garden with low maintenance costs, select materials carefully and consider future operational procedures. Maintain a 7 ft branching height for trees adjacent to pathways; other trees might have lower branches to provide privacy and interest, and attract birds. To create a more relaxed ambiance and also attract birds, allow shrubs to grow and branch out rather than pruning them for a denser appearance.

Refining the Design Considerations

These planning guidelines can form the basis of more extensive discussions about materials, details, and programs.

- *Inclusive programming.* Involve both residents and staff in the programming. Will residents be able to see the garden from their rooms or apartments? Many seniors grew vegetables in their more active years and have fond memories of vegetable gardens. If the garden is properly placed, residents can watch the herbs, fruits, and vegetables grow from inside. Weekly harvests of fresh garden produce can become opportunities for social activities and end-of-season harvest celebrations for residents, families, and staff.
- *Activity areas.* Group activity areas must accommodate participants in wheelchairs and those who need assistance. The design must account for the schedule of activities, storage, carting, and use of materials and equipment. Porches are convenient activity areas with easy access to interior spaces. They should be spacious and provide flexible areas for active and passive uses and clear circulation to and from the garden with minimal disruption or distraction (fig. 5.8). Circulation to, from, and through activity areas should establish clear

Figure 5-8   A porch can be a welcoming, familiar garden element and an important transition between indoor and outdoor space. Its configuration should ensure flexibility in use, separate circulation and activity areas, and, for extended use, provide for light modulation and climate control. *Dirtworks PC Landscape Architecture. Photograph by Bruce Buck.*

destinations and, typically, form a series of looped routes, returning to the main entrance or other landmark.

- *Specialized activity areas.* For programs such as horticultural therapy, determine how many people—therapists, caregivers, and volunteers—will be involved in the activity. The required number of support people depends upon the physical, emotional, and developmental makeup of the group. Six clients may each need a support staffer or caregiver, which will affect the area available for horticultural activities. When groups become larger than 10, the setting is rarely intimate.

- *Paving.* Carefully consider physical limitations when determining the width of pathways and their gradient, the construction materials, seating, and cues. Paving materials should be secure, with sufficient texture for a firm feel underfoot and minimize slipping but not too textured to exhaust garden visitors with limited stamina and those who shuffle their feet while walking. Materials must be low-glare to accommodate individuals with difficulty adjusting to varying light levels. This is particularly important in the transition between indoor and outdoor spaces, under tree canopies, and under garden structures. Avoid strong sun/shade contrasts as they create confusing shadows. Pavement gradients should be about 2 percent to provide for proper drainage, keep water from collecting on walking surfaces, and prevent walkers and wheelchairs from veering from the desired direction.
- *Specialized paving.* Specialized areas with more challenging paving surfaces and gradients allow

occupational and physical therapists to introduce familiar scenarios into their therapeutic regimen. This might involve varied paving surfaces (e.g., brick, cobblestone, stone dust, etc.) as well as steeper pathways, ramps, and steps, and outdoor routines like getting the mail. In close collaboration with staff, introduce a sense of challenge and adventure into the garden experience.

- *Raised beds, planters, and garden amenities.* Plant beds raised to accommodate individual preferences for sitting, standing, or stooping can increase participation in garden activities. Consider varying planter heights in 4 in. increments, from 24–36 in. Raised beds can have indented toe spaces so residents can be closer to the work area. Large planters allow residents in wheelchairs and seated to work with plants easily and to socialize (fig. 5-10).

And don't forget the plants themselves. Is there adequate sunshine for plant growth? Window boxes secured to porch rails with paved surfaces on both sides provide added opportunities for socialization. Tools and materials should be stored—perhaps in a garden shed—near activity areas for easy access and to create a familiar, homelike ambiance. Bird feeders, rain gauges, and other amenities such as a flagpole or hanging baskets can build upon

Figure 5-9   A garden should offer opportunities for varying levels of participation, including areas for passive viewing and participatory activities that provide exercise, such as raising a flag. There can even be a multipurpose area under a trellis. *Dirtworks PC Landscape Architecture. Photograph by Bruce Buck.*

Figure 5-10   Raised planters that vary in height and are easy to navigate invite active participation. Fencing establishes a secure perimeter with a garden ambiance while providing views beyond. *Dirtworks PC Landscape Architecture. Photograph by Bruce Buck.*

familiar daily routines while creating opportunities for exercise and to improve motor coordination skills.

- *Garden furniture.* Base bench and chair selections on their sturdiness, beauty, and whether seat heights allow users to sit down and get up easily. While there should be both chairs and benches in the garden, chairs can be easier for an aging person to use. Benches should be wide enough for two individuals to sit comfortably together for conversation. Consider tables that expand to accommodate varying group sizes and umbrellas, when needed. Wood is often used for its softness, weight, and warmth (particularly in colder climates where metal becomes cold to the touch). Storage for cushions should be protected from rain. Chairs should have sturdy arms that can be used to help a person rise; the chair should be wide enough to accommodate someone who is overweight. Chairs can be moved around easily to accommodate impromptu groups, create privacy, or to capture sun or shade.

- *Fencing and gates.* The garden's enclosure must create a safe, secure setting without producing a sense of confinement, which can lead to frustration, agitation, and confusion. Solid and open-view fencing can be used alone or in combination to achieve specific staff goals. For example, open fencing offers a sense of beyond to an adjacent natural setting; solid fencing blocks views of undesirable activities. Strategically placed plant materials and even grade changes can mitigate the prominence of the garden's edge and fencing, but grade heights and plant varieties must maintain clear views for staff monitoring. Garden amenities and plant displays placed inward focus attention inside the garden. Secured gates out of view might provide easy access for maintenance and special events.

- *Water.* Watering plants can be good exercise that improves upper-body movements. Short hoses that the elderly can manipulate easily lessen the potential for tripping. Watering cans also allow several people to water at the same time. Also consider water to drink and for hand washing.

- *Discovery.* Finally, consider the experiences of residents and visitors using the garden for the first time. Encourage their discovery of the garden by creating clear, identifiable interior signage and other wayfinding strategies. Introduce small display areas within the facility that highlight garden activities or feature what is in bloom to encourage them to explore and enjoy the garden.

CHAPTER 6

BUILDING CODES

Because the health of the aging can be precarious and their safety is paramount, senior housing and care facilities are very carefully regulated. Between the federal and state governments, some new projects are subjected to at least eight to ten codes that govern program areas and the construction of all the major building systems.

In addition, most states have detailed regulations written specifically to govern certain senior housing and care building types, including nursing homes, adult day care, outpatient diagnostic and treatment facilities, and some forms of assisted living. These regulations cover everything from space and environmental standards (also discussed in chapter 2) to resident rights and staffing requirements. Table 6-1 is the table of contents from a typical state regulation for long-term care facilities. Many of these regulations are also available on the Internet.

Table 6-1   Table Of Contents: Typical Long-Term Care State Regulations
1. Definitions
2. License Required
3. Licensing Procedure
4. Licensed Bed Capacity
5. Rights of Applicant If License Denied or Revoked
6. New Construction, Conversion, Alteration, or Addition
7. Administration and Resident Care
8. Admission and Discharge
9. Resident Care Policies
10. Physician Services in Long-Term Care Facilities
11. Nursing Services
12. Dietetic Services
13. Specialized Rehabilitative Services: Occupational Therapy, Physical Therapy, Speech Pathology, and Audiology
14. Special Care Units: General and Respiratory Care
15. Pharmaceutical Services
16. Laboratory and Radiologic Services
17. Dental Services
18. Social Work Services

(*continued*)

Table 6.1 (Continued)
19. Clinical Records
20. Infection Control
21. Reports and Action Required in Unusual Circumstances
22. Transfer Agreement
23. Disaster Plan and Communication
24. Physical Plant Requirements
25. Patient Care Unit
26. Resident Bedroom and Toilet Facilities
27. Equipment and Supplies for Bedside Care
28. Rehabilitation Facilities: Space and Equipment
29. Dayroom and Dining Area
30. Dietetic Service Area
31. Administrative Areas
32. Housekeeping Services, Pest Control, and Laundry
33. Resident Care Management System
34. Resident Status Assessment
35. Care Planning
36. Special Skin Record
37. Geriatric Nursing Assistant Program
38. Medicine Aide: Scope of Responsibility
39. Medicine Aide: Course Requirements
40. Determination of Conditions Warranting Civil Money Penalty, Procedures for Corrective Actions, Determination of Amount, and Procedures for Hearing and Appeal

Regulations promulgated by state licensing agencies go hand in hand with building code requirements and are often even more rigid and resistant to revision. Because building codes specify the conditions for a broad range of building types, they are constantly being questioned, tested, and revised. Licensing standards, on the other hand, are less likely to be scrutinized on a regular basis.

The building design of a nursing home can be required to comply with the basic mandates of all of the following codes and regulations.

CODES AND REGULATIONS
Federal

The Centers for Medicare and Medicaid Services (CMS) is a branch of the U.S. Department of Health and Human Services.

CMS is the federal agency that administers the Medicare program and monitors the Medicaid programs offered by each state. Its mission is to "ensure effective, up-to-date healthcare coverage and to promote quality of care for beneficiaries."[1]

CMS plays a significant role in the regulation of financial reimbursement for Medicare and Medicaid recipients; it can therefore impact a senior housing and care facility's bottom line significantly. CMS is responsible for setting and maintaining quality standards for all long-term care facilities and does so through complex document reporting requirements and a periodic survey. To be reimbursed for services, facilities must be inspected and certified by CMS. The American Health Care Association (AHCA) publishes an annual survey that is utilized by state inspectors to ensure that standards of care are upheld and complied with. The survey, more than 500 pages in length, tracks factors used by the CMS and AHCA to assess the quality of services in long-term care facilities.

The Americans with Disabilities Act (ADA) is a wide-ranging civil rights law that prohibits discrimination based on disability. It sets design standards for access and use of public accommodation for those with disabilities.

The Fair Housing Amendments Act (FHAA) is a law intended to increase housing opportunities for people with disabilities. It sets design standards for access to and accommodations within dwelling units.

State

Each state typically regulates senior living facilities in three ways:

- *Building code:* Typically the International Building Code or a modification thereof.

- *International Building Code:* The International Building Code (IBC) was developed in the 1990s by three regional code authorities to consolidate their regulations into one common code. The IBC has now been adopted in all 50 U.S. states.
- *Modified or expanded international code:* Some states have modified or expanded the IBC to address specifics the IBC does not adequately address.
- *Operations regulation:* Each state provides minimum operations standards for long-term care, assisted living, and adult day care. These regulations set minimum size standards for rooms and establish standards of care. Some states have eliminated their minimum design standards in favor of the American Institute of Architects' (AIA's) *Guidelines for Design and Construction of Health Care Facilities.*
- *Life safety:* Typically integrated as a reference standard within either the building code or the operations code; National Fire Protection Association (NFPA) 101 is typically used, but which year of those standards varies from state to state.
- *Need determination:* Many states require a certificate of need (CON). The process of getting one is intended to contain costs borne by the public through entitlement programs. CONs vary by state and typically control
  - how many beds can be constructed, or services or adult day healthcare participants provided for,
  - project size and programming requirements (gross square foot building area per bed),
  - project cost, and
  - the scope of new construction or renovation.

---

[1] Centers for Medicare and Medicaid Services website, http://www.cms.gov/.

• *Financial security:* Some states have significant regulatory oversight on entry-fee retirement communities, for which they regulate minimum financial standards to protect consumers.

Local

• *Unique local codes:* In the past, many municipalities authored their own building codes. With the advent of strong regional codes and the IBC, most municipalities have abdicated this responsibility, though some cities still impose a unique code or offer amendments to the IBC.
• *Local fire departments:* Fire departments are involved in site plan review to ensure that their firefighting apparatus can access the site, to review a building's hazard level, and to review fire detection and fire suppression systems. They are also becoming increasingly involved in preparation for the support of other, non-fire disasters. Few fire departments have written their own regulations; most have adopted reference standards prepared by others, such as the NFPA. Fire departments typically inspect buildings before they are occupied to ensure that all fire detection, emergency communication, and fire protection systems are fully functional.
• *Local department of health codes:* In most instances, a local health department regulates sanitation. This typically includes swimming pools, commercial kitchens, and water treatment facilities.

Reference Standards

Agencies such as the National Fire Protection Association (NFPA), Underwriters Laboratories (UL), and the American Institute of Architects (AIA) provide reference codes that are referenced by various code authorities. This is especially complicated with the NFPA, which authors NFPA 101 Life Safety, referenced into most codes and regulations. NFPA updates its codes every 3–5 years; NFPA 101 was updated in 2000, 2003, 2006, 2009, and 2012. Different agencies have different processes for adopting updated reference standards. As a result, it is not unusual for multiple versions of the same reference standard to be applied to the same project by different regulators. The AIA's *Guidelines for Design and Construction of Health Care Facilities* provides guidelines for many elements of the design of healthcare and long-term care facilities.

Energy Codes and Sustainable Design Standards

Increasingly concerned with energy efficiency and sustainable design, many states have authored or adopted minimum standards for building envelopes and the energy performance of buildings. Leadership in Energy and Environmental Design (LEED) certification is now mandated by many states and municipalities.

REGULATORY ISSUES

All regulations are directed at eight primary issues:

1. Life safety
2. Space standards
3. Adequate space and equipment for facility programs
4. Appropriate building systems and construction practices
5. Public policy (historic preservation, energy conservation, and accessibility for the disabled)
6. Enforcement
7. Fiscal and bidding controls
8. Land use policy

Life Safety

Life safety is the most important issue behind the development of any code. All state and local codes—as well as enforcement—start with this issue. Key life safety considerations built into the codes include: fire-safety and evacuation standards, environmental safety, and elimination of hazards.

Fire safety

The following are important issues in fire safety.

- Construction materials that reduce the likelihood of fire. For example, wood-frame construction is limited in most states, and the use of flammable interior finishes restricted.
- Reduction of the potential for fire-related structural collapse. While this is more often an issue during firefighting, many codes require structural assemblies that will withstand some period of exposure to fire or require a design that permits one area of the building to collapse during a fire while other areas maintain their structural integrity.
- Early fire detection through smoke and/or heat detectors—particularly in high-hazard spaces such as kitchens and mechanical spaces—is now common.
- Fire and smoke containment through compartmentalization and rated assemblies between floors. High-hazard areas—including mechanical rooms and storage areas—must typically be enclosed by fire-rated walls, floors, and ceilings.
- Fire suppression through mandatory installation of extinguishers, fire suppression systems in high-hazard spaces such as kitchens, and the use of sprinklers to prevent the spread of fire beyond its room of origin. "There has never been a multiple-death fire in a sprinklered health care occupancy in the United States. And that includes nursing homes."[2] For this reason all nursing homes, both new and existing, now must have an automatic sprinkler system to qualify for participation in the Medicare/Medicaid reimbursement program.
- Evacuation in case of fire or other emergency. Almost all codes require two means of egress from most spaces. A choice of evacuation routes—in case one is blocked—is fundamental. Most codes also define the exit widths and aisle or egress width from larger spaces such as the main dining room, large multipurpose room, or other assembly spaces.
- Some codes and/or local and state fire marshals require emergency and fire access to all sides of a senior housing or healthcare building. They usually also establish the location of a standpipe, hydrant, or other devices required for firefighting. Typical requirements call for hydrants located such that any fire can be reached with 500 ft of hose and provided with 500 gallons of water per minute.

Environmental safety

The codes dealing with environmental safety vary from state to state, but almost always address the following common issues:

- Required ventilation (see chapter 9) and indoor air quality standards
- Required removal or containment of asbestos
- Required removal or containment of lead-based paint
- Requirements for food service equipment and food preparation and server spaces

---

[2] Kathleen Robinson, "Long Time Coming," NFPA Journal (National Fire Protection Association, January/February 2013).

- Requirements for safe drinking water and water fountains
- Minimum lighting standards (see chapter 14)

Elimination of hazards

Most state codes, regulations, and departments of health also try to minimize potential hazards. The following are typical mandates, cautions, and prohibitions:

- Flooring materials that minimize slipping
- Marked glazed doors and sidelights
- Safety glass or glazing within 18 in. of the floor
- Minimized pedestrian/vehicular conflicts, especially in drop-off and pickup areas
- Restricted access to high-hazard spaces such as boiler rooms and electrical closets
- Elimination of overhead power lines that cross the property near occupied areas
- Restrictions on the location and use of high-pressure boilers
- A variety of guidelines for natural gas use and distribution
- Protection from resident access to electrical heating devices
- Swimming pool depth and layout standards

Space Standards

Most states establish minimum space standards for resident rooms and program areas in licensed facilities (see chapter 2). Unlicensed facilities are typically not covered by code-mandated space standards, but they are subject to the requirements in building construction codes.

Building Systems and Construction Practices

The vast majority of codes regulate the selection of building systems and methods of construction. While the IBC has become the most widely used building code, many state and local building codes also reference other codes or standards, such as the National Electrical Code (NEC), the American Society of Heating, Refrigerating, and Air-Conditioning Engineers (ASHRAE), or the American National Standards Institute (ANSI). These codes regulate everything from use groups and construction types to energy conservation. There are typically separate codes or sections of the code for mechanical, electrical, and plumbing systems.

Public Policy

As with many other building types, senior housing and care facilities are often subject to laws and codes passed to further some public policy such as historic preservation, energy conservation, or accessibility for the handicapped.

Historic preservation

Preservation regulations vary widely. In some areas, designation as an architecturally or historically significant building comes with few restrictions. In others, a structure designated as a landmark or historically significant, or even a new structure adjacent to or near a designated landmark, may require additional public reviews, restrictions on renovations and additions, or a prohibition against demolition.

Energy conservation and sustainable design

Most states have an energy code that regulates the energy performance of the building envelope, especially the performance of exterior walls, windows, and roofs. Many local codes and, increasingly, client sponsors and user groups, have requirements for trash recycling, water conservation, and other eco-friendly practices. Some client sponsors also want at least some "green" architecture (see chapter 7); LEED certification is being required more and more often.

Accessibility

One of the most discussed—and often misunderstood—code issues is the Americans with Disabilities Act (ADA). Many people think it is a building code, when it is in fact a civil rights law whose intent has now been built into many existing building codes. The general intent of this important legislation is stated in Title II of the law:

> Subject to the provisions of this subchapter, no qualified individual with a disability shall, by reason of such disability, be excluded from participation in or be denied the benefits of services, programs, or activities of a public entity, or be subjected to discrimination by any such entity.

While the law refers only to a "public entity," ADA's supplemental technical guidelines have been referenced by most building codes so that they apply to virtually all buildings serving the public, including all senior housing and care facilities.

This section of this chapter summarizes some of the guidelines that govern the application of this law and the related codes; however, these guidelines have been amended by myriad local and state variations and interpretations. This discussion should not be considered either legal advice or an interpretation of every accessibility code; it is intended as a framework to help in understanding and interpreting this evolving area of building regulation.

While most people are aware of the need to create accessible routes for the mobility impaired, ADA also covers other disabilities, including impairments of sight and hearing. Some of the items covered include curb ramps, elevators, building ramps, toilet and bathing facilities, telephones, and drinking fountains. Installation of fire and smoke alarms suitable for the hearing- and vision-impaired, hardware appropriate for people with hand impairments such as arthritis, and other provisions may be needed as well. The codes in most states establish minimum standards, but the definitions of disability are still emerging.

The degree to which design guidelines should be adjusted to accommodate the aging is hotly debated. Most code officials do not take into account the specific physical limitations and needs of the aging, who may have, for example, limited upper body strength, preventing them from using grab bars located behind water closets.

The main question facing owners of existing facilities is what to do with the barriers in the facilities. The primary issue relates to toilet rooms and bathrooms where existing space constraints make it difficult or impossible to provide fully accessible facilities. This becomes critical when outmoded plumbing fixtures are being replaced and officials require full code compliance as a result.

New buildings constructed or significantly altered after January 26, 1992, had to be designed and built to be "readily accessible to and usable by individuals with disabilities." The federal government references the Americans with Disabilities Act Accessibility Guidelines for Buildings and Facilities (ADAAG), published as 59 Fed. Reg. 31,676 (1994).

In addition, multifamily dwellings must comply with the U.S. Department of Housing and Urban Development Fair Housing Accessibility Guidelines.

Among the special issues of accessibility for the aging are the following:

- Grab bars must be provided at water closets. Codes demand that water closets be placed 18 in. from a sidewall with a grab bar and that a second grab bar be located behind the water closet. These provisions respond to the needs of young adults with good upper body strength who are wheelchair bound. Experts believe that, for the aging, two grab bars that flip down from the wall behind the water closet provide better support—like two armrests on a chair—and work whether the user is right- or left-arm strong. To reduce staff back injuries from lifting a user who requires assistance in transferring to the water closet, the water closet should be located 24 in. from the sidewall to allow two staffers to assist in the transfer.

- Ramps are best avoided. While ramps are permitted if they meet prescribed design criteria, seniors have difficulty maintaining their balance while walking on ramps because their center of gravity shifts as they lean forward or backward. Ramps can also be difficult to negotiate for older persons using walkers or wheelchairs.
- Injuries that result from falls are one of the greatest concerns for aging persons. Falls often occur after tripping at changes in flooring material. While most accessibility codes and guidelines permit a ½ in. high transition strip between flooring materials, the transition strip becomes a barrier for a person using a walker or a wheelchair.
- Vision impairments are common among the aging. Such impairments limit independence and accessibility in ways that include difficulty using a key to unlock one's apartment door to reading menus. In addition to compensating with higher light levels, particularly at entrance doors, electronic options like proximity card readers can facilitate access for residents of senior housing facilities.

Enforcement

Most codes also outline the enforcement procedures that will be employed. However, code officials may have varying interpretations of the statutes in force, which can also differ from city to city and from state to state. And such interpretations are not easily appealed. It is, therefore, important to review design assumptions (especially related to life safety issues), construction type, and firefighter access with code officials early in the design process.

Fiscal and Bidding Controls

When a senior housing or care facility is built with public funds, state laws and other regulations may govern the purchase of design services, construction, equipment, and furnishings. While most states permit qualification-based selection of professional services, construction equipment and furnishings are typically purchased via a competitive bidding process. Though this process can be conducted by a qualification-based construction manager, most other construction, furnishings, and equipment must be purchased through competitive bidding.

Land Use Policy

While land use regulation is typically a local issue (supplemented by some state and federal codes), most new senior housing and care facilities may be subject to some or all of the following:

- Planning and/or zoning board review, which typically focuses on vehicular access, stormwater management, landscape; site planning considerations such as the availability of water and sewer; and compliance with the height, setback, lot coverage, parking, building use, and other provisions of local zoning.

- Coastal zone, state historic preservation office, wetlands, and other reviews typically deal with one of the public policy issues discussed earlier in this chapter.
- A board of architectural review typically deals with the materials and aesthetics of the proposed design
- The state or local department of transportation often governs the road improvements, curb cuts, and other necessities for vehicular access.
- An environmental impact review is often triggered by the expenditure of significant public monies, size of the proposed facility, or locating the facility on an environmentally sensitive site.

WAIVERS

Many innovative senior housing and care facilities have features that do not comply with one or more of the codes. Most codes provide for an appeals process that can lead to relief from a particular code provision. Some of the common subjects of appeals in senior housing and care have been the following:

- Areas such as lounges, dining rooms, and open kitchens that open directly onto corridors in jurisdictions that treat senior living facilities as residential structures (e.g., assisted living)
- Households in long-term care that have fully functioning open kitchens open to other spaces.
- Provision of Dutch doors for dementia-care residential units when a fire-rated partition is required
- Minimum standards for long-term care that do not translate down to the small houses of 10–12 residents (e.g., for a nursing station)
- Delayed or controlled unlocking of egress doors in dementia care facilities to provide security for residents

Typical environmental impact statement issues

1. Land use, public policy, and zoning
2. Natural resources
   Soils, geology, and topography
   Groundwater and surface water
   Ecology
   Air quality
   Noise
3. Hazardous materials
4. Utilities
   Water supply
   Sanitary sewer
   Stormwater management
5. Visual and cultural resources
   Historic structures
   Visual impacts
6. Archaeological resources
7. Traffic and transportation
8. Community services and facilities
   Police
   Fire protection
   Solid waste
   Open space and recreational
      facilities
   Schools

- Water closets and grab bars
- Adaptable provisions in lieu of accessible provisions
- Serving food from bulk deliveries and dishwashing within country kitchens accessed by residents

Standard code compliance procedures do not, unfortunately, lend themselves to alternative approaches. Therefore, promising new solutions are often not formally recognized and tested. Waivers, when granted, are approved on a case-by-case basis. They therefore rarely become the basis for future policy or code reform.

CONCLUSION

Navigating the increasingly complex code and public approval system has become a major task for most the planning and design teams of senior living facilities. It is not unusual for the various reviews to add 6–18 months to the time required to plan, design, and start construction of a senior housing or care facility.

CHAPTER 7

SUSTAINABILITY

Sustainable design has moved rapidly from a narrow specialty to mainstream design practice. Senior-living designers have embraced sustainable design principles and are incorporating them into the communities they design. This chapter explores what sustainable design means, why it is important to this building type, and how to implement successful strategies for weaving these concepts into buildings.

MARKET EXPECTATIONS

Marketing data collected by Gerontological Services, Inc., consultants specializing in market feasibility, research and data based planning of senior living programs and facilities, concludes that of almost 4,400 survey respondents, 71 percent said that energy-saving and recycling programs are very important to them.[1] The data also indicate that the recognition of and value placed on such programs may be generational. Not surprisingly, younger cohorts are significantly more likely to rate these types of programs as "very important" than older ones (see table 7-1 and fig. 7-1).

LeadingAge (formerly the American Association of Homes and Services for the Aging) took the lead with its Quality First mission statement issued in 2003. To enhance the quality of retirement communities, they requested that boards of directors take a "covenant for healthy, affordable, and ethical long-term care" pledge. Sustainable design speaks to each aspect of that pledge,

> We are finding an increasing interest on the part of senior consumers in both sustainability and the use of "green" products. Prospective residents want to be certain that the products used in communities are not toxic and won't cause or compound health problems. Many consumers feel strongly about the environment and are impressed by a sponsor who is committed to sustainable development. Sustainable design resonates positively with the consumer and builds credibility for the sponsor.
> —*Sharon Brooks, President and CEO, SB&A, an integrated marketing company*

and board members of LeadingAge-affiliated communities are beginning to understand that sustainable design relates to their fiduciary and oversight responsibilities.

Ongoing research on the relationship between wellness and the built environment confirms that what we design has a direct

Table 7-1	Environmental Concern, by Age
Age	Rate energy saving and recycling "very important" (%)
Under 65	82
65–69	74
70–74	71
75+	63

---

[1] Maria Dwight and Karen Adams, e-mail correspondence with author, December 3, 2010.

impact on the wellness of the building users. The impact is greater among seniors, who are more likely to have respiratory infections. According to the Centers for Disease Control (2012, p. 98, table 4), over 21 percent of seniors 65 and older have asthma, 29 percent have sinusitis, and more than 10 percent have emphysema; building design must therefore prioritize air quality and lessen the impact of toxins on those in impaired physical condition. Prior to the 2003 renovation of a 70-year-old retirement community for the Felician Sisters Convent in Coraopolis, PA, at least one sister would be taken to the emergency room each month with respiratory difficulties. During the renovation, tactics were employed specifically to address indoor air quality. A post-occupancy evaluation 12 months after construction completion found that not one sister had gone to the emergency room since the renovation.

Risk reduction is also an important argument for sustainable design. Communities may be confronted with legal action when residents face a decline in health due to air toxins produced by carpet glues, cleaning supplies, or the presence of mold.

Cities across the country are offering incentives and adopting codes that will make the incorporation of environmentally sensitive concepts imperative. Such incentives include a waiver for increasing building area or expedited building permit approval. More and more codes are requiring key aspects of sustainable design for a building permit. Following through on the U.S. Conference of Mayors' 2030 Challenge (Resolution No. 50 approved in 2006), which aims to have carbon neutral buildings by 2030, cities are requiring more environmental reviews for zoning approval. California has adopted the California Green Building Standards in 2011; it requires new buildings to meet stringent environmental standards.

Neighbors will also lend more support to a project if they feel sustainable concepts reduce traffic, preserve the habitat, and manage stormwater effectively.

Despite these advantages, some organizations argue that green design raises the project budget beyond what they can afford. But studies show that many sustainable approaches are first-cost neutral or may even save money. For example, a building with additional insulation in the exterior walls may require a smaller, less-expensive HVAC unit. Installing a green roof may reduce the size of the water retention area, allowing a larger building footprint. Such elements must be evaluated as part of a holistic system, rather than individually.

The manufacture of competitively priced sustainable products and systems have reduced costs. In addition, many utility companies offer rebates for projects that implement energy-saving techniques; they realize that it is cheaper and faster to incentivize a project to use more energy-efficient light fixtures or install a geothermal heat pump than to build a new power plant. On a mixed-income project, Esperanza and Park Place, in Seattle, WA, the local utility company rebated the project $181,688 for implementing a mix of energy-saving strategies, including envelope and lighting upgrades.

Most senior living is built and operated by long-term owners: the client operates the building for many years and cost savings therefore accrue over the building's lifetime. In 2003, Ziegler Capital Markets Group determined that utility costs represented approximately 7 percent of a community's budget. Energy required for the operation of senior living environments consists primarily of lighting, HVAC systems, and water management. Energy is also used for vertical transportation, food service, laundry, and for other equipment. Reductions in this large budget item are often easily achieved (fig. 7-2).

CALCULATING COST BENEFIT

There are two commonly used methods for analyzing the costs and benefits of energy conservation strategies: years to payback and life cycle cost.

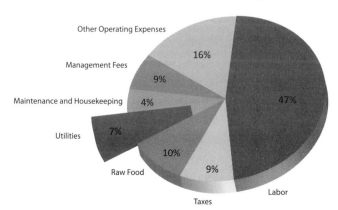

Annual Median Operating Expenses

Other Operating Expenses 16%
Management Fees 9%
Maintenance and Housekeeping 4%
Utilities 7%
Raw Food 10%
Taxes 9%
Labor 47%

◀ Figure 7-2 Utility costs represent 7 percent of a continuing care retirement community's annual expenses. 2003 Ziegler Capital Market Group.

Years to Payback

The years to payback method makes a simple comparison of energy-saving alternatives. The alternative's projected additional first cost is estimated. At the same time, the annual savings—in, for example, gas, oil, or electricity—are converted to a dollar value. The cost of the alternative is then divided by the annual savings to yield a payback period, expressed as the number of years required to recover the capital cost of the alternative through money saved from lower operating costs. The shorter the payback period, the more attractive the alternative. While each sponsor is different, alternatives with payback periods of less than seven years are often considered worthwhile investments.

A variation on this method looks at the full potential cost and benefits of the system under consideration. For example, some calculations factor in projected increases in utility rates and the benefits of utility company conservation incentives. This frequently shortens the payback period, makes the initial expenses cost-neutral, or actually saves money.

Bathroom exhaust heat recovery: less than one year simple payback

First cost: $36,800

Annual savings: $36,084

Incentive return:* $18,400

R20 exterior walls: 2.9 years simple payback

First cost: $95,500

Annual savings: $16,911

Incentive return: $46,649.40

Solarban glass (U = .46 vs. U =. 29): 3.1 years simple payback

First cost: $250,000

Annual savings: $41,229

Incentive return: $123,420.70

*Incentive return: Value of incentives from utility company and other sources.

Life Cycle Cost

The life cycle cost method is used for comparisons of more than first cost and annual savings, including the difference in the life expectancy of the equipment and the time required to maintain the system. The different annual costs of the alternatives are made comparable using "present value" techniques.

A typical calculation for senior living might compare less-efficient, shorter-lived, through-the-wall air-conditioning with a more expensive but longer-lived central system. Energy conservation professionals are often brought in to assist in such calculations.

STRATEGIES FOR SUSTAINABILITY

In the 1970s, architects and owners focused on energy savings because the cost of energy was so high. But a sustainable project addresses a wider range of concerns.

There are five primary strategies highlighted by the U.S. Green Building Council's (USGBC's) Leadership in Energy and Environmental Design (LEED) program, which provides a framework for examining sustainable design strategies.

1. Select and manage the right site.
2. Save water.
3. Reduce or eliminate dependence on fossil fuels.
4. Utilize renewable, nontoxic materials.
5. Create a healthy indoor environment.

Other areas, such as mimicking natural systems and sustainable operations, broaden these core strategies. Many of these features outlined by USGBC (www.usgbc.org) are by now familiar to most designers of buildings, but there are specific features that relate to senior living or that have been used successfully in senior living projects.

Create Sustainable Sites

Site selection

To be truly sustainable, a project should be conceived and defined as such prior to selection of a site. Rather than building on a pristine piece of farmland, where bringing in utility and road infrastructure will be expensive and have a significant environmental impact, it may be preferable to build on an infill site, where much of that infrastructure is already in place. By increasing density, green fields remain untouched, seniors benefit from the range of services available in a higher-density environment, and the community becomes accessible to the staff, particularly if there is public transportation.

The Weinberg Terrace assisted living project (fig. 7-3) is an example of an urban infill development that takes advantage of and reinforces an existing neighborhood. This assisted living project was built over a community center's parking garage on a small urban lot. Adjacency to neighborhood shopping and public transit benefits both residents and staff and allows the building to tap into the existing road and utility infrastructure. By combining community recreational, cultural, and social service uses together with the housing component, the sponsor was able to increase the relative density of the development and make it easier for residents to travel between services.

Transportation

Traffic and parking are major issues for senior living projects. Environmentally sensitive site design can reduce their on-site impacts. Strategies include water-permeable paving, under-building parking (to reduce site disturbance), tandem and/or valet parking (to reduce the total hard surface area per car), and, through negotiations, reduce the amount of parking space mandated by the municipality.

Most zoning codes require more parking than is needed during a typical day at a senior living facility. Use national parking studies to demonstrate to local building officials why there is less traffic at senior living projects and, therefore, why less parking is needed (see chapter 5). Alternatively, document the lower parking use at a similar facility nearby. If zoning officials still insist on a higher parking count than needed, offer to provide a landscaped reserve area and commit to additional parking if actual usage demonstrates need. Some communities are beginning to create car-sharing programs for residents as a way to reduce the parking necessary.

Most senior living communities operate a shuttle bus service to outside activities, doctors' offices, and shopping areas. If a transit station (e.g., bus, trolley, train) is nearby, sponsors should encourage employees to use them. If explored at the planning stage, this can reduce resident and staff parking requirements.

Reduce site disturbance

Every site has unique positive features—a special view, a heritage tree, a favorable solar orientation, an ecosystem of flowers and animals in a supportive habitat. Designers should embrace these natural features and incorporate them into a project. Old trees imbue a community with a feeling of timelessness. Maintaining habitats will engage seniors in the world around them. Keeping the ground sloping to natural watersheds will help gain support from the surrounding community for approvals.

The desire to balance all cut-and-fill onsite and to minimize grading can run counter to providing the easily traversed, barrier-free environment older adults require. In one creative approach to barrier-free circulation on steep sites, individual buildings were tucked into existing grades

▶ *Figure 7-3 Assisted living can be developed on small urban lots. Weinberg Terrace, Squirrel Hill, Pennsylvania.* Perkins Eastman.

and connected by a series of bridges at a single "commons" level. The result is both better for the environment and more convenient for the residents (fig. 7-4).

Save Water

Senior housing and care facilities can be major consumers of water due to high-density housing, a hospitality center with common

◀ Figure 7-4 This retirement community on a steep site used bridges to create a common level. Kendal on Hudson, Sleepy Hollow, New York. Perkins Eastman. Photograph by Chuck Choi.

dining and laundry, or a care center with 24-hour nursing. Conservation has become especially important where water is expensive or scarce. Conservation measures vary somewhat by locality but can include the following:

- Reduce water waste due to leaking faucets and other plumbing-line connections. Although this may sound minor, it is often a major source of waste, especially when all aspects of the plumbing and HVAC systems are considered.
- Install low-flow devices for showers and sinks and low-water-use toilet fixtures.
- Design low-water-use landscaping, whatever the climate. Especially for communities on large suburban sites, the cost of

water used for landscaping can be significant.
- Apply rainwater captured in cisterns, well water if available, or gray water collected from sinks or showers to various tasks, such as landscape irrigation, heating and air-conditioning systems, or flushing toilets.
- At the Felician Sisters Retirement Community in western Pennsylvania, the redevelopment plan included replacing 6 acres of lawn with naturally drought-tolerant plant meadow vegetation, thereby significantly reducing water use and eliminating the need for herbicides or for summertime lawn-maintenance staff. The well water and rainwater collected in rain barrels is used for irrigation. An existing

cistern collects water for an evaporative cooling system providing 48,000 gallons per year of potable water savings.

Reduce Use of Fossil Fuels

There are two strategies for reducing reliance on fossil fuels. The first is to conserve energy through more efficient systems and improved building envelope design. The second is to use alternative energy sources such as photovoltaics, wind, solar, and geothermal energy.

Building orientation

During the conceptual design phase, before mechanical and envelope systems are reviewed, the building should be sited in the correct orientation for the climate. In one building study on a site in a temperate climate, siting a senior residential tower along an east-west axis was compared to siting it along a north-south axis. The building sited along an east-west axis, in which resident windows faced either north or south, produced a 30 percent energy savings over the building sited along a north-south axis, whose windows faced east and west. The energy savings were additionally improved by exterior solar shading devices on the south facade.

Domestic hot water

Domestic hot water uses a lot of energy in a senior living community, and particularly in CCRCs with multiple levels of care. Using high-efficiency domestic hot water heaters for resident areas allows larger boilers to be shut off or eliminated entirely and often has a fast payback. And while some areas, such as dishwashing and laundry, require sanitizing temperatures, reducing resident water use temperatures from 140°F to 120°F can make sense, as residents' reduced skin thickness can make them more sensitive to temperature extremes. Supplementing the

hot water heaters with solar hot water can, in some regions, be cost-effective, with a short payback period.

Heating, Ventilation, and Air-Conditioning

HVAC systems can be the biggest component of total energy use. In response to stricter energy codes and higher operating costs, strategies for limiting HVAC costs include increased insulation, high-efficiency glazing, more efficient heating and cooling equipment, and more localized system controls.

Total energy budgets vary considerably by project type, climatic region, and local utility infrastructure. Energy conservation approaches in senior living environments also vary, depending on who is responsible for paying utility costs— the residents or the operator. This is, in turn, dependent on the balance between private and public space, the cognitive capabilities of the residents, and the level of care being provided. Independent and congregate living projects devote the bulk of the building area to private resident space and often give residents both control over the conditioning of their environment and the responsibility for utility bills that comes with it. In skilled nursing and dementia facilities, the preponderance of public space and residents' limited cognitive abilities typically results in centralized HVAC systems and utility bills apportioned to residents as part of the monthly fees.

When day-to-day energy usage is largely controlled by residents, conservation strategies need to address motivation, ease of operation, and comfort. The elderly population today is more likely than the general population to conserve resources. Residents should be informed about the cost of the energy they are using (for example, how much of their monthly bill comes from air-conditioning) and the benefits to themselves and their environment of even modest conservation measures. These measures can be encouraged by designing the environment to facilitate residents' energy management—for example, by installing windows that are easy to open for a person with limited strength, and by providing easy-to-read thermostats with simple programming options.

It is unrealistic to expect residents to reduce their energy usage to the point of discomfort; comfortable low-energy alternatives need to be provided. Alternatives to air-conditioning can provide valuable yet comfortable energy savings. Rooms with cross-ventilation and high ceilings take advantage of natural cooling. Ceiling paddle fans are a cost-effective alternative that some residents will choose over constant air-conditioning use.

When energy management is the responsibility of the facility operator, the design of centralized building systems and controls has the greatest impact on conservation. There is generally a financial incentive for reducing the use of energy, but energy conservation should not compromise residents' quality of life. Overall building HVAC zoning anticipates both the natural exterior rhythms and the patterns of interior usage.

Many sponsors have implemented measures that have reduced energy costs by 30 percent or more for an investment that is paid for through cost savings in just a few years. The following are some of these strategies:

- Tighten the building envelope, with emphasis on continuous vapor barriers and upgrading insulation levels beyond code standards, especially for roof areas. This should not, however, compromise air quality due to reduced ventilation.

- Improve the performance of glazing systems, including switching to low-E dual-pane glazing. This advanced coating improves window thermal performance and solar shading, permitting the use of larger windows that provide natural light without subjecting residents to drafts and the discomfort of large, cold surfaces.

- Increase personal control of heating and air-conditioning systems and incentive energy conservation. This can be accomplished by the individual metering of water, gas, and electric usage or through flow meters on both domestic hot water and HVAC piping.

- Increase localized zoning and control of heating and air-conditioning within centralized systems, especially for the two-pipe systems most frequently specified for public areas. Zoning perimeter areas by solar orientation and locating thermostats where they can accurately respond to fluctuations in solar load will increase resident comfort while reducing energy costs.

- Specify more efficient boiler systems, which can save energy through flue gas heat recovery, flue dampers, and dual-fuel combustion. Boilers should be selected and sized to operate at peak efficiency throughout the year. Two or three smaller boilers instead of one larger one, although more expensive initially, are better able to keep energy consumption down even during the "shoulder season" and reduced demand periods.

- Use separate systems for kitchens, wellness centers, laundries, auditoriums, and other spaces that have unique utility requirements. Some sponsors outsource food service, which creates an additional incentive to separate the kitchen's energy use from that of the rest of the building. Wellness centers, especially those with large pools or gymnasiums, have energy demand spikes that can be efficiently handled by separate equipment rather than inefficiently inflating the size of centralized equipment. Separate systems for pools from those for other areas is also advisable to limit the potentially adverse impact of humidity and chlorine.

- Reduce the energy consumption of fans, which are often the major energy user in an air-conditioning system. Using high-efficiency variable-speed air supply and ventilation fans as well as variable-volume fans for ducted conditioning areas is a common strategy. Design parking garages that utilize natural ventilation and do not rely on the use of fans.
- Incorporate heat recovery or heat exchanger systems to transfer the heat from exhaust air or return piping to supply air in winter or in the reverse direction in summer.
- Reevaluate design temperature for the thermal comfort of the residents. A mechanical engineer can establish a baseline cooling temperature that deviates from the 68–70°F norm.

Energy management and control systems

Sophisticated energy management and control systems (EMCSs) are used in some newer and larger facilities. While the EMCSs are complex, they are becoming increasingly easier to operate and can also be operated remotely. If the system is complex, it is important to ensure that available staff are able to maintain and manage it.

Lighting and Daylighting

Adequate lighting is essential in senior living design. Light can be delivered in a combination of daylighting strategies and lighting. The trick is to provide more lighting using less energy.

> Older people require three times the amount of light to see as well as younger people, but are more sensitive to glare.[2]
>
> Margaret P. Calkins, Ph.D., expert on design for the elderly.

The first approach to saving energy is using sunlight. Proper daylighting design, including glare control, can eliminate the need for artificial lighting in public spaces during the most active periods of day. Choose the orientation of the glazing carefully. Also, when delivering daylight from above through clerestory or skylights, be sure it does not cast shadows, which can be perceived as a change in floor plane and cause falls. Perimeter design should incorporate drapery or blind pockets inside and exterior shades and trellises, light shelves, and vegetation to help manage the light levels.

Photocell-controlled lighting is a natural complement to daylighting design. It can be used both inside the building and for site lighting, entry canopies, and parking areas. When daylighting is adequate, the photocell turns off the artificial light. If the photocell is controlled by zone, lighting from exterior to interior can be more evenly spread, reducing the effects of glare.

High-efficiency lighting fixtures can provide dramatic cost savings, especially in spaces with higher lumen levels required by older adults. Senior living sponsors have followed the lead of hotel operators by replacing incandescent downlights with compact fluorescent fixtures. Even in spaces such as offices, where fluorescent lights are standard, switching from the older T12 to newer T8 lamps can reduce costs as much as 20 percent.

---

[2] Senior Journal.com, "Lighting an Important Consideration for Senior Citizens' Homes." http://seniorjournal.com/NEWS/Housing/6-05-05-Lighting.htm.

Fluorescents have also replaced incandescent bulbs in decorative ceiling pendants, wall sconces, and table lamps. Thanks to the development of warmer, color-corrected fluorescent lamps, energy savings can be realized without sacrificing residential ambiance. Energy Star bulbs use 75 percent less energy than standard incandescent bulbs and last 10 times longer, with a lifetime savings per bulb of $40.[3]

Staff should be conscientious about turning off lights. To streamline their efforts, a centralized control can be connected through switchable electric outlets. Further incremental reductions in lighting costs can be achieved using occupancy sensors in bathrooms, offices, and other periodic use areas to turn off lights when no one is present, and through multiple circuiting, time-clock switching, and centralized panels that control light levels by time of day and projected occupancy.

Low-energy fixtures are appropriate for some uses, such as light-emitting diode (LED) exit lights and high-pressure sodium lamps for parking lots. LED fixtures have a long life span, and advances in technology are beginning to integrate LEDs in more standard fixtures. Sodium vapor lighting produces twice as much light per watt as mercury vapor lighting and five times as much per watt as incandescent fixtures. The location, mounting height, and orientation of sodium lamps must be carefully controlled to avoid light spill onto neighboring property or glare back into resident rooms. Shading the top of the light and directing all of the light downward reduces light pollution into the night sky.

Alternative Energy Sources

Solar hot water, photovoltaic cells, passive heating and cooling, geothermal systems, fuel cell technology, and wind power are available alternative energy sources; their use depends on a project's location and size. All should be assessed for feasibility, payback, and impact on design early in the design process. For larger projects, installing cogeneration systems can reduce energy costs significantly over the typical useful life of the equipment.

Smart Use of Materials and Resources

Preference should be given to materials that are produced locally, developed from sustainable or rapidly renewable resources, made from salvaged material, manufactured in a way that produces no toxic by-products, and installed in a way that eliminates off-gassing. A few years ago, finding materials that met these rigorous selection criteria was difficult and expensive; now it is a simple matter of specification, and there are numerous practical, good-looking, and competitive products to select from.

Recycled materials

A growing number of projects use recycled materials or content for major portions of floor and wall finishes as well as other parts of the building. Paving materials, structural steel, concrete, roofing, drywall, carpet, tile, ceiling tiles, and wall-covering materials all tout their recycled material content.

Solid waste management

The construction site is the first opportunity to implement solid waste management. Contractors who are savvy about the construction cost savings and impact to local landfills are separating out packaging and excess construction materials, saving a large percentage of the construction waste.

---

[3] "Light Bulbs for Consumers" U.S. Environmental Protection Agency Energy Star website http://www.energystar .gov/index.cfm?fuseaction=find_a_product.showProductGroup&pgw_code=LB

Solid waste management has become increasingly important in municipalities that require or incentivize recycling and composting programs. This requires larger recycling rooms closer to resident living areas as well as additions to space programming for clean supply rooms, soiled holding areas, and trash handling. Maintenance areas also require their own box recycling area and space for separating glass, plastic, paper, and trash. Kitchens may have a composting system; the compost can be used in a vegetable garden on-site.

At a composting program in San Francisco, residents and businesses place food scraps into special bins to turn food waste into compost. The compost is sold to vineyards and local farms. The goal is zero waste into landfill by 2020. "Older residents and senior centers have been enthusiastic about the program, according to city officials."[4]

Adaptive Reuse

Making use of the embodied energy in an existing building is a hallmark of sustainable design. Obsolete schools, hotels, and convents have all been converted into senior housing. A typical former classroom is an appropriate size for an affordable independent living apartment. Several hotel rooms or convent bedrooms can be combined into a good-size assisted living apartment.

Indoor Environmental Quality

Interior air quality is particularly important for frail seniors, who spend long periods of the day indoors. Numerous respiratory aggravators, particularly for more frail seniors include: smoking and second-hand smoke, dirty airways and ducts, chemical cleaning supplies, air intakes adjacent to loading areas, and mold. Some of these must be addressed by policy or operations, but some can be addressed by improving the physical environment.

Senior living communities should avoid building with toxic materials such as paints, sealants, carpet, adhesives, and composite woods containing volatile organic compounds (VOCs) that off-gas. The building should be flushed out prior to occupancy to reduce the levels of any toxins. And the construction process should be organized so that carpets are installed after paint has cured, so the carpets do not accumulate the toxins from the paint and other finishes. Indoor environmental quality does not only apply to air quality; it incorporates strategies that allow seniors to control HVAC, lighting, and window systems. Ample access to views of the outdoors and to natural daylight also qualify as environmental quality strategies.

---

[4] Tauren Dyson, "Making a Big Dent in Landfill Waste," *AARP Bulletin* 51, no. 7.66 (September 210): 6.http://www.aarp.org/home-garden/gardening/info-08-2010/making_a_big_dent_in_landfill_waste.html.

CHAPTER 8

STRUCTURAL SYSTEMS

Senior housing and care facilities have been built using virtually every structural system normally employed in relatively simple structures: wood frame, masonry bearing wall and concrete plank, structural metal stud, steel, precast concrete, poured-in-place concrete, and so on. The selection of the appropriate system or combination of systems is usually the result of an evaluation of at least 13 factors.

CONSIDERATIONS

This chapter reviews these 13 factors and how they govern the choice of a structural system. This section is followed by an overview of the most common systems and the typical issues faced when using them.

Considerations for selection of structural systems

1. Program and concept
2. Applicable codes
3. Potential code changes
4. Flexibility (ability to adapt to future program changes)
5. Soil conditions
6. Lateral forces
7. Impact on finished ceiling and building heights
8. Material delivery and construction timing
9. Local construction capabilities and preferences
10. Ease of construction and schedule
11. Life cycle cost
12. Cost impact on other systems
13. Appearance and aesthetics

Program and Concept

The first factor is the building's program of uses and whether they will be directly above or below one another from floor to floor. A building that contains only nursing units or apartments can employ the simplest systems because the required spans are short. Spaces such as major dining rooms, multipurpose rooms, and pools need longer spans. Public and amenity spaces and apartments are likely to be reconfigured over time, and mid- or high-rise stacking of program components are likely to require more complex structural systems.

Applicable Codes

At least four code issues directly impact the choice of a system: the required live loads, the subsurface soil conditions, the building code use group and related permitted construction type, and special structural requirements to deal with extraordinary conditions (lateral forces) such as a hurricane or earthquake. In addition, the choice of systems can be influenced by fire rating requirements, the ability to run mechanical systems and sprinkler lines, and the assembly thickness when overall building height is an issue. The typical design live loads are 40 pounds per square foot (psf) for residential units and 100 psf for common spaces.

If unusually heavy loading is required in some areas to accommodate special radiology equipment, compact files, rooftop mechanical equipment, or swimming pools located above grade within the building structure, the added loads for these items for that part of the structure can be in the range of

100 psf for mechanical systems to up to 300 psf for some compact file systems. If planned for in advance, these loads can be supported by most systems. However, the more restrictive lateral load requirements being imposed by recent codes make it advantageous to place these unusual loads lower in the building structure or on the ground.

More prescriptive are the use groups and construction types incorporated in most codes. Some states define assisted living, the housing parts of a CCRC, congregate living, and other senior living options as multifamily housing. In many states, housing can be wood-frame up to four stories. In others, wood-frame senior housing is permitted but restricted to one or two stories. As the senior housing industry has matured and senior housing has become more widespread, local code officials have become more sensitive to the resident profiles commonly found in each level of care. As more and more residents are aging in place, code officials are scrutinizing new and existing buildings relative for their ability to accommodate residents who cannot easily evacuate buildings. This may affect the choice of structural systems and the related life safety components of the building.

In addition, a growing number of state and local codes mandate structures that can withstand extreme stresses or loads, such as those generated by hurricanes or earthquakes. In most cases, these requirements point the design team toward more complex and often more costly systems, such as steel or concrete in multistory construction.

Potential Code Changes

The codes governing senior housing and care facilities are of course subject to change, and some of these changes can influence the selection of a structural system. For example, the International Building Code (and related codes for mechanical systems, electrical systems, etc.), which most states have adopted—in whole or with modifications—as their state building code, can affect system choice. In the International Building Code (IBC), assisted living facilities with more than 16 units can be defined as use group I-1 (if the residents are capable of self-preservation in the event of an emergency), and combustible structural frames, such as wood, are permitted for structures up to four stories high, as long as they are sprinklered.

The trend has been toward more code restrictions on the use of combustible structures for frail or confused populations who are hard to evacuate. Some experts argue that the addition of sprinklers as well as smoke and fire protection is far more important than the relative combustibility of the structure, but this argument has not necessarily prevailed.

It is good practice to design to meet any likely future code requirements. This obviates the need for future waivers or upgrades in other systems (such as sprinklers).

Flexibility

Most successful buildings have to accommodate some growth and change. Over the last 20–30 years, senior living environments have had to deal with more change than many other building types. Furthermore, the pace of change has accelerated in the last 10 years, and communities are renovating and repositioning more frequently than ever. Occupants' increasing frailty, their desire for more space and privacy, as well as other factors have required sponsors to reconfigure the basic building blocks of their facilities: resident rooms, nursing units, or apartment units. Some structural systems, such as the use of bearing walls between units (vs. exterior walls and one corridor wall) can be very inflexible. Altering concrete planks can also be problematic if cutting through the floor is necessary, as structural strands generally cannot be cut. Wood frame, steel frame, and larger span structures tend to be accommodate change more readily.

Soil Conditions

A site requiring expensive piles may require the selection of a system such as steel that has longer spans and needs fewer footings and supporting piles. Unstable or variable soils, subject to differential settlement, may preclude less flexible systems, such as bearing walls. In addition, the presence of a high water table may prohibit the inclusion of a basement, especially for buildings over four stories. However, the inclusion of a basement may be financially feasible if poor soil must be removed prior to construction anyway. Some soil types, when located in zones subject to seismic activity, can dictate much of the structure. It is advisable to gather basic geotechnical data prior to making the selection of a structural system or the decision to include a basement.

Lateral Forces

Lateral forces are imposed on a building either by wind loads or by ground shaking (seismic forces). Code changes over the last decade have addressed these factors to make buildings safer and more survivable in a lateral force event.

Recent versions of the International Building Code (IBC) have changed the way seismic forces are dealt with. The ability for a building to resist seismic forces is now judged on two factors: the seismic classification of the region in which the site is located and the ability of the subsurface geology to remain competent and resist forces during a seismic event. Consequently, many sites that previously would not have had to respond to seismic design requirements now

do. As a result, building structures (even for mid-rise buildings) must often have shear walls, braced frames, moment frames, or other structural upgraded to resist ground shaking. In these cases, placing heavy loads (cooling towers, swimming pools, etc.) high in the building is not recommended because they compound the building movements in a seismic event.

The other primary lateral force is wind loading. The taller the building, the higher the forces applied to it by wind loads. This will affect the ability of the building's structural design to resist swaying and twisting, as well as the envelope's design to resist water infiltration, both on the windward and leeward sides of the building. In addition to standard wind loading requirements, there are special ones in various regions intended to help protect the building and its residents during a hurricane or tornado. The Southeast and Gulf Coast have hurricane requirements to improve impact resistance and reduce water infiltration. These may be addressed in part by the structural system. For example, concrete masonry exterior walls are very common in Florida because of their ability to resist impacts by flying debris. In the Midwest and the Plains, where tornados are common, many local codes require a tornado shelter within the building; these have extraordinary structural requirements.

Impact on Finished Ceiling and Building Height

Some structural systems, such as two-way (flat-plate) concrete slabs or bearing walls and concrete plank allow the design team to minimize floor-to-floor height. The floor/ceiling structure is only 7–9 in. thick and can double as the finished ceiling. Other systems, such as wood or steel trusses or structural steel beams, are often 10–15 in.

deeper, and usually need to be covered by a hung ceiling. The result is a floor/ceiling assembly that adds 14–18 in. more than flatplate or concrete plank floors to the overall floor-to-floor height.

Material Delivery and Construction Timing

The choice of a system can have a significant impact on the project schedule. Some structural materials, such as wood, concrete blocks, poured-in-place concrete, and structural studs, are usually readily available. Others, such as structural steel, can have long lead times.

In the past 10-15 years, the global construction economy in places like China and Korea have affected the availability and pricing of various construction materials. In addition, localized catastrophic events like Hurricane Katrina have had short-term impacts on the availability of materials and labor. Furthermore, governmental regulation has caused swings in the availability and pricing of lumber and other eco-sensitive building materials. Involving knowledgeable construction industry professionals in the decision can ensure the proper materials are selected while reducing the impact on the schedule and delivery time.

Local Construction Industry Preferences and Capabilities

There are preferred systems and systems that are rarely used in all construction markets. This is a function of the skills of the local labor pool, the transportation network, and the availability of materials. For some areas, pre-stressed or post-tensioned concrete, for example, is seldom utilized, and in other areas, the use of steel might be uncommon. Going with local preferences and familiarity typically results in lower costs and shorter construction schedules.

Ease of Construction and Schedule

Sometimes systems—particularly wood- or metal framed–buildings—are selected because they are easier to construct in order to diminish the impact of severe winter weather conditions on the construction schedule. If the schedule is such that concrete would be placed or masonry bearing walls built during the winter, selecting the steel-frame or structural-stud building system obviate heating and protecting the structure while concrete or mortar cures.

Some systems that require mixed trades may make sense on paper, but may be difficult to coordinate in the field. For example, a steel frame and concrete plank system is advantageous because it is flexible and can have a low floor-to-floor height. Neverthless, it requires coordination and cooperation between the steel workers and the precast erectors.

Life Cycle Cost

Because of the economics of most senior living projects, first cost is always a major concern. However, the cost of the structural system over the life of the building is also an important factor in the choice of the system. Almost all building owners expect their buildings to last 30 years or more. Most of the structural systems described later in this chapter can perform to that standard.

Some systems are more susceptible to moisture damage and require higher levels of exterior envelope maintenance. Renovating is more economical in buildings that accommodate change more readily.

Cost Impact on Other Systems

The structural system's cost impact on other building systems has not been well understood by many owners and their design teams. The following is information about this impact:

- The systems that add to floor-to-floor height can significantly increase the costs of interior partitions, exterior skin, ductwork, plumbing, elevators, and other systems.
- When systems must be covered, at least part of the cost of the dropped ceiling and soffits should be considered in the structural cost.
- Some systems, such as wood roof trusses in some states, require additional sprinklers and fire protection.
- Most steel systems will require fireproofing, either in the form of concrete fill, drywall wrap, or sprayed-on fireproofing.
- Concrete topping on plank systems should accommodate depressions for showers and level the subsurface for floor coverings.
- Some systems, such as bearing walls and structural steel, can complicate (and increase the cost of) the distribution of ducts, conduits, and other systems.

Appearance and Aesthetics

It is uncommon for the structure to be expressed in most senior living environments, but when it is, its appearance is important. For example, some design teams dislike the exposed ceiling joints inherent in the plank system. Others find the running electrical services and sprinkler lines on the ceilings created by flat-plate concrete slabs to be a significant aesthetic problem, and therefore place these utilities in walls.

There are, however, some opportunities to expose the structural system as an important part of the project's design vocabulary. Larger spaces, such as dining rooms, multipurpose rooms, chapels, and pools present a chance to incorporate the structure as part of the architectural aesthetic. On the exterior of the building, structure is often expressed in the porte cocheres and sometimes, often in wood frame buildings, in the detailing of the skin.

STRUCTURAL SYSTEM TYPES

The following is a brief summary of the issues surrounding the selection of nine of the most common structural systems.

Wood Frame

With the exception of buildings in some urban areas, senior housing has been predominantly wood frame. This system is typically inexpensive, fast, flexible, and can be implemented by a wide variety of contractors. The span limitations can be overcome with trusses, laminated beams, heavy timber, or, in larger spaces, mixing with steel or other systems.

However, wood frame is being dismissed more and more often. The most common reasons are current or probable future code restrictions on combustible structural systems and the potential difficulties for emergency evacuation. And the flooring surface can feel bouncy underfoot in high-traffic areas. Other disadvantages have to do with longevity and quality; wood tends to shrink and swell more than any other system, causing frequent cracks and nail pops. And wood is not a good choice in hot, moist climates, where mold, mildew, rotting, and termites can be an issue. Wood frame construction is generally not allowed in multi-story nursing occupancies.

Structural Metal Studs

The use of steel studs instead of wood is common. It often has a slightly higher material cost, but it is noncombustible. Water damage or moisture, especially in exterior walls, can lead to a loss of structural integrity, even if the steel is galvanized. Its other advantages and limitations are similar to those of wood frame construction.

▶ *Figure 8-1*
Perkins Eastman.

Characteristics of Structural Systems

	Program & Concept Residential Units	Program & Concept Non-residential spaces	Applicable code	Potential code changes	Flexibility	Soil conditions	Lateral forces	Impact on ceiling height	Availability	Local preferences	Ease of construction	Life cycle costing	Impact on other systems	Appearance
Wood frame	O	Ø	Ø	Ø	O	O	O	Ø	O	O	O	Ø	O	O
Metal studs	O	Ø	O	O	O	O	O	Ø	O	O	O	O	O	O
Masonry bearing & plank	O	×	O	O	Ø	Ø	Ø	O	O	O	O	O	×	Ø
Steel frame & plank	O	O	O	O	Ø	O	Ø	Ø	O	Ø	Ø	O	Ø	Ø
Composite steel	O	O	O	O	O	O	O	Ø	O	O	Ø	O	Ø	Ø
Precast concrete	O	Ø	O	O	Ø	Ø	Ø	O	Ø	Ø	O	O	Ø	Ø
Concrete frame; 1-way slabs	O	O	O	O	Ø	Ø	O	Ø	O	Ø	O	Ø	Ø	Ø
Concrete frame; 2-way slabs	O	O	O	O	O	Ø	O	O	O	O	O	Ø	O	O
Concrete frame; post-tensioned	O	O	O	O	Ø	O	O	O	Ø	Ø	Ø	Ø	Ø	O
Long-span structures	O	O	O	O	O	O	Ø	Ø	Ø	Ø	Ø	Ø	Ø	O
Pre-engineered structures	O	Ø	Ø	Ø	Ø	Ø	O	O	Ø	Ø	O	Ø	Ø	O

Ø Usually compatible
O Sometimes presents compatibility issues
× Frequently presents compatibility issues

Structural metal-stud walls can be field-built or panelized in an off-site factory and shipped to the site. The latter speeds erection and enhances quality but is not available in all regions. Because metal stud walls are a bearing wall system, they do not maximize flexibility.

There are three primary floor/roof assembly types associated with metal stud walls: steel joists, light-gauge metal trusses, and long-span metal deck. Steel joists are quick to erect and inexpensive, but they are generally very deep and therefore add to the building height. They also tend to be bouncy as floor structures, and they usually need to be fireproofed, so metal joists are generally only used for flat roof structures.

Light-gauge metal trusses are used for pitched roofs when noncombustible construction is required. These trusses are usually built off-site and shipped to the job. Erection can be difficult, and fire protection is an issue because there are very few UL-listed assemblies for this type of construction.

Long-span metal deck with concrete fill (Epicore) is a good choice for floor systems because it has a low assembly height (typically 6–7 in.) and good sound-mitigation qualities. However, there are few manufacturers of this type of deck, and the lack of competition drives up the price.

Masonry Bearing Wall

A third frequently used option is masonry bearing walls with either steel joists or precast concrete plank floors. It is a simple method, familiar to many contractors, relatively low-cost, and quick to implement.

The span limitations can be overcome by mixing it with other systems for larger spaces. Common problems are its relative lack of flexibility; performance on unstable soil; height limitations (50–70 ft in most construction markets); impact on the distribution of mechanical, electrical, plumbing, and fire-protection systems; and the occasional shortages of masons and/or precast companies. However, concrete plank does have good sound-mitigation qualities and is generally only 8 in. thick, so it minimizes floor-to-floor heights.

Senior housing projects often have many open dining and common spaces on ground-level floors that become difficult to achieve with a bearing wall system. In addition, many design teams object to using the underside of the planks as the ceiling for the space below. When hung acoustical tile or sheetrock ceiling to cover mechanical/electrical distribution systems and the uneven joints between planks are used, some of this system's cost advantages are eroded. Furthermore, concrete planks are heavy, and they complicate the design of the building when lateral forces are considered.

On occasion, steel joists are used as a floor or roof system with masonry bearing walls, in lieu of concrete plank. The advantages and disadvantages of steel joists were discussed previously in the section on metal studs.

Steel Frame and Concrete Plank

This option eliminates some, but not all, of the objections to bearing wall and plank. It has minimal height limitations (as long as the beams are in the same plane as the walls), is quite flexible, performs adequately on unstable soil, and there is rarely a lack of skilled manpower to install it. On the other hand, steel requires fireproofing, and hung ceilings (or at least soffits and bulkheads) are almost always required. There can be long

delivery times with steel, and coordination between the steelworkers and the precast erectors is an issue for the contractor.

Composite Steel

Composite steel (steel and poured-concrete deck) has somewhat the same characteristics as the steel and plank system, but it is more costly and the system depth is greater due to the inclusion of intermediate beams. This system also has advantages: it can accommodate long spans, it can be core drilled in the future to accommodate changes in program, it can be designed to resist lateral forces, and it is lighter than most other noncombustible systems, which mitigates the building's contribution to problems with lateral forces.

Precast Concrete

Precast concrete is not a typical building material in senior living communities. Its most common application is for exterior wall panels (mostly in urban high-rise locations), or in parking garages. It is also sometimes used for columns, beams, and bearing walls and as a structural choice for site bridges and other simple, long-span, heavy-load structures. Some areas, however, are not served by a nearby sophisticated precast company. Moreover, many senior living facilities do not have the scale and degree of repetitiveness necessary for precast to be cost-effective.

Concrete Frame

Concrete is used in many parts of the country. It is especially common for when building structures must be noncombustible or withstand significant lateral loads, such as those produced by hurricanes. It is also relatively easy to build in most local construction markets, and it can produce a building flexible enough to renovate easily in the future. Concrete-frame construction is generally used only for mid- and high-rise buildings. An increasingly common application is for a concrete parking podium that has a low- or mid-rise apartment building on top of it built out of a more economical construction type.

There are three typical forms of concrete-slab construction, all of which have poured-in-place concrete columns: one-way concrete slabs, two-way/mild-steel reinforced concrete slabs, and post-tensioned concrete slabs.

A one-way concrete slab typically has a rectilinear column grid, with the spans longer in one dimension than the other. Slab thickness is minimal, but there are "ribs" in one direction that frame into beams in the other direction. The ribs and beams are 16–20 in. deep (including slab thickness), depending on the spans, and cannot be penetrated by any utilities. This system is uncommon compared with the other two concrete systems.

A two-way, flat-slab concrete structure is a frequent choice for taller residential buildings since it minimizes floor-to-floor height, is fast to build, creates a finished ceiling with the underside of the slab, permits flexible column placement, and is relatively easy to brace or stiffen for lateral loads. This option, however, requires substantial reuse of forms (usually created by a mid- to high-rise program) and an experienced structural concrete subcontractor to make the cost feasible. Even when these conditions are met, flat-plate structures are substantially more expensive than other options. Two-way slabs are relatively easy to core-drill for future program changes, and spans can be increased by thicker slabs and/or shear caps at the columns.

Post-tensioned concrete has some of the same advantages and disadvantages of two-way flat-plate construction. Depending on the skills of the labor pool available, this system can be less expensive than traditional mild steel–reinforced construction. Post-tensioned systems can be thinner than flat-plate systems, and spans can be longer. This type of system is not prevalent in all regions. The slabs are not easily cut or core-drilled in the future because of the stressed tendons in the slab; cuts can only be made after careful x-ray or sonogram studies of the slab, which is expensive and inconvenient.

Long-Span Structures

Long-span structures are not typically needed for senior living facilities. Long spans are generally limited to some of the larger amenity spaces such as multipurpose rooms, dining rooms, swimming pools, and, sometimes, parking garages and porte cocheres. These are often the very same elements that might be expressed architecturally.

The most common long-span structures are fabricated wood or timber trusses, precast concrete, fabricated steel trusses, deep steel beams, or fabricated steel truss girders.

Pre-Engineered Structures

The use of pre-engineered structural systems in senior housing is uncommon, and there are very few total pre-engineered structural systems available. Most pre-engineered structural elements are actually individual components rather than full systems. The most common pre-engineered structural components are roof trusses and panelized, light-gauge, metal-stud walls. These are built in a factory and engineered by the manufacturer based upon the structural engineer's performance criteria. The panels are shipped to the site ready to erect, often with windows and exterior sheathing already installed.

A pre-engineered component gaining favor, especially in sustainable architecture, is structural insulated panels (SIPs). SIPs are composite panels of a foam core sandwiched between two sheets of oriented strand board or some similar product. SIPs can be used as bearing walls, long-span floor sheathing, and long-span roof sheathing. They have excellent insulating and sound-mitigating properties, and they are quick to erect. They are combustible, however, and their use is limited to those overall structural systems for which combustible elements are allowed by code.

Combined Systems

It is common to employ two or more systems in a single project. In some CCRCs, for example, poured-in-place concrete has been used for the foundations, precast concrete in the garages, structural stud for residential wings, and structural steel for the common areas.

213

CHAPTER 9

MECHANICAL, PLUMBING, FIRE-PROTECTION, AND ELECTRICAL SYSTEMS

This chapter discusses four systems:

1. Mechanical systems, specifically heating, ventilation, and air-conditioning (HVAC) systems. HVAC systems condition the space—providing temperature, humidity and draft control—within the building shell.
2. Plumbing.
3. Fire-protection systems. In this chapter, the focus is on sprinklers and other fire-suppression systems.
4. Basic power distribution, emergency power, and fire alarm systems.

These systems account for significant parts of both the construction and operating costs of senior housing and care facilities. Their design should be carefully focused on the typical comfort, convenience, and safety needs of older adults.

THE INTERIOR ENVIRONMENT AND COMFORT FOR AN AGING POPULATION
Mechanical/HVAC

Perceptions of what is comfortable can be quite different for the aging, as they are more sensitive to changes in temperature, drafts, and extreme cold and heat. This sensitivity is partially related to loss of strength and to cardiovascular strain. In addition, the brain reflex that controls perspiration does not function as well in the aging, making them less able to adapt to extreme temperatures. An older person can perceive even the movement of warm air as cold. Therefore, a controlled interior temperature that is

higher than the norm for younger people is usually appropriate for this population.

The way older people perceive temperature can also be influenced by variables such as

- their activity level,
- the type of clothing they are wearing,
- side effects of medication they are taking,
- colors and textures in their immediate environment,
- the climate where they lived or visited frequently, and
- specific activities. (Assisted bathing, for example, can make the elderly feel cold despite the presence of heat lamps.)

Noise generated by mechanical and plumbing systems can also be an issue. Systems that generate significant background noise can cause hearing problems for older residents with hearing loss. Finally, there are safety issues. Heating sources should be protected so that confused residents cannot burn themselves, and mechanical rooms should be accessible only to facility staff.

Plumbing

Anatomical changes in older adults govern the design and specification of the plumbing fixtures in senior living facilities. Reduced body height and upper body mobility and loss of dexterity due to arthritis or stroke influence the specifications of faucets, switches, and toilet, bath, and shower controls (see also chapter 1). Hot water temperatures should be moderated so residents cannot scald themselves; at the same time, the rapid delivery of hot water is important.

Fire Protection

Virtually all federal and local codes require the use of sprinklers and heat- and smoke-detection systems in all senior housing and care facilities. Because rapid evacuation is infeasible, early detection and suppression is essential.

Electrical

A building's electrical power network must be an invisible, silent support mechanism for virtually all the systems in a senior living facility. Electrically powered systems have a direct impact on the comfort of a community's residents. Audio systems affect the ability to distinguish important audible signals from noise, lighting levels are key to functioning independently, and numerous low voltage systems ensure convenience, safety, and entertainment.

PROGRAM AND CONCEPT

The program and concept of each project are the most significant drivers in the selection of systems. Small renovation and new construction projects are less likely to have central mechanical plants because there are no economies of scale to support large infrastructure costs. Larger projects are more likely to have higher-voltage electrical distribution systems because of the long length of feeders.

Other factors, such as the desired degree of energy efficiency, the levels of care that a project will accommodate, and individuals' ability to control their own environment (something that "silent generation" residents did not require but that baby boomers demand) all affect the choice of systems. Many sponsors want their residents to have control over their own unit's heating and cooling;

safety, operational efficiency, and the physical and cognitive capabilities of the typical resident put limits on how close they come to this goal. Sponsors increasingly want to meter utility costs individually in order to control operating expense. This single decision often has a large impact on the design of HVAC, plumbing, and electrical systems.

APPLICABLE CODES

There are numerous codes and standards that affect the systems design for senior housing facilities, and as the level of care progresses from residential to institutional, the code requirements and layers of regulation increase.

In addition to basic engineering code requirements, there are numerous energy-efficiency requirements (irrespective of whether a project desires LEED certification) and health-related requirements that help prevent sick building syndrome and promote overall wellness.

Mechanical and HVAC

Depending on jurisdiction, the design of mechanical and HVAC systems is governed by several overlapping sets of codes (see chapter 6). The American Society of Heating, Refrigerating, and Air-Conditioning Engineers (ASHRAE) and the International Mechanical Code (IMC) are the best sources for an overview HVAC systems. The 2008–2011 *ASHRAE Handbook* (each of the four volumes is updated in successive years) provides an introduction to the major issues.

Mechanical ventilation is required by code in all senior housing communities. The *ASHRAE Handbook* recommends ventilation rates for different spaces and different levels of care. The latest version of ASHRAE Standard 62.1 and addenda should be consulted as the basis for the ratios in codes.

The more regulated levels of care, such as assisted living and skilled nursing, also have requirements for emergency heating and sometimes for emergency cooling in hotter climates. This is often accomplished by providing a large public amenity space, such as a dining room or multipurpose room, with separate HVAC systems connected to emergency power. If the rest of the building loses HVAC, residents can gather in this climate-conditioned space.

Plumbing

Plumbing system design begins with the International Plumbing Code (IPC) and Americans with Disabilities Act or Federal Housing Administration guidelines. In skilled nursing and medical offices, the Facility Guidelines Institute publication *Guidelines for Design and Construction of Health Care Facilities* (2010) also comes into play. Additional local clarifications usually specify the types of materials usable in different piping situations.

The IPC has very specific requirements for the number of plumbing fixtures to be provided to support a community's public amenity spaces. These requirements can often be reduced during discussions with the local code officials, if the majority of the users of these spaces are residents of the building who have their own private bathrooms elsewhere.

The *Hospital and Health Care Facilities Guidelines for Nursing Facilities*, Table 4.1-2, "Hot Water Use-Nursing Facilities," lists recommended temperatures and hot water consumption for resident care areas, dietary services, and laundry.

Fire Protection

The National Fire Protection Association Life Safety Code (NFPA) 101, NFPA 13 and 13R, and the International Fire Protection Code are the basis for fire-protection system design, but local codes may vary significantly in their requirements for fire-resistive walls and doors, allowable compartment sizes, and sprinkler head location and coverage. Flow tests must be performed to determine whether sprinklers can be supported by the public water system without a fire pump.

Local fire departments have a strong influence on building design; design professionals must therefore meet with local fire officials early and then often throughout the course of a project. Since most fire protection systems are designed using a design-build approach, these systems are reviewed and approved twice by local officials. The first time, the general layout and performance criteria of the system, designed by the engineer of record, is reviewed during the building permit process. The second time, the shop drawings, which include hydraulic calculations, pipe sizes, valve details, and specific sprinkler head details, are submitted by the design-build contractor for approval.

Electrical

Consult the following codes: NFPA 70 (the National Electric Code); NFPA 72, Fire Alarm and Signaling Devices and NFPA 110, Emergency Systems; and the International Electrical Code (IEC).

PROGRAM IMPACT ON SYSTEM SELECTION

The space required for central mechanical systems depends on project location, site size, sponsor preference, and local construction practices. Enclosing all equipment within the building reduces mechanical, electrical, and plumbing (MEP) life cycle costs but enlarges the total project size, which usually results in a larger total project development cost. Although most boilers, chillers, cooling towers, pumps, exhaust fans, and electrical switch gear are available in exterior applications, extreme climates or the need to control noise emissions may preclude their use.

The size of central mechanical plants also varies by program type. Primarily residential settings, such as congregate care and independent living, tend to have very limited central services, while settings for skilled nursing or continuing care communities generally have larger central plants. When a central system requiring mechanical rooms is selected, the normal allocation varies from 2–4 percent of total area for independent living to 5–7 percent for a continuing care retirement community (CCRC) with a full complement of healthcare, social, dining, and activity spaces.

In addition to the central plant area, shaft spaces are required for vertical piping, plumbing, cabling, and duct distribution. Floor space may also be required for local mechanical rooms housing air-handling units. The area required will vary considerably depending on the number of floors and the complexity of the program.

The area required for residential space HVAC systems depends on the system selected. Package units and individual hot water heaters appropriate for large independent living apartments may require a closet of 8–10 sq ft per unit; in-the-ceiling fan coils, used for dementia and skilled nursing, require no floor space at all. Regardless of what system is selected, some developers tend to include these mechanical spaces within the area of the apartment, thereby avoiding any loss in overall area efficiency.

Mechanical and HVAC

The mechanical and HVAC systems have the largest space requirements of all the engineering systems in the building, and their distribution requires the most coordination, since ductwork is large and cumbersome. The design and location of major pieces of equipment (chillers, cooling towers, rooftop units, energy recovery units, etc.) is critical from structural, architectural, and noise and vibration standpoints, since this equipment is large, heavy, and has rotating parts.

Furthermore, the ability to move air, refrigerant, or other coolants from this equipment to the rooms with the heating and cooling loads requires careful coordination with the architectural, structural, plumbing, fire protection, and electrical (primarily lighting) systems in the building. Most coordination issues that result in either change orders or less than desirable ceiling conditions are a result of poor HVAC systems coordination. Penetrations through rated ceilings, walls, and shafts require dampers, and access panels are usually required to reset these dampers, all of which have cost and aesthetic implications.

Plumbing

Plumbing systems do not take up as much space in a building as mechanical systems, but their configuration may still have an impact on building design and programming. The most important single decision regarding the building plumbing systems is whether to use a centralized hot water system. Centralized systems require more distribution piping, have larger central plant equipment (boilers, storage tanks, and pumps, which need a room to house them), and require more sophisticated maintenance staff. However, centralized systems are more economical to operate, have lower maintenance and replacement costs, and provide quicker hot water delivery than decentralized systems.

Fire Protection

The primary space considerations regarding fire-protection systems have to do with the incoming service to the building, backflow preventers, and fire pumps, if necessary. The backflow preventer can often be located in the incoming water service room, along with the water meter to the building.

Fire pumps are either diesel or electric. Electric pumps can be located inside and must be powered by the emergency generator, which requires upsizing the generator. Diesel pumps should be located outside and require fresh air, fuel tanks, venting, and spill containment.

Electrical

There are significant cost and space requirements associated with the design of the electrical distribution system. The on-site location of the transformer(s) drives the location of the switchgear room, which is typically the largest single electrical room in a project. From the switchgear room, electrical service is distributed to various closets throughout the project. Depending on the selection of the distribution voltage, these closets may require step-down transformers, which have space and ventilation requirements. Sometimes, these closets can be shallow, with doors that gain access from a corridor. However, if these closets become small rooms, then National Electric Code clearance requirements and accessibility requirements come into play.

FINISHED CEILINGS AND BUILDING HEIGHT

Designers should understand all the MEP systems located above various types of spaces before setting floor-to-floor heights. The need to coordinate the overlap and penetration of structural components such as beams, HVAC piping and ducting, the

potential transfer of plumbing risers from above, electrical cabling, recessed light fixtures, and sprinkler mains dictates requirements for ceiling spaces. While ceiling spaces can often be eliminated above the main portions of individual resident rooms, 2 ft or more are often required above the finished ceiling to accommodate HVAC, piping, and ducting, as well as the other systems above main public spaces, such as dining, service areas, and kitchens.

Mechanical and HVAC

Ductwork and suspended HVAC equipment will have the largest impact on overall building height and the ceiling treatments of all the systems. In addition to the actual size of the ductwork, other details, such as ductwork insulation, connecting flanges, hangers, and supports all affect the finished ceiling height. Ducts will often be concealed in bulkheads or soffits to keep the main ceilings in a room higher or free for lights and other utilities. In addition to basic supply ductwork, ductwork crossings should be minimized with return ducts, exhaust ducts, and other specialty ducts such as dryer exhausts.

Plumbing

The most significant plumbing issue for ceiling heights is piping from above coming down into a finished ceiling space below. This usually occurs as a result of roof drains (in the case of a top floor condition) or from kitchens or bathrooms not stacking between floors. The result is almost always a furred-down ceiling condition of a minimum 8 in. and usually 12 in. This is why most senior housing communities are designed with the bathrooms and kitchens lined up along the corridor walls, creating a continuous zone of lower ceilings along the corridor. This then allows a taller zone of unencumbered ceilings near the windows of living rooms, dining rooms, and bedrooms.

Fire Protection

Typically, fire-protection (i.e., sprinkler) systems do not present great challenges for floor-to-floor heights, since sprinkler piping is under pressure and the routing of much of the piping can be adjusted with elbows to avoid other systems. Coordinate the routing of the sprinkler main (usually a 3 in. diameter pipe) on each floor and wherever it crosses corridors or wraps around stairwells or elevators

Frequently, the piping to serve individual heads can be run in partitions or concealed in the same low-ceiling zone mentioned above for the other plumbing; the heads can then be mounted for sidewall discharge.

Electrical

Electrical distribution components are the smallest of all the systems and have the least impact on floor-to-floor heights. The primary concern for coordinating the vertical dimension has to do with lighting fixtures. Recessed lighting can interfere with ductwork, plumbing, and sprinkler piping, and ceiling-mounted fixtures can interfere with door swings and other headroom clearances.

Flexibility

Most sponsors want a system that can provide both heating and cooling as required. The design team must find a system that can accomplish this cost-effectively. Using life cycle cost analysis will help a sponsor select the most appropriate option.

In a phased project, whether a renovation or new construction, early phases may not encompass the entire build-out. In such cases, the design team must determine if it will scale the systems to accommodate only the early phases or the full long-term

project. Both of these choices have design implications for connection points and space for multiple systems; the latter burdens the project's early phases with the cost of the capacity for future phases.

CONSTRUCTION
Materials Delivery and Timing

The primary concerns related to MEP systems are the availability of major pieces of equipment and their delivery schedule, especially on small, fast-paced projects for which the equipment is required early in the project schedule. It is advisable to write long lead times into the project specifications and require shop drawings to be submitted for review early in the construction process.

Local Construction Capabilities and Preferences

What are the skill sets of the contractors that will install the MEP systems, and what are the local preferences? In suburban and urban markets, where there is a lot of commercial construction, it is easy to find subcontractors who can install almost any kind of system. However, in rural markets, it may be difficult to find subcontractors who can install a chilled water plant, a variable refrigerant volume HVAC system, or some other complex or new technology. In such cases, it will cost more to import labor to the site—and operations and maintenance will still be problematic. Local installers and maintenance and operations staff must be able to operate and maintain the selected system.

Ease of Construction and Schedule

The ability to install systems quickly and efficiently is closely related to the local capabilities and material delivery issues. The more complicated the system, the longer it will take to install. Since extended general conditions and other time related expenses are costly, it is always advantageous to complete a project as quickly as possible. The length of the planned installation schedule should, therefore, always be a factor in selecting a system.

First Cost and Life Cycle Cost

Senior living environments are occupied 24 hours a day. Therefore, a system selection informed by life cycle cost analysis can ensure that all comfort-related objectives are met and that the best economic payback is realized. Concerns about high first costs lead too many owners to selecting systems with unnecessarily high operating and maintenance costs.

HVAC systems typically make up 7–12 percent of total construction costs. The percentage varies by program type; it is slightly lower in less complicated congregate and independent living settings. Costs also vary significantly by region. Plumbing systems typically make up 5–8 percent of total construction costs; fire protection systems, 2–4 percent; and electrical systems (exclusive of low-voltage specialty systems), 6–10 percent.

Sponsors usually see payback for the energy savings achieved by installing a more efficient system in 5–10 years. The expected life span of most senior housing is at least 30 years, making this rate of payback attractive.

Cost Impact on Other Systems

The choice of MEP systems and the location of major pieces of equipment have an effect on the cost of other building systems—primarily the structural system, the building envelope, and the building life safety components.

Locating large, heavy pieces of equipment on the roof can increase the cost of the structural system because the system must then accommodate greater gravity loads and

lateral forces. Large ducts may require structural components like beams and lintels to be shorter to minimize floor-to-floor heights; this, in turn, causes structural components to become heavier and more costly. Increased floor-to-floor heights also raise the cost of all vertical components, including columns, bearing walls, and the exterior envelope, interior partitions and finishes, stairwells, and elevator shafts; they will also increase the height—and cost—of the MEP systems themselves.

Finally, depending on the routing of duct shafts and other utilities, fire and/or smoke dampers and other life safety components may be required. A large number of dampers can add significantly to project costs.

Appearance and Aesthetics

With very few exceptions, such as exposed round spiral ductwork in a pool area or wellness gym, most MEP systems should be concealed from view. The only visual signs of the systems are HVAC grilles and diffusers, receptacles, light switches and light fixtures, and plumbing fixtures and sprinkler heads. After these devices are specified by the engineers, the architect must consider their aesthetics. The placement of major pieces of rooftop- or ground-mounted equipment should be similarly reviewed to ensure they are adequately screened.

Noise and Vibration

The noise and vibration produced by mechanical systems must be controlled. This topic is dealt with more fully in chapter 12.

Controls

Controls are an often overlooked component of engineering design, but proper controls can improve energy efficiency and staff efficiency, and boost residents' comfort and convenience.

Today, electronic (i.e., digital) control systems have replaced almost all older analog or electro-pneumatic systems. Such systems can be as simple as a stand-alone thermostat that controls an individual HVAC unit or as complex as a full direct digital control (DDC) building management system (BMS). Digital controls can be programmed to automatically control environmental comfort without constant manual adjustment.

Electrical controls are usually more specific to lighting and dimming design, and are covered in chapters 7 and 14, on sustainability and lighting, respectively.

MECHANICAL AND HVAC SYSTEM OPTIONS

HVAC systems in most senior housing and care projects are not very complex. Most consist of only a few basic components:

- A central heating and cooling plant serving the entire complex, including boilers, chillers, cooling towers, and pumps that supply hot and chilled water to resident rooms and common areas
- Decentralized HVAC systems, including supplemental heating, for resident rooms
- Air-handling systems to provide ventilation and conditioning for common and service areas, including large rooftop-mounted units
- Specialized and/or independent HVAC systems for commercial kitchens, fitness areas, pools, and other spaces with unique occupancy needs
- Automated temperature-control systems for equipment monitoring and control, which are often integrated with life safety, security, and telecommunications networks

The sections below describe the most common HVAC systems found in senior housing communities and some pros and cons associated with each. There are, of course, significant regional variations.

Packaged Terminal Air-Conditioning Units

Packaged terminal air-condition units (PTACs), or through-wall units, are the most common HVAC system in senior housing communities, especially in older communities. They provide individual room control. PTACs come with a variety of concerns.

- They are the most inexpensive to install.
- They are generally noisy.
- They can use energy inefficiently.
- Poor installation can cause leakage into the exterior wall cavity.
- The compressors have to be replaced frequently, often every 7–10 years.
- PTACs intrude on the clear floor area within the room, and they have louvers on the exterior wall that present design challenges.
- Horizontal PTACs only have one point of air discharge, which makes it challenging to control the temperature in the entire room.

PTACs come in horizontal (console) or vertical arrangements. Horizontal units are the most common. Vertical units are generally built into a closet in an exterior corner of the room; this provides some acoustic isolation. Vertical PTACs are more expensive but have more capacity. They are used for larger spaces such as whole apartments. Console units are generally used for single rooms. Most recent PTAC installations use remote wall-mounted thermostats, which give the unit a less commercial, hotel-like feel.

PTACs generally come in four configurations. They all use electricity for cooling.

Characteristics of MEP Systems

	Interior Environment and Comfort	Program and Concept Residential Units	Program and Concept Non-residential Spaces	Applicable Codes	Potential Code Changes	Impact on Ceiling Height	Flexibility	Availability	Local Preferences	Ease of Construction	Life Cycle Costing	Appearance	Noise and Vibration	Controls
PTAC's	Ø	O	×	O	Ø	O	O	O	O	O	×	×	×	O
Packaged Rooftop Units	Ø	×	Ø	O	Ø	Ø	Ø	O	O	O	Ø	O	Ø	Ø
Air-to-air Heat Pumps	Ø	O	×	O	Ø	O	Ø	O	O	O	Ø	O	Ø	O
Water Source Heat Pumps	O	O	O	O	O	O	O	O	O	O	O	O	Ø	O
Geo-thermal Heat Pumps	O	O	O	O	O	O	O	Ø	O	O	O	O	Ø	O
VRV	O	O	Ø	O	O	O	O	Ø	Ø	Ø	O	O	O	O
2-pipe Fan Coils	Ø	O	O	O	O	O	O	O	O	Ø	O	O	O	Ø
4-pipe Fan Coils	O	O	O	O	O	O	O	O	O	Ø	O	O	O	O
Radiant Heating and Cooling	O	O	O	O	O	O	O	Ø	Ø	Ø	O	O	O	Ø

Ø   Usually compatible
O   Sometimes presents compatibility issues
×   Frequently presents compatibility issues

For heating, there can be a simple electric heater strip, which is very energy-inefficient. Most recent PTAC installations are heat pumps, which are more energy-efficient but may not deliver comfortable temperatures in colder climates. Two less common variations that deliver warmer heating temperatures are electric A/C with hydronic heating coils and electric A/C with gas-fired heat. The hydronic coils only make sense if hydronic heat is being used elsewhere in the building. Gas heat is more prevalent in vertical PTACs than in horizontal ones, and does not require the installation of a flue.

Packaged Rooftop Units

Packaged rooftop units come in the same mechanical configurations as PTACs, and they have the same strengths and drawbacks. Rooftop units can be specified with significant capacities and can serve areas of the building 5,000 sq ft or more. Rooftop units are generally used in three different ways.

First, they can be used as an overall building A/C system. This is uncommon but is seen in older, inexpensively built nursing facilities. One or more rooftop units have major trunk ducts that either distribute above the roof or in the ceiling space and supply a number of different spaces. This design has several drawbacks: each space does not have individual control, and it is not possible to simultaneously heat and cool different spaces served by the same unit. Installing variable air volume (VAV) boxes in the ductwork solves the individual control issues, allowing any spaces served by one VAV box to be controlled separately from other VAV boxes. This is expensive, and, therefore, not often done.

Rooftop units can also serve the larger common spaces in a building while PTACs or heat pumps are used for the resident rooms.

Finally, rooftop units can provide conditioned ventilation air to common spaces and corridors while the heating and cooling of these spaces is handled by heat pumps.

Air-to-Air Heat Pumps

In addition to the air-to-air heat pumps discussed above, a typical residential-style heat pump is often used for cottages, and sometimes, for apartments. These systems consist of a ground- or rooftop-mounted compressor unit and an indoor evaporator unit. The two must be connected by insulated refrigerant lines, the length of which is limited. These systems are house-size systems and cannot handle more than about 2,500 sq ft of building area. Nor can they provide comfortable heating when outdoor temperatures are below freezing, so an auxiliary electric resistance strip is used. Alternatively, a hydronic coil can be placed in the air handler, or electric or hydronic baseboard heating is used to supplement the heat pump.

This system is not uncommon in multifamily buildings. It requires space for all the refrigerant line sets to run to the compressor farm. Locate the compressor farm on the roof to free up the ground plane for landscaping and to keep the noise from all the compressors away from residents' windows. These systems do allow individual control in each apartment, and some can run in cooling mode at the same time that others can run in heating mode. This is a maintenance-intensive system, and it does not allow for energy balancing, since all the units run independently.

Water Source Heat Pumps

Water source heat pumps (WSHP) have gained in popularity for senior housing communities no matter what level of care they provide. They have several advantages: they are energy-efficient; each space or apartment can control them individually; they provide good comfort levels, even in cold climates; and their noise levels are acceptable.

A WSHP system is a central plant system and therefore more expensive to install than any of the systems previously discussed. It also requires a higher level of skill to operate and maintain. Nevertheless, water source heat pumps are the system of choice for many current projects, moreover, they are easily adapted to geothermal heating and cooling sources.

WSHP systems consist of a heating plant, a cooling plant, a distribution system, and terminal units. The main mechanical room for a WSHP system contains boilers to reheat the main condenser water loop, a series of pumps, and sometimes a heat exchanger. The main mechanical room is about 1–2 percent of the gross square footage of the building. The cooling plant either consists of an open-cell cooling tower (in which case a heat exchanger is not used) or a closed-circuit fluid cooler (in which case a heat exchanger is used). This equipment maintains a constant condenser water loop temperature of approximately 55–60°F; the water is then piped out to all the terminal units. These units are 14–16 ft tall; if roof-mounted, they must sit on dunnage and must therefore be screened.

The terminal units for WSHPs come in four different physical configurations; all consist of a compressor and air-handling unit. Each terminal unit requires inlet and outlet condenser water piping connections and a condensate drain connection.

Terminal units do not require fresh air connections but can be designed to accommodate fresh air ductwork on the return side of the unit.

Console units can be used in a variety of locations to handle small loads, such as individual rooms, nursing resident rooms, and single rooms within independent living apartments. Console units are uncommon and come with the same space issues that console PTACs do.

Vertical units stand in the corner of a room and take up about 24 sq in of the full height of the room. They can be stacked easily and designed to accommodate a limited amount of ductwork so that air is distributed to more than one room. Vertical units are often furred in with drywall construction to enclose them, with the return air panel on the face of the unit as the only service access point.

A third WSHP configuration is ceiling-mounted. Similar to console units, such units do not have a large capacity and can serve only one room. They are designed to have very low profiles (10–12 in.) so they can be mounted in areas with furred down ceilings.

The last configuration of WSHPs are closet-mounted. These can fit in a small closet (typically 36" × 42") within an independent living apartment, with ductwork that runs out to all the spaces in the apartment. Closet units can also be specified with significant capacity levels to serve larger areas of a building (3,000–4,000 sq ft) and do not have to be mounted on the floor in closets. They can also be suspended in ceiling spaces.

Geothermal heat pumps

Geothermal heat pump systems are a type of water source heat pump system. In a geothermal system, the terminal units are the same as in a standard WSHP, as is the piping distribution system, the primary method of adding or rejecting heat to the condenser water loop differs.

In a standard heat pump system, the boiler plant adds heat to the condenser water loop when the loop temperature gets too low, and the cooling tower rejects heat from the loop when the loop temperature gets too high. In a geothermal system, the ground is used as a heat sink for moderating the temperature of the condenser water loop, essentially providing free energy. So except for running pumps, there are no central plant energy costs for heating or cooling the building. The system also eliminates the first costs for installing a boiler plant or cooling tower. However, depending on the type of geothermal system used, there can be significant first costs for installing a well field as well as operating and maintenance costs related to the required pumps and other components.

There are two types of well fields used in geothermal systems: open-loop and closed-loop. Open-loop fields rely on a large, perpetual source of groundwater. The groundwater is pumped out of wells, just as domestic water would be, and run through a heat exchanger in the building, where temperature of the condenser water loop is moderated by the temperature of the groundwater.

A closed-loop system requires an extensive well field, where the condenser water runs through a manifold of pipes that connect a number of deep wells in order to moderate the temperature of the condenser water loop. Such a system is not as dependent on groundwater supply, but it does rely on the temperature conductivity of the soils surrounding the wells. This factor determines the number and depth of wells required.

Variable Refrigerant Volume Systems

Variable refrigerant volume (VRV) systems are a relatively new technology popular in Europe and Asia. VRV systems run several terminal units from a central ground- or roof-mounted compressor unit. The compressor can run at a range of capacity levels, depending on the demand put on it by the terminal units. If only one terminal unit is calling for refrigerant, then the compressor runs at very low capacity; if all the terminal units are calling for refrigerant, then the compressor runs at high capacity. Like a water source heat pump system, if some terminal units are calling for heating and others for cooling, the loads balance out. VRV systems are therefore very efficient.

The terminal units are much like fan coil units: all they have is a fan and a (refrigerant) coil, so there are limited maintenance requirements. However, VRV systems are not very common, and their installation requires special skills that not all HVAC contractors have. Also, the refrigerant distribution piping system is a highly engineered system designed by the manufacturer.

VRV systems are very good for retrofits, especially for skilled nursing facilities and assisted living facilities where a sponsor wants to replace a packaged terminal air-conditioning system but does not want a water source heat pump system.

Fan Coil Systems

Fan coil systems have long been considered the Cadillac of HVAC systems. They are efficient to run; they provide great comfort levels; the terminal units are very quiet; and compressors are not distributed throughout the building (as with WSHPs), thereby reducing maintenance. However, fan coil systems are expensive to install and may require licensed operating engineers, and the central plant requires a significant amount of space.

Fan coil systems come in two configurations; two-pipe systems and four-pipe systems. The latter are more expensive to install because there are two sets of piping—hot water supply and return, and chilled water supply and return. This configuration allows each terminal unit to provide either heating or cooling whenever the resident desires, and it allows some terminal units to provide heating while others provide cooling. Few facilities can afford four-pipe systems.

Two-pipe systems are less expensive to install because there is less piping involved, but this compromises comfort levels. The entire building must be switched over twice each year, from heating to cooling and back again. Therefore, an individual resident cannot have air-conditioning if the building is in heating mode, and vice versa. However, if the terminal units are equipped with electric resistance heating strips, it is possible to provide heat to some units when the building is in cooling mode.

The terminal units in a fan coil system are very quiet because there are no compressors in the rooms; this also reduces maintenance. Fan coils come in a variety of sizes, configurations, and capacities, so there are applications for almost any requirement. The central plant in a fan coil system requires a boiler plant and a chiller plant, sometimes with a cooling tower. Operating such a plant often requires a licensed operating engineer, and mechanical rooms can be 2–4 percent of the overall building area. The chillers require vibration isolation, and the boilers have flues and combustion air requirements.

Dehumidification Systems

Dehumidification systems are used mainly in moist environments like pools, which do not need to be cooled.

Radiant heating/Cooling

Radiant heating is accomplished through electric strip heaters or hot water (hydronic) coils. Such systems do not have any moving parts, like fans, although hydronic systems do have pumps to move the hot water through the building. In its simplest form, radiant heat can be used as supplemental heat under windows or in rooms in a baseboard heater configuration. Radiant heat can also be used as a building's primary heating source by running a hot water coil through the slab. This form of heating is very comfortable since there are no drafts and all rooms/floors feel warm although the actual air temperatures is not too warm. Radiant heating systems are efficient to operate and simple to maintain, but a separate air-conditioning system is required.

Solar Collection Panels

Solar collection panels are generally used as a supplemental source of heat to augment the building's domestic hot water system or the hydronic heating system. Solar collection panels are typically mounted in an array on a roof, facing south, although they can be mounted on the ground, too. Water piping is run from panel to panel, and as the piping is exposed to sunlight, it is heated. Frequently, the heated water is run through a heat exchanger, since the water in the solar panels often has antifreeze in it and must be kept separated from domestic uses.

There are many rebate and tax credits available for the installation and use of solar collectors. Designers should be aware of all such state and federal programs to help a sponsor decide whether to pursue collectors.

VENTILATION
Fresh Air Requirements

Most spaces within a senior living facility have significant fresh air (ventilation) requirements, and research has shown that higher levels of ventilation are healthier. In independent living apartments, natural ventilation can be achieved through operable windows. Functionally, this will satisfy code requirements. For nursing units and public spaces, fresh air needs to be ducted to each space. In these cases, a rooftop unit or other high-capacity mechanical equipment is typically used to condition the outside air (heat, cool, humidify, or dehumidify) and then distribute it to each space. This is in addition to the basic heating and cooling systems that serve each space.

Filtration

As sustainable design has gained in popularity and acceptance, one of the areas of focus has been indoor air quality. A component of healthy indoor air quality is the level of filtration achieved at each air handling unit. All air handling units (regardless of configuration) have filters on the return side of the fan. Filters can be specified in a various levels of effectiveness. A well-accepted measurement of a filter's effectiveness is called its minimum energy reporting value, or MERV, rating. The higher the MERV rating, the more effective it is. An average MERV rating is 5–7, an above-average MERV rating is 8–12, and an exceptional MERV rating is 13 and above. Air handling units must be designed to a specific MERV rating, because the higher the MERV rating, the higher the static pressure the filter puts on the fan. If an air handler is designed for a filter with a lower MERV rating, using a higher rated filter will restrict the overall airflow, which will affect comfort levels and cause premature failure of the fan motor.

The location and access of filters is a primary consideration in the design of a ventilation system. Filters need to be replaced or cleaned (if reusable) regularly, and poor access will cause poor maintenance, which in turn will negatively affect comfort, health, and equipment longevity.

General Exhaust

Toilet rooms, janitor's closets, trash rooms, mechanical rooms, electrical rooms, and similar spaces are not provided with supply or return air ductwork but do have general exhaust systems. Exhaust fans draw stale or warm air out of these rooms and exhaust it to the exterior. This exhaust is typically conditioned fresh air that is ducted to other spaces in the building and finds its way into the exhausted spaces through louvers, door undercuts, or other passages that are part of the overall air balance calculations. The amount of fresh air introduced into the building must be more or less equivalent to the amount of air exhausted from the building. Some spaces will be balanced to have a positive pressure, and others will be balanced to have a negative pressure, generally for odor or infection control. Positive and negative pressure differentials should be low so that doors are not hard to open and so damp, exterior air is not constantly being drawn into the building through cracks in its exterior skin.

A recent technology now commonly employed as part of building's ventilation systems is the energy recovery unit (ERU). This is typically a roof- or attic-mounted machine connected to the building's exhaust system. The ERU extracts heat from the exhaust stream before exhausting the air to the exterior. Then the recovered heat energy is returned to the overall HVAC system (usually a water loop). ERUs are large pieces of equipment and require careful placement. They are not required, but usually have a reasonably quick payback period—2–7 years in most parts of the country.

Kitchen Exhaust/Grease Ducts

One of the most challenging ventilation considerations in a senior housing facility is the kitchen exhaust. This is a high-volume exhaust duct and fan associated with the kitchen hood. Typically, these ducts are made of galvanized steel to prevent rusting and to contain a grease fire should one occur. Kitchen grease ducts require cleanouts if there are changes in ductwork alignment, and they are sprinklered to extinguish grease fires. They also have heat detectors to actuate the sprinkler system.

The kitchen grease duct connects two major pieces of equipment: the kitchen hood and the exhaust fan. The fan must be designed and located so that the grease does not land on any nearby architectural finishes (some roofing products decompose in the presence of grease) and to ensure that odors from the kitchen do not adversely affect nearby spaces, such as resident apartments. The fan must be visually screened in some cases, since it is typically a large, shiny piece of equipment that protrudes up higher than most adjacent roofs. The hood itself is designed to capture the heat and fumes from the main cooking battery in the kitchen, and large volumes of air are exhausted through the hood. A separate makeup-air unit will therefore accompany the hood and supply an amount of air to the hood equal to the amount that the exhaust fan removes from the kitchen. This balance will help prevent the doors from the kitchen to the dining room from swinging open or shut when the exhaust fan is running. Depending on the climate, the makeup air unit may heat or cool the makeup air, but some just introduce raw ambient air under the kitchen hood.

Laundry and Lint Traps

Many facilities have a commercial laundry; this has its own ventilation considerations.

The side of the operation where incoming (soiled) laundry is handled is kept under negative pressure. This helps contain odors and bacteria. Washing is done in this room. Once the laundry is cleaned, it is moved to a clean room kept under a positive pressure, also to help keep odors and bacteria away from the clean laundry. Drying is done in this room.

The dryers have a large fresh air requirement, since the drying process requires moving large volumes of air through the dryers. If the dryers are gas-fired, combustion air must be introduced into the drying room. All this air is generally direct-ducted into the dryers from an outside air louver and then exhausted to the exterior through a lint trap. Lint traps should be located where they can be easily cleaned because dirty lint traps are a fire hazard. The termination of the laundry exhaust duct must be located where stray lint or laundry odors will not affect adjacent uses.

PLUMBING
Fixtures and Fittings

Seniors must be able to use the kitchen and bathroom comfortably to maintain their independence. There are many legislated accessibility criteria that govern the design of kitchens and bathrooms, but most of these laws are not specifically formulated to support seniors. Designing for seniors requires additional considerations, and sometimes these conflict with federal or state rules. The design team must understand these conflicts so it neither leaves residents unable to use kitchen and bathroom fixtures and fittings or leave the sponsor noncompliant with state and federal statutes.

Hot Water Distribution

There are two basic configurations of hot water distribution systems: centralized and decentralized. Communities without independent living apartments generally use a centralized system. Such a system requires large hot water heaters or boilers. These are usually gas fired but can also be electric. The heated water is stored in large hot water tanks in a mechanical room and is then pumped to the various spaces that require hot water. When hot water must be delivered to different spaces (such as the commercial kitchen and laundry) at different temperatures, there are separate storage tanks for the different temperatures.

Decentralized hot water systems are typically used in residential occupancies, such as independent living. In these systems, each unit has its own hot water heater, which is usually electric (gas is often unavailable in these buildings). Each resident uses only what he or she needs but does not have an unlimited supply of hot water, as is the case with centralized systems. Decentralized systems are less expensive to build because duplicate piping throughout the building is not required, but they require more maintenance because of the proliferation of water heaters. Decentralized systems lend themselves to individual metering.

In a decentralized system, small, single-use restrooms in public areas and other small water loads, such as coffee stations and hand sinks, use local "instant-hot" hot water heaters instead of traditional tank-type hot water heaters.

Metering

Most senior housing communities rely on a single water meter for the entire community; it is usually located in the incoming water service room, at the backflow preventer. Some sponsors install individual meters for each residential unit to help manage water use and costs. Although it is possible to meter just cold water usage when a building has a centralized hot water system, all water usage can be metered if a building has a decentralized hot water system.

Rainwater

Rainwater is carried away from buildings either by a system of gutters and downspouts or by internal roof leaders (drain pipes). Gutters and downspouts are used on low- and mid-rise buildings with sloped roofs. They are typically made of copper or prefinished or painted aluminum. Downspouts either spill out to grade or are tied into boots that then lead to the site's storm drainage system. Internal rain leaders require roof drains and internal piping (usually cast iron, although they can be PVC) that runs down the building and either spills out to grade or is tied into the site's storm drainage system. In either case, the building plumbing engineer of record is usually responsible for the design of the roof drainage system to a distance of 5 ft outside the building footprint. In a growing number of new senior communities, rainwater is captured and used for landscape irrigation and other on-site uses.

FIRE PROTECTION
Fire Alarm

An automatic fire alarm system is a code requirement for all facilities. In most jurisdictions, fire alarm design goes through a design-build process. The design engineer lays out the system's basic requirements in a performance specification and locates the annunciator panel and the fire alarm control panel. Then the design-build contractor submits detailed shop drawings, including sequence of operations, to the local fire officials for review and comment. This allows the local officials to tailor the system to the skills and capabilities of the firefighters and equipment that would respond to any emergency. In a small number of jurisdictions, the full fire alarm design must be prepared

by a licensed engineer as part of the construction documents. The scope of work for the engineer of record should be matched to the project requirements early in the design process.

All new fire alarm systems are digital and fully addressable, which allows each device to send a location-specific message to the fire alarm control panel. This is invaluable to staff and fire officials responding to an emergency. Digital systems can also communicate with other communications and alert systems, such as e-call, pagers, and scout phones, alerting staff right away when a device senses trouble. New systems also have battery backup built in to the fire alarm control panel. There will typically be an annunciator panel just inside the main entry to the facility to tell emergency responders where the trouble is. The fire alarm control room must be located at the main entry, usually with a separate door to the exterior, especially in high-rise buildings.

The specific function of the fire alarm system depends on the building's occupancy classification and licensing requirements. If a facility has more than one occupancy classification, the fire alarm system must be zoned accordingly. For example, in residential occupancies such as independent living, the smoke detectors in each residential unit are not typically tied to the central system, so if a resident burns toast in the kitchen, the whole building does not go into alarm. In skilled nursing, all smoke detectors are tied to the central system, and evacuation to an area of refuge is handled with staff assistance.

Fire Pumps and Backflow Preventers

All new skilled nursing facilities and virtually all other senior housing facilities are required to be sprinklered by a fully automatic system. In fact, many local jurisdictions now require single-family homes (including independent living cottages) to be sprinklered. In low-rise buildings, there is often enough water pressure in the municipal water system to support a sprinkler system without a pump, but in some cases, a fire pump is required. A fire pump can require a significant amount of power to provide adequate pressure and volume of water to the highest and farthest reaches of the building. There are code minimums for these pressures and volumes, which are also dependent on the types of sprinkler heads used.

Fire pumps can either be electric- or diesel-powered. On rare occasions, fire pumps can be natural gas–fired as well. If a fire pump is electric, it will likely be the largest load placed on the emergency generator. Diesel-powered fire pumps raise many issues: fuel storage, containment, pumping and transport, fuel tank ventilation, combustion air, noise control, exhaust piping, maintaining a diesel engine, and so on. For these reasons, electric fire pumps are preferred.

A fire service room will include a backflow preventer, a fire pump (if required), valves, and often the facility water meter. The backflow preventer is required in order to keep stale water retained in the sprinkler piping from contaminating the domestic water supply. In small communities, this device will be 3–5 ft long and 3 ft high. In larger communities, the backflow preventer will be 10–12 ft long and 4–5 ft high. An electric fire pump does not require very much space; usually the same amount as the backflow preventer. So the overall size of the incoming water service room is usually about 100 sq ft for a small community and 200–300 sq ft for a larger one.

Wet Systems

The majority of sprinkler systems in senior housing facilities are wet systems. Each length of pipe and each sprinkler head are under constant water pressure so that if a head is actuated, there is an immediate flow of water.

The design engineer must decide whether the system will be NFPA 13 or 13R (a code decision), the type of piping to be used (black steel, chlorinated polyvinyl chloride, etc.), the type of heads (fast response, normal response, extended throw, sidewall, pendant, etc.), and which finish to employ (chrome, white, recessed, semi-recessed, etc.). The design-build contractor will automatically locate the heads according to the coverage capabilities of the specific heads, so if the architect wants them placed differently for aesthetic reasons, their locations must be specified.

Dry Systems

Dry sprinkler systems are similar to wet systems, but they are generally reserved for areas where a wet system is subject to freezing, such as parking garages, canopies and porte cocheres, attics, crawl spaces, and other unconditioned spaces. Black steel piping cannot be used for dry systems because it rusts, so galvanized steel piping or chlorinated polyvinyl chloride piping must be used.

Dry systems have a compressor that maintains a charge of compressed air within the portion of the system that is "dry." This compressed air keeps water from flowing into the dry system until a sprinkler head is actuated. Then the air charge will empty through the sprinkler head, followed by water under pressure. Dry systems do not work instantaneously—it can take several seconds for water to begin flowing through the sprinklers. The compressor must be maintained and connected to emergency power.

ELECTRICAL DISTRIBUTION
Transformers

The utility supplying power to the site will have specific requirements for the arrangement of the incoming service, transformer, and metering. In most cases, the utility will provide the primary cable from the street to the transformer (within length limits), and the customer will be responsible for the conduit or duct bank and transformer pads. Secondary cable from the transformer to the switchgear is expensive; transformers should be located close to the switchgear.

The location of incoming supply, rate schedule, and service date are all important to facility design and critical to proper electrical system selection and life cycle analysis; they should be discussed with the supplying utility early in the design process.

Switchgear

Primary supply voltage is usually high, with the transformer supplying secondary voltage to the facility at 480/277V. A secondary voltage of 208/120V may be available on request and should be considered for smaller facilities, particularly where mechanical cooling and heating are not powered by electricity. In smaller facilities, the switchgear is sometimes located in a closet (3–4' × 10–12') with pairs of doors that open wide, either to the exterior or to an interior space. In larger communities, the switchgear may be part of an overall incoming service room about 300–400 sq ft. Code may dictate two exits from the switchgear room.

Metering

Most facilities have a single utility meter for all electrical energy consumed. Rate analysis identifies demand and energy costs, seasonal variations, daily on/off peak variations, and any penalty for power factor. This important information is needed to project overall energy cost for the facility and is a major component in the decisions leading to HVAC system selection.

Individual metering of the resident units should be evaluated in the initial stages of the project, since it will impact HVAC system selection as well as the electrical distribution system arrangement. Individual metering is best suited to independent living facilities, where resident energy use is significant and varies among occupants. New technologies (electronic metering) makes individual metering easier than the older mechanical meter banks, which take up considerable space. Electronic metering also allows communities to take advantage of bulk metering while preserving their ability to bill residents individually for their utility usage.

Any jurisdiction's regulatory restrictions should be confirmed before implementing any private sub-metering arrangements.

EMERGENCY POWER

An emergency power-supply generator may be required depending on the type of senior living facility and level of care provided, the local authority that has jurisdiction, and the state or federal regulations governing the facility's license. Independent living facilities are less likely to require an emergency generator; skilled nursing facilities are certain to have such a requirement. At a facility with different levels of care, the more stringent requirement will apply, although not necessarily to the entire community. One of the biggest emergency power needs is for a central place where residents can gather during a power outage, be kept warm or cool, and be fed.

At minimum, egress and exit lighting and fire alarm systems must have an emergency power source. Where generators are not mandated, battery-supported equipment can be used. Elevators may have battery-lowering packs or be on the generator.

Battery equipment, where used, must accommodate seniors' longer egress time.

Typical emergency lighting fixtures have a 90-minute capacity, with degrading performance over that time. When applied as supplemental battery packs to normal lighting fixtures, the initial illumination is about 40 percent of the normal fixture output, with degradation similar to that of separate battery fixtures.

Emergency generators are usually located on the ground or on a roof. They are large and may need to be screened so they do not detract from the image of the building or site. And they need to be tested on a regular basis, so their proximity to residential units or public spaces is an issue because they are also noisy. Fuel storage, containment, and transport also come into play. If the generator is located on a roof or in a garage, then the way fuel will be pumped to the generator must be determined. Fuel tanks must be vented. Proper spill containment is required by the Environment Protection Agency.

LIGHTING

See chapter 14 for details on lighting design for seniors.

CHAPTER 10

COMMUNICATIONS AND LOW-VOLTAGE ELECTRICAL SYSTEMS

Communications and low-voltage electrical systems are playing an ever-increasing role in settings for older adults. Advances in wireless technology, phone systems, and automated reporting are streamlining operations, enabling staff to spend more time in direct contact with residents, and facilitating detailed record-keeping, which in turn minimizes liability problems.

Many of the early low-voltage systems were stand-alone systems for nurse call, emergency call, fire alarm, and building perimeter control. These are being replaced by integrated networks whose capabilities increase every year. Resident expectations, especially in independent and assisted living settings, have grown since the advent of the Internet, and high-bandwidth connectivity is rapidly becoming a standard feature in apartment design.

This chapter deals with current mainstream communications and information technology (IT) systems. For a discussion of emerging technologies, see chapter 11; for a discussion of lighting, see chapter 14.

SYSTEMS PROLIFERATION

The following are some reasons for the propagation of communications and low-voltage electrical systems in senior housing and care facilities:

- Marketplace expectations for technology have increased as residents and sponsors have become more sophisticated about available options. Their presence makes a facility more competitive.
- Economic pressures have led to the adoption of technologies that reduce overall costs by increasing efficiency. These technologies allow for the following:
  - The provision of more services to more residents and lower staff costs.
  - Better business analysis through information gathering and study, for example, tracking consumables and intelligent purchasing.
  - More efficient building management and, therefore, lower operating costs.
  - "Just-in-time" (JIT) or stockless inventory—the arrangement of supply deliveries so that materials needed for one day's work arrive at the start of the day and are consumed during the day, reducing or eliminating inventory. JIT is especially useful for larger facilities, which then need less staff and space to accommodate inventory.
- Security concerns have increased.
- Sponsors and care providers must keep a greater number of records to defend themselves against accusations of malpractice and to comply with practice standards. Record-keeping systems help staff keep track of services provided, and wandering systems help monitor cognitively disabled residents.
- The very old and frail increasingly rely on user-friendly communications equipment; such devices help residents remain autonomous despite their physical limitations.

- Technology must address the needs of the aging and everyone involved with their care:
  - Volunteers
  - Potential residents
  - Potential staff
  - Existing staff (for continuing education, staff retention, etc.)
  - Users of home healthcare (for logging to fileservers to maintain schedules of home health aides, access billing and medical information, etc.)
  - Residents' families (especially those who are out of town) to access resident information such as bills or medical records
  - Caregivers (for access to medical information)
  - Residents
- Technology has become a part of everyday life for the residents for whom communities are currently being designed and renovated:
  - Easy-to-use Internet, telephone, and cable TV systems
  - Access to lifelong learning opportunities
  - Streamlined billing and financial transaction processes
  - Ease of movement while still maintaining security

Communications and low-voltage systems have also grown more complex, and senior living communities now routinely have an information technology (IT) professional on staff. In larger communities, an IT department may be necessary to ensure that these systems operate smoothly.

Emergency Response/Nurse Call

A full-featured emergency call system contributes to residents' sense of security. Early technology included wired pull cords in toilets and adjacent to beds in skilled care environments. At one time, most codes mandated hard-wired systems in these locations. Today, some states allow the use of radio-frequency (wireless) systems for nurse call. However, not all new equipment is rated by Underwriters Laboratories, a requirement in most jurisdictions. Code requirements also depend on the level of care the facilities provide. Skilled care environments have the most regulations; assisted living settings have fewer regulations, and independent living settings often have none.

Important features of such systems include voice-to-voice communication between staff and residents and flexibility in call station locations. Many skilled nursing environments still have fixed call station locations at a resident's bedside and in the bathroom, although these can be wireless in some jurisdictions. In assisted living and independent living settings, personal wireless transmitters, such as a pendant necklace or wristband that communicates with a telephone-based transmitter, are common. Pocket paging devices are used like cell phones. Fall, movement, and wander alert systems monitor a resident's activity; such technology is still developing. (These systems are discussed in more detail in chapter 11.)

Movement alarms

Elopement prevention systems, which keep staff informed about the location of each resident, are a technological response to the wandering behavior of some dementia care residents. (See chapter 2 for ways to help prevent the hazards of such behavior through designing the building plan and program to suit their needs.)

Elopement prevention systems supply residents prone to wander with an electronic device that interfaces with door hardware or proximity detectors. The device is usually an unobtrusive bracelet, watchband, or anklet equipped with a small transmitter. The transmitter alerts a receiver when the resident approaches a receiver, usually located at a stairwell, exit, and elevator doors and doors leading to unsecured building areas. The receiver may lock the door when a wandering resident approaches, sounds an alarm, and sends a message to the staff phones. (To comply with code, exit door hardware unlocks in an emergency that triggers the fire alarm system or by constant pressure on the exit hardware.)

Most wander alert systems interface with the emergency alert system, so when a wander alert message is sent, staff receive the same resident profile information they do through the emergency alert system, and they receive the alert through the same equipment (monitors, cell phones, pagers, etc.). Some companies offer an integrated product line that incorporates emergency call and wander alert functions. New technologies include GPS and triangulation locators.

Access Control

Access control (primarily door security) was at one time as simple as using brass keys to unlock doors. But keeping track of keys, replacing lost keys, and rekeying doors when a resident moved or a staff member left was costly and time-consuming. Today's access control systems are electronic and able to interface with any or all of the following systems: time and attendance systems, visual monitoring systems (see below), wander alert systems, TV systems, and fire alarm systems.

Visual Monitoring

Visual monitoring systems (closed circuit television, or CCTV) fall into three different categories: surveillance, remote access, and monitoring. A CCTV system's primary function is surveillance. Cameras are located

in numerous locations throughout a community and its grounds (e.g., loading docks, entry points, remote site locations, gatehouses, etc.) and communicate to a central monitoring point. Most cameras are wireless. Signals from the main control station can direct the cameras to tilt, pan, or zoom and relay the visual data. A digital record is kept of all signals sent by the cameras to aid the security staff if there is a security breach.

Visual monitoring systems are also used for remote access. These are standalone systems with a small camera and push-to-talk button. They are located at a gatehouse or the main entrance to a building and used whenever these locations are not staffed. A monitor is located at a location staffed 24/7, allowing staff to verify someone's identity before buzzing him or her in.

CCTV systems are also used as a monitoring aid for staff, particularly in skilled nursing environments. There are still jurisdictions that require nursing staff to be able to visually monitor the entry door to every resident's room and see the dome lights above those doors. These line-of-sight requirements run counter to the movement to deinstitutionalize skilled care environments by shortening corridor lengths, eliminating nursing stations, and clustering rooms in neighborhoods. When permitted by code, CCTV systems can meet direct line-of-sight requirements in non-institutional facilities.

Telecommunications

Telecommunications is one of the fastest-growing segments of the low-voltage family of systems, and a telecom system often serves as the backbone for a community's other low-voltage systems. In fact, there may be several independent or integrated telecommunications systems that incorporate the resident and staff voice systems, internet/intranet, fax machines, and single-use auto dialers (e.g., elevators, fire alarms, security systems, etc.).

Resident Voice Systems

Should phone service be managed by the sponsor or by a telephone company? A sponsor-controlled service can be a source of income for the facility; however, residents may demand the ability to select their phone service provider. Especially in large communities, the sponsor is rarely involved with the resident voice system, and provides the residents only with a connection point.

Staff Voice Systems

A staff phone system can be as small as a dozen handsets or as large as 100 or more. Anticipating potential growth by purchasing a scalable switch will ensure that the system can handle future needs.

Most staff voice systems integrate a call-tracking (cost accounting) system to assist management in controlling costs. Other features, such as voice mail, intercom, and call forwarding, are standard.

Television

Telecommunication companies now generally provide both phone and basic cable TV service as well as Internet access. This makes the decision on a provider impactful on cost and service flexibility. Most providers now fully wire for cable TV to allow choices in internet/cable companies.

Internet Access

Internet access is an integral part of most people's lives.

- For residents, access to the Internet is a means to stay connected with friends and family, to manage personal finances, to do research, and to shop. Physicians will increasingly be able to access residents' medical records via the Internet.

- For sponsors, Internet access can aid in education and training, marketing and referrals, business logistics, and support services.
- For families, Internet access is a way to stay in touch with the senior living community and even monitor their loved ones' health.

Networks and Intranets

Networks and intranets link the computers, websites, and databases involved in various functions, including purchasing, medical and social services record-keeping, education, time and attendance, accounting, and point of service (see below), as well as e-mail. They can also monitor building systems such as lighting and heating.

In small communities, the server room can be as small as a 10 sq ft closet; in larger communities, it can be a 200–300 sq ft room. This room will require a dedicated air-conditioning unit and an emergency power source. The server room may also house the main phone switch and other low-voltage head-end equipment. There will be considerable bundles of cable exiting this room and distributed throughout the community.

The residents may be able to access the community's intranet for functions like billing, events calendars, online classes—even to watch reruns of community events. At some communities, residents use the intranet to make reservations for dinner or at the spa or salon, sign up for classes, and even order room service.

Wireless Technology

Most electronic devices will likely use wireless technology making hard-wired cabling obsolete other than for carrying large amounts of data, such as the cables handling building-wide services such as Internet access and cable TV.

Audiovisual

The complexity of a community's audiovisual systems depends on the different types of spaces within that community and the sponsor's requirements. Audiovisual systems are found in boardrooms, classrooms, multipurpose rooms, and theaters; they are also used for background music. The design and operation of these systems must account for the seeing and hearing changes that occur with aging.

Background music

Background music systems are used in public areas (e.g., corridors, lobbies, and dining rooms) and provide warmth and ambiance. The music must not be intrusive or become distracting; it can impact mood and behavior both positively and negatively, especially in skilled care and dementia care environments. Noise canceling technology is useful in dining rooms and quiet rooms and to minimize and mitigate agitation.

Boardrooms and classrooms

Audiovisual technology in boardrooms and classrooms usually involves a large-screen monitor or a projector and screen for presentations. The computer(s) may also be connected to the Internet. A small audio system is often used to amplify the presenter or broadcast the audio. These systems require a small closet for equipment, and, typically, ceiling-mounted speakers.

Multipurpose rooms and auditoriums

The audiovisual system in a multipurpose room must be coordinated with its design, lighting, and acoustics to properly serve the needs of the elderly. Most multipurpose rooms employ a beefed-up version of the systems found in boardrooms and

classrooms. An audiovisual designer can enhance the audio system to deliver better music quality, install fixed-mount cameras or connections for portable ones so events can be recorded and broadcast on in-house TV channels, and even design a recording studio where radio shows and in-house videos can be produced.

Theaters

Some communities employ audiovisual designers for 25–50 seat theaters with sophisticated, high-quality surround-sound audio and large, high-definition viewing screens, as well as theatrical acoustical and lighting controls.

Point-of-Sale Systems

In the past, point-of-sale (POS) systems were used mainly as a way to track how many meals a resident on a fixed monthly meal plan had eaten. Today, POS systems can be expanded to cover a variety of venues where residents can purchase services.

Operations Systems

While some of the systems discussed above may be necessary to support the staff, it is mainly the residents who interact with all of them. Operations systems are used exclusively by staff. They are installed by the vendor, and their design does not involve the architect or engineer. However, these systems do require power and network connections (unless they are wireless).

The most common operations systems are discussed below.

Management systems

Management systems are used for bookkeeping and accounting, accounts payable and receivable, the payroll, human resources management, resident profile management, facilities management, purchasing, sales and marketing, and medical records management.

These software suites are network-based and do not involve any physical infrastructure. One such system, Answers on Demand, integrates all of these functions into a single software package; communities can use one, several, or all of the functions the software handles.

Medical records management

Medical records management systems facilitate caregiving by centralizing the storage of medical records in digital form. Electronic medical records can be retrieved by staff and external physicians from a computer with network or intranet access. These systems can track charts, medical status, medications, even the use of consumables. This saves time, increases accuracy, improves cost-control, and, most importantly, enables staff to provide better care while ensuring compliance with regulations and privacy laws.

Time and attendance systems

Electronic timekeeping systems are standard in most communities. Time clocks are located in one or more places throughout the community; the most common location is near an employee entrance, close to the locker rooms to minimize the time between clocking in and beginning the work day.

TRENDS

Trends in electrical and communications systems design fall into two broad areas: the expansion of services available to residents and the development of staff communications systems.

High-speed Internet access and "smart house" systems that automate utilities and appliances have engendered new practical and code requirements for power receptacles and wiring density, increasing electrical construction costs of resident units. A typical one-bedroom independent living apartment built in 1990 might have required a single 20 amp incoming electrical circuit sufficient to power the refrigerator, stove, general lighting, one telephone, one TV outlet in each room, and outlets spaced every 15 ft along the walls. The same apartment built in 2013 may require as much as 100 amps of incoming service to power all the appliances, technology, and in-unit HVAC systems. The increased power will accommodate a dishwasher and microwave and twice the number of electrical outlets. Final installation will include multi-outlet receptacles that combine telephone, TV, high-speed Internet, separate fax line, and accessory power.

Improvements in hardwired and wireless communications technologies are changing staffing patterns, the location of support spaces, and management policies and procedures.

How should designers respond to these changes? Consider the following:

- Where possible, use standards-based products and systems. Systems that are based on open (nonproprietary) protocols are more readily interconnected. The most common protocol is Internet protocol (IP), the language of the Internet. Any system that uses IP will be more easily interfaced with other systems.
- Recognize that technology has a short life cycle:
  - Infrastructure (equipment buried in walls, wiring, etc.): 15 years
  - Central telephone equipment: 10–15 years
  - Hardware: 5 years
  - Software: 3 years

What is considered state-of-the-art will change at least twice during a 5-year development and construction period, so it is prudent to recognize and plan for these changes during the design and construction phases of a project.

CHAPTER 11
SPECIAL TECHNOLOGIES

In any living or care environment, the ability of staff, residents, and families to contribute novel and useful ideas and solutions to everyday problems is often more important than a high-tech gadget. Nevertheless, new technological solutions are steadily improving the lives of older adults. What were once cutting-edge technologies are now mainstream; many are discussed in chapter 10. The following leading-edge technologies, while not yet widely implemented, are examples of innovative strategies.

REMOTE BIOMETRIC MONITORING SYSTEMS

A promising new technology continuously measures health-related information unobtrusively, making it easier to predict changes in health. Industry giants such as GE and Intel, as well as smaller, private companies, such as VirtualHealth, have developed such systems. The technology measures body weight, sleep patterns, repeated activities within an apartment (e.g., trips to the bathroom)—even how many times a resident flushes the toilet or opens the door. Some monitor blood sugar levels and blood pressure. The more sophisticated systems even provide real-time videoconferencing for resident-specific assessments and health education.

These data are gathered through wireless sensors; the information is sent to a computer that analyzes it. Reports identify changes to care staff. For example, a reported reduction in body weight over time might indicate poor eating habits. An increase in trips to the bathroom at night might indicate some sort of infection or change in digestive function. A resident might not report such things, but if staff is aware of them, they can diagnose and treat them more quickly than would otherwise be possible. Family members can view the same history and reports as staff via a secure web portal, allowing them to be more involved in their loved one's healthcare (fig. 11-1).

A key advantage to these systems is privacy. Most require no cameras, so no pictures are ever taken. In others, a camera and voice link is provided to allow the senior to speak directly to a triage nurse about any health concerns (see the section on telemedicine, below). An added benefit of these systems is that some can also track a resident's whereabouts using personal locator technology.

Personal Locator Systems

Personal locator systems use either GPS or, more frequently, a series of antennas or infrared sensors to triangulate a resident's location. The accuracy of these systems can be impressive—sometimes, to within a few feet. They can track a resident within a room, identify which room the resident is in, or where the resident is outside the building.

These systems require the resident to wear some sort of a transceiver—usually a wristband or pendant. A system's range depends on the number and spacing of the sensors or antennas. On large sites, full coverage is often not possible due to the high cost of installing many antennas. Another drawback is that they cannot track height accurately and can at times misrepresent location in a multistory building.

▶ *Figure 11-1 New technology like tele-health allows patients to proactively monitor their health and transmit test results to their doctor through the Internet. This particular patient is pre-diabetic and uses tele-health to measure her blood sugar levels.* Photograph courtesy of Virtual Health.

Personal locator systems are often developed in conjunction with wander alert and emergency response systems. Some companies make an integrated package that allows a resident to signal for help and a staffer to determine the resident's location and condition.

GPS location technology is also built into smartphones. Commonly used to track the whereabouts of children, it can also be used for seniors; they must, however, remember to take their cell phone with them for it to work, a drawback for the memory-impaired.

Fall Detection

What happens when a senior living alone falls? Frequently, he or she cannot get up or summon help. New technologies incorporating triaxial accelerometers can detect a sudden change from a vertical to a horizontal position. A device worn on the resident's wrist and tied in to an emergency alert system can warn staff of a potential emergency automatically. Combined with personal location technology, it lets staff know if a resident is in trouble as well as where he or she is.

Telemedicine

Telemedicine is the diagnosis or treatment of an individual by a healthcare provider in a remote location. Telemedicine is used in rural areas where long distances make in-person access to medical professionals difficult and in underdeveloped countries with an insufficient medical infrastructure. It is now being used with seniors who have difficulty getting to a doctor's office.

The two most common forms of telemedicine are remote monitoring and interactive monitoring. Remote monitoring relies on the resident to wear or use a device to transmit information to a medical professional. Wireless technology transmits this data via the Internet in real time so someone can interpret it and act upon it. When wireless transmission is not possible, devices such as cardiac event monitors are able to store the data digitally. Other remote monitoring equipment lets a senior measure his or her blood pressure, blood sugar, or vital signs and transmit the results automatically. This allows health professionals to track trends and abnormalities and respond to them quickly.

Using interactive telemedicine, a medical professional can be in direct contact with the patient via telephone or the Internet. The patient is sometimes in the company of a visiting nurse or family member. The key benefit is that the patient does not need to leave home for the appointment. For seniors without transportation or in remote areas, telemedicine is becoming a vital tool in maintaining health and wellness.

Very little infrastructure is required to conduct telemedicine. For patients without Internet access, the telephone is often sufficient for many telemedicine interventions.

Web Portals

Providers and sponsors recognize that a partnership between themselves, the resident, and the resident's family is the best way to care for a resident. Sharing data via the Internet allows a resident's family to participate fully in their loved one's care.

Access to fileserver-based databases can be granted to anyone with an Internet connection. With the proper security in place, web portals providing patient information can give family members access to their loved ones' financial and medical records, to information about their activities and movements throughout the community, to data from biometric sensors—even to information from the POS system about what a resident is eating. The ability to monitor a resident's health and wellness is limited only by the sophistication of the technology a sponsor is willing to install.

Virtual Reality Therapy

Many communities extol the virtues of the Wii and similar virtual gaming technologies,

as the best wellness device to be introduced in many years. Residents not only get much needed exercise but they find the activities enjoyable because they are social and not conducted in a clinical setting.

This type of technology, specially adapted to discrete therapeutic modalities, is now popular in progressive therapy settings. Therapists coach residents through simulated activities like walking, bicycling, driving, or even more strenuous sporting activities. Cameras capture the resident's image performing these activities and project that image onto a simulated background (e.g., a moving sidewalk, a roadway, a sporting venue, etc.). Sensors measure the resident's strength and reaction times, and the technology generates objective reports that show the resident's progress toward stated goals. These systems show promise in their ability to shorten the recovery times and overall therapy regimens and provide good outcomes in conjunction with or in contrast to standard manual therapies. For residents who cannot participate in a group setting, the entire technology package can be brought to them on a rolling cart.

Remote Learning

Remote or online learning is not a new technology: thousands of people use it every day to pursue degrees. But there are new technologies for seniors with limited computer skills that enable them to take advantage of remote learning opportunities. Companies such as It's Never 2 Late have developed interactive software that is used in conjunction with touch-screen monitors. After entering a virtual classroom, residents can converse with others in the class, listen to instruction, and view examples (fig. 11-2). This type of interactive environment keeps seniors engaged and vital, in contrast to sedentary activities like watching TV.

▶ *Figure 11-2 A resident and her companion engaged in remote learning activities. Courtesy of It's Never 2 Late.*

Circadian Lighting

Circadian lighting has been used for some time to help individuals with seasonal affective disorder, a condition that occurs in winter when there is less sunlight during the day. The disorder causes depression and other symptoms.

The patient is exposed to a high light level for a short period of time on a regular basis. By inhibiting melatonin production, this technology improves mood and activity levels.

Derivations of this technology are now used to help control the circadian cycles of individuals with Alzheimer's disease and other dementias. By introducing graduated full-spectrum light levels in the morning, individuals can be awakened naturally, and will in turn be more focused and energetic throughout the day.

In the evening, the color temperature of the lighting changes and lighting levels are gradually decreased, stimulating the production of melatonin, which induces sleepiness. This simulation of the natural circadian rhythms can moderate agitation in confused individuals who are no longer oriented to time of day.

CHAPTER 12

PRODUCTS AND EQUIPMENT

Senior living facilities make use of a wide range of supportive products and equipment particular to the industry that enhance innovative care and the activities of daily living. As the amortization of capital costs often represents at least 30 percent of a facility's operating budget, equipment and products must be selected with care. The following are examples of key products and equipment that can positively impact senior living design.

MEDICAL EQUIPMENT

Specifics about medical equipment are beyond the scope of this book. Whatever the equipment and its function, staff must be comfortable with and knowledgeable about its use.

Future technology will reduce injuries due to medical errors, which contribute to approximately 100,000 deaths annually. According to some studies, better medical records, computer-assisted prescribing, and similar technological improvements will reduce this number[1].

UNIVERSAL DESIGN

Universal products are designed to serve the entire population regardless of age, stature, size, or physical ability. These products include the following:

- Door and window hardware
- Kitchen and laundry appliances
- Cabinets
- Bathroom fixtures
- Climate and lighting controls
- Stairway lifts and elevators
- Gardening tools
- Tableware
- Kitchenware

The design of most universal products are modifications of designs originally intended to help people with physical limitations live more comfortably.

For example, grab bars and handrails finished in stainless steel, once common in institutional settings, are now made from many materials, including colorful plastics, plastics that look like wood, and wood moldings that resemble a component of millwork. Many residents use towel bars for support, which can be dangerous. So new strong but decorative grab bars are now used in their place. This prevents the collapse of a towel bar not designed to support a person's weight.

Kitchen design for independent living units should incorporate universally designed accessories to prolong independence and support aging in place: cabinets with pull-out shelves or drawers in lieu of doors with fixed shelves, lazy Susan carousels in corner cabinets, pull-down shelving units in upper cabinets, and pull-out pantry units to make the contents easily accessible. The cabinet box core construction should support additional accessories that can be mounted as needed, such as pull-down

---

[1] Kathleen Sebelius and David Cote, "Taking on Medical Mistakes" Philadelphia Inquirer (April 25, 2011). http://www.hhs.gov/secretary/about/opeds/phillainquirer20110425.html

shelving units installed in the upper cabinets. Appliances in the following configurations are appropriate for senior living facilities:

- Refrigerators with the freezer on the bottom
- Induction cooktops, to reduce the risk of burns from electric or gas burners
- Drawer style dishwashers
- Microwaves that open like a drawer and are mounted under a countertop rather than at eye level

Two resources for universal design accessories are *The Directory of Accessible Building Products*, published by the National Association of Home Builders Research Center, and Lighthouse International, a center for education, research, and product recommendations for the visually impaired.

MOBILITY DEVICES

The senior population in residential environments use walkers, canes, and motorized carts more frequently than wheelchairs (figs. 12-1 and 12-2). But accessibility codes have been written to accommodate the needs of wheelchair users with at least some upper body strength. The mobility variations among the aging and the space needs for their mobility devices warrant special consideration. (See chapter 6 for more information about accessibility.) These considerations include corridor width so that two individuals using mobility devices can pass one another easily, storage and battery-charging space for carts, and areas adjacent to dining and activity rooms for cart parking.

In long-term care environments, advanced wheelchairs are being used to assist staff in helping frail and immobile residents.

FOOD SERVICE

Meal delivery has evolved from the traditional hospital model to residential and hospitality models. The designers of senior dining spaces have become more attentive to issues of acoustics, comfortable furnishings, lighting, room size, and the quality and character of finishes (see chapters 13, 14, and 15 for descriptions of dining spaces and interior design).

Food service delivery now focuses on maintaining food quality, texture, and temperature, as well as on promoting a congenial dining atmosphere. Dining is one of the most important activities of the day and is scrutinized by prospective residents and their families. The ways in which food service delivery impacts the various senior living environments is described below. Note that some concepts, such as the country kitchen or family-style model, can create a more familiar setting in many senior living environments.

Adult Day Care

Food delivery depends on whether the facility is standalone or connected to a larger campus. Facilities may use any of the systems discussed below, depending upon the type of client they serve.

Long-Term Care

Most long-term care residences are still largely reliant upon tray service, but a growing number are opting for country kitchen or family-style models, as described below in the section on assisted living. In long-term care, residents' restrictive diets and their need for assistance with eating must be accommodated.

◀ *Figures 12-1 and 12-2   As mobility devices have become more affordable, their use has increased.* Image (left) courtesy of Sunrise Medical.

The following are ways to enhance traditional tray service. (See chapter 15 for a description of the furnishings appropriate to such a setting.)

- *Green House/small house model:* The food is cooked by the care staff in the house.
- *Bulk delivery:* Some facilities deliver food in bulk to a nursing unit or household and then plate it individually for the residents. This keeps food at the appropriate temperature and gives food service a residential feel.
- *Mixed meals:* This Canadian concept has been introduced in the United States, France, Belgium, and Spain. These reconstituted meals utilizing minced and pureed foods resemble their normal counterparts so closely that their modified texture is only apparent when tasted. Technology

preserves most of the foods' natural flavor and appearance but allows patients with dysphagia (difficulty swallowing) to enjoy an appetizing meal.
- *Cook-chill:* This is a tray-based method used in environments where meals must be served in large quantities or where meals are distributed from a kitchen remote from the dining room. Its advantage is the higher quality food that results from the cook-chill process: the food is prepared, rapidly chilled for safety and quality control, and then reheated or restored to the proper temperature as needed. Conduction and convection "re-therm" (reheating) systems provide computerized temperature and time controls and automate the schedule for reheating food. This system has a high first cost, but in some places this is balanced by lower labor costs, since all

three meals can be prepared during one shift. Its critics refer to it as the "airline food" approach but it can provide quality meals.

Assisted Living

- *Main dining:* In some assisted living residences, the hospitality/restaurant concept has turned mealtime into show time. Every day, the chef fixes a meal in front of residents. Equipment includes a presentation area with sink, warming devices, and a meat-carving area. The event is designed to appeal to the senses, provide entertainment, and encourage dialogue by bringing kitchen teams into the dining rooms. It improves residents' appetites and the relations between residents and food service staff.
- *Decentralized dining:* Country kitchen and family-style models rely on a residentially appointed warming pantry. Food is plated from either a hot/cold cart transported from the main kitchen or from built-in food wells supplied with food in bulk from the main kitchen. This enhances the experience of the meal's aromas and fosters a residential atmosphere. Some facilities serve a hot breakfast in decentralized spaces within each resident cluster and lunch and dinner in the main dining room.

Independent Living

Many independent living residences offer both formal and informal options for dining; the latter are gaining in popularity. Features of an informal setting include a salad bar or even a cafeteria tray line. Café or bistro environments have also been integrated into the social atmosphere of the lobby. Equipment for these settings might include a bar/sink, an espresso maker, an ice cream freezer, and a blender. Formal settings may include the equipment necessary for presentations by a chef and for carving meat within the dining space.

Special Care and Dementia

Such facilities deal with the following:

- *Irregular schedules:* Not all residents will eat at the same time, so food must be kept at the appropriate temperature for longer periods of time. Depending upon health department regulations, some meal preparation—especially the preparation of eggs, toast, and other foods for which maintaining the textural quality is important—can occur adjacent to the dining room, remote from the main kitchen. See the section on assisted living, above: the country kitchen/family-style dining model is especially appropriate to this setting.
- *Smaller group size:* Groups of 10–14 are recommended for special care dining.

See chapter 2 for further discussion of the needs of special care residents and of those with dementia.

Kosher Preparation

The local rabbinical council will have specific requirements for maintaining a kosher kitchen for observant Jewish residents. The specific requirements will vary but typically require a main kitchen at least 60 percent larger than a non-kosher kitchen for the following reasons:

- There must be separate preparation, storage, and cleaning areas for meat and dairy. The storage space for equipment and utensils used to prepare meat and dairy must be separate as well.

- There must be storage and preparation space dedicated exclusively to Passover meals.

BATHING EQUIPMENT

See chapter 15 for descriptions of bathing spaces and their finishes. Although bathing equipment has become easier to use and looks more like familiar residential fixtures, the floor plan configurations and care practices traditionally found in long-term care settings focus on hygiene rather than on comfort. But residents may think of bathing as a calming retreat at the end of the day, a vigorous shower after exercise, or a romantic occasion, not simply a way to get clean. The resident may prefer a shower to a bath, or vice versa, making a mandatory experience elsewhere uncomfortable.

A spa is one model of bathing. Applications include recessing a therapeutic whirlpool tub into an archway or creating a defined space for the tub and decorative light fixtures, shower curtains, draperies, artwork, or mosaic tile. Thick, heated towels and a selection of beverages, music, scents, and soaps can be offered. Services can include massage, pedicure, facials, and other beauty services handled separately from the facility's barber shop and beauty parlor. For example, the textures of a back brush, loofah sponge, or towels of different textures and colors all affect residents' perceptions of the bathing experience. Equipment might include an electric towel warmer, whirlpool tub, piped-in music, or aromatherapy diffusers (fig. 12-3).

Tubs

Of all environmental features, tubs likely have the strongest influence on resident and caregiver satisfaction with the activities of

personal hygiene. The tubs and bathing equipment typically found in institutional environments are unfamiliar to most residents, and some equipment has even been likened to that of a spaceship.

Frequently cited tub-related problems and complaints include the following:

- Slow-filling tubs chill residents.
- Complex controls make operation or control of spray strength or temperature difficult.
- Unfamiliar, oversize institutional equipment upsets many residents, as does noisy equipment and the sound of high water pressure flowing through pipes.
- Lifts, transfer devices, and moving tubs can be disorienting and a source of anxiety.

Like clothing, there is no one tub that fits all. Facilities should therefore provide more than one type of tub, if feasible. The following are desirable features:

- Easy entering and exiting
- Nonslip floors and temperature-control systems that prevent scalding are essential.
- Tubs for assisted living residents or those with early- and mid-stage dementia should allow for independent entry and for bathing in the sitting position. Tubs for long-term care residents or those with advanced dementia must accommodate both a sitting and reclining position so a caregiver can assist in bathing the resident comfortably and easily (fig. 12-4).
- Some models offer jets of warm air for resident comfort while the tub fills, but many older residents perceive the movement of air as a cold draft. An integrally

▶ *Figure 12-3 Many sponsors are moving away from institutional bathing settings by creating spa-like environments. Foulkeways at Gwynedd, Gwynedd, Pennsylvania. Reese, Lower, Patrick & Scott, Ltd. Photograph by Larry Lefever.*

▶ *Figure 12-4 This tub, with a pull-up side and a built-in seat, facilitates entry and exit for the frail elderly. Courtesy of Arjo Inc.*

heated sitting surface, similar to heated seats in luxury cars, may solve any problems created by moving air.

- Some models now provide a water reservoir that can deliver warm water gradually in a shorter time period than filling from a faucet once the resident has been seated.
- Ceiling-mounted lifts may be needed to ease the transfer of long-term care residents from bed to bath (fig. 12-5).

Showers

While many residents and staff prefer showers to tubs, this may be due in part to a lack of satisfaction with bathing equipment as well as shifting generational preferences.

Common shower-related issues include the following:

- Slipping is a common hazard in shower areas.

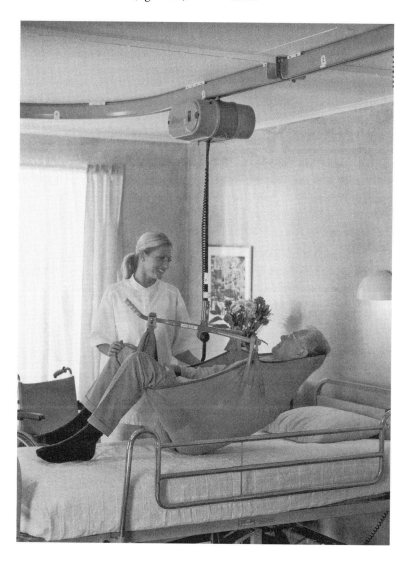

◀ Figure 12-5 For residents who are completely immobile, ceiling-mounted lifts are used in acute-care services.
Courtesy of Arjo Inc.

- Negotiating a shower threshold can be difficult, so roll-in showers are more commonly used. Sloping the floor for proper water drainage is essential for safety and to handle water that runs out of the shower area.
- Integrally molded seats and fold-down seats are often too small, sometimes difficult to fold up and down, are too far from the shower controls, and make it difficult for staff assisting a resident to reach all parts of his or her body. However, they are required by some state and local codes.

Desirable features include the following:

- An adjustable handheld shower nozzle that gives the user more flexibility, avoids a harsh or noisy shower spray, and supports autonomy.
- An adjustable mounting system provides for flexibility in the placement of grab bars, the shower seat, and accessories such as those available with the systems from Pressalit Care, a manufacturer of home products for the disabled (fig. 12-6).
- Although a raised threshold does not always meet accessibility requirements,

▶ *Figure 12-6 The slim, flat rail system and easily mounted accessories provide flexibility in the placement of the assistive devices. Hebrew SeniorLife: NewBridge on the Charles, Dedham, Massachusetts. Perkins Eastman. Photograph by Sarah Mechling.*

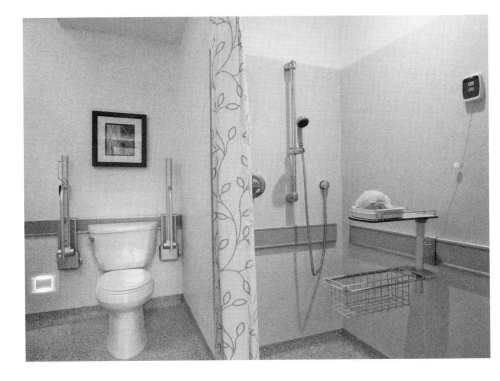

such a threshold can contain water within the shower. Such thresholds should collapse when stepped on or rolled over by a wheelchair.

- A freestanding plastic shower chair is an inexpensive way to increase flexibility and can actually be safer than an integral seat.
- American National Standards Institute (ANSI) standards, upon which most accessibility codes are based, require dimensions of 36" x 36" for a transfer-type shower stall and 30" x 60" for a roll-in shower stall, although some states require a 48" depth. To comfortably assist a resident, a shower depth of at least 36" and a width of at least 48" are desirable.

Both tubs and showers must include adequate space immediately adjacent to the fixtures for toiletries, robes, and clothing. This shortens the time the resident must take to dry off, cover up, and get dressed after bathing. It also supports a resident's independence and privacy. A shelf within the bathing enclosure should be large enough to hold several bottles and soaps, with a continuous surface rather than open slats, so that contents remain stable.

CHAPTER 13
ACOUSTICS

Many people experience hearing loss as they age. Nearly two-thirds of Americans over 70 suffer from hearing loss that ranges from mild to severe[1]. Poor acoustical design in a senior living facility can make it difficult for residents to hear and be heard, cause social discomfort, and contribute to fear, embarrassment, depression, and isolation.

Even those who wear hearing aids are affected by background noise. Although new developments in hearing-assistance technology have helped to minimize this problem, some older hearing aid models still amplify background noises along with messages, making it difficult for hearing-assisted individuals to distinguish what is being said to them. It is therefore essential that senior living spaces be designed to deal with the way sound travels to accommodate hard-of-hearing and hearing-assisted residents.

The acoustical design of a space involves attenuating unwanted and disturbing sounds and enhancing desired sounds so they can be heard properly. Some factors—for example, a rise in exterior noise levels due to a change in nearby noise sources—are beyond the control of the design professional. Architects and other design professionals rely on simple acoustical design procedures when specifying floor, wall, and ceiling finishes.

For the more demanding design and engineering of multipurpose, dining, or other large, high-occupancy spaces or for the analysis of exterior mechanical equipment to meet the code requirements for noise reduction, an acoustician should be retained. Several software programs model the acoustical performance of spaces before they are built. In addition, criteria for the acoustical design of spaces are widely available in textbooks and technical publications such as *Architectural Acoustics* by M. David Egan.

Healthcare industry studies indicate that high noise levels affect staff performance and fatigue patients (Joseph and Ulrich 2007). If high noise levels can have such significant consequences in a short-term environment, they can impact long-term living conditions even more.

KEY ACOUSTICAL CONSIDERATIONS

Key acoustical considerations include

- excessive noise levels,
- the transmission of noise from one space to another,
- the privacy of individual spaces, and
- the intelligibility of speech against background noise.

Three issues shape how effectively an individual can hear and understand: distance from the source of the sound, the level of background noise, and the effects of reverberation. Designers can improve signal-to-noise ratio and thus increase speech intelligibility by controlling background noise levels and reverberation times (fig. 13-1).

---

[1] Roni Caryn Rabin, "Aging: Hearing Loss Is Common but Often Ignored," *New York Times*, March 3, 2011.

▶ *Figure 13-1 Carpeting and other sound-absorbing materials, such as acoustic tile ceilings, window coverings, and upholstered seating, are important factors in creating a comfortable dining room. Amsterdam at Harborside, Port Washington, New York. Perkins Eastman. Photograph by Sarah Mechling.*

Background noise from HVAC systems, conversations, telephones, paging devices, kitchen equipment, and many other sources interferes with effective listening because it competes with the spoken message. Louder speech signals are required to overcome high background noise values across the frequencies of speech (500–2,000 Hz). Background noise (or ambient noise) design criteria are typically expressed as a range between two noise criteria (NC) curves, which plot sound levels across eight standard frequencies. A sound meter is used to test sound levels at these frequencies.

The NC rating for a room is typically between 5 and 10 points below the decibel (dBA) reading. Design engineers can specify HVAC equipment with low noise ratings and limit the sound generated by system operation in a variety of ways. Rooms and spaces can be protected from unwanted exterior sound by mass, insulation, and isolation in wall and slab construction, and by minimizing (or sound-protecting) openings.

Reverberation—reflected sound that persists within a room or space—also masks the sound of the spoken message and increases background sound levels. Reverberation is

Table 13-1 Definitions
Sound absorption: The process of removing sound energy, or the ability of materials, objects, and structures (e.g., a room) to absorb energy.
Reverberation: The persistence of sound after the cause of sound has stopped, or the ear's reaction to echoes in an enclosed space, giving an impression of "liveness" or "deadness."
Noise criteria (NC) curves: A set of spectral curves used to obtain a single number rating describing the "noisiness" of environments for a variety of uses, and generally used to describe the maximum allowable continuous background noise. NC curves plot sound levels across the frequencies between 63 and 8,000 Hz, the speech perception range.
Room criteria (RC) curves: Developed to measure background noise from HVAC systems, RC curves are adjusted at very low and very high frequencies to avoid annoying mechanical sounds.
Noise reduction (NR): Either the reduction in sound-pressure level caused by some alteration to a sound source or the difference in sound-pressure level between two adjacent rooms caused by the transmission loss of the intervening wall (i.e., the difference in background sound level between a source on one side of a wall and a receiver on the other).
Noise reduction coefficient (NRC): A single-number rating of the sound absorption of a material equal to the arithmetic mean of the sound-absorption coefficients in the 250, 500, 1,000, and 2,000 Hz octave frequency bands rounded to the nearest multiple of 0.05.
Sound transmission loss (STL): The decrease or attenuation in sound energy of airborne sound as it passes through a building construction. Generally, STL increases with frequency.
Sound transmission class (STC): A single-number wall or other assembly rating describing the sound-insulating properties in the 100–4,000 Hz range, used mainly to assess speech transmission through a structure.

Definitions are taken from: William J. McGuinness, Benjamin Stein, and John S. Reynolds *Mechanical and Electrical Equipment for Buildings* (New York: John Wiley and Sons, 1980); Charles M. Salter, *Acoustics: Architecture, Engineering, the Environment* (San Francisco: William Stout, 1998); Federal Register 36 CFR Chapter XI, "Architectural and Transportation Barriers Compliance Board: Petition for Rulemaking; Request for Information on Acoustics."

expressed in seconds (the time it takes for the sound to decay) and can be controlled by manipulating the absorbent surfaces within a space and the proportions and volume of the space itself. When reverberation time and background noise are controlled, speech effort and sound levels decline, leading to a reduction in room noise.

Noise Reduction Coefficients

A noise reduction coefficient (NRC) rating is a single number indicating how effectively a material absorbs sound. With a range from 1.00 to .00, an NRC of .99 indicates almost total absorption, and .01 virtually none. The higher the NRC of a particular material, the more effectively it will absorb sound.

Sound Transmission Class Values

The sound transmission class (STC) rating of a particular assembly (such as a wall, partition, or screen) is a single number that indicates effectiveness in preventing sound transmission. The higher the STC value, the more effectively the assembly blocks sound transmission.

Table 13-2 Noise Reduction Coefficients (Nrc)	
Material	NRC
Bare concrete floor	.05
Tile or linoleum on concrete	.05
Carpet (1/8" pile)	.15
Carpet (1/4" pile)	.25
Carpet (7/16" pile)	.40
Plaster ceiling	.45
Metal pan acoustic ceiling	.60
Partition system surfaces	.55–.80 (.60 typical)
Carpet over padding	Up to .65
Acoustic ceiling system	Up to .99

Source: Pile 1988, p. 484.

Table 13-3 Sound Transmission Class (Stc) Values	
Material	STC
3/16" plywood	19
Open-plan furniture screen panel (typical)	21
1/4" Plexiglas sheet	27
5/8" gypsum wallboard	27
22-gauge steel plate	29
Wood 2" x 4" stud partition	35–39
Staggered stud partition	45
6" concrete block wall	46
Steel-stud partition with two layers of wallboard on each side	55

DESIGN GUIDELINES FOR SPECIALIZED SPACES

Lobbies

A lobby greets the public and is an important first impression for future residents, community outreach programs, and the welcome mat for visitors. Acoustic control methods like ceilings with articulation, including large-scale acoustic panels; wood-slat ceilings; and floating curved sound-absorbing panels can make visitors feel comfortable immediately. The lobby is a high-traffic area that warrants the use of a durable, hard-surface flooring such as stone or ceramic tiles. Carpet set in at seating areas will reduce the sound reverberation caused by such materials, as will hanging tapestries, woven textiles, and fully upholstered furniture (fig. 13-2).

Dining Areas

Among the largest areas in most residential senior settings, dining spaces produce high noise levels, often making it difficult for hard-of-hearing seniors to converse. Hard surfaces such as tile floors, plaster walls or ceilings, and glass and metal do more than reflect noise—they also generate noise as feet and chairs scrape on floors or dishes rattle on tabletops. (Think of how difficult it is to hear and be heard in a restaurant designed exclusively with hard surfaces: by the end of the meal, the excess noise can be agitating and tiring.)

One solution is the creation of smaller dining rooms within the larger eating area. Smaller spaces provide some separation from background noise without completely isolating those within. The best way to limit excessive ambient noise is to select sound-absorbing materials for walls, floors, ceilings, and even for furniture and window treatments. Soft, absorbent materials such as carpet, fabric upholstery, and drapery; linens on tabletops; absorbent

◀ Figure 13-2 Acoustic control elements such as a wood-slat ceiling, "soft" artwork, carpet insets, and textured stone walls reduce noise levels when integrated into the design. C.C. Young: The Point, Dallas, Texas. Perkins Eastman. Photograph by Chris Cooper.

wall surfaces; and acoustical ceiling tiles can all attenuate unwanted noise.

Carpeted floors are widely used in dining rooms, even those in skilled nursing facilities, although carpet tile or a more resilient surface may be required to protect against spills. If hardwood or tile floors are used, the minimum NRC for other surfaces should be 0.8, and the design team should consider the use of wall hangings or other absorbent surfaces to improve the acoustics.

Eating areas should be separated from kitchens and serving areas. If they must be adjacent, sound-absorbing material or appropriate planning can isolate noise sources like cooking hoods and commercial dishwashers.

Isolating noise is particularly challenging in "display cooking" dining rooms that require noisy equipment such as exhaust hoods and refrigeration equipment with large compressors. The combined decibel ratings of all the equipment must be evaluated to properly design the sound-absorbing finishes required. The proper sizing of ducts attached to the exhaust hoods can significantly reduce decibel levels (fig. 13-3).

Multipurpose Spaces, Spiritual Areas, Auditoriums, and Media Theaters

Senior living facilities often provide a chapel and a multipurpose performance space such as an auditorium. The spectrum of sound in these spaces runs from speech at one end to music at the other. The installation of variable acoustics is very expensive and thus impractical for most senior housing. Instead, auditoriums should be designed to the middle of the spectrum, with a reverberation time between the optimal times for speech and music. Various

factors, including the volume of the room, affect the reverberation time. Extraneous noise (like noise from the mechanical system serving the space) must be eliminated or reduced by the rooms' design.

Once a room's reverberation time is established, acoustic materials can be designed to achieve the desired reverberation time and provide sufficient reflecting surfaces to project sound and absorbent surfaces to prevent sound reflections (figs. 13-4 and 13-5).

Sound systems, microphones, and loudspeakers are required in almost all such spaces in senior environments and should be part of the design of the space from the start. Hearing-assistive systems have become more readily available and less expensive. The hearing loop, a technology used mainly in northern Europe, is now gaining ground in the United States. It permits the transmission of signals directly into hearing aids without the use of headphones. "The basic technology, called an induction loop, has been around for decades as a means of relaying signals from a telephone to a tiny receiver called a telecoil, or t-coil, that can be attached to a hearing aid."[2]

Bathing Areas and Other Hard-Surfaced Spaces

Bathing areas require hard surfaces, which reflects the noise created by running water. Limiting the use of ceramic wall tile and using resilient flooring in lieu of ceramic floor tile can mitigate the problem somewhat. The limited use of acoustic ceiling tile designed for high humidity above tub areas is an additional means of reducing reverberation. This is especially important for residences specializing in the care of persons with Alzheimer's and related dementias.

---

[2]John Tierney, "A Hearing Aid That Cuts Out All the Clatter" *New York Times*, October 23, 2011.

◀ *Figure 13-3 Proper acoustic design can reduce noise from equipment within the dining area. Collington Episcopal Life Care Community, Mitchellville, Maryland.* Perkins Eastman. Photograph by Edward Massery.

There are also tubs and whirlpool baths specially designed to reduce noise. Avoid the use of uninsulated polyvinyl chloride (PVC) pipes and plumbing fittings, which create noise when water runs through them. (In many jurisdictions, the use of PVC piping for interior applications is no longer code-compliant.)

Indoor Pool Spaces

It is very difficult to control the acoustics in an indoor pool space because all the materials must be moisture-resistant and non-corrosive; most soft acoustic materials cannot be used. Rather than gypsum board ceilings a hung acoustic tile ceiling system designed to withstand the humid environment can provide some noise reduction.

Mechanical and Electrical Systems and Mechanical Rooms

Noise-producing mechanical rooms should not be placed near residential or noise-sensitive activity spaces. The structural density of the floor slab in mechanical rooms adjacent to acoustically sensitive spaces must be great enough to enable the slab to act as a barrier to airborne sound and rigid enough to provide a stable platform for operating equipment. If the foundation is not sturdy it will resonate, and the mountings for equipment will be less effective than specified.

Air-handling systems serving multipurpose spaces require special design, with low-pressure fans, slower-than-average air velocities (less than 1,000 ft/min), and grilles and diffusers

▶ *Figure 13-4 Wood-slat ceilings with acoustic design enhance the experience of the residents during large functions. Grand Rapids Dominican Sisters: Marywood Center, Grand Rapids, Michigan.* Perkins Eastman. Photograph by Chris Barrett/ Hedrich Blessing.

sized at a maximum noise criterion rating of 20, based on designed air quantities.

The volume of air circulating in a space can produce noise. Insulation around ducts can reduce noise levels. In addition, using insulation and staggering the construction of solid walls helps to keep noise levels to a minimum.

Since the human voice lies midrange in the sound frequency spectrum, drywall construction is preferable to masonry for speech privacy because it attenuates higher-frequency sounds more effectively. With proper design, almost anything can be programmed over a mechanical space without designing an expensive, acoustically isolated structure. Whenever practicable, however, avoid direct adjacencies.

In addition to mechanical equipment, electrical equipment such as telephones, paging systems, and office equipment also

generates noise. Wireless communications systems reduce environmental noise considerably and create a less institutional setting as well.

HEARING-IMPAIRMENT GUIDELINES AND CODE REQUIREMENTS

Under the Americans with Disabilities Act (ADA), the departments of Justice and Transportation are responsible for issuing regulations for the implementation of accessibility standards in newly constructed and altered facilities. The regulations currently include ADA Accessibility Guidelines (ADAAG) 1–10.

Rules governing the transmission and receipt of acoustic testing are developed and maintained by several private sector organizations. The acoustical performance

◀ *Figure 13-5 Ceiling forms, stage curtains, and stepped upholstered seating reduce noise in a theater. C.C. Young: The Point, Dallas, Texas. Perkins Eastman. Photograph by Chris Cooper.*

▶ *Figure 13-6 The hard surfaces of most indoor pools present special acoustical challenges. Saint John's on the Lake, Milwaukee, Wisconsin.* Perkins Eastman. Photograph by Chris Barrett.

of equipment installed in buildings and other facilities is regulated by the American Society of Heating, Refrigeration, and Air-Conditioning Engineers (ASHRAE). The American National Standards Institute (ANSI), in conjunction with the Acoustical Society of America (ASA), has established several protocols for the measurement of room sound levels, including ANSI S12.2 Criteria for Room Noise Measurement. Foreign and international standards also exist.

Model codes contain both standards and requirements for sound-rated construction components in multifamily housing and other occupancy types. The developers and operators of medical and housing facilities typically set similar acoustical standards for sound transmission through floors, walls, structure, and HVAC systems.

CHAPTER 14
LIGHTING DESIGN

For lighting design to enhance the independence of residents of senior housing, it must respond to the difficulties inherent in the biological process of aging as they relate to the aging eye and the loss of light perception (fig. 14-1). Human vision declines with age, as discussed in chapter 1. Although there are neural losses, the decline is due mainly to changes in the eye's optics. The pupil shrinks, allowing less light to enter the eye. The pupil's response to dim light also decreases with age and becomes virtually nil by age 80, so the elderly have significant vision problems in low-light environments. Figure 14-2 illustrates how vision changes with age.

◀ Figure 14-1 The Bivins Foundation: Childers Place, Amarillo, Texas. Perkins Eastman. Photograph by Chris Cooper.

▶ *Figure 14-2 Human vision at age 20 (left), age 60 (middle), and age 75 (right).* Courtesy of AIGA. Paul Nini, "Typography and the Aging Eye," AIGA website, January 23, 2006. http://www.aiga.org/typography-and-the-aging-eye/.

Impaired visual perception can be worsened by improper lighting design, which can create hazardous conditions that impede mobility and affect equilibrium. A proper light level can make a space come to life. Good lighting helps with color recognition, makes food look more appetizing, and encourages contact by allowing residents to recognize people and see spaces more clearly. Integrating the proper use of daylighting can also enhance a person's mood and health.

There is a difference between quantity and quality of illumination. Lighting that is too bright can be as inappropriate as lighting that is too dim. Seniors with cataracts have great difficulty seeing in overly bright spaces. The source of light should not produce glare; bare bulbs should not be visible, and bright spots should not be created. Fluorescent lighting is the lamping of choice. New technology offers many types of full-spectrum triphosher lamps. The T8 (1 in. diameter fluorescent tube) replaces the larger and older workhorse T12 (1.5 in. diameter fluorescent tube), and the newer, sleeker T5 (5/8 in. diameter fluorescent tube) and compact fluorescent double, triple, and quadruple tubes are more sustainable alternatives. Color temperature of a bulb is stated using the Color Rendering Index (CRI), which measures its ability on a scale of 1–100 to accurately render all

frequencies of the color spectrum when compared to a reference light at the same color temperature. The higher the CRI rating, the more accurately colors will be reproduced. These newer lamps can provide a color rendition index (CRI) of over 80, enabling residents to recognize color more reliably. The designer can conserve energy at the same time by selecting higher-wattage fluorescent lamps, as discussed in chapter 7.

The integration of decorative fixtures not only helps residents find their way, it also adds to the sought-after residential ambiance, particularly in long-term care settings. Avoid the shadeless fixtures that use clear candelabra bulbs, which create glare. Decorative wall sconces can be used as accent lights but not as the primary source for ambient lighting, since they do not produce sufficient footcandle (fc) levels. These fixtures typically produce readings of 5fc in corridor applications when the recommended minimum level is 20 fc and the ideal is 30. Budget constraints often force the quality of the lighting package to be reduced. The designer must limit the cost of fixtures yet not compromise lighting levels to save money. When project budgets are cut, it is better to eliminate wall covering or other interior features than to reduce the quality of lighting.

LIGHT LEVELS, REFLECTANCE VALUES, AND GLARE

Codes for specific facility types and recommendations by such groups as the Illuminating Engineering Society of North America should be considered minimums for senior housing. Light levels must be increased or made more efficient to compensate for the loss of visual acuity that occurs during the aging process. The fc goal for corridors is 20, but the level residents prefer is 30 fc or more. Indirect lighting systems that produce less glare and fewer shadows will provide adequate illumination for most spaces, sometimes at lower fc levels.

Light levels are affected by the light-reflectance values of the finishes in the room: carpet absorbs more light than resilient flooring; light colored walls and ceilings reflect more light while darker colors absorb more. A flat-white ceiling finish will yield the most efficient indirect lighting output. Ceiling reflectance should be 85 percent for direct lighting schemes and 95 percent for indirect and daylighting schemes (Bonnema et al., 2010).

Table 14-1 Minimum Maintained Average Illuminance		
Space	Ambient Light (fc)	Task Light (fc)
Administrative (active hours)	30	50
Activity areas (day only)	30	50
Visitor waiting (day)	30	
Visitor waiting (night)	10	
Barber/beautician (day)	50	
Chapel or quiet area (active)	30	
Hallways (active hours)	30	
Hallways (sleeping hours)	10	
Dining (active hours)	50	
Exterior entrance (night)	10	
Interior entry (day)	100	
Interior entry (night)	10	
Exit stairways and landings	30	
Elevator	30	
Medicine prep	30	100
Nurses station (day)	30	50
Nurses station (night)	10	50
Physical therapy area (active hours)	30	50
Occupational therapy (active hours)	30	50
Examination room (dedicated)	30	100

(Continued)

Table 14-1 (*Continued*)		
Space	Ambient Light (fc)	Task Light (fc)
Janitor's closet	30	
Clean/soiled utility	30	
Commercial kitchen	50	100
Food storage (non-refrigerated)	30	
Staff toilet area	20	60
Resident room Entrance Living room Kitchen	 30 30 30	 75 75 50
Bedroom	30	
Makeup/shaving area	30	60
Shower/bathing area	30	

Older adults include persons 60 and older and people of all ages with some form of visual impairment.

Ambient light levels are minimum averages measured at 30" above the floor in a horizontal plane. Task lighting levels are minimums taken on the visual task.

For makeup and shaving, the measurement should be taken on the face in a vertical position.

Daylight is encouraged in entryways to smooth the transition between outside and interior illumination levels.

Lamp color: The lamp should have a CRI of 80 or higher.

Examination room lighting should be 90 CRI or higher.

These values are minimums. Optimally, task lighting should give the user control over the intensity and positioning of the light source to meet his or her individual needs.

Source: Illuminating Engineering Society of North America. From RP-28–07, Recommended Practice for Lighting and the Visual Environment for Senior Living.

LAMPING OPTIONS
Linear Fluorescent Lamps
T-8 and T-5 are the most commonly used linear fluorescents; all major lamp manufacturers produce low-mercury versions. The lamps should be specified with a CRI of at least 80. T-5s reduced the use of natural resources (glass, metal, phosphors) and en- able the use of smaller luminaires than comparable T-8 systems.

Compact Fluorescent Lamps
To meet energy codes, pin-based compact fluorescent lamps (CFLs) can be used for downlighting, accent lighting, and wall-washing. (Screw-based lamps can be

replaced with an incandescent lamp and are therefore not compliant with most energy codes.) Many lighting manufacturers can modify incandescent fixtures to accept fluorescent lamping.

Halogen Lamps

Halogen lamps are more difficult to maintain and should therefore be used sparingly for public areas such as dining rooms or bars.

Other Lamp Types

New and improved lamp options are coming on the market every day. LED lighting, which provides good color rendition, is on average more expensive than fluorescent lighting, but their price is decreasing and will soon be competitive with that of fluorescent fixtures. When affordable, LED fixtures are preferable. Cold cathode fluorescent lamps are also becoming popular; they have a shorter warm-up time and a better CRI than traditional fluorescents.

Another technology relatively new to the market is the electron-stimulated luminescence (ESL) light bulb. Mercury is not used in their manufacturing process and users report that their light is of better quality than that of either the LED or the CFL[1]. At present they are made to fit recessed fixtures but as their price lowers and availability expands they could become an increasingly attractive option.

WINDOWS AND DAYLIGHTING

Good lighting design distributes light evenly and ensures similar light levels from one space to the next. A brightly lit area adjacent to a dimmer area will make the two areas appear lighter and darker, respectively, than if the areas were separate. Because the aging process slows down the eye's ability to adjust to changes in light levels, balanced lighting design and daylighting will contribute to residents' health and well-being.

When a daylit space is adjacent to a windowless area, two levels of lighting design are required: one for daylight hours and a lower fc level for nighttime. This is similar to the lighting at the entry to tunnels, which is designed to ease a driver's transition between very bright sunshine and the darker tunnel. Window coverings are an essential part of controlling light levels and glare.

DESIGN GUIDELINES FOR SPECIALIZED SPACES
General Guidelines

The following are essential to the design of a successful lighting system for any space utilized by seniors:

- Energy-sensitive design as described in chapter 7
- Evenly distributed light levels on floor surfaces that do not create visual barriers of dark and light spots
- Non-glare light sources
- Fc levels 15–20 percent higher than those for younger adults
- Consistent light levels from one area to the next
- Transition areas that give the eye time to adjust to spaces with different light levels

---

[1]Matt Hickman. "Will ESL Light Bulbs Beat LEDs?," *Eco-nomics: Stories from the Mother Nature Network* (November 22, 2010) http://www.forbes.com/sites/eco-nomics/2010/11/22/will-esl-light-bulbs-beat-leds/

Common Areas

When designing lighting for common areas, consider the following:

- Integrate natural and artificial light sources to achieve proper fc levels (fig. 14-3).
- Utilize a variety of light levels, particularly in the large multipurpose areas, by specifying different light sources, such as cove, decorative, and downlighting. Mix incandescent lighting in decorative fixtures with more energy-efficient fluorescent fixtures. Some fluorescent light sources come with dual switching and dimming capabilities.
- Use lighting to highlight architectural features such as vaulted ceilings, beams, and wood ceilings.
- Budget appropriate funds for decorative light fixtures.

The following are guidelines for the lighting design for specific common areas.

- *Lounge areas:* These spaces should not rely solely on accessory lighting from table and floor lamps because bulbs are not always replaced swiftly. Accessory lighting should supplement minimum general light levels of 35 fc.
- *Activity rooms:* Indirect lighting is the best source for these activity rooms because it provides the most even distribution of light on work surfaces without creating glare or shadows; this significantly reduces the fc levels required to see clearly.
- *Library:* For aisles of shelving, stack lighting is the most efficient way to light the aisles and wash the face of the books. There should be general illumination of approximately 30 fc. Use directed

▶ *Figure 14-3 The use of both natural and artificial light in areas like this lobby provides a smooth transition for an aging resident whose ability to adjust to changing light levels has diminished. Hebrew SeniorLife: NewBridge on the Charles. Perkins Eastman. Photograph by Chris Cooper.*

◀ *Figure 14-4 The light levels in dining areas and restaurants should be at least 50 fc so residents can see the color of the food clearly. Indirect light minimizes glare and shadows. Leonard Florence Center for Living, Chelsea, Massachusetts. DiMella Shaffer. DiMella Shaffer. Photograph by Robert Benson Photography.*

task-lighting over tables or floor lamps at the proper height next to seating.

- *Dining areas:* Downlighting in dining areas can create unflattering shadows on the face; indirect lighting often works better (fig. 14-4).
- *Spa/salon:* While the best light source for general illumination is downlighting, it can create unflattering shadows on the face and strong glare while looking up at the ceiling (when, for example, residents are getting their hair washed). Use indirect lighting with some decorative sconces instead. Lighting on both sides of a mirror provides the most even light for viewing the face. Use lamps with a color rendition closest to natural light for the most flattering quality of light (fig. 14-5).

- *Therapy areas and exercise rooms:* Indirect is also the preferred type of light source for these areas because residents often undergo physical therapy on tables looking up at the ceiling (fig. 14-6).
- *Pool areas:* Use indirect lighting for pool areas as well. To facilitate maintenance, do not position lighting directly over the pool (fig. 14-7).

Corridors

When designing lighting for corridors, consider the following:

- The fc requirements in codes are minimums. Some state codes require only 20 fc in the corridors of long-term care

▶ *Figure 14-5 A combination of lighting types (direct and indirect) works well in a spa or salon. Lighting on both sides of the mirror provides proper light levels. C.C. Young: The Overlook, Dallas, Texas. Perkins Eastman. Photograph by Chris Cooper.*

▶ *Figure 14-6 Indirect lighting is particularly important in therapy areas, where the resident may spend time looking up at the ceiling. Nash Healthcare Systems: Bryant T. Aldridge Rehabilitation. Perkins Eastman.*

◀ Figure 14-7 The ability to maintain and easily change lamping over a pool area is critical. Cross Keys Village: The Brethren Home Community: Harvey S. Kline Wellness Center, New Oxford, Pennsylvania. Reese, Lower, Patrick & Scott, Ltd. Photograph by Larry Lefever Photography.

facilities, even though residents prefer designs with 30–45 fc.

- A variation in light source will make corridors look shorter (fig. 14-8). The integration of lighting with architectural features creates visual cueing and areas of interest that support wayfinding. Space recessed downlights 6 ft on center with a minimum of two 26-watt compact fluorescent lamps.
- Decorative sconces at unit entries support wayfinding and provide supplemental lighting so residents can read the room number, find their keys, and locate the keyhole. Alternatively, highlight unit entries by installing a recessed cove over the door, bathing the entry in accent lighting.

Resident Living Spaces

Long-term care resident room

The following guidelines are for the lighting design of resident rooms in long-term care facilities. Codes vary from state to state; not

all of the following approaches will be code-compliant in all states.

- There should be a ceiling fixture for general lighting as well as a supplemental light source such as a table lamp on the bedside cabinet.
- Table lamps should have a toggle switch located on the column rather than the customary knob at the bulb. Some table lamps can be bolted to the bedside cabinet and are offset for mounting at the rear of the cabinet surface in order to provide a work area and space for personal belongings. Most manufacturers will modify bedside table lamps to allow the lamp to be bolted to the nightstand or secure the bulb and shade (fig. 14-9).
- Night-lights assist the resident in finding the path to and from the toilet. Their design should direct light to the floor surface, and the cover should not permit light leaks that could disturb sleep.

▶ *Figure 14-8 Lighting can make corridors look shorter, highlight unit entries, and reduce glare. The Tradition, West Palm Beach, Florida. Perkins Eastman. Photograph by Edward Massery*

▶ *Figure 14-9 Table lamps attached to bedside tables both create a residential ambiance and take safety precautions into account. Air Force Village: The Mission, San Antonio, Texas. Perkins Eastman. Photograph by Casey Dunn.*

- Over-bed lighting can combine direct and indirect light sources with different switching options. Nursing units that provide higher levels of care, bedside treatments, and medical evaluation in the resident's room require a supplemental light source over the bed or mounted on the wall.
- Ceiling-mounted fixtures with multi-function light sources for ambient, reading, examination, and night light are available from several manufacturers. Specular aluminum reflectors provide precise light control and a glare-free environment; fixtures may be recessed or surface-mounted.

◀ *Figure 14-10 Use under-cabinet lighting in addition to general illumination in areas with upper cabinets. Hebrew SeniorLife: NewBridge on the Charles, Dedham, Massachusetts. Perkins Eastman. Photograph by Chris Cooper.*

- The use of floor lamps as a supplemental source is controversial because they can easily tip over. Always use lamps with weighted bases. Bulbs should be enclosed so that if the lamp falls, the bulb will not shatter.

Assisted living residential unit

The abundance of options for the lighting design of assisted living residential units means decisions are largely budget-driven.

Ceiling fixtures

How many ceiling fixtures should be used? Should they be controlled by a switched outlet? The choices will affect hundreds of fixtures.

Switched outlets can be problematic because residents may not understand that the light must be turned off at the wall switch rather than at the lamp, nullifying the advantage of being able to switch them on upon entry.

Specific rooms

What follows are lighting design guidelines for specific areas within a residential unit:

- *Tea kitchen:* Provide a light source upon entry as well as general illumination for the tea kitchen and adjacent closet. Overhead lighting at the sink counter will cast shadows on the work surface, making under-cabinet lighting at the sink and counter area essential.
- *Living room:* Living rooms are rarely equipped with a ceiling fixture; a switched outlet is provided instead. If the resident turns the lamp off at the source rather than the switch, there is usually sufficient light spillover from the entry area to allow the resident to find a table lamp.
- *Bedroom:* Some facilities provide a ceiling fixture in the bedroom, but a switched outlet is typical. However, the bedside lamp plugged into the outlet linked to the switch will always be turned off at bedside, thus eliminating the ability to turn on the light at the doorway, so ceiling fixtures are recommended in the bedroom. Reasonably priced fixtures will have a standard incandescent "A" lamp or a less efficient fluorescent circline lamp. More energy-efficient fluorescent lamps tend to be more expensive. If the bedroom has no ceiling fixture, all closets should have their own light sources.
- *Bathroom:* The majority of senior falls occur in the bathroom[2]. As a result, light must be evenly distributed so the resident can clearly see the all assistance devices (like grab bars); he or she must

also be able to read the labels on items stored in the medicine cabinet.

An indirect light source will minimize glare. Fluorescent lamping will provide the higher CRI ratings necessary for color recognition and image clarity and provides higher light output at lower wattages. Accessibility guidelines call for large toilet areas for senior populations, so the light source placed over the vanity may not provide enough light for the bathing area, which should therefore have a light source as well.

A heat lamp not only warms the area but serves as additional task-lighting for drying and dressing. Combination units include the exhaust fan, useful if there is no central exhaust system. A night-light will illuminate the path to and from the bathroom at night.

Independent living unit

The guidelines for assisted living units apply to independent living units as well. Lighting upgrades are sometimes offered at the time of sale. Such upgrades include ceiling fans with lights in the kitchen and dining areas and bedrooms, the addition of dimmers and rocker switches (which are much easier to use than standard toggle switches), and motion sensors to activate lights in the bathroom upon entry.

CONCLUSION

The following eight suggestions apply to the lighting design of all senior living and care environments:

1. Provide lighting that responds to the needs of aging eyes.

---

[2] Seitzer, Michelle. "Bathroom Safety Tips For Home, In Assisted Living" (October 16, 2012) http://www.seniorsforliving.com/blog/2012/10/16/bathroom-safety-tips-for-home-in-assisted-living/ and Centers for disease control. "Nonfatal bathroom injuries among persons aged ≥15 years — United States, 2008" (June 10, 2011 / 60(22)) http://www.cdc.gov/mmwr/preview/mmwrhtml/mm6022a1.htm?s_cid=mm6022a1_w

2. Use energy-efficient lighting products such as fluorescent lamping and incorporate lighting controls.

3. Provide uniform illumination and eliminate glare.

4. Improve color rendering by using appropriate lamping types.

5. Keep transition zones between adjacent spaces at similar brightness.

6. Raise overall light levels only slightly above standard, as overly lit spaces can produce glare.

7. Incorporate task-lighting without causing glare or significantly increasing energy use.

8. Provide access to natural daylight.

Appropriate lighting contributes to an environment that maximizes the abilities of older adults and also prevents accidents, thereby increasing their independence and quality of life.

CHAPTER 15

INTERIOR DESIGN

THE DESIGN PROCESS

Successful interior design integrates the landscape and architecture, creates seamless transitions between levels of care, defines a sense of place, reflects a lifestyle, embraces senior living standards, develops a brand, and aids in the environment's marketability. The design of interior spaces can also impact behavior, evoke emotion, assist in cognitive awareness, allow for aging in place, and aid in accessibility.

For many older adults, the interior design of their home or senior living environment can be more important than any other aspect. It defines who they are, where they come from, and what is important to them.

◀ Figure 15-1   The gallery lobby incorporates a variety of flexible seating areas that activate the space and offer opportunities for different kinds of events, exhibits, and gatherings both large and small. The reclaimed wood ceilings provide warmth while articulating the art wall and circulation throughout the space. Saint John's on the Lake, Milwaukee, Wisconsin. Perkins Eastman. Photograph by Chris Barrett.

It offers the familiar contrasted with the new and innovative.

The interior design of a project should reflect the resident and the environment where the project is located. A design concept and defined goals can tie the entire project together and inform every design decision.

The plan and systems are important, but the interior detailing is critical to a facility's success as an appropriate setting for the aging. For example:

- The wrong mounting height for an appliance or handrail can make it unusable.
- An incorrectly shaped handrail, especially one that is too narrow, can be hard to grasp for someone with arthritis.
- Floor patterns with strong contrast can be perceived as a hole or step, impeding mobility for those with poor vision.
- Poorly chosen lighting fixtures can create glare that effectively blinds residents.
- Many chairs and sofas are too deep or do not have arms that permit an older adult to rise from them without assistance.
- The wrong carpet will trap stains and odors created by spills and incontinence.

These are just some of the hundreds of interior design issues that a sensitive, informed interior design must address. This chapter discusses some of the most important.

From a process standpoint, fully integrated interior design begins with the confirmation of the program and space plan. Interior design team members must be part of the design process from the project's inception. Understanding and sharing in the development of the design concepts and project goals ensures an integrated team approach.

Interior design team members can provide the following services:

- Space planning
- Programming
- Adjacency diagrams
- Furniture layouts
- Budgeting
- Finish and material selections
- Decorative lighting selections
- Decorative plumbing selections
- Casework/built-in design and detailing
- Millwork detailing
- Furniture selection (indoor and outdoor)
- Window treatment selection
- Interior landscape
- Interior signage
- Art selection
- Accessory selection
- Bidding documents
- Installation coordination

Trends

The interior design of today's senior living environments is influenced by the lifestyles of the consumer, the residents' family members and friends, and the provider's staff and leadership team. The following is a discussion of the trends impacting interior designers.

Hospitality focus

Senior living environments should no longer look or feel institutional. The overused term *homelike* has long been used to describe designers' goals for spaces, finishes, and furnishings in older senior living environments. The term is still used to describe residents' private environment and small public spaces like elevator lobbies and resident corridors. But the larger, multifunctional public spaces found in senior living communities—and the quality of their finishes and furniture—have taken on the look and feel of hospitality-focused environments such as hotels and resorts. Dining environments should look like the restaurants in the surrounding community (fig. 15-2). A beauty shop should mirror a salon or spa. The fitness room should resemble a health club.

Historically, communities updated, remodeled, and repositioned their spaces every 10 to 15 years. Due to increased competition and increasingly discriminating consumers, senior living communities are following the hospitality industry and updating their environments on a shorter cycle closer to the hotel industry's normal of 7 years. This has an impact on the selection and life cycle costs of materials, finishes, and furnishings and the financial planning for future capital improvements.

Casual living

Consumers and influencers are swayed by the advertising and marketing for commercial products. Martha Stewart, Starbucks, Crate & Barrel, and countless other consumer product companies are inundating consumers with branded design and new maintenance-free products that fit into a contemporary lifestyle. Casual living is comfortable, fun, usable, and typically more affordable. Formal dining and living rooms are being replaced with great-rooms integrated with gourmet kitchens and outdoor areas where families and friends gather. Special occasion china, silver, and crystal have been pushed aside for carefree dinnerware and specialized dining and serving items. Formal restaurants requiring business attire have been replaced with casual, interactive display kitchen restaurants. The design of the

◀ Figure 15-2 An underutilized multipurpose room was repositioned to create the Sky Lounge Piano Bar. This destination bar and restaurant attracts residents from Air Force Village Campus I and II and their guests. Air Force Village, San Antonio, Texas. Perkins Eastman. Photograph by Casey Dunn.

residential units and public spaces in senior living environments must reflect these trends. Because these trends are ever-changing, designs must also be flexible and adaptable (fig. 15-3).

Outdoor living

Outdoor living and dining areas are increasingly popular and include both public and private spaces. The increased desire for outdoor living reflects the desire for healthier lifestyles, new environmental awareness, renewed appreciation of nature, and the influence of European cafés and bistros.

The industry has responded with maintenance-free, comfortable outdoor furniture, art, textiles, audiovisual entertainment equipment, and heating and cooling devices that add comfort and increase enjoyment of the outdoors. Outdoor living and dining environments can be integrated into senior living communities easily. Special considerations for older adults include the creation of microclimates that address potential discomforts and problems created by glare, heat, cold, and wind.

Wellness and biophilia

Biophilia should inform the planning, architecture, and interior design of sustainable senior living environments with a wellness philosophy. Harvard biologist Edward O. Wilson defined the concept of biophilia as "the inherent need of humans to interact and affiliate with nature to achieve and maintain optimum health and well-being."[1]

▶ *Figure 15-3 The casual and comfortable living room in a skilled care facility is welcoming and facilitates interaction among residents, family, and staff. The Bivins Foundation: Childers Place, Amarillo, Texas. Perkins Eastman. Photograph by Chris Cooper.*

[1] Quoted in Julie Stewart-Pollack, "Biophilic Design," *Ultimate Home Design* 4, July/August (2006).

Biophilic design is important because the "elements have real, measurable, benefits relative to…productivity, emotional well-being, stress reduction, learning, and healing" (Kellert et al., 2011)

The design attributes of biophilia include

- the dynamic use of daylight,
- natural ventilation,
- visual and acoustic proximity to water,
- frequent and spontaneous interaction with nature,
- physical and sensory connections to nature,
- a connection between interior and exterior space,
- fundamental natural forms, and
- the use of local, natural materials.

Incorporating these elements into a design benefits the older adults, staff, and visitors who live and work among them.

Sensory stimulation
The seven senses are sight, sound, touch, smell, taste, balance, and motion. The senses continuously provide information about the environment and contribute to emotional, spiritual, and physical well-being. Designing to address the senses of the aging allows older adults to remain independent, age in place, and most importantly, experience life.

Regional and community-based design
Homogeneous environments and designs assume that the lifestyles and preferences from city to city and region to region are the same. A unit plan and the material selection for a project on the East Coast may not be marketable on the West Coast. Understanding consumer expectations is critical in order to set a project apart from the competition's and make it reflect consumers' wants and needs. Through focus groups and questionnaires, the design team can assess expectations on unit design, materiality, programs, restaurant venues, and lifestyle. The information gathered will benefit the design, marketing, and leadership teams. Involving the community and outside partners in the design process enables the development of a unique design (fig. 15-4).

Repositioning
Negative first impressions are hard to overcome. Many senior living facilities are suffering from old, dated buildings, amenities, and interior finishes and furnishings. An interior master plan can comprehensively reposition a facility's amenities and spaces . The master plan can establish the scope, phasing, and budget necessary to execute the project. Repositioning a senior living community by redoing its interior design is an investment that can improve marketability, resident satisfaction, and employee retention.

Affordability
From affordable to luxury markets, consumers are looking for environments that reflect their lifestyle. Design that addresses the client's needs and expectations transcends market. For example, affordable veterans' housing that not only reflects their needs but their life experiences as well will set the housing apart from other affordable options in the marketplace.

A key to designing any interior space is matching the budget to the client's expectations. This is especially important when designing affordable environments. Begin with evaluating the spaces. Which spaces will make the first impression? These are the priority. Develop three finish levels based on cost: high, medium, and low. For affordable projects, the high-cost finish areas may be limited to one or two first-impression spaces.

Figure 15-4 Movable glass wall partitions connect the lobby to the landscape beyond, bringing the desert into the space. The materials, colors, textures, furniture, art, and accessories create a sense of place and a connection to the Southwest. Westminster Village, Scottsdale, Arizona. Perkins Eastman. Photograph by Chris Cooper

This approach to finish levels for common spaces should also be considered when determining finishes throughout all levels of care as defined as basic, average, and above average (see table 15-1).

		Floor	Base	Wainscot	Wall below Wainscot	Wall above Ceiling
Table 15-1 FINISHES						
Long Term Care						
Resident room	Basic	VCT*	RB or VB	P	P	ACT
	Average	VS	RB or VB	P	P&DVP	GYP &ACT
	Above Average	VS or CPT	WD	P	P&DVP	GYP
Resident bathroom	Basic	VS	VS/B	P	P	ACT
	Average	VS	VS/B	P	P	GYP
	Above Average	CT	CT/B	P	CT/P	GYP
Resident corridor (with handrail)	Basic	VCT*	RB or VB	P	P	ACT
	Average	VS	RB or VB	P	P	ACT &GYP
	Above Average	CPT	WD	P	VWC or DVP	ACT &GYP
Assisted Living						
Resident room Kitchenette	Basic	CPT*	RB or VB	P	P	ACT
	Average	VS	RB or VB	P	P	GYP
	Above Average	CT	WD	VWC	P &CT/W	GYP &ACT
Bathroom	Basic	VS	VS/B	P	P	ACT
	Average	CT	CT/B	CT or P	P &CT/W	GYP
Living room	Basic	CPT	RB or VB	P	P	GYP
	Average	WD	WD	P	P	GYP

(Continued)

Table 15.1 (Continued)						
Independent Living						
Resident unit						
Foyer	Basic	CPT	RB or VB	P	P	ACT
	Average	LVT	RB or VB	P	P	GYP
	Above Average	WD	WD	P	P	GYP
Kitchen	Basic	LVT	RB or VB	P	P	ACT
	Average	CT	RB or VB	P	P	GYP
	Above Average	WD	WD	P	P & CT/W	GYP
Living/ dining	Basic	LVT	RB or VB	P	P	GYP
	Average	CPT	RB or VB	P	P	GYP
	Above Average	WD	WD	P	P	GYP
Bedroom	Basic	CPT	RB or VB	P	P	GYP
	Average	WD or CPT	WD	P	P	GYP
Bathroom	Basic	LVT	RB or VB	P	P	GYP
	Average	CT	CT/B	P	P & CT/W	GYP

* Other products to consider for a more sustainable option are a corn or flax seed based product.

ACT=*acoustic ceiling tile*; P=*paint*; VWC=*vinyl wall-covering*; CT/W=*ceramic wall tile*; DVP=*decorative vinyl panel*; CPT=*carpet*; CT= *cermic tile*; WD= *wood*; VB= *vinyl base*; RB= *rubber base*; CT/B=*ceramic tile base*; VS/B=*flash cove base (integral with flooring)*; CT=*ceramic tile*; VS= *sheet vinyl*; LVT= *luxury vinyl tile*; VCT=*vinyl composition tile*

COLOR THEORY

Color can create interest, provide contrast, define volume, elevate mood, invigorate the senses, inspire, improve the appearance of skin tones, enhance the taste of food, and even stimulate the appetite. "Color and light, when combined with pattern and texture, provide some of the most important elements…to enhance architecture and environmental details" (Baucom 1996).

Everyone perceives color differently. As it ages, the cornea begins to yellow, which impacts color. "The yellowing of the cornea turns blues into grays and whites into yellow[s]. Purple also appears grayer, and blue and green often become less distinctive and run together" (Regnier 2002). Understanding the aging eye and the use of colors and patterning will impact material selections positively.

WAYFINDING

The wayfinding system in any building is important to the comfort of residents and visitors, especially those who feel insecure in their environment. For older persons, who are not as agile and facing a significant change in their lifestyle, finding their way around their environment should be effortless.

A wayfinding system should go beyond simple signage; it should be a multilayered system of spatial cues. Multiple wayfinding cues reinforce a sense of security for residents, who might otherwise feel intimidated by spaces they cannot navigate easily. Residents who know their way around will venture out of their home more often, gather, and be more physically active.

There are no off-the-shelf solutions for wayfinding. It is the coordination of various architectural and interior design tools, including signage, lighting, finishes, artwork, floor coverings, accent furniture, objects, and even people. Wayfinding is a complete system and should be thought through in the initial planning and design sessions.

Begin with the facility's overall layout. Organize the layout in a supportive configuration that responds to function, program, and circulation in a logical progression, guiding residents from space to space. If the basic plan is puzzling—creating, for example, a maze of corridors—wayfinding devices will not work effectively.

Visual cues are an essential aspect of wayfinding. For example, interior windows and half-height partitions permit residents to see into adjacent spaces. The integration of specialty pieces such as display cabinets and artwork and recognizable objects at decision-making intersections become cues that orient residents.

Flooring can also be used to assist residents. The color of the flooring product can be varied from floor to floor or area to area. The carpet product used in the public spaces can have a different appearance from the carpet located in the resident wings. Accent colors, artwork, and carpet design features such as a border around the circumference of the elevator lobby are all part of the multilayered system of wayfinding devices.

Lighting design and wall finishes should also be integrated into the wayfinding plan. A decorative sconce at the entry to each unit not only provides additional light but also marks the location. The ceiling design and lighting can create a recognizable event at a cluster of resident entries. A change in wall finish signals entry into a new area (fig. 15-5).

Persons with Alzheimer's benefit from a wayfinding system with multiple layers and cues that include staff stations where familiar caregivers are visible, major landmarks (for example, a grandfather clock), and cues that engage other senses (such as the sense of smell).

MATERIALITY

Finishes provide the backdrop for an environment. Aesthetics are, of course, primary; however, cost, appropriate construction for the area's function, durability, maintenance requirements, the visual effects of patterns, and the mobility constraints of the surface must be considered as well. Keep the following in mind when selecting interior products selection:

- *Durability and appropriateness:* While some residential products can be used, commercial-grade products are best for senior living environments.
- *Maintenance:* Most products come with specific maintenance guidelines that must be followed to ensure their longevity.

▶ *Figure 15-5 Artwork, accent furniture, lighting, and interior architectural detailing aid in wayfinding. Sun City Ginza East, Tokyo, Japan. Perkins Eastman. Interiors by Barry Design Associates. Photograph by Milroy and McAleer Photography.*

▶ *Figure 15-6 The reception area at Conleys combines a variety of materials, textures, patterns, and art that together develop the theme for the restaurant. C.C. Young: The Overlook, Dallas, Texas. Perkins Eastman. Photograph by Chris Cooper.*

- *Life cycle costs:* What are the initial, maintenance, and operating costs over the useful life of the material?

INTERIOR DESIGN GUIDELINES

Most experienced designers of senior living facilities follow a number of industry-wide goals:

- A safe, comfortable environment that is supportive of the resident's need to maintain independence
- Design that seamlessly incorporates the necessary support devices (such as grab bars and handrails) in an unobtrusive manner
- An interior environment that avoids the institutional stigma associated with traditional medical and hospital settings
- A design that addresses the six characteristics of aging: loss of balance; cognitive impairment; loss of strength; visual impairment; hearing impairment; and increased sensitivity to cold, drafts, and direct sunlight

There are at least ten major types of living and care environments for the older adults. Although there are many differences among the types, all interior spaces should be designed to meet the needs of this population:

- Distribute non-glare lighting with appropriate footcandle levels specific to tasks by area (see chapter 14).
- Provide contrast between the horizontal and vertical planes for better visual discrimination to improve the sense of balance. For example, residents may perceive a corridor whose floor and wall finishes are a similar color and value as a muddy river. Without contrast between the planes, it becomes difficult to determine where the wall ends and the floor begins.

- Be sensitive to acoustics when designing and selecting finishes; choose those that reduce background noise to improve hearing at social gatherings (see chapter 13).
- Ensure flush transitions from one flooring material to another. Plan for slab recesses where necessary to reduce trip hazards.
- Avoid sharp corners or edges in millwork, wood trim, furniture, hardware, and other interior elements.
- Choose flooring products that have patterns without high contrast and with colors close in value; otherwise, there is the potential for vertigo and falls.
- Select durable textiles and wall coverings with inherent or added moisture barriers like Nano-tex and Crypton.
- Specify colors that are not so dark that they are perceived as black or so subtle that they appear dreary to the aging eye.
- Choose floor finishes that are not slippery or that have a high-gloss appearance.
- Install carpets with fiber construction and moisture-barrier backing systems appropriate for people with incontinence (see chapter 1).
- Limit the use of mirrors on walls that create the illusion of space, as this can cause confusion and disorientation.
- Incorporate the necessary support devices (such as grab bars and handrails) in an unobtrusive manner.

Also consider the following:

- Contrast can improve seniors' ability to locate assistive devices such as grab bars in the shower and in doorways. Color is more than a decorating tool: used properly, it can be a visual identification system. Too many bathrooms are white on white, making it difficult to clearly see grab bars and the exact location of the toilet or the edge of the shower.

- Integrate wall-protection systems such as corner guards and lean rails into the design of high-traffic areas so they do not detract from the residential feeling of the interior.

Flooring

Soft finishes and carpets

The first interior finish selected is usually the flooring. There are two types of carpeting: broadloom (rolled product) and carpet tile. Both have their place in senior living environments. Broadloom has less seams and a more monolithic character. Although carpet tiles come in various sizes, they have multiple seams; however, they can be replaced easily if they become stained.

Both broadloom and carpet tile come with several options: fiber types with soil-repellant treatment, antimicrobial treatments, releasable adhesives, and improved backing systems. These backing systems increase the tuft bind rating of loop carpet, so pulling a single loop does not cause the carpet to zipper or unravel; it is also a moisture barrier against spills and incontinence. Carpeting also comes in a variety of patterns and controls noise transmission.

Dense loop carpet is the best walking surface for the frail. It provides sufficient friction to reduce slipping and has a soft yet firm surface for shuffling feet without impeding the use of wheelchairs or walkers. Use a minimum of 4,500 (density) for high-traffic areas and a loop face weight of 26–32 oz. For further information about matching carpets to specific locations, consult the Carpet and Rug Institute or individual manufacturers.

Carpet considerations

- *Carpet construction:* Consider the backing, fibers, type of pile (loop or cut), and weight.
- *Slab treatment:* Carpet with moisture-barrier backing guards against spills and incontinence. However, the backing might require special installation and a special, compatible adhesive. Some gypsum sealant products, for example, absorb moisture that is locked between the slab and the waterproof carpet, causing the sealant to degrade and crack.
- *Volatile organic compounds (VOCs):* Minimize the use of products and sealants that off-gas, as frail seniors are particularly susceptible to airborne contaminants, which may cause irritation to eyes and respiratory systems.
- *Installation guidelines:* Follow the manufacturer's installation procedures, or the warrantee may be voided. For example, some moisture-barrier carpeting is perforated for easier rolling and shipping and must be resealed with a special adhesive when installed. Failure to use the appropriate adhesive voids the warranty and renders the moisture barrier ineffectual.
- *Cost:* There are ways to achieve the desired aesthetics even within a limited budget. These include reducing the face weight of carpet, selecting all products from one mill to increase price negotiating position, and meeting mill minimum yardage requirements, which may allow for the purchase of custom-colored carpet for the same price as carpet in a standard color.

Sheet vinyl and luxury vinyl tile

Advances in technology have led to vinyl sheet and plank flooring in a wide range of patterns, colors, and textures; low-maintenance, enhanced performance, and sustainable options are also available. Aggregates within the sheet flooring make it slip-resistant and therefore ideal for wet areas, high-traffic areas, and high-maintenance areas such as resident bathrooms, bathing spas, commercial kitchens, employee areas, and locker rooms. Vinyl flooring is often more hygienic and provides a softer surface than other hard surface flooring, and it is not cold to the touch.

Vinyl flooring that looks like wood, tile, and stone can appear authentic and is a less expensive alternative to the real products. Vinyl sheet flooring is also low-maintenance; most floors do not need to be waxed. Finally, moisture resistant vinyl floors are often preferred by providers concerned with incontinence, spills, and stains.

Vinyl floor considerations

- *Glare:* A high sheen often signifies cleanliness. However, high-sheen flooring materials produce significant glare and are thus inappropriate for senior housing facilities. There are low-luster finish products that reduce glare and increase traction to prevent slipping. Since vinyl flooring typically does not need waxing, glare usually is not an issue.
- *Cost:* Cost usually drives product selection. Vinyl composition tile (VCT) has the lowest first cost of the available options. However, VCT requires frequent cleaning and buffing, making its life cycle cost high. The first cost of other types of resilient flooring such as vinyl sheet product, vinyl plank or linoleum can be as much as three times the first cost of VCT, but they require less maintenance.
- *Slip and water resistance:* In wet areas, use flooring materials with a slip-resistant coefficient (relevant codes include the Static Coefficient of Friction Guidelines of the Americans with Disabilities Act). Slip-resistant products require more maintenance because their rough surfaces are more susceptible to collecting dirt and they are more difficult to clean.
- *Slab treatment:* See above section about moisture-barrier carpets.
- *Seaming:* Heat and chemical seals may be used for sheet goods, depending upon the product.
- *Transitions:* Transitions between flooring materials keep the edges of the material in place and prevent loose edges that create tripping hazards. Designers should use vinyl or metal transition materials that create a smooth, gradual transition appropriate for wheeled traffic. In addition, flooring materials must be carefully cut and adhered, and transitions properly installed.
- *Base materials:* When sheet goods are selected for wet areas and for their low maintenance requirements, install a flash-coved base. This base is integral with the floor, avoiding a seam between wall and floor. If a flash-cove base is not used, a resilient base composed of rubber, vinyl, or a combination can be utilized instead. Specify a minimum $1/8$" thick base to avoid telegraphing irregularities in wall surfaces.

Select vinyl base in continuous rolls, because vinyl shrinks and seamed lengths will eventually separate, leaving gaps between pieces. The traditional approach is to use a flat resilient base with carpet. However, the irregularities of gypsum-board partitions and the difficulty of cutting carpet make it virtually impossible to match the edge of the carpet with the base along its entire length. When using a higher pile carpet, the carpet itself obscures gaps between the carpet edge and base. With lower face weight and tight loop construction, gaps will be obvious, and a vinyl cove base should be considered. If a cove base is ruled out aesthetically, use a tapered base product: it will look like a flat base but still cover any irregularities between carpet and wall.

- *Maintenance:* VCT is high-maintenance because it is more porous, a result of the high volume of composition relative to the volume of vinyl in the product. Products that feature a solid vinyl wear layer are more scratch-resistant, less porous, and require less sealing and no buffing. These products therefore cost less to maintain, and the maintenance is less disruptive to residents.

Stone and wood
Natural stone and wood flooring are durable, natural, and can be very attractive. Natural stone flooring is considerably more expensive and generally not slip resistant when wet. Determine the slip coefficient for flooring both wet and dry to ensure the product is appropriate. If necessary, a sealer can be applied to meet slip-resistant coefficient requirements. Confirm on a sample that the sealer does not alter the character of the natural material. Low-luster options reduce glare and often increase traction and reduce slipping.

While potentially maintenance intensive, natural or engineered wood floors provide a warm, welcoming, and familiar aesthetic. Select hard woods to avoid dimpling and gouges, and specify VOC-free stains and sealers. The thickness of the product and sub-products can make transitions between wood flooring and other flooring material problematic; the choice of flooring may require slab depressions, which add cost. The inherent flammability of wood may be a code issue.

Ceramic and porcelain
Ceramic and porcelain pavers can be used in high-traffic areas because they are so durable.

The come in a variety of shapes, sizes, colors, and textures. These products are commonly manufactured sustainably and made with recycled content.

Ceramic and porcelain flooring considerations
- *Grout color and treatment:* Because grout is porous, it absorbs urine. Therefore, use grout with additives that make it less porous; epoxy grout, though more expensive, is another option. Select a dark color that will not show dirt or traffic patterns.
- *Slope and size:* In floor areas with drains, use tiles that can accommodate floor slope. To accommodate the slope in shower stalls, 2" × 2" tile works best; kitchen floors have a more gradual slope and can therefore accommodate larger tiles.
- *Slip resistance:* For entryways and showers, follow the manufacturer's information on slip resistance. For example, tile should have a minimum slip-resistance coefficient of friction of 0.06.
- *Slab treatment:* If ceramic tile is used in a wet area, a waterproof membrane should be installed in accordance with the Tile Council of America guidelines.

Other floor coverings
Other flooring options that are environmentally friendly and low maintenance include cork, bamboo, rubber, and stained concrete; this eco-friendly alternative can create interesting aesthetics within a space. Refer to the manufacturers recommendations on appropriate uses and specifications.

Wall Coverings
Vinyl
Vinyl wall covering is durable and resistant to stains and abrasion. Fabric-backed vinyl is

more durable and stain-resistant than paper-backed vinyl and vinyl-coated paper coverings, and, because the fabric adheres to the hanging surface, more stable; the fabric backing increases the resistance to abrasion as well.

There are three types of vinyl wall coverings:

- Type I: light-duty wall covering (7–13 oz/sq yd) is used for residential applications. For example, it can be located above a chair rail where it is not exposed to cart or wheelchair traffic.
- Type II: medium-duty wall covering (13–22 oz/sq yd) is specified for commercial areas where there will be a lot of cart or wheelchair traffic.
- Type III: heavy-duty wall covering (22+ oz/sq yd), which is the most expensive, is reserved for high-traffic areas such as public spaces and food service areas. In high-traffic areas such as loading or service areas, crash rails are used to protect the walls.

Vinyl wall covering considerations

- *Environmental issues:* Despite being used widely in senior housing and care facilities, its use is of environmental concern. Avoid vinyl wall coverings that off-gas. Vinyl or polyvinyl chloride (PVC) production produces dangerous inhalants.

  Its disposal is also problematic. Vinyl can leach chemicals into landfills, polluting nearby water sources. If it is incinerated or catches fire, those chemicals pose a risk to firefighters and incineration-plant workers. Though PVC is recyclable, very little of what is produced actually gets recycled.

  Manufacturers of vinyl wall coverings are exploring more environmentally friendly means of manufacturing. Its durability and affordability continue to make it a top choice for most projects. (See chapter 7 for more information about sustainable design.)

- *Removal:* Walls must be prepared properly before vinyl wall covering is hung. With such preparation, it can be easily removed for a renovation; improper installation makes removal difficult. For information about locating qualified wall covering installers, consult the National Guild of Professional Paperhangers (NGPP) or the Better Business Bureau (for general contractors).
- *Maintenance:* Vinyl is often chosen specifically because it is easy to clean and requires little other maintenance. Because different coverings and finishes are compatible with different cleaning products, always consult the manufacturer's cleaning suggestions.
- *Cost:* Prices range widely. Vinyl is very cost-effective if evaluated on a life cycle cost basis.
- *Customization:* Most manufacturers will only customize the colors and patterns on vinyl wall covering if the pattern is specified in sufficient quantity—for use throughout an entire facility, for example.
- *Mold:* To avoid mold, many designers, owners, and operators are no longer using vinyl wall covering on exterior walls, especially in coastal and very humid environments where moisture can develop between the wall covering and the substrate, creating an environment conducive to mold growth.

Paint

Paint continues to be a popular wall finish. Like vinyl, paint is durable and low-maintenance, but choose the right type of paint for the area. For example, using the wrong paint in bathing and shower rooms or kitchens can lead to cracking, flaking, chipping, and fading because they are hot and humid, causing surfaces to expand and contract.

Paint is made up of three basic ingredients, which influence its performance:

- *Binder:* Suspended particles that enable paint to form a finishing film; affects durability, adhesion, and color retention.
- *Pigment:* Suspended particles that give paint color and body.
- *Solvent:* The liquid component in which the other two components are suspended; makes paint spreadable.

The higher the proportion of solid components, the more expensive the paint, because the paint will be more durable and retain color better.

Paint considerations
- *Environmental:* The paint should be VOC-free to eliminate foxing.
- *Color:* Painted walls should be a different color than floors.
- *Types and location:* Choose the right paint for the right location. Bathrooms require a washable paint surface. High-gloss paint is more durable and stain-resistant but creates glare, which can be hard on aging eyes. Eggshell finishes are therefore best for most walls in senior housing.
- *Surface preparation:* Although paints differ in quality, an improperly prepared surface can shorten the life of even the most expensive high-quality paint. The surface to be painted should be smooth, clean, dry, and stain- and mildew-free. Use primer to ensure the wall surfaces are consistent.

Fabric wall covering
Fabric is often used to reduce sound; it can be used on both walls and ceilings. The inherent acoustical property of fabric-wrapped rigid panels greatly improve the acoustical characteristics of a space. These panels can be attached using Z clips. Another, more expensive method is to stretch the fabric over soft or rigid acoustical material on a track system that facilitates replacement and maintenance. The fabric—polyester is best—must meet flame-spread requirements and be easy to clean.

Ceramic and porcelain tile
Tile provides a washable surface; however, the porous grout joints tend to absorb liquids and odors. Grout must be sealed around toilets and urinals. Using larger tiles reduces the amount of grout necessary. Seamless sheet vinyl flooring with an integral cove base is a common alternative to ceramic tile floors in bathing and toilet areas.

Ceramic wall tile considerations
- Pattern (define horizontal and vertical planes)
- Cost and size
- Transitions with other materials

Wood trim
As with wood flooring, wood accents and trim create a warm, welcoming atmosphere. Wood can be used for standing and running trim such as moldings, baseboards, handrails, and window trim, as well as for paneling, cabinetry, millwork, and ceiling treatments. A wood ceiling can be tongue-and-groove or pre-manufactured.

Wood considerations
- *Cost:* Wood is a more expensive option for wall covering, though its cost varies greatly depending on regional, availability, species, grade, and the way in which it is cut and joined. Standard profiles in standing and running trim are less expensive than custom cuts.

- *Finishes:* Painting, staining, and varnish techniques
- Flammability
- Code compliance

Wall protection

Corner guards, crash rails, bumper guards, handrails, door frame covers, door protection, and wall panels are employed in skilled care environments to protect walls against damage from carts, walkers, wheelchairs, and beds. These materials can be color-matched to the wall so they blend in, or they can contrast and become an aesthetic statement. Many of these materials are available in wood-like finish. Corner guards come in several lengths and can be surface mounted or recessed. Bumper guards are typically mounted 12–18 in. from the finished floor.

Windows and Window Coverings

Daylight contributes to the quality of a space and connects it to the outdoors. Window treatments are used to control glare and the amount of light in a space. Decorative window treatments can give a room a residential or hospitality ambiance. When selecting window treatments and coverings, durability, maintenance, fading, code requirements, and fire-resistance ratings should be considered.

Base window coverings for both public and residential spaces include manual or motorized roller shades and panels, blinds and louvers, and solar and glare-control window films. Decorative window treatments include wood and faux wood blinds; fabric-wrapped cornice boards and valances; sheers, panels, and curtains; fabrics shades; and custom draperies.

FURNITURE AND FURNISHINGS

Furniture and furnishings are the finishing touches in the interior design of a project; without these items, spaces will look incomplete. Avoid being locked into buying arrangements or to preferred vendors when making selections. Through an open bid process, the owner can usually obtain preferred pricing on furniture and furnishings.

Definition

Furniture, fixtures, and equipment (FF&E) are defined as the products within the environment that are not fixed to the building. This includes furniture, decorative window treatments, decorative pillows and cushions (soft treatments), art, signage, accessories, interior landscaping, and portable lamps. Other items that may either be provided by the owner or part of the FF&E include fitness equipment, salon and spa equipment, movable stages, podiums, audiovisual equipment, dishware and linens.

Trends

Furniture and furnishings should reflect the architectural aesthetic, the setting and location of the project, and the lifestyles of the residents. Interior designers should review an array of products and specify those that embrace the overall design concept.

Many commercial furniture manufacturers now design newly interpreted lines that support senior living design principles. David Edward's Aspen wing chair is one example: the chair is a transitional take on the familiar, traditional wingback chair that features a higher density foam cushion, senior-friendly dimensional proportions, and an optional wood arm cap for durability.

Restaurant-style dining venues require a variety of seating types. Combining easily accessible banquettes (for independent and active adult environments) with different styles of armchairs and table sizes creates a more interesting setting with various seating options for the residents. It also breaks up a large dining venue into smaller, more personal spaces.

Unique, eclectic, conversational furniture pieces scattered throughout a project give a room character. These pieces can be antiques or one-of-a-kind art pieces or reflect the local aesthetic. Art, accessories, decorative pillows, and interior landscape pull together the design and give a room a finished look.

Specifications

In the programming and planning phases, use test layouts to determine the proper dimensions for furniture and to plan an area with the proper accessibility clearances for wheelchairs and supportive devices like walkers. Do not use the furniture templates provided by computer-aided design (CAD) or building information modeling (BIM) software, particularly for dining and activity spaces. The chairs in the templates are typically only 18" square; a chair with arms is actually 22" square or more. Multiply this 4" difference by 60 or 80 occupants, and the furniture becomes too large to fit in the room. Similarly, templates for a table for four are typically only 36" square. But tables as large as 48" square are often required in formal settings. The food delivery system affects table size in dining areas and, therefore, the square footage per occupant ratio used for planning.

Provide a variety of seating choices that accommodate two, four, and six or more persons, like a table for four with leaves that flip up to create a round table for six. If a table for two has at least one dimension in common with a table for four, they can be joined for additional flexibility. Ensure that table heights are accessible to wheelchair users. While adjustable-height tables are available, the bases are typically unattractive,

although some manufacturers have introduced adjustable wooden pedestals.

Furniture selection for each level of care within a senior living community should reflect the physical abilities of the frailest users, as aging in place is common in such facilities. The physical effects of aging can be addressed by furniture that meets the following criteria:

- *Proper dimensions:* The seat height should be a maximum of 19"; seat depth a maximum of 21"; and arm height a maximum of 26".
- *Style of arm:* The arms must extend to the front of the seat so they will support the weight of residents who lean on them in order to stand or sit unassisted.
- *Density and firmness:* The cushions must be supportive so that the bottom of the seat will not sink lower than the height of the occupant's knees.
- *Upholstery:* There are several treatments on the market that repel stains and prevent the moisture from passing through the cushion. Nano-Tex and DuraBlock offer an alternative way to treat more complex, higher-quality fabrics. Nano-Tex builds permanent spill- and stain-resistance into the fiber structure. DuraBlock laminates a durable liquid barrier to a textile that prevents liquids from penetrating the fabric. They can be used separately or together, giving the designer flexibility in choosing fabrics that both match the aesthetic and perform as needed.

Crypton is another moisture-barrier technology that comes standard on many textiles. The tactile experience of these specialized fabrics has improved greatly over the years. Crypton leather is available through manufacturers such as Edelman

Leather. It is cleanable, stain-resistant, and water-resistant and provides antibacterial protection. A less expensive alternative to leather is polyurethane. It has the embossed grain of leather but a softer feel. A vinyl, polyurethane, or leather seat is typically used in high-traffic areas and dining and lounge areas where food and beverages are served.

Textile colors and patterns should contrast from those of the floor and the surroundings to help seniors with poor eyesight see the outline of the furniture.

- *Durability:* Although a residential or hospitality appearance is desirable, the construction must be of commercial quality, with bracing and sturdy joinery. Chairs for dining should have cross-support stretchers to prevent their legs from loosening, as the residents of senior living facilities push and pull chairs frequently as they sit and rise. Casters can be added to the front legs to reduce the stress on the structure of the frame and make it easier for residents to pull a chair up to the table. (For safety, casters should only be used on the front legs.) A crumb release—a reveal between the chair back and seat—prevents food particles and crumbs from collecting in the seams and creases of the chair.
- *Weight:* Furniture for rooms with multiple functions, such as stackable chairs, must be light enough for the occupant to move while still providing a safe, stable frame with arms that will not tip over when the occupant rises. Folding tables must have mechanisms that lock in place for stability and without any sharp edges or movable parts that could cut or pinch.
- *Rockers, swivel chairs, and recliners:* Studies have shown that these chairs have a positive effect on the well-being of senior populations. However, these chairs can

be a tripping hazard or rock over someone's foot. Ensure that rockers do not tip forward when the occupant uses the arms for support to stand.
- *Tables:* The glass tops of occasional tables should be tempered and edged in wood or metal so the glass contrasts with other materials and can seen easily. Dining tables can have a wood or laminate top with a hardwood edge and a metal "X" base, which is both sturdy and easy to clean. Wood tabletops should have a high-wear finish coat. Avoid tables with aprons; they are difficult for residents who use mobility.
- *Glides:* Furniture glides need to be specified appropriately for the type of flooring material the chair is placed on. Teflon glides are used on carpeted, vinyl, or rubber flooring; a rubberized, nonskid glide is best for use on hard surfaces like stone or porcelain tile.
- *Code:* In skilled nursing, state health codes often mandate the minimum furniture to be provided in each resident room: typically, a bed, a wardrobe or dresser, a chair, and a nightstand.

Sustainability

Consider aesthetics, performance, and cost when selecting green materials. Embodied energy and life cycle analysis are two methods used to evaluate materials. Embodied energy calculates the total energy consumption embedded in a material from its raw state through manufacturing to transportation to the point of use. Life cycle analysis investigates the health and environmental impact at each stage of a product's life.

The Business and Institutional Furniture Manufacturer's Association (BIFMA) has invented a sustainability standard called Level that allows designers and architects to evaluate the environmental impact of furniture transparently. Level addresses a product's sustainability from many perspectives. Some of the considerations are

- Climate neutrality;
- efficiency of material usage;
- biodegradability;
- rapidly renewable materials;
- sustainably harvested woods and veneers;
- solvent-free and low-VOC adhesives, paints, and finishes;
- formaldehyde-free substrates;
- alternatives to hardwoods (such as wheat panel);
- high-pressure laminate that contains recycled content or recycled fibers;

- water-based stains and finishes;
- recycled steel and wire for springs;
- soy-based foams or latex rubber;
- pesticide-free cotton batting;
- fabrics with recycled content or natural fibers; and
- PVC alternatives, such as rubber.

PROCESS

On the most successful projects, the interior design team begins work early in the process: the interior designers should begin work in the schematic design phase at the latest. Interior design professionals are often part of the programming phase that tests adjacencies, room shapes, volumes, and sizes.

CHAPTER 16

RENOVATION, RESTORATION, AND ADAPTIVE REUSE

Many senior living facilities have become outdated and will have difficulty marketing themselves to the next generation of residents and their adult children. These older facilities cannot support contemporary care programs, and they lack the hospitality ambiance necessary to keep them competitive and financially viable. Given their antiquated hospital-like or "old age home" design model, these older facilities will also struggle to recruit and retain good healthcare workers. These problems can sometimes be solved through restoration or renovation.

LONG-TERM CARE FACILITIES

The following are problems commonly faced by existing long-term care facilities:

- Skilled care bedrooms are for two and sometimes three or more persons, offering residents little privacy.
- Skilled care toilet rooms are not handicapped accessible.
- Support functions, such as clean and soiled utility rooms, are remote from resident rooms. As a result, staff must make long trips to reach them, and soiled linen carts stack up in the corridors, creating an institutional environment.
- Nurses stations are isolated behind hospital-like counters. Enclosed nurses stations with high partitions or 36" high counters separate caregivers and wheelchair-bound residents.

- Insufficient lounge and activity space results in a line of residents in wheelchairs, usually near the nurses station. This creates congestion and a depressing, institutional environment.
- Heating, ventilation, and air-conditioning systems are old and noisy, with soiled filters and without resident-accessible controls.
- Smoke and fire alarm systems and emergency call systems are antiquated and confusing to residents with dementia.
- Corridors, dining, and activity rooms have glossy vinyl composition tile floors, 2" × 4" acoustic tile suspended ceilings with non-louvered fluorescent light fixtures, antiquated paging systems, and little or no natural light. They are institutional, cold, unattractive, and unappealing to potential residents and their families.
- Congested communal shower and tub rooms provide little privacy or dignity for residents and are neither well-ventilated nor illuminated properly. The flooring is not slip-resistant.
- Dining is centralized in large, institutional multipurpose rooms. As a result, residents do not enjoy dining and do not eat properly. And staff must spend too much time transporting residents to and from their rooms (fig. 16-1 and 16-2).
- There is little or no easily accessible outdoor sitting or activity space for residents and their families.

▶ Figures 16-1 and 16-2
Before and after photos of a
large dining room. After the
space is divided into four
separate restaurants,
residents have a choice of
venue and menu. Westminster
Village, Scottsdale, Arizona.
Perkins Eastman. Photograph
(right) by Chris Cooper.

ASSISTED LIVING FACILITIES

The following are problems commonly faced
by existing assisted living facilities:

- Small resident rooms are not much more
  than sleeping spaces.
- Bathing areas are shared by several
  residents.
- Resident bathrooms are neither homelike
  nor handicapped accessible. Many lack a
  countertop sink with space for towels
  and toiletries.
- Units lack tea kitchens, and residents or
  their children are unable to fix a snack or
  a simple meal.
- There is little or no space in units for residents to store their books or keep their
  television, knick-knacks, and memorabilia.
- There are few or no spaces for families to
  gather.
- There are insufficient activity spaces.

- Large, school-like, cafeteria-style dining
  rooms create an institutional atmosphere.
- There is little or no space for home
  healthcare aides and other nursing and
  housekeeping staff.
- Individuals cannot control the air temperature or velocity within residential units.
- There are no easily accessible outdoor
  sitting areas.

INDEPENDENT LIVING FACILITIES

The following are problems commonly faced
by existing independent living facilities:

- The bathroom in small residential apartments is not located in the bedroom and
  is not handicapped accessible.
- Residential apartments do not have
  washer/dryers, under-counter microwaves,
  dishwashers, or adequate countertops,
  closets, or storage.

- Residential apartment balconies are too small to accommodate a table and chairs for residents and guests.
- Residential apartments are too small to accommodate residents' furniture or technology.
- Residential apartments are connected to the main dining venues and educational rooms by long, badly lit corridors, making it difficult for residents to age in place.
- Inadequate activity, fitness, aquatic, or wellness facilities fail to meet residents' expectations.
- Communal resident entrances are unprotected from the elements.
- Lobbies and living rooms are not handicapped accessible and have an institutional ambiance.

If the basic structure and systems are sound, and the resident rooms, dining areas, and bathing areas are sized appropriately, the solution to many of these typical problems may be minor or cosmetic. In other cases, a moderate renovation and expansion can address them. But more and more facilities require a major renovation—or must be replaced—to resolve these issues.

COSMETIC RENOVATION

All heavily used facilities need regular rejuvenation; a major cosmetic asset upgrade every five to eight years is typical. Senior living and care facilities, however, usually cannot afford to renovate on such a short cycle, and they begin to show their age within ten years.

Sometimes a modest renovation can give an older facility new life. The most common approaches are to reprogram underutilized spaces; change floor, wall, and ceiling finishes; remove inappropriate elements; and upgrade the lighting. Taking an oversize lobby at the front door of the town center and creating a hotel-like living room with a fireplace, computers, and a small coffee shop creates the ambiance that marketing staff can use to overcome some of the community's other shortcomings (figs. 16-3 and 16-4). Indirect lighting, window treatments, and senior-friendly furniture and carpets can drastically alter an environment (figs. 16-5 and 16-6).

MODERATE RENOVATION

Cosmetic changes, however, may not address the issues that leave the facility unable to compete in the marketplace, merely postponing the inevitable. Many older facilities were designed for a younger, ambulatory population that had lower expectations for home-like or hospitality environments, restaurant-style dining, and apartment amenities and space. As a result, moderate changes must be made to accommodate both existing and future residents, including those who use assistive walking devices or wheelchairs. Future residents will demand more privacy and engaging program spaces nearer to their rooms or apartments.

A typical complication is that the facility must remain occupied during renovation. This may require constructing new wings or decreasing the population enough to free up space for a phased renovation. By navigating these significant challenges, moderate renovations can result in dramatic improvements.

MAJOR RENOVATION

In some cases, only a major reconstruction will reposition the facility to meet current functional, aesthetic, and market expectations, and make it code-compliant. Major renovations can cost as much as a new construction.

▶ *Figures 16-3 and 16-4*
Before and after photos of a
remodeled lobby that incorp-
orates a wi-fi café, lounge,
and music venue. Air Force
Villages, San Antonio, Texas.
Perkins Eastman. Photograph
(below) by Casey Dunn.

◀ *Figures 16-5 and 16-6*
Before and after photos of an
unused multipurpose room
on the eighteenth floor. It was
repurposed into a five-star
lounge and restaurant with a
wine bar and private dining
room. Air Force Villages,
San Antonio, Texas.
Perkins Eastman. Photograph
(below) by Casey Dunn.

Answer the following 12 questions before committing to either a major renovation or the construction of a new facility.

Key Questions

1. Will a major renovation or construction of new additions trigger a lengthy, expensive public land use review or amendment process or challenge grandfathered covenants?
2. Will a major renovation or new construction trigger mandatory compliance with new fire and accessibility codes, disrupting the entire facility or increasing costs?
3. Are there asbestos, lead paint, or other hazardous materials that will add costs or complicate renovation?
4. Are the resident apartments or skilled care rooms appropriately sized or can they be expanded or combined to create an attractive, competitive facility?
5. When finished, will the facility be competitive with or superior to existing or future facilities in the same market area?
6. Will the reuse of the existing structure leave the facility with an inefficient plan and insufficient space? Larger but unmarketable units? Will it involve extra costs resulting from too little floor-to-floor height? From creating a barrier-free environment?
7. Will any retained mechanical, electrical, plumbing, or fire-protection (MEPFP) systems result in excessive operating, maintenance, or replacement costs?
8. Will enough of the existing superstructure and MEPFP systems be reused to realize real savings compared to new construction?
9. Has the building envelope (foundation, windows, roofs, and exterior walls) been properly maintained, or have there been leaks and other problems that might have created hidden MEPFP or structural problems?
10. Is there a construction phasing strategy that will maintain occupancy economically and feasibly?
11. Can the residents' and staff's quality of life be maintained? Will the campus remain attractive enough to be marketed during the renovation?
12. Will the time saved by reusing all or parts of the existing facility create significant short- and long-term savings?

The answers to these questions can justify renovation. But owners should not be surprised if new construction turns out to be more cost-effective.

Integrated Scenario Planning

A unique planning process brings together the client and all the consultants very early on: it is called integrated scenario planning (ISP).

The process begins with the adoption of a strategic plan by the facility's board or management. Then a list of ideas, or an action/program list, is formed; those ideas will be tested on the existing campus.

A financial model of the campus's existing operations is then constructed. The model must be flexible enough to change in real time as new scenarios develop—the addition of programs or square footage, for example. Then any deferred maintenance items related to the short- and long-term building life cycle are allocated.

After touring the campus and buildings, focus groups are held with the current and future residents, department heads, and board members. These focus groups will define what programs are needed for the next generation of consumers as well as the issues that were identified in the strategic plan. The action/program and project parameters are then translated into a global spatial requirements matrix that describes square footage, quality of materials, and phasing criteria.

Each department head must then prioritize the program component and assist in the creation of values for a pricing exercise performed by the construction manager or general contractor. The financial feasibility consultant or the organization's CFO then runs the financial scenario model on all the continuum components identified in the matrix.

Once a model successfully meets the organization's financial objectives—such as the debt coverage ratio—the sponsor can green light the project and proceed to master planning.

ISP allows all stakeholders to identify a successful renovation or remodeling project without the cost of weeks of drawing concept plans that may never pan out.

ADAPTIVE REUSE

Recycling existing structures into modern independent living, assisted living, and long-term care facilities is another option. Elementary schools, buildings on college campuses, hotels, motels, and convents have all been adapted to meet the needs of the aging. These adaptive buildings might also be in locations that are more acceptable to the next generation of seniors.

To determine the feasibility of an adaptive reuse, analyze not only the twelve key questions for major renovations, above, but also seven additional questions that arise when changing the use of an existing structure.

Key Questions

- Is the building envelope and structure code-compliant, or can it be upgraded to be code-compliant, with the new intended senior use?
- Will the local land use and state and national building code officials support the adaptive reuse for ambulatory and non-ambulatory seniors?
- Is the building location and surrounding setting appropriate for seniors?
- Is the building's image appropriate? If not, can it be upgraded, made more residential, or otherwise changed to be appropriate?
- Are the building's existing floor plan, footprint, and dimensions appropriate? Are there creative ways to deal with excessive width (such as in a typical office or industrial building) or other floor plate issues?
- Will the configuration of the existing footprint permit a layout adapted for a particular use, adequate unit size for skilled care, and appropriate adjacencies? Are there creative ways to overcome any inefficiencies?
- Does the existing exterior fenestration enable an efficient layout, or can additional openings be created?

Answering the questions about renovation and reuse can be a creative way to develop a new environment for seniors in a setting that allows for urban or intergenerational integration.

CHAPTER 17

INTERNATIONAL CHALLENGES

The sociological, political, and economic challenges of an aging society are not confined to the United States. Worldwide, the number of people over 60 is expected to triple to two billion by 2050 (United Nations 2011, p. 11), making aging a concern for countries both rich and poor. In fact, the impacts of aging will be more pronounced outside the United States. The United Nations estimates that although the U.S. population's median age is expected to rise from 37.2 today to 41.7 by 2050, Germany's median age may rise to 51.7 and Japan's to 55.1 by that date[1].

Our planet provides both challenges and opportunities for senior living community design. Although the developed countries of Europe and North America, as well as Japan, have entrenched medical, health, and welfare policies and systems, most countries in the developing world do not. This is problematic, but it is also an opportunity to help newly emerging aging societies create social, political, and economic systems that avoid the mistakes that have been made elsewhere. The struggling economies in these countries would make European-style, state-sponsored social welfare models hard to replicate. In developing countries, the private sector will have to meet more of these needs.

The physical and mental impacts of the aging process are universal, as is the need for specialized senior housing. Aging Japanese,

for example, develop Alzheimer's, arthritis, and other impairments that make living in an apartment with tatami mats impractical. Moreover, many of their children live far away, and moving to live with them is not feasible. And even Japanese who expected to care for their aged parents are investigating other options. The situation is similar in other countries as well.

In the past, much of the innovation and many of the best models for senior housing and care were found in the United Kingdom and Scandinavia. However, the relatively small, stable populations in these countries make these models impractical for larger countries with a rapidly growing aging population. As a result, sponsors in other large countries often look to the United States and Canada, where larger models exist.

Does Western senior living design expertise translate to other countries? Although the physiological and cognitive changes in the elderly are similar worldwide, each country develops unique responses to aging

> In Europe, countries became rich before they became old. But in the developing world, countries are growing old before they become rich.
>
> *Gro Harlem Brundtland, former director general, World Health Organization[2]*

---

[1] "The Median Age of 1950-2050 (an animated interactive map)" http://www.datapult.info/en/content/median-age-1950-2050-animated-interactive-map

[2] Economic Commission for Latin America and the Caribbean, *Population Ageing in the Caribbean: An Inventory of Policies, Programmes and Future Challenges,* May 11, 2004, p. 3.

Table 17-1 Global Aging						
	Number of Residents 60+ (in thousands)		Percent of Total Population 60+		Percent of Total Population 80+	
	2002	2050	2002	2050	2002	2050
USA	46,960	106,660	16	27	21	8
China	134,243	436,980	10	30	9	23
India	81,089	324,316	8	21	8	15

United Nations, Population Division, Department of Economic and Social Affairs, "Population Aging 2002."

based on social customs and traditions, politics, existing health systems, and legal and regulatory situation.

Many of the examples cited in this chapter are from recent experiences in Asia, because the wealth and sophistication of a growing number of countries there have opened up a potentially large market for experienced North American architecture and design firms. Europe, and some other developed regions have their own seasoned firms, but only a few countries in the developing world have the financial wherewithal to import design expertise for this building type.

China and India in particular have recently begun to explore and develop new models of policy, education, service delivery, and facility design to address their rapidly expanding elderly population. While their demographic shifts are of different makings,

Today's problems with the oldest old appear to exist in North America, Europe, and Japan. However, by 2025, China and India will push the U.S. into third place in the 80+ population.

Regnier 2002, p. 8.

the situation in both will dramatically remake their society.

Often perceived as a country of young and inexpensive labor, China's working-age population will actually begin to contract in 2015, and the number of Chinese over 65 is trending to over 400 million by 2050.

India, while younger overall, is also beginning to see both the benefits and societal responsibilities of increasing numbers of elderly. Life expectancies are approaching 70, and over 64 million Indians were 65 or older in 2010. This number will rise to over 97 million in 2020.

What does retirement look like in countries where the concept was all but unknown only decades ago? With retirement ages ranging from 55 to 60, both China and India face additional challenges as large numbers of relatively healthy and active individuals leave the workforce to retire. The notion of what "old" is in each country, increasing life spans, and younger retirement ages than those found in the West will affect how designers and developers approach retirement housing.

When North American design teams do work overseas, they have to be educators as well as designers. Though the United States has senior living facilities more than 100 years old, and almost all Americans have had a relative or friend who has lived in a long-term care setting of some sort, the same is not true overseas: the typical resident of the growing number of facilities in Tokyo, Osaka, and Kyoto is the first person in his or her family to move into a senior living community. Educating the client, local opinion leaders, regulators and politicians, staff members, and potential customers and their families is central to any international design opportunity.

SERVICE DEVELOPMENT

Working overseas offers an opportunity to do something different. Differences in regulatory and reimbursement environments demand more flexible thinking about what services to provide and how to provide them. The long list of settings for older adults described in chapter 2 was developed from historical and current U.S. regulations, reimbursement practices, and traditions. Assisted living, for example, became popular as a non-institutional residential response to the shortcomings and deficiencies of traditional nursing homes. Key to assisted living's rapid development was the private sector's ability to convince potential customers and their adult children that this new approach was kinder and more compassionate, and therefore worth both the paying of higher monthly charges and foregoing potential governmental support such as Medicaid.

But what if government reimbursement did not draw artificial distinctions between independent living, assisted living, dementia care, and skilled nursing, as in Japan? There, the *kaigo hoken* system focuses on aging in place, and a menu of care options allows residents to choose the one that responds to their own needs, setting few limits on what services are performed in any particular

place. As a result, the U.S. model, with its rigid regulation of services and facilities, is inappropriate.

The leading sponsor of new senior living options in Japan has used foreign design teams that have had to evolve new service models. For example, Tokyo's Sun City Chofu, 3-story, 118-unit "life care" project built in 2004 combines 94 independent and assisted living units on the top two floors with 24 beds with 24-hour monitoring for dementia and skilled nursing on the ground floor. The result is a new business model where pricing, including entry and monthly fees, is tailored to individual circumstances. Entry is based on the customer's physical and cognitive situation.

On average, residents enter a U.S. independent living facility in their late 70s. But with retirees leaving the workforce at 55, India's first-generation communities have focused on the active adult market, and the design and operations differences between the Indian and American facilities are significant. For example, in the United States, security concerns are a significant motivation for seniors' decision to move into a purpose-built community. In India, younger customers shift the focus to protecting their finances, whereas in the United States and Japan, the priority is healthcare. As a result, accommodations in most of India's senior housing offerings are sold to residents, and the communities provide very little care programming, dining options, or other amenities.

China's propensity to think big about most development initiatives is resulting in continuing care retirement communities (CCRCs) of 1,000, 2,000, or even more resident units. While perhaps necessary to address the scale of China's burgeoning aging population, communities of this size challenge heretofore commonly held standards for operational models and the creation of successful communities of seniors. Is there such a thing as "too big" for a senior community?

The urban high-rise retirement community is a U.S. invention whose development and perfection may occur overseas. In contrast to the low-rise settings of most U.S. senior living products, senior housing in the large cities of Asia and around the world call for high-rise solutions. The Ginza East Tower, which opened in 2006, is an early example. This life care community's 31 floors include 276 independent living apartments, a 120-bed care center, a health club, two restaurants, and other social clubs and cultural spaces. Security, planning for efficient staffing, and designing for an in-town population likely to be five years older and more frail than those in the suburbs were key issues in the design process (fig. 17-1).

The availability and cost of labor differs widely from country to country in Asia. Countries with low labor costs are able to offer lower staff-to-resident ratios than most developed countries. But in Japan—a young country just 60 years ago but now one of the world's oldest societies—labor costs are high and the workforce is shrinking. Japan is therefore increasingly relying less on staff and more on technology to assist with bathing, personal mobility, and communications (fig. 17-2).

PROGRAMMING AND DESIGN

How people live, eat, bathe, and socialize makes program requirements for international projects different from their counterparts in the United States. And sometimes these traditions are at odds with the changing needs of older adults, making the designer's task more difficult. The traditional Japanese lifestyle, for example, where a large proportion of time is spent on tatami mat floors, is ill-suited to older adults with a declining range of movement, inflexible knee joints, poor balance, and increased susceptibility to drafts. And although Japanese love to soak in a tub at day's end, deteriorating upper-body strength may make it impossible to get out of the tub afterward. Before starting any overseas assignment, an architect should spend some time getting to know local lifestyles firsthand, even staying with a family, if possible.

A big factor in designing for seniors in Japan, for instance, is the very small size of personal living spaces. Apartments are roughly half the size of corresponding units in the United States, and independent living units typically range from 450–850 sq ft. However, the Japanese entertain in an amenity-rich common space, not a smaller private one. This arrangement can benefit the overall community, as a greater density of living units allows for a larger, richer common space program and common space costs can be spread across a larger number of residents. Denser communities also result in shorter walking distances to dining and other amenity spaces.

Food is as important overseas as it is in the United States, but cultural differences impact space requirements, staffing, operations costs, soft development costs, and kitchen programming For example, in Japan it is traditional to change dishware with the seasons and holidays, requiring more than twice the dish storage space of an American community of the same size. Different cookware and utensils are used for fish than for meat and vegetables. Daily deliveries from a large number of suppliers are typical. This reduces long-term stock space but complicates the choreography and staffing for delivery, preparation, service, and trash removal.

◀ Figure 17-1 Many of the overseas retirement communities in large Asian cities must be developed on small urban sites. This 427,000 sq ft CCRC in Tokyo was built on a 50,714 sq ft site. Sun City Ginza East, Tokyo, Japan. Perkins Eastman. Photograph by Milroy and McAleer Photography.

Some of the first CCRCs in India are planned to have at least one servant living in each of the independent living units and assume that the servant's duties include meal preparation and service in the unit itself.

Bathing, health, and beauty are closely related in many places around the world. Until recently, senior communities in both Asia and Scandinavia placed much greater emphasis on bathing-related programs than

▶ *Figure 17-2 Rooftop Japanese ofuro (tub) with lift-equipped bathing pool in the foreground. Hatsutomi Royal Care Garden, Hatsutomi, Japan.*
Perkins Eastman.

did those in America, although the increasing numbers of healthy aging is forcing the United States to catch up. Japanese settings for older adults, even at the skilled nursing level, provide significantly more space for *onsen*-style bathing. This increases both total space requirements and construction costs. An American 350-unit CCRC might devote about 10 sq ft per unit to swimming pools, Jacuzzis, exercise areas, and locker rooms; Tokyo's Sun City Kanagawa, a typical upscale Japanese product, allocates 30–35 sq ft per unit to these uses.

In low-cost-labor countries such as India and Thailand, depending on personal staff for cooking, cleaning, and other assistance is common. Early senior community programming studies in both countries suggest that residents may expect that personal staff to accompany them to a senior community.

What, then, is the interaction between and division of responsibilities between facility staff and resident staff? What accommodations must be made for personal staff? What are the implications for programming and construction costs when the effective population of a community is larger than that with a Western staffing model? "Assisted living" may mean something quite different in this context.

Asian cultures share a variety of beliefs about geomancy and feng shui that impact room layouts, building-to-building orientations, and even site selection. South-facing units are preferred or even required in countries with a cooler climate, like China and Japan. This can lead to inefficient single-loaded corridors, increased walking distances, and deep, narrow apartments. In countries with hot climates like India and

Thailand, residences must have shelter from the midday sun, which impacts site strategies and building geometries.

Vastu in India is comparable to feng shui, but its guidelines necessitate a different design response. For climatic reasons, *vastu* requires the highest part of a building complex to face southwest, to shelter the rest of the building from the the sun's heat at the hottest time of day.

SERVICE AND SOCIALIZATION

Design concepts are impacted by differences in values and beliefs about staff roles. While many U.S. and European communities encourage residents to participate in community governance, the current generation of Asian customers may expect a more hotel-like environment.

Even in a CCRC, independent living residents may not want to interact with or even see residents of the care center, which is therefore hidden or located out of the way. But in some senior communities in the United States, operators follow the philosophy of the Pennsylvania-based Kendal Corporation. In their communities, all residents are part of one community, and all areas and amenities are available and accessible to all. The "one community" view seems more popular in societies that traditionally revere the aged.

PROCESS

Client-consultant relationships and communications, project delivery, and economics can vary considerably from the American model.

Communication differences are by far the most important and include not only language barriers but those resulting from cultural traditions, government–private sector relations, religion, and family values. Designers contemplating international design

opportunities will succeed only if they are committed to meeting clients at least half-way, with staff fluent in the home country's language. This is especially important because the designer will be an educator as well, called upon throughout the design, construction, and startup process to explain the community's objectives, its design, the details of its program, and the essence of its operation to widening circles of client, staff, politicians, regulators, local architects, contractors, subcontractors, operations staff, and possibly customers and their families.

Whenever possible, communications should be simple, direct, and clear. Use images and charts and keep words to a minimum. Always explain the goals and objectives behind a recommendation and how it fits into the project as a whole.

European and American concepts of professional training and qualifications are not uniformly employed elsewhere in the world. In many areas, hierarchical relationships are the norm and put architects at the bottom of the client-designer-builder triumvirate. Designers should research the local situation and the client thoroughly. By and large, U.S. architects have been most successful overseas when contracted directly by the client, and the U.S. team's responsibilities and authority in relation to local architects and contractors must be clearly delineated. The client has enlisted U.S. experts in senior living design because there is a lack of similar knowledge locally. This usually means the client expects the U.S. team to take responsibility for the design, function, quality, image, and sales success of the finished senior living product.

U.S.-style construction documents, bidding, and document-intensive construction administration are rare outside North America. In some countries, design-build approaches shift a large percentage of design detail and construction system definition to the contractor. In others, the local architects and engineers handling the construction documents are not used to the interior detailing required by high-quality senior living environments. The result is often local permit documents that are less detailed than the U.S. team's design-development set. This practice can create serious design coordination problems among the architects and engineers and make any early cost estimates less reliable. Successful U.S. designers have had to be more specific than usual in the early stages and provide a clearer and more complete set of design-development drawings and specifications. They also plan considerably more time for the later phases to answer to frequent phone calls, faxes, e-mails, and texts seeking clarification of drawings and specifications.

Building codes in Asia range from equivalent to U.S. standards to substandard for the specialized requirements of designing for seniors; setting appropriate standards up front is therefore critical. This may involve educating all team members, from the client to the local design associate, and especially the U.S. team itself. When local standards and practices fall short of life safety requirements for similar facilities in the United States, it may be in everyone's interests to build to U.S. standards. Indeed, doing so may prove to be a valuable advantage when marketing to well-traveled seniors who have lived or stayed in Western accommodations and seek similar quality in their retirement housing.

Project budgets will vary considerably with location, the economics of local real estate, and client motivation. Senior living communities are a balance of housing, hospitality, and healthcare. Senior living sponsors in different countries are responding to their market perceptions differently, but all know that market expectations are evolving

rapidly. As senior living markets evolve, the perception of senior living communities by increasingly sophisticated consumers will change as well.

Early senior living developments in Taiwan, for example, have been perceived primarily as a special kind of real estate—a sort of serviced apartment for retirees. In India today, the residents want to own their unit. In China, seniors are often satisfied with small, spartan units to which they are accustomed, but it is unlikely such units will satisfy the next generation of retirees. All of these views are likely to evolve as the need for supportive senior living is better understood by the next generation of seniors.

In Japan, life care communities attract customers interested in purchasing peace of mind in a society whose public welfare health insurance system faces bankruptcy, and accessible design is becoming standard for all independent living apartments. In a development outside Seoul, Korea, the emphasis on hospitality required regrading the site to incorporate a full-scale health club. With gymnasium, swimming pool, racquetball courts, and golf practice tees to complement the aerobics rooms, weights, and exercise equipment, the club is available to all residents of Korea's first CCRC as well as families in the adjacent Samsung housing estate. And for the designer, consumers' interest in purchasing may mean a focus on sales-to-area ratio; developers may forego full handicapped accessibility for bigger closets or add units instead of programmable public space.

AGING AT HOME

In the coming decade there will be an increase in the cross-pollination of new ideas about senior living design between Asia, North America, and Europe. Ten years from now, a list of the most exclusive retirement communities in the world may include facilities in Tokyo, Shanghai, Singapore, and Hong Kong (fig. 17-3). Western Europe will expand its existing options, while eastern European countries will look for affordable solutions, with the private sector taking a larger role than it has historically in northern Europe. In South America, the private sector will respond to the limited but growing demand for senior living options for the middle class and the wealthy. Limited public budgets will probably delay response to the need for government-supported programs.

But with one in five Americans now born overseas, part of the international challenge begins at home. Foreign-born residents of American facilities for the aging will stimulate flexible thinking, the ability to design across cultural differences, and the search for more creative programmatic responses to the needs of an increasingly diverse population.

COUNTRY-SPECIFIC ISSUES

The following is a brief examination of some of the challenges that shape senior living

planning and design overseas. The discussion of China, Japan, India, and Thailand illustrates the significant differences among countries even beyond these four.

China

As Table 17-1 illustrates, by the middle of this century, China's population of seniors will exceed the current population of the United States. An increasing life expectancy and China's one-child policy have already made quality senior living a major issue. As the number of seniors increases, the traditional caregiver population—the children—is in decline. Moreover, government policy requires women to retire in their fifties and men to retire in their early to mid-sixties, and retirees' pensions are meager. The government has recognized the crisis but is asking the private sector to respond to it since there are many other problems competing for government resources.

In China, children have traditionally been expected to care for their aging parents; failing in that duty is even considered

◀ Figure 17-3 Some wealthy seniors are opting to retire in resort settings, such as this resort-based active adult and retirement community west of Shanghai. Landgent Moganshan, Zhejiang, People's Republic of China. Perkins Eastman.

shameful. However, the strict enforcement of the government's one-child-only policy has created what has come to be called the "4-2-1 problem." As reported in the *New York Times*, "In part because of the one-child policy, soon a single person in China will be expected to help support two parents and four grandparents,"[3] an overwhelming responsibility by any standards. Moreover, many adult children have moved far away from their parents to find employment; their parents' pensions are tied to their current place of residence, making a move closer to their children impossible. Concerned about adult children who shirk their responsibility to their parents, China even proposed a law requiring children to visit their parents "regularly."[4]

Unlike the Japanese and citizens of other more developed Asian countries, Chinese elderly are rarely wealthy. Due to the economic turmoil that extended through the Cultural Revolution, in the 1960s and 1970s, most older Chinese have few resources. Most wealth is in the hands of those under 50. Retired government workers, senior military officers, and senior managers of both state-owned and private industries; the parents of adult children now part of the new middle and wealthy classes; and overseas Chinese returning to China to retire can usually afford market-rate senior living options (fig. 17-4). But the vast majority of the elderly in China cannot. While there are some very limited programs for those without adequate income, the need for affordable options is a big problem in China, and

it is getting bigger. In 2011, only 1.3 percent of China's seniors lived in state retirement homes.[5]

The private sector is beginning to mobilize. Insurance companies and private developers have been studying the market and are committing to their first projects. Because they "make no little plans" in China, many of these companies plan to roll out a program of 100 or more large-scale senior living communities. Too many of these companies see senior living as a real estate opportunity, but a growing number understand that it is a business requiring new management, care, and operations skills.

Several things ensure that successful Chinese models will differ from those in more developed countries, including the very low cost of skilled labor, the relatively low cost of construction, the high cost of land, rapid urbanization, and a culture that reveres the aged. As a result, some Chinese senior living communities are likely to be intergenerational: parents *and* their children will live there. Care will initially be provided primarily by home healthcare workers, more communities will occupy high-rise buildings in urban settings, and most of the initial models will be concentrated in the wealthier cities of the eastern coastal provinces.

The private sector's response is complicated by likely changes in resident expectations. The current cohort of seniors grew up in an era when entire families lived in one room and had a very modest outlook on life. But many adult children now live in modern apartments or homes that rival the size and

---

[3] David Barboza, "China, in a Shift to Acceptance, Takes On Its Alzheimer's Problem," *New York Times*, January 13, 2011.

[4] *China Daily*, "Debate: Aging Population," p. 9.

[5] Patti Waldmeir, "China Looks Forward To Age Of The 'Silvertown'" *Financial Times*, April 29, 2011, p. 8.

◀ Figure 17.4 Entirely new lifestyle communities are being planned to attract seniors and their families. This community near Beijing contains a broad range of senior housing and care facilities. Eco-Town, Hebei, People's Republic of China. Perkins Eastman.

amenities of those in developed countries. Moreover, there is an almost complete lack of successful senior living models and experienced operators (and of consulting resources to guide the development of successful models); a shortage of experienced caregivers; and limited consumer awareness of senior living options. As a result, some of the early projects have been poorly conceived and have not achieved the level of success that would inspire other developments.

The lack of local experience and options is particularly apparent when it comes to more complex senior living needs. The *New York Times* reported that Shanghai has over 120,000 seniors with Alzheimer's and almost no facilities designed to provide appropriate care. "To cope with a severe shortage of nursing homes, Shanghai is proposing what it calls the 90-7-3 plan, which means 90 percent of the elderly will be cared for at home, while 7 percent make occasional visits to a community center and 3 percent live in nursing homes."[6]

These factors have created a significant opportunity for international design firms, consultants, and operators. Yet only a few international firms have taken up the challenge. But those firms that do get involved find an enormous market for their services —and come up against the many challenges of doing business in China. Because of this market's complexity, involvement demands a

---

[6] David Barboza, "China, in a Shift to Acceptance, Takes On Its Alzheimer's Problem," *New York Times*, January 13, 2011.

commitment to learning what it takes to be successful, from respect for *feng shui* to regional food preferences.

Japan

Japan is the pioneer in Asia in addressing the needs of the aging and is two decades ahead of its neighbors in devising and implementing strategies for integrating the needs of its aged into national planning and adapting international models to its own culture (figs.17.5 and 17.6). With this head start, Japan's experiences along the way can provide valuable lessons for other Asian countries now contemplating the needs of their growing numbers of seniors.

With a population that peaked in 2005, Japan is facing unprecedented challenges: one in five Japanese is 65 or older, and there are now over 50,000 Japanese over the age of 100 [7].

At the policy level, the centerpiece of the Japanese safety net for seniors is the *kaigo hoken*—long-term care insurance (LTCI). These services are available to seniors in their own homes or in facilities located in their communities. The successor to the Gold Plan introduced in 1990, the LTCI program is intended to provide a more stable long-term financial foundation than its predecessor. While a great success of the Gold Plan was the shifting of senior care from an extended-stay hospital model to a community-based, in-house model, the strong demand for these taxpayer-funded services and the lack of effective cost-controls threatened its viability. Reforms in the *kaigo hoken* introduced in 2000 included levying insurance premiums on all workers over 40 and shifting the program's administration to municipalities.

All Japanese over 65 are eligible for LTCI benefits; eligibility for specific services is determined through a questionnaire plus a review by a committee of experts. Once that eligibility is established, a care manager is assigned and a program that meets the individual's needs is devised. Four levels of care are available: preventative, home visits, community day care, and skilled nursing. Individuals are expected to cover 10 percent of all services costs. The program's emphasis is on aging in place—in an individual's own home—and housing, food, and other domestic costs are not reimbursed.

The program seems to be successful in keeping the elderly at home: the Tokyo Municipal Government reports that the number of residents utilizing home healthcare services increased more than threefold from 2000 to 2008, while facility-based services only increased twofold during the same period. One factor in this disparity is that demand for nursing home beds has exceeded supply, and some long-term care facilities have waiting lists. Nonetheless, with 75 percent of all LTCI beneficiaries using home healthcare, the commitment to, and embrace of, the home healthcare model is clear.

Expecting the government to provide attractive reimbursements, a large number of private companies entered the senior living business when the government opened the market in the mid-1990s. Instead, competition and spending controls have kept costs in check, and the market has proven to be quite challenging for private providers.

India

India's demographics certainly point to a robust opportunity for an innovative senior living concept that combines housing with

---

[7] Yoree Koh, "Japan Centenarian Population Tops 50,000," *Wall Street Journal Japan*, September 14, 2012.

supportive living services, manages healthcare needs, and provides access to a vibrant and unique lifestyle. The Westernization of the culture and changing social patterns of family-based elder care also suggest that there will be new demands for supportive living services for seniors. Limited property, home ownership and wealth in much of the over-65 population will challenge traditional senior living financial models. Lack of government regulation, reimbursement, or policy are an opportunity for creative solutions to India's dearth of services for the aging.

In 1950, the life expectancy in India was 38 years; today it is almost 70. There were 44 million people over 65 in 2000, 64 million in 2010, and will be a projected 97 million in 2020. The current unit count for old age homes for the poor is 75,000 to 80,000, while the total number being developed for the middle class is 5,000.

Many of the existing senior living offerings for the middle class are niche real estate schemes targeting active seniors over 55. Ownership security is the primary selling point, and little attention is given to community-building or the care needs of residents as they age. However, interest on the part of developers and investors, as well as the government, has increased significantly in the last decade.

Indian seniors place a very high value on family and social networks, and the collective family care model is still largely in place. However, a study by HelpAge India on the state of the Indian family suggests that this model is not keeping up with society. Insecurity, loneliness, and boredom are major complaints by survey respondents, and 93 percent find the concept of senior citizen's homes, senior citizen's clubs, and senior citizen's associations either excellent (29 percent) or good (64 percent). Personal

needs are changing with urbanization and lengthening life spans.

India is a nation of extreme contrasts. There is a large, highly educated elite and middle class, but there is a much larger number of extremely poor. As is true in most developing (and many more developed) countries, the market for senior living design services is focused almost exclusively on the upper-income segment of the population. This group tends to have fewer children, many of whom live or work abroad, and the wealth to consider alternatives to traditional multigenerational family living arrangements.

The private sector is beginning to respond to the growing demand for senior living communities, but the response is complicated by consumers' lack of knowledge, the lack of operational expertise, high land costs, the higher returns possible with other types of development, and other factors, all of which have slowed the development of senior living in India. But it is coming. In the interim, it is a growing market for Western firms that can provide more than traditional planning and design services. Moreover, some leading Indian corporations have decided to enter the field, and in 2011, several innovative projects were in development (fig. 17-7).

Labor costs are low in India, and a family might hire help for housekeeping, laundry, meals, gardening, and driving. While one theory holds that the rich will simply hire all the help they need to age in place, it is difficult to manage a household staff. Turnover, unreliability, and a lack of training in eldercare all underscore the attractiveness of a senior community.

Non-resident Indians (NRIs) may become an important determinant in the development of senior community models. Some adult children living and working abroad will

▶ *Figures 17-5 and 17-6*
Japan is adapting
international models to its
own culture. Sun City
Takatsuki, Takatsuki, Japan.
Perkins Eastman. Photographs
by Chuck Choi.

Figure 17-7 *A growing number of senior living options are being developed in India, including this large CCRC in a resort setting.* Antara Senior Living Community, Dehradun, India.
Perkins Eastman.

fund their parent's retirement back in India; others will return to India to retire. Either way, Western money and Western expectations will influence the communities targeted to an NRI population and their parents. Understanding these expectations is key to providing options responsive to the needs of the entire Indian family.

Thailand

Thailand's demographics are similar to those of other Southeast Asian countries. The population is relatively young; by Western standards, the percentage of those over 65 (8.7 percent) is small. With a population of 66 million, 70 percent of which is rural, Thailand's economy has only recently begun to mature. With a significant decline in birth rate in the last two decades, the percentage of elderly will rise steadily in the years ahead.

The Thai economy and the country's demographics suggest that a middle-class market for senior living communities is years away. An early market entrant should therefore be targeted to upper-income clientele, who must currently choose between relying on untrained personal staff and family or expensive stays in a high-quality private hospital for care. Although many expatriates from the West and Japan move to Thailand to retire, most live on their own, as there are few senior living communities.

Thailand has always been a medical tourism destination. Patients come from around the world for affordable medical procedures and elective surgeries. In the process, patients and their families are exposed to the warm climate and low cost of living. A government program through the Tourism Authority of Thailand is attempting to increase the number of long-stay visa foreigners over 50, a market already interested in ready access to high-quality healthcare. The program targets visitors who stay between one and six months per year. Because they cannot remain for the rest of the year, this market is limited to those interested in a second home retirement for active adults. Currently, strict visa limitations are placed on people with disabilities or the aged with significant care needs, though the potential for a senior living industry targeted at foreigners is greater in Thailand than in its neighbors.

The Americas

Many countries in the Americas are also becoming markets for senior living development. Canada, of course, is already responding to the needs of it senior citizens in a manner similar to the United States. It is in the countries south of the border where adapting U.S. experience presents the biggest opportunities.

According to projections by the Latin American and Caribbean Demographic Centre (CELADE), the base of the population pyramid is shrinking rapidly due to declining birth rates, and the number of elderly is increasing due to longer life spans. There were approximately 43 million individuals over 60 in 2000. This number is projected to rise to over 100 million (15 percent of the population) by 2025 and to over 180 million (over 24 percent of the population) by 2050. Many of these seniors will be supported by their families, but a growing number will not. Moreover, there are a significant number of sophisticated consumers in many of the Latin American and Caribbean countries who will be looking for the same options as U.S. seniors. It is likely that the development responses will look to U.S. models.

In addition, Latin America and the Caribbean have become retirement destinations for seniors from the United States.

▶ *Figure 17-8 Northern Europe has developed innovative new environments for the aging. Humanitas-Bergweg, Rotterdam, Netherlands.*
Courtesy of Humanitas-Bergweg.

Mexico and Costa Rica, in particular, are becoming home to a rapidly growing number of American seniors seeking affordable retirement options in a warm climate. As this trend continues, it is likely that U.S. design professionals will become involved in building new communities and facilities.

Europe
In the more prosperous European countries, the development of senior living is mainly the province of the local design and development firms, and European models continue to be worthy of study (fig. 17-8).

CONCLUSION
The rapid growth of the number of aged is a worldwide trend. While many countries will be too poor or focused on other social challenges to respond, design firms should look to the countries and regions discussed in this chapter for opportunities to meet the growing demand for senior living internationally.

CHAPTER 18

OPERATION AND MAINTENANCE

The first cost of the building is a fraction of the total cost of that building and its operation and maintenance. In staff-intensive facilities such as nursing homes, the debt service for the money borrowed to build the facility may be less than 20 percent of the annual operating budget. Therefore, most experienced sponsors want to minimize the cost of staffing, operating, and maintaining their facilities.

INTRODUCTION

A well-designed senior living community must be easy to operate and maintain and require lower-than-average investments in daily cleaning, operations staff, utilities costs, and routine and long-term maintenance. In addition, well-designed communities limit the hospitality and care staff needed to provide the desired level of resident services. Thus the design for operations and maintenance has three goals: reduce ongoing running costs, maximize durability, and support high-efficiency staffing.

Operating costs fall into the following categories:

- Labor-related
  - Administrative
  - Dietary
  - Housekeeping
  - Maintenance
  - Care staff
  - Marketing
  - Other departments
- Non-labor-related
  - Taxes
  - Insurance
  - Raw food
- Utilities
- Marketing
- Repairs and maintenance
- Housekeeping
- Management fees
- Other

Many of these expense categories can be controlled or reduced by careful facility planning and design.

Labor costs are the largest part of operating costs. These costs can vary significantly by region, code mandate, level of service, degree of unionization, and building type. A survey conducted by the American Seniors Housing Association (ASHA) illustrates the range of full time equivalents staff (FTEs) by category of senior housing (table 18-1).

As table 18-1 illustrates, the staffing in many operations areas varies by 50–100 percent between facilities. Older, inefficient facilities staffed with unionized labor in higher labor-cost regions often struggle financially.

The same wide ranges in operating costs are found in other cost categories as well. Total utilities costs by resident day, for example, are illustrated in the *State of Seniors Housing 2010* survey results (table 18-2).

These costs have been rising steadily and have fueled the growing interest in the long-term savings achievable with sustainable design (see chapter 7).

Repairs, maintenance, and housekeeping costs are also significant. The same study notes that these three categories average between 8–11 percent of total expenses across the same three building types. Long-term, low-maintenance materials and systems

Table 18-1 FTEs per Resident by Labor Department and Property Type									
	Independent Living			Assisted Living			CCRC		
Department	Lower Quartile	Median	Upper Quartile	Lower Quartile	Median	Upper Quartile	Lower Quartile	Median	Upper Quartile
Administrative	0.02	0.03	0.05	0.03	0.04	0.05	0.01	0.02	0.03
Dietary	0.08	0.10	0.12	0.06	0.10	0.13	0.11	0.12	0.15
Housekeeping	0.03	0.03	0.03	0.02	0.03	0.04	0.04	0.06	0.07
Maintenance	0.01	0.01	0.02	0.01	0.02	0.02	0.02	0.03	0.05
Marketing	0.01	0.01	0.02	0.01	0.01	0.02	0.01	0.01	0.01
Assisted Living	0.06	0.08	0.12	0.19	0.28	0.37	0.03	0.04	0.08
Skilled Nursing	***	***	***	0.03	0.04	0.09	0.11	0.13	0.21
Other	0.00	0.02	0.03	0.01	0.02	0.03	0.02	0.05	0.09
Total	0.16	0.24	0.32	0.41	0.50	0.62	0.39	0.48	0.60

*** A minority of independent living properties reported nursing-related revenue in properties without licensed skilled nursing units, which is likely indicative of the provision of temporary private-duty nursing services to independent living residents.

Source: American Seniors Housing Association, 2010, p. 63.

Table 18-2 Total Utilities by Resident Day by Community Type: Quartile Analysis			
	Lower Quartile ($)	Median ($)	Upper Quartile ($)
Independent Living	3.97	4.67	5.67
Assisted Living	4.10	4.81	5.79
CCRC (all)	4.84	5.67	8.45
CCRC (for-profit)	5.26	5.59	7.59
CCRC (nonprofit)	4.35	5.51	7.11
All Communities	4.12	4.86	5.94

Source: American Seniors Housing Association 2010, p. 69.

choices can significantly reduce these expenses.

OPERATIONS COSTS

Real estate, staffing, and operations and maintenance costs vary considerably depending on resident needs and services offered. Operations and maintenance costs are divided into three components: running and maintenance costs, including building operations staff; repair and replacement costs, including phased replacement of both mechanical equipment and finishes; and utilities costs.

In senior living, staffing and real estate costs are inversely related. As the level of service increases, the impact of real estate costs (land, building construction, FF&E,

financing, and taxes) diminishes. Whereas a 10 percent increase in real estate costs is likely to have a similar impact on total costs in independent living, its impact is only one-third as large in dementia care. On the other hand, a design that saves one full-time nursing staff member on each shift can save over $120,000 and cover the debt service on $1.5 to 2 million of capital costs (fig. 18-1).

ONGOING OPERATING AND MAINTENANCE COSTS

Ongoing operating and maintenance costs include cleaning, scheduled and routine maintenance for building systems, and operations (facility management) personnel. Operations-friendly community design includes locating primary mechanical and electrical equipment in just a few, easy-access locations; locating all major controls for building equipment, elevators, fire alarm, emergency/nurse call, and telephone/data systems in one area near administration or nighttime security staff; providing elevator access to rooftop equipment areas to facilitate parts replacement; and providing access

hatches to subfloor pit areas for the maintenance of plumbing drains.

Design teams should not select overly complex controls and technology, such as advanced facility management systems, which are costly and require highly trained personnel to operate and maintain. The complicated computer-based management of mechanical systems, for example, may be too complex for the maintenance staff that operate and maintain most senior housing and care facilities. Sometimes, simpler is better.

At a smaller scale, operations-friendly design includes locating light switches in central locations for easier after-hours control; providing switched outlets so that table and floor lamps can be controlled from central locations; specifying light fixtures that minimize the number of different types of bulbs required; providing positive drainage in both paved and landscaped areas; specifying low-maintenance ground cover in place of grass; and installing low-glare site lighting such that bulbs can be changed using a ladder rather than a lift (fig. 18-2).

Cleaning costs are directly related to materials specifications for floors and walls. While

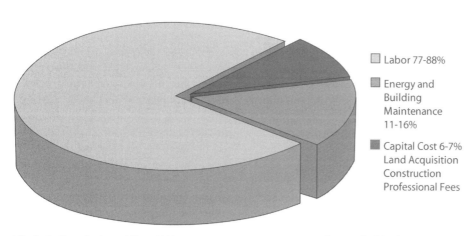

Life Cycle Costs Projected Over 40 Years

Labor 77-88%

Energy and Building Maintenance 11-16%

Capital Cost 6-7% Land Acquisition Construction Professional Fees

Source: Perkins Eastman

◀ Figure 18-1 Life cycle costs projected over 40 years. Perkins Eastman.

▶ *Figure 18-2 Appropriate interior design details can make a resident's room easier to occupy for residents and easier to maintain for staff. Perkins Eastman.*

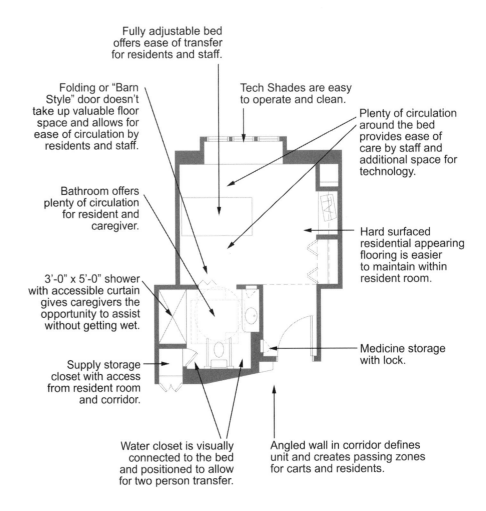

Fully adjustable bed offers ease of transfer for residents and staff.

Folding or "Barn Style" door doesn't take up valuable floor space and allows for ease of circulation by residents and staff.

Tech Shades are easy to operate and clean.

Plenty of circulation around the bed provides ease of care by staff and additional space for technology.

Bathroom offers plenty of circulation for resident and caregiver.

Hard surfaced residential appearing flooring is easier to maintain within resident room.

3'-0" x 5'-0" shower with accessible curtain gives caregivers the opportunity to assist without getting wet.

Supply storage closet with access from resident room and corridor.

Medicine storage with lock.

Water closet is visually connected to the bed and positioned to allow for two person transfer.

Angled wall in corridor defines unit and creates passing zones for carts and residents.

using harder materials can reduce cleaning costs, they can be dangerous for residents and may come with liability insurance costs that outweigh first-cost savings. With both carpets and wall coverings, modest first-cost investments in stain-resistant or tear-resistant materials can keep daily maintenance problems from becoming repair and replacement candidates, lengthening useful life by 50–100 percent. A detailed discussion of some of these products appears in chapter 15.

Cleaning costs for window coverings and upholstery can vary by 100 percent or more depending on the type of product and material selected. High-tech fabrics such as Avora are available in a variety of weights and textures, can be printed to look like jacquards or blends, are machine washable, and do not shrink; the savings over traditional fabrics, which require dry cleaning, are significant. In hard-use areas, Crypton is an alternative to both laminated fabrics and vinyl. As an upholstery fabric, it offers the easy cleaning properties of vinylized fabric but is softer to the touch and much more comfortable to sit on for long periods.

DURABILITY, USEFUL LIFE, AND REPLACEMENT COSTS

The durability of building products and equipment is directly related to the expenditure of staff maintenance time and the life cycle costs of the building's systems. The table on pages 330–32 lists the expected useful lives of major building systems as well as recommended cycles for thorough inspection and maintenance.

Some common materials have a wide range of maintenance and replacement cycles. For example, carpets vary in yarn type, pile height and density, weaving technique, and backing and therefore must be carefully matched to their intended use to balance first cost, maintenance costs, and marketing concerns. Residential areas often get simple, low-tech materials because there is a marketing advantage to installing replacement carpet for new long-stay residents. Conversely, dementia or skilled care settings require high-tech yarns and backings due to the high levels of wear and cleaning these areas must endure.

Lower parts of walls and corners must withstand considerable abuse; special consideration should be given to wall bases, corners, chair rails, and doorframes. A higher wall base than normal should be specified for areas with significant cart and wheelchair traffic. Many providers require a 10–12 in. high base, tall enough to keep wheelchair foot plates from gouging walls. Chair rails, lean rails, and handrails provide similar protection at 30–34 in. above the floor. Exposed corners are often fitted with corner guards, especially in service areas or where circulation is narrow. Painted metal doorframes, standard in many senior living communities, can be protected with color-coordinated plastic guards in vulnerable areas. All of these "cart catchers" receive their share of abuse, but they keep problems away from expensive-to-repair walls, reducing maintenance and replacement costs and extending useful life.

Including "attic stock"—additional product or material—in the construction and furnishings contracts is an easy way to reduce repair and replacement costs in the first few years. Experienced operators require their contractors to leave on-site, rather than throw away, all carpet remnants longer than 6 feet.

OPERATIONAL EFFICIENCY

With staffing, operations, and maintenance costs contributing up to 75 percent of resident charges, design for operational efficiency is paramount. Sizing the project to make maximal use of expensive senior staff is a given; setting the size of units or floors to maximize the utility of day, evening, and night staff is crucial but often overlooked. Design facilities so staff can operate efficiently among smaller groupings of residents during the day and then supervise and support larger groupings at night. Locating clean linen, soiled utility, and charting rooms close to residents reduces staff walking distances, maximizes staff's direct contact time with residents, and improves quality of care.

Staffing levels vary according to differences in regulation, sponsor programming, residents' frailty, and other variables. When does the staffing level peak? This question will be asked during the land use approval stage. Typically, it is during the day shift (7 AM to 3 PM). The figure informs the sizing of staff lounges, locker rooms, and similar spaces. And most planning and zoning boards use this figure to assess parking needs and traffic impacts.

Day-shift staffing levels for facilities offering a high level of care and services are as follows (from American Seniors Housing Association 2010):

Table 18-3 Expected Life and Recommended Inspection/Maintenance Cycles for Major Systems		
	Approximate Expected Life Span*	**Recommended Inspection/ Maintenance Cycle****
Exterior Envelope		
Foundation		
Block	Indefinite	3 Years
Concrete	Indefinite	5 Years
Structure		
Steel	Indefinite	7 Years
Concrete (poured-in-place or precast)	Indefinite	5 Years
Masonry bearing wall	Indefinite	5 Years
Structural metal stud	Indefinite	If leaks discovered, inspect studs.
Wood	Indefinite	3 Years
Exterior Wall		
Masonry	Indefinite	3 Years
Stucco	40 Years	2 Years
Painted wood	30 Years	3–5 Years
Stained wood and wood shingles	30 Years	3–5 Years
Exterior insulation finishing system (EIFS)	20 Years	Annually
Vinyl	20 Years	3–5 Years
Cementitious plank	30 Years	3–5 Years
Windows		
Aluminum/steel windows— long-life finish	40 Years 5-Year Warranty	Annually including weather stops, glass, & hardware lubricator
Aluminum/steel windows— (field) painted finish	40 Years 20-Year Warranty	Annually including weather stops, glass, & hardware lubricator
Aluminum-clad wood	20 Years	Annually
Wood windows	40 Years	Annually, including weather stops, glass, and hardware lubricator

Table 18-3 (Continued)		
	Approximate Expected Life Span*	**Recommended Inspection/ Maintenance Cycle****
Vinyl-clad wood	20 Years	Annually
Roof		
Slate shingles	Indefinite	Annually
Copper roofing	50 Years	Annually
Painted metal	20 Years	Annually
Fiberglass shingle	25–40 Years	Annually
Asphalt or wood shingle	20–25 Years	Annually
Built-up	20+ Years***	Semiannually—spring and fall, always after a major storm
Single-ply	20+ Years****	Semiannually—spring and fall, always after a major storm
Spray-foam system	15–20 Years	Annually (typically for repair/ restoration)
Building Systems		
Mechanical		
Incremental mechanical systems (through-wall air-conditioning units)	15–20 Years	Annually
Exterior mechanical equipment (exposed rooftop heating and air-conditioning units)	15–20 Years	Quarterly
Boilers/central mechanical systems with interior mechanical rooms	25–50 Years	Annually
Piping	10–50 Years	Annually (depending on material)
Ductwork	20–50 Years	Annually
Electrical	15–20 Years	Annually (limited by technical upgrades)
Plumbing	20–50 Years	Annually
Fire protection	15–50 Years	Semiannually

(Continued)

Table 18-3 (Continued)		
	Approximate Expected Life Span*	Recommended Inspection/ Maintenance Cycle**
Interior Envelope		
Walls		
Paint	2–4 Years	As required
Painted wood	15–20 Years	As required
Stained wood	15–20 Years	As required
Vinyl wall covering	10 Years	As required
Painted metal frame	2–4 Years	As required
Floors		
Carpet	10-Year Warranty	Regularly
Vinyl composition tile (VCT)	5-Year Warranty	Regularly
Sheet vinyl	5-Year Warranty	Regularly
Rubber	5–10-Year Warranty	Regularly
Ceramic	10–20 Years	As required
Wood	20–30 Years	Dust mop, sweep, or vacuum daily
Stone	30–50 Years	As required (with mild soap and water)
Slate	20–30 Years	As required (with mild soap and water)
Ceilings		
Drywall	Indefinite—dependent upon use and location	Depends on surface
Acoustic ceiling tile	10–15 Years depending upon how often ceiling is accessed	Remove surface dirt by vacuuming or light brushing.

* If properly maintained.

** Greater frequency may be appropriate in extremely hot and cold climates or frequent freeze/thaw cycles.

***10–20-year warranty with two-year installer's warranty.

**** 10–15-year warranty with two-year installer's warranty.

Source: Perkins Eastman.

- Adult day care (40–50 participants/day): 10–12 full-time employees (FTEs)
- Assisted living (80–100 units): 20–25 FTEs
- Skilled nursing facility (120 beds): 60–100 FTEs
- Skilled nursing facility (280 beds): 125–200 FTEs
- CCRC: .4–.6 FTEs per resident

The small house movement (see chapter 2) has had a dramatic impact on traditional staffing levels. Typical small house staffing (10–15 residents/house) is as follows:

- Medium-acuity long-term care
  - Two certified nursing assistants (CNAs) for each of two shifts
  - One registered nurse (RN) visit per shift
  - Director of nursing (DON) and administration remote
- High-acuity long-term care
  - 2 or 3 CNAs for the day and evening shifts and 1 or 2 CNAs at night
  - RN visit each shift
  - DON and administration remote
- Short-term rehab
  - Two CNAs on each of two shifts
  - Rehab therapist during the day shift
  - RN visit on each shift
  - DON and administration remote

Designs should reduce the required staffing without diminishing the quality of care. Clients and design teams now model required staffing before arriving at the preferred plan.

Technological advances have led to widespread reliance on wireless communications in senior housing and care facilities; they increase staff flexibility, reduce costs of hardwiring each unit to control

panels for nurse call, emergency response, fire alarms, and perimeter alarms. Electronic medical records (EMR) permit flexible access to core information without the need to track down paper files or notebooks.

When specifying digital technology, design teams should consider the owner's knowledge and resources, the size and configuration of the facility, and the availability of backup systems. In some locations, two reliable independent systems, each doing a portion of the nurse, emergency, and fire communications work, may actually yield lower long-term operating costs than a single integrated system, even if the two overlap and duplicate functions in some areas. (For more about such systems, see chapters 9 and 10.)

CLEANLINESS, OPERATIONS QUALITY, AND DESIGN

Senior living communities are rich in services. But unlike the building itself, the hospitality and care service components are hard for prospective customers to see. Given that, potential residents and their families often equate cleanliness with quality operation, compassionate care, and high-level hospitality. Design that makes it easy to keep the community looking clean and well cared for is therefore essential.

Strategic goals for operations
- Making the most of every minute of staff time (e.g., minimizing the number of staffed entrances, locating materials/supplies near where they are used)
- Flexible technology systems that prevent data duplication and reduce paperwork
- Communication systems that allow caregivers to support each other as needed

- Overhead lifts that save time and reduce the number of people required
- Infrastructure to support aging in place
- Efficient mechanical, electrical, and plumbing systems that reduce utility and maintenance costs (see chapter 9)
- Durable interior finishes that can be maintained inexpensively (see also chapter 15)

Trends and opportunities for innovation

- *Skilled nursing:* Employ operating models that reduce management staff positions by giving frontline caregivers more responsibility.
- *Subacute operations:* Balance rehab therapists' valuable time with ensuring a good patient experience.
- *CCRCs:* Unbundle services such as food, fitness and wellness programs, and concierge services, and charge only for those a resident utilizes.
- *Payment:* Institute a declining balance system, long in use at country clubs and now popular on college campuses.
- *Budgeting:* Plan for capital replacements every five to eight years.

CHAPTER 19

COST MANAGEMENT

Cost management is a set of complex tasks the owner and the design and construction teams must tackle. A comprehensive review of those tasks is beyond the scope of this chapter. Instead, this chapter presents general guidelines for effective cost management of a building program. Those guidelines include

- an outline of the basic steps in a cost management program,
- an introduction to the relative costs of typical building systems choices,
- a discussion of value engineering and life cycle costing

COST MANAGEMENT PROGRAM

An effective cost management process involves setting a realistic budget, developing conservative and careful cost estimates, and making adjustments to ensure that the design can be executed within the budget. The key tasks in a cost management program are discussed below.

1. Retain a design team, professional cost estimator, and/or construction manager with an up-to-date and proven cost estimating database and cost management capabilities for specific continuum of care components. An expert in healthcare projects is not necessarily qualified for a skilled care, assisted living, or independent living project.
2. Start the budgeting process during the initial program phase; do not wait until the schematic and design development process. An experienced team should be

able to translate a space program and evaluation of building conditions into a realistic concept budget. In well-managed projects, this budget covers not only construction costs but also the many other expenses (fees, financing costs, land, furnishings, marketing, administration, etc.) that make up the project's total cost.

3. Prepare detailed cost estimates at four points in the design process:
   - The end of schematic design
   - The end of design development
   - The midpoint of the construction document phase
   - The end of the construction document phase

The first two estimates are more useful because it is easier to adjust the design to ensure the building program remains within budget during these stages. The in-depth detail of the later estimates, however, also helps to identify potential budget challenges, facilitates final design or material choices, and helps to keep the project within budget. The detailed estimates also aid in the analysis of construction bids. If the project is using a negotiated bid contractor, the later estimates help identify possible problems in subcontractor proposals, such as unavailable building system expertise, inadequate subcontractor interest, or misunderstanding of the contract documents.

4. Factor a project's cost and phasing into the evaluation of major design and

marketing decisions. Experienced owners and construction teams evaluate both the first cost and the life cycle cost inherent in the design decision.

5. Use value engineering to achieve the proper balance between cost, marketability, sustainability, and perceived quality. Value engineering is a process often misused for cost-cutting when it should be used to achieve the same or slightly modified program, quality, and design goals less expensively.

RELATIVE COSTS

Building and site costs are always a function of local factors (local labor and material costs, contractor availability and interest, building systems required by local climate or site conditions, etc.) as well as regional and national factors. For example, in 2010, a new 3-story assisted living residence in an open-shop construction market that permits wood-frame construction might cost less than $150 per square foot, but it might cost over $300 per square foot in some high-cost urban areas with more stringent codes and unionized labor.

Regardless of location, however, the choice of building systems and materials, as well as development challenges inherent in the site, can have a significant impact on cost. The chart that follows compares the relative costs of some common choices. It should be noted that costs vary significantly over time and between locations; the chart itself is not meant to be comprehensive.

VALUE ENGINEERING AND LIFE CYCLE COST ANALYSIS

Value engineering is often confused with cost cutting. The term was coined to describe a technique for seeking design options that achieve the original design

objectives at a lower cost. Some owners and design teams even use a formal process to develop and evaluate value engineering ideas. At the very least, most owners expect to see construction and operating or life cycle cost comparisons of the major building system alternatives.

The following questions are common in the design of facilities for the aging:

- Should the owner use low-maintenance finishes, such as vinyl wall covering, or lower first-cost finishes that require regular maintenance, such as paint?
- Will installing long-life light fixtures that have a higher first cost and bulb-replacement cost gain the benefits of the lower energy usage, reduced maintenance load, and lesser heat-gain impact on the air-conditioning?
- Will a central mechanical system (vs. a decentralized system of package units) justify a higher first cost with lower replacement, energy, and other costs?
- Should the owner use more durable exterior finishes that require less maintenance, such as brick in lieu of wood siding or exterior insulation and finishing systems?
- Should the owner use more expensive clad or aluminum windows with a baked-on long-life finish and high-performance glass or less expensive vinyl windows with clear glass that require periodic repair and result in higher heating and cooling energy costs?
- Should the owner build a new, more efficient building or renovate an older, less efficient building?

Always update the drawings and re-coordinate to confirm any new designs can actually be executed. For example, a common value engineering suggestion is to lower

Table 19-1 RELATIVE COSTS		
STRUCTURAL		
Economic Costs (Low)	**Average Costs (Medium)**	**Above-Normal Costs (High)**
• Unclassified earth excavation, minimal elevation deviations (contractor takes the risk) • Stockpiling excavated material on-site • Balanced site cut-and-fill • Uniform spread footings • Continuous wall footings, non-stepped • Concrete-block or poured-concrete foundation walls • Concrete slab-on-grade • Wood frame with wood roof trusses (if permitted by code) • Bearing wall and simple joist roof framing	• Unclassified earth excavation, some variance of grade elevations • Stockpiling excavated materials on-site • Balanced site cut-and-fill • Spread footings of generally uniform dimensions with some oddities • Continuous wall footings with stepped requirements • Poured-concrete foundation walls • Concrete slab-on-grade • Some interior foundation wall requirements or thickened slabs • Uniform bay size layouts for structural system, including variances for special conditions • Masonry bearing wall and concrete plank construction • Structural steel frame, with spray-on fire protection and metal deck/concrete or precast plank floors • Generally more complicated building shape with breaks, corners, and some cantilevers • Heavy-gauge steel wall and floor (generally proprietary system) • Light-gauge metal roof trusses	• Classified earth excavation such as hardpan, clay, boulders, rocks, organic matter, etc. • Great variations in grade • Dewatering problems • Bracing and shoring required during construction • Unbalanced cut-and-fill resulting in need for borrowed or exported material • Foundation complications requiring footings of varying sizes and shapes; special foundations, such as piles • Grade-beam requirements more often than usual, continuous wall footings and foundation walls • Structural slab not on grade • Waterproofing of basement areas and slab surface water drainage • Interior requirements for foundation walls and footings • Varying bay sizes • Complicated reinforced concrete frame and slab; structural steel frame encased in concrete fireproofing • Detailed precast concrete, architectural concrete, or cast-stone detail • Complexly shaped structure requiring unique structural design solutions or high-caliber contractor • Design for future expansion

(continued)

Table 19-1 (Continued)		
ARCHITECTURAL		
Economic Costs (Low)	**Average Costs (Medium)**	**Above-Normal Costs (High)**
• Simple building shape with minimal architectural features • Clapboard, shingle, or vinyl exterior • Exterior brick or block with stock window shapes, some stone-work or precast trim, low ratio of windows • Residential-grade vinyl- or aluminum-clad windows (senior friendly) • Drywall partitions in most areas • Resilient tile floors, VCTs, standard carpet predominantly with vinyl base. • Suspended ceilings with 2' x 2' or 2' x 4' ACT in corridors and offices • Standard millwork cabinets • Simple pitched roofs with residential-grade shingles • Flat roofs with parapets • Simple waterproofing requirements • Limited use of ceramic tile • Simple program requirements • Low ratio of interior work • Wood or hollow metal doors and bucks at normal heights • Simple stair exiting and fire-protection requirements • Minimal provisions for future flexibility • Minimum circulation space, double-loaded corridors • Hydraulic elevators with single-side open doors	• More complex building shape expressing architectural features • Concrete stucco, brick, architectural concrete exterior; larger ratio of windows; special-size windows; moderate use of stonework, cast stone, and other special exterior materials • More expensive interior finishes such as vinyl wall coverings, especially in public areas • Resilient tile floors, VCT., or similar products; some custom carpeting or other more costly finishes; some painted base • Greater requirement for hung accent "cloud" ceilings, simple suspension system and economic use of acoustical tile • Higher-grade millwork cabinets • Flat roofs with some setbacks on different levels; pitched roofs with complexities • More complex waterproofing requirements • Greater use of ceramic tile on walls and floors in toilet and wet areas • More complex program requirements, modular design • Greater density of interior work • Solid wood doors and metal bucks; heights vary according to need and location • Greater fire-protection and exiting requirements • Modest provisions for future flexibility • More circulation space requirements	• Complex building shape requiring architectural treatments such as overhangs, setbacks, rounded corners, etc. • Exterior walls expressing and accentuating architectural aesthetics, utilizing stonework, complex precast or architectural concrete units, special window shapes and details, high ratio of glasswork, high-quality windows with long-life finishes and low-e glass, greater use of metal alloys for trim and decorative purposes • Extensive use of designer vinyl wall coverings; stain-grade trim and base • Greater use of hung ceilings with dry wall or high-quality 2' x 2' acoustical tile in most areas; architectural ceiling treatments with pop-ups and cove lighting • Extensive interior custom trim (crown moldings) • Extensive custom millwork and cabinets • Multilevel roofs, setbacks, penthouses, promenade decks; green roofs; complicated roof shape such as standing seam roofs • Complex damp-and-waterproofing requirements • Ceramic tile or glazed block on floors and walls in wet areas • Complex program requirements for multipurpose occupancy • High-density requirements for interior work; single-loaded enclosed corridors • Expensive fire-protection requirements, large exiting needs • Large circulation and public areas, single-loaded corridors • Need for large mechanical equipment space

Table 19-1 (Continued)		
ARCHITECTURAL		
Economic Costs (Low)	**Average Costs (Medium)**	**Above-Normal Costs (High)**
	• Greater need for mechanical equipment space • Modest use of varied materials for interior finishes • Limited use of movable partitions • Electric side-motor vertical-lift elevators with single-side open doors	• Expensive vertical and horizontal transportation equipment • Flexibility in layout and design to accommodate future changes and requirements for mechanical and electrical trades • Large movable partitions • Electric high-speed hoist elevators and lifts with dual-side open doors
PLUMBING		
Economic Costs (Low)	**Average Costs (Medium)**	**Above-Normal Costs (High)**
• Gravity sanitary and storm system using PVC pipe and fittings if code permits • Domestic hot and return water systems using submerged tankless coils in boiler • Gas-fired, self-contained HVAC units; PTAC units • Economical toilet layouts, (i.e., typical in-line facilities) • Fire standpipe system, if required • Insulation for mains, risers, water lines, and horizontal storm drains in finished areas • Economical plumbing fixtures • Fire sprinkler system only in occupied areas	• Gravity sanitary and storm system using cast-iron pipe and fittings • Sump and ejector pump systems • Hot water generator • Domestic water recirculating system • Emergency generator gas connections • Standard plumbing fixtures • Attic fire sprinklers (dry system)	• Sanitary and storm systems using cast iron above and below grade • Foundation drainage systems • Preheater for domestic hot water • Water treatment, if required • Gas piping for multiple users • Heavy central commercial kitchen work • Fire pump • Insulation of all domestic water and heating piping • Luxury plumbing fixtures • Sprinklers in all concealed spaces • Piped oxygen and suction • Graywater from shower, bath, and kitchen for irrigation systems • Solar hot water collection system
HVAC		
Economic Costs (Low)	**Average Costs (Medium)**	**Above-Normal Costs (High)**
• Low-pressure, one-pipe hot water system • Through-the-wall electric incremental units • Gas-fired, self-contained HVAC units • Ventilation of interior areas (toilets)	• Central station heating and air-conditioning (single zone) • Multi-zone heating and air-conditioning systems with reheat coils • Fan coil system, two-pipe • Water-source heat pump	• Four-pipe central HVAC systems • Variable air-volume system with mixing boxes or terminal reheats • Humidifier systems • Dust-collection systems • Heat reclamation • Radiant ceilings and floors

(continued)

Table 19-1 (Continued)		
HVAC		
Economic Costs (Low)	**Average Costs (Medium)**	**Above-Normal Costs (High)**
• Forced-air heat only • Self-contained boiler rooms • Limited insulation of piping and supply ductwork	• Kitchen and "simple" exhaust of spaces requiring ventilation • Mechanical equipment rooms, including converters, chillers • Acoustic lining • Pneumatic controls, electronic controls • Basic rooftop heating/cooling ventilation equipment, limited ducted distribution	• Snow removal systems • Water treatment systems • Boiler feed system • Remote power plant installation • Central station computerized monitoring for automatic temperature controls • Sound attenuation systems • Design requirements for future expansion
ELECTRICAL		
Economic Costs (Low)	**Average Costs (Medium)**	**Above-Normal Costs (High)**
• One main distribution panel serving simple 120/208V • Feeders: runs feeding one or more panels at a time • Lighting fixtures: fluorescent and few incandescent fixtures, economy products • Branch circuit work: one light switch per average room, receptacles per code • Motor work: individually mounted starters furnished by others • Sound system: master amplifiers with microphone and page common to all speakers • Emergency lighting: wall-mounted battery units with headlamps • Security system with local audible alarm • Hardwired emergency call system • Central emergency call station • Internet connection provided through telephone system	• Service and panels: one main distribution board serving light and power panels; simple 120/208V service • Feeders: runs feeding one or more panels at a time • Lighting fixtures: basic 2' x 2' fluorescent fixtures, few incandescent fixtures; low-voltage or LED lighting where necessary plus some architectural lighting for aesthetics • Three-way switching; more generous employment of receptacles, both duplex and special • Motor work: motor control center furnished by electrical contractor • Sound system: master amplifiers with microphone and page common to all speakers • Television system: cable or antenna amplifier and receiving outlets • Emergency lighting system: emergency generator and autotransfer switch feeding one emergency panel	• Service panels: 480/277V service into building, one or more freestanding main distribution board 480/120-208V transformers, subdistribution panels, light and power panels • Feeders: multiple sets of feeders between main distribution boards and from main distribution boards to subdistribution panels. Single feeder runs from subdistribution panels to light and power panels. Possible use of bus duct for main feeders • Lighting fixtures: low-glare and up/down fluorescent and PL fixtures. Specialty lighting where necessary plus some architectural lighting for aesthetics. Some dimming. High-intensity lighting for special areas • Three-way switching. Generous number of receptacles, both duplex and special • Motor work: motor control centers plus intricate interlocking and control devices, fan shutdown coupled with fire alarm system

Table 19-1 (Continued)		
ELECTRICAL		
Economic Costs (Low)	**Average Costs (Medium)**	**Above-Normal Costs (High)**
	• Security system with door alarms tied to report at a central security station • Zone-specific wireless emergency call system • Central emergency call station plus wireless staff pages/displays • Dedicated Internet wiring in addition to phone system	• Sound system: master system plus subsystems in other facilities interconnected for selective paging • Television system: cable and/or antennas, amplifiers, and receiving outlets throughout, plus program originating and sending facilities. Possible television studio • Emergency lighting system: emergency generator plus complete system of feeders and panels to all areas • Telephone system with features (voice mail, etc.): complete system of feeder conduits, terminal cabinets, and outlets • Intercom telephone system: automatic exchange plus handsets • Lightning protection • Security system with door alarms tied to report at a central security station and connected to staff communication receivers and surveillance cameras • Location-specific wireless emergency call system tied to the telephone system • Central emergency call station plus wireless staff communicating phones/display • Building-wide network for high-speed Internet with wireless connectivity • Design for future expansion

floor-to-floor height. But this can result in beam penetrations, soffits, or other measures to permit mechanical, plumbing, and fire-protection distribution that no longer fit in the ceiling plenum.

Cost management is essential because virtually all projects push the budget envelope, which is usually tight due to the complex economics of senior housing and care facilities.

CHAPTER 20
FINANCING AND FEASIBILITY

Access to capital is essential to all successful senior housing and care facilities, and virtually every form of financing has been employed for such projects. Public/private partnerships, philanthropy, publicly offered tax-exempt and taxable bonds, real estate investment trusts (REITs), conventional construction loans and mortgages, and government grants and mortgage guarantees are just some of the many methods employed.

This chapter discusses—generically—the steps in the financing process, describes the primary participants, and provides examples of the most common financing approaches. Also included are benchmarks and financial terminology for the most common building types.

TEN STEPS TO FINANCING
Most projects go through the following 10 steps. Completing them successfully to secure adequate financial resources to build and open the facility often takes longer than planning, programming, design, and construction documentation.

1. Preliminary feasibility planning and analysis
   a. Assembly of an experienced project feasibility team
   b. Preparation of debt capacity analysis for the sponsoring organization
   c. Evaluation of market demand and competition
   d. Preparation of a preliminary financial model for the project
2. Identification of potential capital structures and sources of financing and equity

   a. Equity from organization's own assets
   b. Predevelopment or venture capital from external sources
   c. Capital campaign funding
   d. Debt financing options (Tax exempt bonds—fixed and variable rate, HUD 232, bank debt, etc.)
      i. Evaluate potential for credit rating
   e. REIT or other build/lease options
3. Selection of financing team and method of financing
   a. Determine whether construction financing followed by permanent financing or going straight to permanent financing is most appropriate
   b. Compare underwriting criteria
4. Evaluation of government approvals necessary for project to proceed
   a. State department of insurance for continuing care retirement communities (CCRCs) in some states
   b. Certificate of need for projects involving a nursing facility or other regulated program in many states.
   c. Other regulatory approvals
5. Determination of level of financial and market feasibility studies
6. Underwriting process with financing sources
   a. Evaluate key financial ratios for the project
      i. Debt service coverage ratio
      ii. Debt service coverage ratio, revenue only
      iii. Cash-to-debt ratio

      iv. Days cash on hand
       v. Loan-to-value ratio
     vi. Debt-to-equity ratio
  b. Seek preliminary approval by financing sources
  c. Credit enhancement
7. Prepare for closing of financing
8. Closing
9. Monitoring project costs and covenants during construction
10. Ongoing reporting of performance and covenant compliance

Preliminary Feasibility Planning and Analysis

This step is a test of a potential new facility's viability: Is there a suitable site? Is there a real market? Can it be financed? Is it self-supporting? A feasibility consultant (a team that includes both market and financial feasibility analysts), investment bankers, and an architect/planner assist the sponsor with this first hurdle.

The expansion and/or renovation (sometimes referred to as "repositioning") of existing campuses or buildings also require a feasibility analysis to ensure that phasing, lost or new revenue, relocation costs, and temporary operational and capital costs are accounted for.

Market research is critical to defining the product, its service offerings, and the up-front investment necessary to successfully capture the market. Market research that merely defines the market by numbers of age- and income-qualified seniors will not identify the key factors that position the project for long-term success; religious affiliation, organizational brand awareness, ownership/contract type, program and service offerings, and price point (value) must also be assessed.

A thorough preliminary feasibility analysis tests the project's potential for success against such variables as interest rates, occupancy and fill rates, unit sizes and pricing, and total unit complement. (See chapter 4 for further discussion of feasibility planning and analysis.)

Potential Capital Structures and Sources of Financing and Equity

Developing the capital structure for a project requires creativity and awareness of successful debt and equity structures. Virtually all projects require the sponsor to commit some cash, other tangible assets such as land, or guarantees to enable the project to attract an optimal financing package. The amount required varies based on the following variables, among others:

- How conservative the project and sponsor are
- Conditions in and perceptions of the financial markets
- The feasibility of the project, including the reliability of the project's projected income
- The availability of predevelopment capital. Sometimes a sponsor needs or prefers outside predevelopment capital. Also called seed or venture capital, predevelopment capital is a way for a sponsor to fund project costs that must be incurred before more traditional financing is locked in. Typical costs incurred prior to financing relate to planning and feasibility, architecture, preconstruction services, marketing, and site engineering
- The potential of a capital campaign. Nonprofit sponsors often conduct a capital campaign to assist with project funding.

Potential sources of debt

In many states, tax-exempt bonds for senior housing can be issued by counties, cities, and municipalities. Many states and municipalities have also created entities that can issue tax-exempt debt for senior housing and care projects, including state and local housing agencies and authorities and industrial development bond programs. Many sponsors, both for-profit and nonprofit, also look to other financing sources: banks, REITs, insurance companies, pension funds, and so on. Other popular sources for permanent financing are HUD programs that offer fixed long-term rates, mortgage insurance, or outright grant subsidy.

Each of these sources has different lending requirements, and a sponsor must determine which ones are appropriate for the proposed project and whether their requirements (percentage of equity, debt-coverage ratios, liquidity ratios, time to close, credit enhancement or guarantees, restrictions on admissions, rental or entry fees, etc.) are acceptable. Going too far down the road with an inappropriate funding source can seriously delay a project. If they have not already assembled a core financing team, many sponsors retain investment bankers or other financial advisers specializing in senior living finance to guide them through this process.

Equity formation

Most sponsors can develop very few projects without at least some equity investment. This can come from an infusion of cash from the sponsor's endowment or corporate resources, limited or full guarantees of the project debt, the contribution of land, public grants, and/or fundraising. The amount required is generally based on risk tolerance and financing requirements.

Of the sources of equity, fundraising for a nonprofit is the most complex and time-consuming. If the amount to be raised requires a formal campaign, the organization should seek advice from fundraising consultants, who do not raise the money but rather plan and guide the process. Such advice will include how the financing institutions will evaluate pledges due in the future vs. cash contributions.

Many formal campaigns follow four steps:

1. A preliminary analysis to determine the fundraising potential of the supporters of the sponsoring entity
2. Preparation of the fundraising materials, which often include plans, renderings, cost estimates, and the answers to donors' potential questions about the need for the project and the project itself
3. A quiet campaign among a limited list of the largest potential donors (usually to raise at least a third of the project's total)
4. A full campaign to the rest of the potential donor list

Financing Team and Method

At the same time that potential capital sources are being identified, the sponsor will expand the team that will guide the project financing. For tax-exempt bonds, this team consists of bond counsel, borrower's counsel, a financial feasibility consultant, a financial adviser, the investment bank or underwriter, the underwriter's counsel, and an issuing municipality or agency for the debt. This team guides the sponsor through the steps and prepares the documents necessary to obtain project financing.

The financing institution may undertake a wide-ranging evaluation beyond a basic feasibility study. It can dictate financial parameters; the obligations of other affiliated organizations and their products (particularly important for multi-building/multi-site clients); and the terms of recourse to the sponsor or affiliated foundations. It can even demand changes to corporate and operational structure. Financial covenants requiring the sponsor to meet and maintain certain financial thresholds by certain dates are increasingly common.

Government Approvals

All projects require many government approvals; time for getting them must be built into the project planning timeline. This chapter focuses on two key approvals. First, if the project involves independent living with entrance fees, approval from the state's department of insurance or similar state agency may be required before any marketing of the project can begin. Second, if a nursing or other regulated facility is involved in the project, a certificate of need or similar approval may need to be obtained from the appropriate state agency before the project can be built.

Financial and Market Feasibility Study

Every financing source has different requirements for the independent feasibility analysis. Some banks will be satisfied with a compiled projection or forecast for the project and a separate market study. The compilation report confirms that the projected or forecasted financial statements are presented in the proper format and do not include an evaluation of the underlying assumptions.

National banks and virtually all tax-exempt bond financings require a full feasibility study by a regional or national accounting firm with recognized experience in senior living. Feasibility studies include a financial forecast and market study. The report issued by the accounting firm is called an examination. The examination includes procedures for evaluating whether management has a reasonable basis for their assumptions in the forecast.

Sponsors with strong financial results and balance sheets may not be required to have a feasibility study, but a study is still recommended.

Underwriting

Evaluate key financial ratios

Financial ratios are key underwriting criteria for financing sources. Financial covenants in loan agreements are generally less stringent than the underwriting criteria. Sponsors develop internal underwriting criteria that set a higher performance expectation than outside sources may require. This will grow the financial strength of the project.

The most important financial ratios and underwriting criteria are as follows:

i. *Debt service coverage ratio:* Demonstrates the provider's ability to fund their annual debt service payments with cash flow from net cash revenues and net entrance fees.

ii. *Debt service coverage ratio—revenue basis:* A measure of a provider's ability to meet the debt service from revenue.

iii. *Liquidity:* Liquidity ratios measure a provider's ability to meet the short-term cash needs of its ongoing operations. The three most common ratios to measure liquidity are cash-to-debt, days cash on hand, and the cushion ratio.
   a. *Cash-to debt ratio:* A measure of available cash and securities divided by the project's debt.
   b. *Days cash on hand:* The number of days a provider can continue to operate using only its own unrestricted cash, cash equivalents, and marketable securities.

iv. *Loan-to-value ratio.*

v. *Debt to equity ratio.*

Seek preliminary approval by financing sources

The financial team usually begins with the preparation and submission of the materials necessary to obtain a preliminary or conditional commitment from the source of financing and/or credit enhancement—typically a feasibility study, cost estimates, and marketing projections that the project can achieve 95 percent occupancy in an acceptable period (often two years or less) as well as generate enough cash flow to safely cover projected operating costs and debt service and maintain adequate cash balances.

GLOSSARY

Debt service coverage ratio: Measures a provider's ability to fund annual debt service with cash flow from net cash revenues and, when applicable, net entrance fees:

> Income (loss) + interest, depreciation, and amortization expenses
>
> – Amortization of deferred revenue
>
> + Net proceeds from entrance fees
>
> = Annual debt service

Debt service coverage ratio—revenue only: Measures a provider's ability to cover debt service exclusively from operating revenues and non-operating revenue:

> Income (loss) + interest depreciation, and amortization expenses
>
> – Amortization of deferred revenue
>
> = Annual debt service

Cash-to-debt ratio: Measures a provider's position in available cash and marketable securities in relation to its long-term debt, less current portion.

> Unrestricted cash and investments and long-term debt
>
> – Current portion of debt
>
> = Cash-to-debt ratio

Days cash on hand: Measures the number of days of cash operating expenses a provider could cover with its unrestricted cash, cash equivalents, and marketable securities on hand.

> Unrestricted cash and investments (operating expenses, including interest expense)
>
> – Depreciation/amortization
>
> ÷ 365
>
> = Days cash on hand

Loan-to-value ratio: Measures the fair market value of the asset to the value of the loan.

> Loan amount
>
> Appraised value of property

Debt-to-Equity Ratio Measures a provider's financial leverage.

> Long-term debt equity or net assets

2010 Financial Ratios and Trend Analysis of CARF-CCAC Accredited Organizations

Credit enhancement

Many projects financed with tax-exempt bonds are required to have credit enhancement, which is a guarantee from a financial institution or government agency that improves the credit status and marketability of the bonds. Sometimes this is accomplished through a letter of credit issued by a bank or other financial institution that guarantees the debt. In other cases, the guarantee is provided by a government entity. The Department of Housing and Urban Development's Federal Housing Administration Section 232 Mortgage Insurance Program (HUD 232) is one such source of credit enhancement. This program provides mortgage insurance as the credit enhancement for as much as 90–95 percent of the project value. Bank letters of credit typically provide credit enhancement for as much as 80 percent of the project's value; however, banks are less interested in providing letters of credit for senior living projects in recent years.

Preparing for Closing

Following preliminary approval, most sources of financing require a number of items prior to closing the financing; these typically include the following:

- Complete plans and specifications, often with all public approvals and land use and building permits
- For some products, particularly independent living, proof of pre-leasing/pre-sales of 70–80 percent of the units
- A lump-sum or guaranteed-maximum-construction price contract from a contractor with a performance bond
- Loan agreements, mortgages, and other financing documents that provide security to the financing source (lender or investor) and specify the terms of repayment
- Bond-offering documents for bond sales to investors when tax-exempt bonds are the source of financing

If conventional financing sources are used, this phase can take 60–90 days from the time all of the requirements are met until the financing is in place. Institutions offering government-backed financing vehicles take much more time. While there have been efforts to shorten this timeframe considerably, 6–12 months or longer is still the norm.

Closing

Once the lender's requirements have been met and documents are finalized—and, in the case of bond financing, the bonds have been sold—the entire project team meets so the documents can be executed and the financing funded.

Project Costs and Covenants

Key metrics and milestones should be monitored monthly during construction and fill-up. An independent firm representing the owner will often keep close tabs on project costs and timing to ensure project is delivered on time and within budget. Delays can have a dramatic negative impact on filling up the project. Financing covenants must be adhered to during construction and fill-up.

Ongoing Reporting of Performance and Covenant Compliance

Once a project is built and opened to residents, most financing structures require adherence to financial and other covenants. Generally, covenant compliance is monitored quarterly. The project's financing source(s) establish these covenants to protect their financial interests. Meeting or exceeding the performance levels required by the covenants provides assurance that the project is achieving acceptable results. If covenants are violated, the financing source (bondholders, bank, REIT, etc.) typically have the right to require the hiring of an independent consultant to analyze the situation and suggest ways to cure the violation.

Meeting or exceeding forecasted performance is the ultimate goal. Forecasted performance is generally significantly better than that required by the financial and other covenants. Strong performance and timely reporting enhances the sponsor's image with financing sources and puts the organization in good position for follow-on financing.

FINANCING VARIATIONS FOR SENIOR SETTINGS

There are many variations on the steps summarized above, and many sponsors have found unique ways to fund their building programs. Nevertheless, there are typical approaches relevant to some of the more common building types. Among these are the following:

Assisted Living

Many for-profit chains have arranged conventional financing for their building programs, and they sometimes use this credit to build and operate until profitability is achieved. Then the completed project is sold to an investor group, REIT, or other entity (with the sponsor retaining the management contract) to free cash for future projects. Others have financed their building programs with the proceeds of a public stock offering or the cash generated from existing facilities.

Nonprofits typically follow the ten steps outlined above. Some start with land and supplement their equity with fundraising. There are a variety of financing vehicles available for assisted living. Some nonprofits have endowments that fund some or all of the entire project. Some enter into partnerships with for-profit companies to develop and/or operate the facility. And HUD 232 credit enhancement is often used.

Skilled Nursing Facilities

New or renovated skilled nursing facilities generally operate at 90 percent occupancy or greater. Their revenue is usually a mix of Medicare, Medicaid, and private pay. Medicaid reimbursement is usually the predominant source of revenue for established nursing facilities. However, new or renovated facilities are designed to attract Medicare and private-pay residents. The feasibility of a skilled nursing building program is usually gauged from detailed projections of the income sources and the related expenses. Lending sources usually consider Medicaid reimbursement a risky source of revenue because states can reduce their Medicaid budgets or payment methodology. Some nursing facilities have philanthropic support or endowment income that improves their operating statements. Many projects use HUD 232 credit enhancement in their financing.

Independent Living

The federal government's HUD 202 program funds low-income housing units for seniors. HUD also provides public housing subsidies and Section 8 funding for low-income seniors. In addition, some states run subsidized housing programs for seniors with limited incomes as well as joint programs with HUD.

Middle- and upper-income independent living projects are typically financed using the same conventional sources as other market-rate multifamily housing developments. These projects depend largely on the financial strength of the sponsor and positive market and financial feasibility studies.

Continuing Care Retirement Communities

The structure of financing for CCRCs depends on the structure of resident fees. The most common resident fee structure is an entry fee, which can be substantial, plus a monthly service fee. The entry fee may be fully refundable when a resident dies or leaves, partially refundable, or decline in value each month. Many CCRCs offer several entry fee refund options.

If the CCRC is a life-care community, the entry and monthly fees typically cover the costs of the residents' care regardless of where they reside in the community (independently, in assisted living, or in the nursing center) for the rest of their lives. In other CCRCs, there are limits on the number of days that residents are allowed to stay in the CCRC nursing facility without paying additional fees, and services are provided on a fee-for-service basis. Some CCRCs require residents to have long-term healthcare insurance.

Entry-fee CCRCs are frequently financed with little equity from the sponsor when 70 percent or more of the independent living units have been reserved with 10 percent deposits before the closing of the financing. The pre-sales demonstrate the strength of the CCRC market, and the entry fees act as a restricted form of equity and create financial reserves.

UNIT TYPES AND SIZES FOR SENIOR LIVING

UNIT TYPE	UNIT SIZE RANGE	AVERAGE UNIT SIZE*	NOTES
	Typical Unit Area	Typical Unit Area	
Independent Living	Low to High	Net sq ft	
Studio apartment	320–735	660	Rarely used today in market-rate projects
One-bedroom apartment	650–900	800	
One-bedroom plus den apartment	850–1200	950	Usually includes an additional 1/2 bath
Two-bedroom apartment	1,100–1,400	1,200	
Two-bedroom plus den apartment	1,200–1,800	1,400	Usually includes an additional 1/2 bath
Three-bedroom apartment	1,200–2,000	1,600	
One-bedroom plus den cottage	900–1,200	1,100	
Two-bedroom Cottage	1,200–1,800	1,400	Usually includes single-car garage minimum
Two-bedroom plus den cottage	1,200–2,000	1,800	Can include two-car garage
Three-bedroom cottage	1,400–2,500	2,100	Can include two-car garage
Assisted Living			
Studio/alcove unit	350–375	350	
One-bedroom unit	450–600	500	
Two-bedroom unit	800–1,000	850	A few provided for couples
Long-Term Care			
Private room	230–320	250	Most market-rate projects and CCRCs are all private
Large private room	320–425	390	
Semi-private room	350–500	425	Newer models with shower in bathroom
Dementia/Memory Care			
Private room	230–320	250	Shower in bathroom
Semi-private room	350–500	425	Only a few typically recommended

*See Figure 2-1 for measuring unit area. Above areas do not include attached garage, carport, or covered porches.

APPENDIX B

BUILDING NET-TO-GROSS FACTORS FOR SENIOR LIVING

The net-to-gross factor is used to accommodate unprogrammed space such as circulation (corridors, stairs, elevators) structure/walls (columns and wall construction not measured in room/unit areas), and mechanical/electrical (vertical chases, electrical panel closets, miscellaneous pipe chases).			
Building Type	**Range**	**Net-to-Gross Factor**	**Notes**
Independent living apartments	1.25–1.5	1.3	Site- and configuration-driven
Assisted living	1.35–1.6	1.4	Corridor width and configuration varies.
Long-term care	1.40–1.6	1.45	Dependent on care philosophy
Memory care/ dementia (AL)	1.35–1.6	1.4	Corridor width and configuration varies.
Community spaces in a CCRC	1.25–1.5	1.35	Scope of unprogrammed circulation and not including circulation within departments
Clinics/adult day care	1.3–1.5	1.4	Corridor width and configuration varies.

Notes

Cottages and duplexes have a net-to-gross factor of 1.0.

Structured parking ranges from carports to underground garages.

APPENDIX C

GERIATRIC CLINIC: TYPICAL PROGRAM COMPONENTS

Type of Space	Typical Code Minimum Area (sq ft)	Recommended Minimum Area (sq ft)
Clinic Spaces		
Waiting area	20–30/ exam room	60–70/ exam room
	10–15/person	20–25/ person + escorts
Clerical/staff work	N/A	200+
Records/dictation	N/A	10–15/exam room
General exam room	90–110	110–130
Procedure room	100–120	140–160
Dental exam/procedure	90–110	140–150
Dental workroom	50–100	50–100
Hearing/speech testing	N/A	110–130
Radiological exam (if provided)	N/A	200–250
Neuro/psych testing	80–90	100–110
Patient consult/staff meeting room	N/A	140–160
Staff office	100–110	110–140
Patient toilet room (ADA)	50	50
Pharmacy (if provided)	N/A	450 & up
Lab prep/medication supply	50–100	100 & up
Soiled utility room	50–85	50–75
Clean utility room	50–60	50–75
Therapy Spaces		
PT gym/open equipment area	N/A	1,200 & up
Hydrotherapy area (limb tanks only)	N/A	120–150
Equipment storage	N/A	100 & up
OT program area	N/A	250–300
ADL suite (kitchen, bedroom, bath)	N/A	300–400
Training toliet/shower room	80–100	80–100
Staff observation/work area	N/A	200 & up
Staff office	100–110	120–130
Patient consult/staff meeting room	N/A	100–150
Patient toilet room (ADA)	50	50

APPENDIX D

SAMPLE LARGE OUTPATIENT CLINIC PROGRAM*

Space	Area (sq ft)	Space	Area (sq ft)
Entry/Reception		**Staff/Support Areas**	
Main waiting, 20–30 seats	900	Medical records/dictation (high-density filing)	200
Clerical/reception (3–4 person station)	250	Financial counselor office	160
Accessible restrooms (2 @ 50 sq ft)	100	Business manager office	120
Subtotal entry/reception	1,250	Nurse manager office	120
Typical Exam Cluster		Neuro/psych office	120
Subwaiting room	150	Staff conference room	300
Check-in/out room	100	Open staff work area ("bullpen")	300
Shared toilet room	50	Staff workstations (+/– 12 @ 50 sq ft/ea.)	600
Standard exam room (5 @ 120 sq ft)	600	Nurse station (3–4 person station)	250
Large exam room	160	Medication/pixus room	80
Toilet room (adjoining large exam)	50	Staff toilet room	50
Family consult room	150	Soiled supply room (2 @ 80 sq ft)	160
Subtotal for 4 exam clusters	5,040	Clean supply room (2 @ 50 sq ft)	100
Shared Patient/Specialty Exam Areas		Staff lockers	100
Blood-drawing room	120	Janitors closet	50
Procedure room	80	Equipment storage	80
Neuro/psych testing	160	General/supply storage	140
Radiological exam	240	Subtotal staff/support areas	2,930
Subtotal for shared exam areas	700		
		Total usable square feet	**9,920**
		Total program area (1.4 net/gross factor)	**13,888**
		(average @ +/– 580 sq ft/exam room)	

*24 exam room cluster model

APPENDIX E
SAMPLE ENHANCED RETIREMENT COMMUNITY CLINIC PROGRAM

Space	Area (sq ft)
Waiting room (seating for 8–10)	180
Reception/clerical	140
Small exam (2 @ 120 sq ft)	240
Large exam/procedure	160
Dental exam/procedure	160
Dental workroom	65
Lab prep/supply	100
Soiled (1 @ 80 sq ft)	80
Clean supply room (1 @ 50 sq ft)	50
Patient toilet room (2 @ 50 sq ft)	100
Patient/family consult	150
Staff office (2 @ 135 sq ft)	270
Medical supply	80
Subtotal usable square feet	**1,775**
Total program area (1.4 net/gross factor)	**2,485**
(average @ +/– 620 sq ft/exam room)	

ADULT DAY CARE: SAMPLE PROGRAM FOR 50 PARTICIPANTS

Description	Space Count	Proposed Users	Net Square Feet		Notes
		total	each	total	
Entry/admissions/reception					
Waiting and reception	1	4–5	150	150	
Interview/meeting room	1		150	150	
Coat/drinking fountain/telephone	1		80	80	
Wheelchair storage	1		40	40	
Public toilet	1		50	50	
Common Activities					
Dining/recreation	1	50	40	2,000	Net of circulation
General activities	1	10	25	250	
Activities of daily living (ADLs): Kitchen /Work Area	1		250	250	
Special Programs					
Physical therapy room	1	3–4	400	400	
Exam/treatment room	1		160	160	
Private counseling room	1		120	120	
Quiet room	1		180	180	
Staff Area					
Director's office	1		120	120	
Staff Workstations	10		30	300	
Staff lounge/multipurpose room	1		200	200	
Support Areas					
Medical records/files	1		50	50	
Copier/fax station	1		50	50	
Pantry	1		200	200	
Storage	1		100	100	

Description	Space Count	Proposed Users	Net Square Feet		Notes
		total	each	total	
Toilet Rooms					
Toilet room	4		50	200	
Toilet room and shower	1		100	100	
Staff toilet	1		50	50	
Washer/dryer	1		20	20	
Janitors closet	1		50	50	
Mechanical/electrical/telephone	2		0	0	Base building
Total usable square feet				**5,270**	
Total program area (x 1.4 net/gross factor)				**7,378**	
(average @ +/- 150 sq ft/participant)					

LONG-TERM CARE GROSS AREA PER BED GUIDELINES

Long-Term Care Model	Total GSF / Bed	Resident Living Area*	Common Areas	Admin/Office	Back-of-House MEP
Nursing unit	635–925	480–600	50–150	25–50	80–125
Clusters	655–925	500–600	50–150	25–50	80–125
Neighborhoods	705–965	550–700	50–150	25–40	80–125
Households	735–985	600–750	50–150	25–30	60–100
House: freestanding (1 story)	670–880	670–880	N/A	N/A	N/A

*Guidelines based on predominantly private rooms and a 120–160 bed long-term care facility.

APPENDIX H
TYPICAL LONG-TERM CARE PROGRAM COMPONENTS

Space Description	Typical Code Minimum Area (sq ft)	Recommended Minimum Area (sq ft)
Dining	15 per resident	30–40 per resident / 20–30 residents max per dining area
Lounge/activity/living room	10–15 per resident	20–35 per resident
Central bathing (fixture = tub or shower)	150; 1 fixture per 15 residents	250; 1 fixture per 15 residents
Clean utility	40–60; 1 per unit	50–75; 1 per 15–20 residents
Soiled utility	40–60; 1 per unit	60–100; 1 per 15 residents
Clean linen	15–25; 1 per unit	15–25; 1 per 15 residents
Nurses station/care base	150–250	150–250 decentralized
Medication room	25–40; 1 per unit	50–75; 1 per 15 residents
Resident toilet near dining	Not required	50 sq ft recommended / multiple single-use rooms
Public/visitor toilet	Required	50 sq ft recommended / multiple single-use rooms
Staff toilet	Required	40–50 sq ft required
Resident toilet with bathing	Required	1 per bathing suite
Staff office	Not required	1–2 per unit for nursing supervisor and/or social worker

Notes:
Central bathing should include tub & shower.
Central bathing should be spa-like.
Private resident rooms should include a personal shower if possible.

APPENDIX I

SAMPLE PROGRAM: LONG-TERM CARE, 126-BED, 4-STORY (AND BASEMENT) NEIGHBORHOOD/HOUSEHOLD MODEL

Long-Term Care Neighborhood: 42 Residents				
14-resident household	**Qty.**	**Size**	**Total**	**Notes**
Large private resident room with full bath	2	285	570	
Typical private resident room with full bath	10	250	2,500	
Shared suite room: two sleeping rooms with one bath	1	425	425	
Living room	1	300	300	
Dining	1	480	480	
Household kitchen	1	300	300	
Pantry	1	50	50	
Alcove for resident scale	1	25	25	
Coat closet at entry	1	25	25	
Storage closet	1	25	25	
Housekeeping closet	1	60	60	
Linen cart storage	1	25	25	
Clean utility	1	60	60	
Soiled utility	1	100	100	
Laundry (personal clothing)	1	100	100	
Staff workstation with charting and medication	1	120	120	
Lift/shower chair alcove	1	25	25	
Wheelchair storage alcove	1	25	25	
Public toilet	1	50	50	
Electrical closet	1	60	60	
Communications closet	1	25	25	
Subtotal			**5,350**	
Total for three households			**16,050**	

Long-Term Care Neighborhood: 42 Residents				
Shared areas for neighborhood of three households	**Qty.**	**Size**	**Total**	**Notes**
Great-room	1	600	600	
Family meeting/care planning/conference/private dining	1	240	240	
Staff work room (hotelling desks for four) with copier/fax	1	150	150	
Offices (unit director, social worker, coordinator of nursing services, swing office)	2	100	200	2 offices/ neighborhood = 4 offices/floor = 4 positions to be distributed
Public toilet	1	50	50	
Elevator lobby	1	240	240	
Holding area at freight elevator	1	100	100	
Equipment alcove	1	40	40	
Equipment storage (code cart/oxygen)	1	75	75	
Soiled utility room with chutes	1	75	75	
Electrical closet/communications	2	60	120	
Housekeeping/janitorial closet	1	60	60	For common spaces
Subtotal for shared areas			**1,950**	
Total for 4-resident neighborhood			**54,000**	x 3 floors

APPENDIX I (*cont.*)

Entrance and Public Spaces	Qty.	Size	Total	Notes
Entry vestibule	1	200	200	
Lobby	1	650	650	
Reception/concierge desk	1	120	120	
Security office	1	100	100	
Admissions suite	1	400	400	
Public toilet	4	200	800	
Auditorium/multipurpose room	1	1,500	1,500	
Chair/table storage	1	200	200	
Coats	1	50	50	
Gallery prefunction	1	400	400	
Studio: arts, crafts, gardening	1	400	400	
Library	1	400	400	
Meeting rooms	2	200	400	
Bistro/kitchen	1	850	850	
Bistro/café serving counter	1	250	250	
Bistro/café seating for 25	1	850	850	
Convenience store/gift shop	1	350	350	Next to bistro serving counter (shared cashier?)
Spa/salon	1	350	350	
Meditation room	1	400	400	
Clergy office	1	100	100	
Total entrance and public spaces			**8,770**	

APPENDIX I (*cont.*)

Clinical Support			
Rehab Suite and Clinic	**Qty.**	**Size**	**Total**
Toilet	2	50	100
Waiting	1	150	150
Reception/business office/nurses station	1	150	150
Rehab director's office	1	120	120
Rehab staff work room/charting	4	30	120
OT/PT suite	1	800	800
Speech suite	1	200	200
Exam rooms	2	120	240
Clinic director's office	1	120	120
Large exam/procedure	1	120	120
In-suite toilets	2	50	100
Housekeeping	1	60	60
Clean utility	1	50	50
Soiled utility	1	80	80
Storage	1	100	100
Files/copier/fax	1	100	100
Subtotal			**2,610**

APPENDIX I (*cont.*)

Administration Support			
Administrative Suite	**Qty.**	**Size**	**Total**
Reception/waiting	1	200	200
Receptionist/admin.	1	100	100
Storage	1	120	120
Executive director	1	180	180
Assistant director/nursing home administrator	1	150	150
Small conference	1	150	150
Large conference	1	300	300
Director of operations	1	150	150
Director of nursing	1	150	150
Director of finance	1	150	150
Finance offices	2	120	240
Offices	2	120	240
HR director & office	2	120	240
Medical director (if not in clinic)	1	120	120
Staff coordinator/scheduling	1	120	120
Supply/copy/workroom	1	300	300
Education training coordinator	1	120	120
Staff toilets	2	50	100
IT office	1	120	120
IT workroom/equipment/storage	1	250	250
Medical records	1	300	300
Files/storage	1	200	200
Classroom	1	400	400
Subtotal: administration			**4,400**
Staff Support			
Men's locker room	1	300	300
Women's locker room	1	500	500
Prep kitchen/vending	1	400	400
Staff dining room	1	400	400
Subtotal staff support			**1,600**

APPENDIX I (*cont.*)

Services / Support	Qty.	Size	Total	Notes
Kitchen	1	2,800	2,800	Includes storage; assumes no tray makeup or dishwashing
Dry storage	1	300	300	
Dietary offices	2	100	200	
Central supply				
Stores	1	500	500	
Manager's office	1	75	75	
Mailroom	1	150	150	
Patient equipment cleanup room	1	120	120	
Patient equipment holding	1	200	200	
Receiving/loading dock/trash	1	1,000	1,000	
Linen staging				
Clean linen holding	1	200	200	
Soiled linen holding	1	300	300	
Laundry	1	500	500	
Morgue	1	100	100	
Grounds maintenance: JHE storage	1	0	0	
Resident storage	1	1,200	1,200	Per licensure code
Central housekeeping storage (with supervisors workstations)	1	400	400	
Maintenance workshop (repair)	1	600	600	
Maintenance shared office space	1	120	120	
Maintenance supply	1	400	400	
Facilities director's office	1	120	120	
Mechanical/electrical	1	3,500	3,500	
Elevator equipment room	1	120	120	
Subtotal: services/support			**12,905**	
Subtotal: usable square feet			**84,285**	
Total program area (1.45 gross/net)			**122,213**	
(Average @ +/– 970 sq ft / bed)				

FREESTANDING 75-UNIT, 3-STORY ASSISTED LIVING FACILITY WITH 20-BED MEMORY-SUPPORT NEIGHBORHOOD

Space Description	Space Count	Proposed Users		Net Square Feet
		total	each	total
Assisted living resident units for 55				
Studio	13		350	4,550
One-bedroom	40		500	20,000
Two-bedroom	2		800	1,600
Subtotal: AL residential units				**26,150**
Resident cluster common areas for 15–20				
Sitting areas/dens/game rooms	3		250	750
Resident kitchen with sitting area	1		400	400
Resident laundry	3		75	225
Guest toilet	3		50	150
Subtotal: Cluster common areas				**1,525**
Resident cluster support areas for 15–20				
Linen supply	3		15	45
Housekeeping closet	3		50	150
Trash room	3		50	150
Electrical closet	3		25	75
Subtotal: Cluster support areas				**420**
Resident common areas				
Vestibule	1		110	110
Lobby (Note: may include an open stair)	1		900	900
Mail	1		150	150
Dining prefunction/carts	1		100	100
Dining	1	55	1,935	1,935
Private dining	1		280	280
Library/living room	1		500	500
Large activity/multipurpose	1		800	800

Space Description	Space Count	Proposed Users		Net Square Feet
		total	each	total
Spa bathing with toilet	1		250	250
Toilets near dining	4		50	200
Special activity room	1		400	400
Hair care/salon	1		250	250
Subtotal				**5,875**
Administration				
Administrator	1		180	180
Admissions with meeting area	1		200	200
Activities director	1		120	120
Business office (for 2)	1	2	75	150
Receptionist/waiting	1	3–4	150	150
Workroom	1		220	220
Conference room	1	4–5	150	150
Care team workroom with medications	1	3–4	400	400
Subtotal				**1,570**
Dementia / memory support neighborhood for 20				
Household 10				
Resident rooms	10		250	2,500
Living room	1		200	200
Dining area	1		350	350
Linen supply	1		15	15
Subtotal				**3,065**
(x 2 households)				**6,130**
Shared areas				
Open kitchen	1		400	400
Staff work area	1		150	150
Resident/visitor toilets	2		50	100
Housekeeping closet	1		50	50
Electrical closet	1		25	25
Soiled utility	1		80	80
Clean supply	1		50	50
Staff office/workroom	1		120	120
Laundry	1		75	75
Activity room	1	10-15	400	400
Subtotal				**1,450**

(continued)

APPENDIX J (*cont.*)

Space Description	Space Count	Proposed Users total	each	Net Square Feet total
General support				
Staff lounge/lockers/toilet	2		250	500
Commercial kitchen	1		1,500	1,500
Housekeeping storage	1		300	300
Housekeeping supply	1		300	300
Central clean linen	1		250	250
Central soiled linen	1		300	300
Mechanical/electrical/pumps	1		1,500	1,500
Maintenance shop	1		300	300
Elevator machine room	1		80	80
Resident storage (4' x 4' x 4' cubicle)	1	75	20	20
Cart wash	1		40	40
Loading/receiving	1		250	250
Trash	1		150	150
Telephone closet	1		50	50
Subtotal				**5,540**
Total usable square feet				**48,660**
Total program area (1.4 net/gross factor)				**68,124**
(average @ +/– 910 sq ft/unit)				
Optional Spaces				
Common spaces: resident				
Ice-cream parlor/café	1		500	500
Multipurpose/theater	1	20	20	400
Wellness center				
Waiting/reception	1		120	120
Exam room	1		120	120
Office	1		120	120
Toilet	1		50	50
Exercise/meeting	1	20	20	400
Support : general				
Laundry	1		500	500

APPENDIX K

SAMPLE PROGRAM FOR 40-PERSON MEMORY-CARE RESIDENCE

Space Description	Space Count	Proposed Resident total	Net Square Feet each	total
Residential areas, 4 houses of 10				
Single rooms with bathroom	10	10	250	2,500
Living room	1		250	250
Dining room for 10	1		350	350
Linen closet	1		15	15
Subtotal		**10**		**3,115**
x 4 households		**40**		**12,460**
Shared areas for each cluster (2 of 20)				
Household kitchen/staff area	1		400	400
Laundry room	1		75	75
Soiled utility	1		80	80
Housekeeping	1		50	50
Resident/visitors toilet	2		50	100
Electrical closet	1		25	25
Subtotal				**730**
x 2 neighborhoods				**1,460**
Activitys/program areas				
Great-room	1	20–25	700	700
Shared living room	1	10–15	400	400
Arts and crafts/messy activity	1	10–15	400	400
Private dining/activity	1	8–10	280	280
Toilets	2		50	100
Staff workroom/records/medication	1	3–4	300	300
Haircare and spa with toilet	1		250	250
Subtotal				**2,430**

(continued)

APPENDIX K (*cont.*)

Space Description	Space Count	Proposed Resident total	Net Square Feet each	total
Administration / public				
Vestibule	1		100	100
Lobby/reception/waiting/secretary	1	3–4	350	350
Public toilet	2		50	100
Staff toilet	1		50	50
Director's office	1		180	180
Marketing/admissions office	1		140	140
Recreation/activity director's office	1		120	120
Professional development/conference room	1	4–5	150	150
Workroom/copy/supply/file/storage	1		220	220
Subtotal				**1,410**
Service support				
Kitchen	1		1,200	1,200
Storage	1		400	400
Soiled holding (assumes bulk laundry elsewhere)	1		150	150
Clean holding/supply	1		150	150
Housekeeping storage	1		150	150
Mechanical/electrical/telephone	1		1,200	1,200
Staff lounge/retreat	1		280	280
Staff lockers/resident storage	2		80	160
Resident storage	1		200	200
Subtotal				**3,890**
Total usable square feet				**21,650**
Total program area (1.4 net/gross factor)				**30,310**
(average +/– 760 sq ft/person)				

APPENDIX L

SAMPLE PROGRAM FOR INDEPENDENT LIVING WITH SERVICES BUILDING— 150 UNITS, 4 STORIES, 2 WINGS

	Space Count	Proposed Users total	Net Square Feet each	total	Notes
Independent living: resident units					
IL-1BR, 1 bath	25		800	20,000	
IL-1BR,1.5 bath, den	50		950	47,500	
IL-2BR, 2 bath	60		1,200	72,000	
IL-2BR, 2 bath, den	15		1,400	21,000	
Subtotal				**160,500**	
Resident wing: support areas					
Housekeeping/closet (1 per wing)	8		50	400	
Trash room	8		50	400	
Telephone/CATV closet	8		25	200	
Electrical closet	8		25	200	
Subtotal				**1,200**	
Administration					
Receptionist/waiting	1		150	150	
Administration office	1		180	180	
Business office	2		120	240	
Office (activity/social work)	2		120	240	
Marketing office with meeting area	1		200	200	
Administrative assistant	1		80	80	
IT director/fileserver	1		300	300	
Director of HR	1		120	120	
Conference room	1	8–10	280	280	
Copy/workroom	1		220	220	
Storage	1		100	100	
Coat closet	1		10	10	
Staff toilet (M/F)	1		50	50	
Subtotal				**2,170**	

(continued)

APPENDIX L (*cont.*)

	Space Count	Proposed Users total	Net Square Feet each	total	Notes
Resident common areas					
Vestibule	1		120	120	
Entry lobby	1		900	900	
Reception	1		100	100	
Mail/package room	1		350	350	
Coffee shop/casual dining (convenience store)	1	20	50	1,000	
Public toilet	2		180	360	
Dining room (assumes multiple seatings)	1	100	30	3,000	
Private dining	1	10–12	280	280	
Game room	1	30–35	800	800	
Library/media room	1		400	400	
Gathering lounge with fireplace	1	35–40	1,000	1,000	
Community room with stage	1	50–60	1,200	1,200	
Storage (table/chair)	1		100	100	
Activity/crafts room	1	20–25	600	600	
Activity/supply storage	1		75	75	
Media room	1	25	20	500	
Hobby room	1	10–15	400	400	
Barber/beauty shop with toliet	1		350	350	
Branch bank/personal finance	1		200	200	
Toilets	2		120	240	
Subtotal				**11,975**	
Resident wellness					
Reception/nurse/files	1		200	200	
Treatment room (exam / massage)	2		120	240	
Wellness director's office	1		120	120	
Toliet (unisex)	1		50	50	
Lab/supply room	1		65	65	
Exercise coordinator/lifeguard	1		80	80	
Exercise/lap pool/spa	1		2,500	2,500	
Pool equipment and storage	1		80	80	

	Space Count	Proposed Users total	Net Square Feet each	total	Notes
Pool mechanical room	1		240	240	
Fitness room	1		800	800	
Changing/showers/lockers/toliets (women)	1		400	400	
Changing/showers/lockers/toliets (men)	1		250	250	
Subtotal				**5,025**	
Service/support: food service					
Kitchen	1		2,800	2,800	
Dry storage	1		300	300	
Storage	1		300	300	
Housekeeping closet	1		50	50	
Director of food service office	1		120	120	
Dietician office	1		90	90	
Dining room manager	1		75	75	
Staff lounge/vending	1		275	275	
Staff lockers	2		350	700	
Subtotal				**4,710**	
Service/support: housekeeping					
Director of housekeeping office	1		75	75	
Central housekeeping supply	1		325	325	
Central laundry	1				Offsite service
Maintenance shop	1		450	450	
Maintenance storage	1		250	250	
Office	1		100	100	
Mechanical rooms	1		4,000	4,000	
Elevator equipment room	2		120	240	
Central building storage	1		800	800	
Resident storage (4' x 4' x 4' cubicle)	1	150	15	3,000	
Receiving/loading dock/trash/ compactor	1		500	500	
Subtotal services/support				**9,740**	

(continued)

APPENDIX L (*cont.*)

	Space Count	Proposed Users total	Net Square Feet each	total	Notes
Total usable square feet				**195,320**	
Total program area (1.35 net/gross factor)				**263,682**	
(average +/– 1760 sq ft/unit)					
Parking					
Garage and/or surface					
Resident (1.0/unit)	1		150		
Staff	1		50		Garage or surface parking is a local market, site and budget issue. Zoning/public transportation and facility transportation all impact parking quantity.
Visitor	1		30		
Total parking			**230**		

APPENDIX M
CCRC PROGRAM

Space Description	Space Count	Proposed Users total	Net Square Feet each	Net Square Feet total	Notes
Apartments					
1 bedroom, 1 bath	20		800	16,000	
1 bedroom with den, 1.5 baths	50		950	47,500	
2 bedroom, 2 baths	100		1,200	120,000	
2 bedroom with den, 2 baths	30		1,400	42,000	
Subtotal: apartments	**200**			**225,500**	
Subtotal (1.3 net/gross factor)				**293,150**	
Cottages					
1 bedroom with den, 1.5 baths	6		1,100	6,600	One-car garage @ 200 sq ft
2 bedroom, 2 baths	30		1,400	42,000	Two-car garage @ 400 sq ft
2 bedroom with den, 2 baths	20		1,800	36,000	Two-car garage @ 400 sq ft
3 bedroom	4		2,100	8,400	Two-car garage @ 400 sq ft
Subtotal: cottages	**60**			**93,000**	
Note: Cottages net/gross = 1.0					
Common areas					
Resident wing support areas (4 stories/2 wings)					
Housekeeping closet (1 per wing or floor)	8		50	400	
Trash room	8		50	400	
Telephone/LAN	8		25	200	
Electrical	8		25	200	
Subtotal: support areas				**1,200**	
Resident common areas					
Lobby	1		800	800	
Vestibule	1		150	150	
Reception	1		100	100	
Public toilets	2		225	450	

(*continued*)

APPENDIX M (*cont.*)

Space Description	Space Count	Proposed Users total	Net Square Feet each	total	Notes
Mailboxes/package room	1		350	350	
Formal dining	1	50	35	1,750	
Bistro/casual dining	1	100	30	3,000	
Bistro display kitchen	1		800	800	
Coffee bar	1	20	35	700	
Bar/takeout	1	20	35	700	
Service bar	1		600	600	
Private dining	1	15–20	400	400	
Community room with stage	1	125–150	2,250	2,250	
Gathering lounge / library room with fireplace	1		800	800	
Coat room/cart storage	1		200	200	
Store	1		400	400	
Media room/movie theater	1	30	20	600	
Library	1		600	600	
Billiards/game room	2		350	700	
Activity/art room/painting studio	2	15–20	350	700	
Greenhouse	1		150	150	
Hobby room	1	15–20	400	400	
Classroom/meeting room	1	30–35	600	600	
Resident bank	1		200	200	
Guest suite	2		350	700	
Miscellaneous toilets	2		300	600	
Community room storage	1		200	200	
Subtotal: resident common areas				**18,900**	
Resident wellness (see Exhibit E for enhanced clinic and rehab programs)					
Reception/nurse/files	1		250	250	
Treatment rooms/massage/exam	2		120	240	
Speciality exam/treatment	1		160	160	

Space Description	Space Count	Proposed Users total	Net Square Feet each	Net Square Feet total	Notes
Medical director	1		150	150	
OT/PT suite	1		750	750	Near long-term care
Toilets	4		50	200	
Lab/workroom	1		100	100	
Records/workroom	1		150	150	
Wellness director office	1		120	120	
Exercise coordinator office	1		80	80	
Exercise/lap pool/spa	1		3,000	3,000	
Pool equipment/storage	1		100	100	
Pool mechanical	1		300	300	
Fitness equipment room	1		800	800	
Aerobic room	1		800	800	
Changing/shower/locker (women)	1		400	400	
Changing/shower/locker (men)	1		250	250	
Subtotal: resident wellness				**7,850**	
Central administration					
Executive director	1		180	180	
Asistant director/nursing home administrator	1		150	150	
Director of social work/ admissions	1		120	120	
Director of finance	1		120	120	
Director of development	1		120	120	
Director of resident services	1		120	120	
Clergy office	1		150	150	
Business office	1		200	200	
Administrative support	1		225	225	
Marketing director	1		150	150	
Marketing reception/waiting	1		150	150	
Marketing coordinator	1		120	120	
Human resources office	1		100	100	
Human resources coordinator	1		120	120	

(continued)

APPENDIX M (*cont.*)

Space Description	Space Count	Proposed Users total	Net Square Feet each	Net Square Feet total	Notes
Human resources waiting	1		150	150	
Workroom/copy/supplies	1		150	150	
Conference (large)	1	8–10	300	300	
Conference (small)	1	4–5	150	150	
Staff toilets	2		50	100	
Subtotal: administration				**2,875**	
Subtotal: Common Area usable square feet				**30,825**	
Subtotal (1.35 net/gross factor)				**41,614**	
Assisted living program, 30 units (assumes 2 floors)					
1-bedroom units	30		500	15,000	
Cluster den/game room/living room	1		250	250	
Resident kitchen with sitting area	1		400	400	
Resident laundry	2		75	150	
Guest toilet	2		50	100	
Linen supply	2		15	30	
Housekeeping closet	2		50	100	
Trash room	2		50	100	
Electrical closet	2		25	50	
Entry/lobby/waiting/reception	1		400	400	
Mail	1		50	50	
Dining prefunction/personal services	1		50	50	
Dining	30		35	1,050	
Private dining/meeting	1	8–10	280	280	
Library/living room	1		300	300	
Spa bathing with toilet	1		250	250	
Toilets rear dining	2		50	100	
Special meeting room	1	8–10	300	300	
Director office	1		180	180	
Care team workroom with medications	1	2–3	300	300	

Space Description	Space Count	Proposed Users total	Net Square Feet each	total	Notes
Office (sw or activities)	1		120	120	
General storage	1		300	300	
Soiled linen holding	1		80	80	
Clean supply	1		50	50	
Resident storage (4' x 4' x 4' cubicle)	1	30	20	600	
Subtotal: Assisted living usable square feet				**20,590**	
Subtotal (1.4 net/gross factor)				**28,826**	
Dementia/memory-care program for 20 (assumes 2 households)					
Private room	20		250	5,000	
Linen closet	2		15	30	
Living room	2		250	500	
Dining room for 10	2		350	700	
Household kitchen/staff work area	1		400	400	
Laundry room	1		75	75	
Soiled utility	1		80	80	
Housekeeping closet	1		50	50	
Resident/visitor toilet	2		50	100	
Electrical closet	1		25	25	
Arts and crafts/messy activity	1	10–15	400	400	
Director office	1		140	140	
Care team workroom with medic	1		300	300	
Haircare and spa with toilet	1		250	250	
Secure entrance	1		100	100	
General storage	1		200	200	
Clean supply	1		50	50	
Subtotal: Memory care usable square feet				**8,400**	
Subtotal (1.4 net/gross factor)				**11,760**	

(continued)

APPENDIX M (*cont.*)

Space Description	Space Count	Proposed Users total	Net Square Feet each	total	Notes
Long-term care program for 40 beds (assumes 2 neighborhoods)					
Private rooms	40		250	10,000	
Linen closet	2		15	30	
Living room	2		250	500	
Dining room for 20	2		700	1,400	
Household kitchen	2		400	800	
Staff work area/alcove	2		150	300	
Laundry room (resident personals)	2		75	150	
Soiled utility	2		80	160	
Clean utility	2		80	160	
Housekeeping closet	2		50	100	
Resident/visitor toilet	2		50	100	
Electrical closet	1		25	25	
Arts and crafts/messy activity	1	15–20	400	400	
Shared living room/library	1	15–20	400	400	
Greatroom/large gathering	1	25–30	700	700	
Private dining/meeting room	1	6–8	200	200	
Director's office (nurse?)	1		180	180	
Care team workroom with medication	1	4–5	400	400	
Office (social work, activity, therapy)	1		120	120	
Medical records/unit clerk	1		120	120	
Haircare, spa with toilet	1		250	250	
Entry/lobby/waiting/reception	1		400	400	
Toilets (public, visitor)	2		50	100	
Toilet staff	1		50	50	
General storage	1		300	300	
Central soiled linen holding	1		80	80	
Clean supply	1		50	50	
Resident storage	1		800	800	
Wheelchair storage	1		50	50	
Subtotal: Long-Term Care usable square feet				**18,325**	
Subtotal (1.45 net/gross factor)				**26,571**	

Space Description	Space Count	Proposed Users total	Net Square Feet each	total	Notes
Service / Support					
Kitchen	1		3,500	3,500	
Director of food service	1		120	120	
Dry storage	1		300	300	
Dietrician's office	1		90	90	
Dining room manager	1		100	100	
Director of housekeeping	1		75	75	
Training classrom	1		400	400	
Plant manager / assistant plant manager / plans	1		200	200	
IT manager / fileservers	1		400	400	
Maintenance shops and storage	2		600	1,200	
Central storage	1		800	800	
Resident storage (4' x 4' x 4' cubicle)	1	200	20	4,000	
Staff locker rooms with toilets	2		300	600	
Staff lounge/vending	1		500	500	
Housekeeping/ supply	1		600	600	
Director of housekeeping office	1		75	75	
Body holding	1		100	100	
Cart wash	1		100	100	
Trash holding	1		150	150	
Central laundry	1		800	800	
Elevator equipment room	3		120	360	
Receiving / loading dock / trash	1		1,500	1,500	
Mechanical	1		5,000	5,000	
Subtotal: Service/Support usable square feet				**20,970**	
Subtotal (1.3 net/gross factor)				**27,261**	
Grand total GSF				**522,182**	
Maintenance building (grounds equipment)	1		1,500	1,500	

(continued)

APPENDIX M (*cont.*)

Space Description	Space Count	Proposed Users total	Net Square Feet each	total	Notes
Parking	1.25/unit	250	450	112,500	Garage or surface parking is a local market site and budget issue. Zoning / public transportation and facility transportation all impact parking quantity.
Garage (residential units)					
Cottages	1.0/unit	6	200	1,200	
(6) 1-bedroom with den	2.0/unit	108	400	43,200	
(54) 2-bedroom or 2-bedroom with den	.1/unit	26		surface	
Visitor/guest (not in unit driveway)		**390**		156,900	
Subtotal					
Assisted living (resident/visitor)	.33/bed/unit	17		surface	
50 units		**17**			
Subtotal					
Healthcare (visitor/private duty aides)	.33/bed	13		surface	
40 units		**13**			
Subtotal					
Central building	1/peak shift staff	120		surface	
Staff	.1/unit	26		surface	
Visitors (IL/commons)		**172**			
Subtotal		**566**			
Total parking					

APPENDIX N
ENHANCED CCRC THERAPY PROGRAM

Description	Space Count	Proposed Users total	Net Square Feet each	total
Waiting room	1	6–8	200	200
OT/PT director's office	2	–	120	240
Staff observation/work area	1	–	200	200
PT open gym area	1	–	550	550
PT mat/table area	2	–	140	280
PT weights/exercise area	1	–	140	140
PT hydrotherapy area	1	–	100	100
OT program area (including ADL kitchen)	1	–	300	300
Audiology/speech therapy	1	–	140	140
Resident toilet/shower	1	–	100	100
Public toilet	1	–	50	50
Equipment storage	1	–	200	200
Subtotal usable square feet				**2,500**
Total program (1.4 net / gross factor)				**3,500**

PT – Physical therapy
OT – Occupational therapy

GLOSSARY

Accreditation A process whereby a program of study or an institution is recognized by an external body as meeting certain predetermined standards. For facilities, these standards are usually defined in terms of physical plant, governing body, administration, and medical or other staff. Organizations that grant accreditation are usually created for the purpose of assuring the public of the quality of the accredited institution or program. Federal and state governments can recognize accreditation in lieu of or as the basis for licensure or other mandatory approvals. Public or private payment programs often require accreditation as a condition of payment for covered services.

Active adult communities Resort-like residential communities geared to younger retirees (55 years and up) who are physically active.

Activities of daily living (ADLs) Basic activities that are important to self-care, such as bathing, dressing, using the toilet, eating, and getting in and out of a chair. ADLs are used to measure a person's level of independence.

Acute care Care that is provided for a short period of time to treat a specific illness or condition.

Adult care homes Residences for aged and disabled adults who require 24-hour supervision and assistance with personal care needs. Previously called domiciliary homes, they differ from nursing homes in the level of care and the qualifications of staff.

Adult day care This is a senior care setting that provides social interaction, medical care, and/or Alzheimer's care for a limited number of hours per day to frail physically or cognitively impaired older persons who require some supervision and care during the day but are able to reside in the general community.

Age-associated memory impairment A decline in short-term memory that sometimes accompanies aging; also called benign senescent forgetfulness. This is distinguished from dementia and Alzheimer's disease in that it does not progress to further cognitive impairments.

Aging in place A process by which individuals remain in their living environment despite any physical and/or mental decline or increased need for supportive services that occur as they get older. For aging in place to be successful, an individual must have access to services that respond to his or her changing needs.

Alcove A small recessed space opening directly into a larger room.

Alzheimer's disease A neurological disease named for the German physician who first described it, Alois Alzheimer. This disease is marked by the development of dense deposits of neuritic plaques around the nerve cells in the brain, as well as twisted strands of fiber called neurofibrillary tangles within the nerve cells. This degeneration of brain cells produces a progressive, irreversible decline in memory (especially in the ability to store new memories), the performance of routine tasks, time and space orientation, language and communication skills, abstract thinking, and the ability to learn and carry out mathematical calculations. Other symptoms include personality changes and impaired judgment. Alzheimer's is the most common cause of dementia among older people. It is incurable, although numerous treatments have been used with varying success.

American Society for Testing Materials (ASTM) Organized in 1898, ASTM International is one of the largest voluntary standards development organizations in the world. ASTM International is a nonprofit organization that provides a forum for the development and publication of voluntary consensus standards for materials, products, systems, and services.

Americans with Disabilities Act (ADA) A civil rights law passed by Congress in 1990 intended "to establish a clear and comprehensive prohibition of discrimination on the basis of disability." This law has had extensive repercussions on building codes.

Assisted living A coordinated array of supportive personal and health services, available 24 hours a day, to residents who need those services in a residential setting. Assisted living promotes self-direction and participation in decisions that emphasize independence, privacy, and dignity in homelike surroundings.

Assistive devices Tools that enable individuals with disabilities to perform essential functions. These include telephone headsets, adapted computer keyboards, and enhanced computer monitors.

Behavioral symptoms of Alzheimer's This category of symptoms of Alzheimer's disease is particularly troublesome for caregivers. It includes wandering, pacing, agitation, screaming, and aggressive reactions.

Building codes Regulations, ordinances, or statutory requirements of a government unit that relate to building construction and occupancy, generally adopted and administered for the protection of public health, safety, and welfare.

Building envelope The exterior structure of a building that separates the interior environment from the exterior environment.

Building-related illness According to the Environmental Protection Agency, the term "building-related illness" (BRI) describes situations in which building occupants experience symptoms of diagnosable illness that can be attributed directly to airborne building contaminants such as lead paint or asbestos. Also known as "sick-building syndrome."

Caregiver Anyone who provides support and assistance to a physically or cognitively impaired person. This can include family members, friends, neighbors, and professionals.

Carpet backing Fabrics and yarns that make up the back of the carpet as opposed to the carpet pile or face. In tufted carpet, the primary backing is a woven or nonwoven fabric into which the yarn is inserted by tufting needles. The secondary backing is a lamination that is applied to the back of the carpet to reinforce and increase dimensional stability.

Carpet pile The visible surface of carpet consisting of yarn tufts in loop and/or cut configuration. Sometimes called "face" or "nap."

Certificate of need (CON) A certificate issued by a government body to a healthcare provider who is proposing to construct, modify, or expand facilities or to offer new or different types of health services. A CON is intended to prevent duplication of services and overbedding and to provide quality assurance. Granting of the certificate indicates that the proposal has been approved.

Chronic care Care and treatment given to individuals whose health problems are of a long-term and continuing nature. Rehabilitation facilities, nursing homes, and mental hospitals are considered chronic-care facilities.

Chronic organic brain syndrome An alternate term for dementia or dementing illness.

Cognitive functions The mental activity by which an individual is aware of his or her environment, including all aspects of thinking, perceiving, reasoning, and remembering.

Cognitive impairment Damage or loss of intellectual or mental functioning. This can include impairment of short- or long-term memory; orientation as to person, place, or time; and deductive or abstract reasoning skills. Alzheimer's disease is the most common cause of cognitive impairment in older adults.

Color-rendering index A scale used to measure the color-rendering capabilities of lamplight: how much of the color spectrum is represented in the light and in what amounts compared to the perfect reference lamp of the same color temperature. The color-rendering index, ranging from 1 to 100, measures how well a lamp will render colors and determines the suitability of light for any given purpose.

Community-based services Services designed to help older people remain independent and in their own homes; they can include senior centers, transportation, delivered or congregate meals, visiting nurses or home health aides, adult day care, and homemaker services.

Congregate care The precursor to assisted living, congregate care was the first alternative to custodial care on one end of the continuum of care spectrum and complete self-sufficiency on the other. Congregate care provides supportive services to accommodate the changing needs and varied populations in a residential environment for the aging. There can be broad differences in size, services, staffing, and social programs between facilities.

Continuing care retirement community (CCRC) A residential community setting offering housing and health-related services for life or for longer than one year that includes access to coordinated social activities, transportation, dining services, and multiple levels of healthcare should the need for those services arise. It may also include full or efficiency units, villas or cluster homes, and community dining and recreational areas. CCRCs usually offer independent living, assisted living, and skilled nursing care facilities so that residents may receive the level of care they require while still aging in place. Also referred to as "life care."

Continuum of care The entire spectrum of specialized health, rehabilitative, and residential services available to the frail and chronically ill. The services focus on the social, residential, rehabilitative, and supportive needs of individuals as well as needs that are essentially medical in nature.

Contrast The difference in brightness between light and dark areas.

Dementia An organic mental disorder characterized by a decline in cognitive functioning severe enough to interfere with a person's normal daily activities and social relationships. It includes loss of memory, impaired judgment and abstract thinking, and changes in personality.

Design development The second phase of the design process, during which the architect prepares more detailed drawings and finalizes the design plans, showing correct sizes and shapes for rooms. Also included is an outline of the construction specifications listing the major materials to be used.

Disability The limitation of normal physical, mental, or social activity. There are varying types (functional, occupational, learning, physical), degrees (partial, total), and durations (temporary, permanent) of disabilities. Benefits are often available only for specific levels of disability, such as total or permanent.

Elevation A two-dimensional scale drawing of the three-dimensional vertical face of a building.

Environmental psychology An area of psychology that studies the relationship between human behavior and the physical environment for the purpose of designing work or living areas.

Feasibility study An analysis of a project's financial, market and/or operational likelihood of success.

Fire-rated A part of a construction (such as a wall or door) that takes a certain number of minutes to burn—usually 20, 60, or 90. Fire-rated items are often required by building codes for certain uses.

Fire retardant A chemical compound used on or in textiles to reduce flammability.

First cost The initial investment required for the construction of a facility.

Flammability A product's capacity for combustion with respect to flame spread, fuel contribution, smoke generation, and other factors.

Footcandle A measure of light falling onto an area and onto a given object.

For-profit Organization or company in which profits are distributed to shareholders or private owners.

Functionally disabled A person with a physical or mental impairment that limits his or her capacity to live independently.

Geriatric medicine The branch of medicine that deals with the diagnosis and treatment of diseases and problems specific to the aged.

Gerontology The comprehensive study of aging and the problems of the aged. Unlike geriatrics, gerontology is not limited to the biological but also includes psychological and sociological issues.

Glare An intensely bright, blinding light.

Green architecture Sustainable or environmentally friendly architecture. See "sustainable architecture."

Green House A registered name for a small house or part of a larger facility where small groups of residents receive support from a team of caregivers. In these settings there is no nursing unit nor are there nurses stationed in each house. The Green House movement was started in Mississippi by Dr. William Thomas and is now influencing projects nationally.

Home health agency A public or private organization that provides home health services supervised by a licensed health professional in the patient's home, either directly or through arrangements with other organizations.

Home healthcare Includes a wide range of health-related services, such as assistance with medications, wound care, intravenous (IV) therapy, and help with basic needs such as bathing, dressing, and mobility, delivered at a person's home.

Hospice A philosophy of care that focuses on the relief of symptoms, pain control, and providing personal, emotional, and spiritual support to dying patients and their families.

Hue The property that enables color perception. Hue is determined by the dominant wavelength of the light.

HVAC Heating, ventilation, and air-conditioning.

Independent living facility Rental units in which services are not included as part of the rent, although services are often available on-site and may be purchased by residents for an additional fee.

Intermediate care facility A nursing home, recognized under the Medicaid program, that provides health-related care and services to individuals who do not require acute or

skilled nursing care but who require care and services above the level of room and board.

Level loop A carpet construction in which the yarn on the face of the carpet forms a loop with both ends anchored into the carpet back. The pile loops are of more or less the same height and uncut, making a smooth, level surface.

Level of care (LOC) Amount of assistance required by consumers, which may determine their eligibility for programs and services. Levels include protective, intermediate, and skilled.

License/licensure Permission granted to an individual or organization by a competent authority, usually public, to engage lawfully in a practice, occupation, or activity.

Life care A type of contract that guarantees that continuing care retirement community residents will receive the amount of healthcare appropriate to their needs as they age.

Life cycle cost A complicated mathematical calculation of the cost of a design decision over the course of its lifetime. This calculation is usually used for decisions involving complex cost analysis, such as the purchase of an HVAC system that includes both heating and cooling, with overall costs varying with season and over time.

Long-term care A range of medical and/or social services designed to help people who have disabilities or chronic-care needs. The services may be short- or long-term and may be provided in a person's home, in the community, or in residential facilities such as nursing homes or assisted living.

Low-E glazing/low-emissivity glass A special type of glass that has a transparent material fused to its surface that acts as a thermal mirror, reflecting heat so as not to increase the internal temperature of a building. This saves energy in the cooling season.

Medicaid (Title XIX) A joint federal and state program that provides medical care to low-income individuals. Specifics vary between states.

Medicare (Title XVIII) The federal health insurance program for persons 65 and over and some people who are disabled regardless of age. Medicare pays for skilled care in certified skilled-nursing facilities for up to 100 days following hospitalization in a calendar year. Beneficiaries are required to pay part of the bill for care after the first 20 days. Medicare does not provide benefits for intermediate or custodial care.

Mobile care A truck equipped to provide medical exams and minor treatments.

Nonprofit/Not-for-profit An organization that reinvests all profits back into that organization.

NORC Naturally occurring retirement community.

Neighborhood A grouping of two or more household sized units within a larger senior living facility.

Nursing facility or home A facility licensed by the state to provide residents with personal care as well as skilled nursing care 24 hours a day. It also provides room and board, supervision, medication, therapies, and rehabilitation.

Occupational therapy Therapy designed to help participants improve their

independence with activities of daily living through rehabilitation, exercise, and the use of assistive devices.

Operating cost The cost of operating a facility. This includes staffing, utilities, maintenance, upkeep, and other ongoing expenses.

Orientation An awareness of the parameters of one's immediate physical environment, including time, place, and other people present, achieved through cognitive and sensory input.

Personal care Also called custodial care. Assistance with activities of daily living as well as with self-administering medications and preparing special diets.

Perspective drawing A type of drawing that gives a 3-D view of a building or space using a specific viewpoint and vanishing points.

Photovoltaic cell A semiconductor device that converts the energy of sunlight into electric energy. Also called a solar cell.

Physical therapy Therapy designed to restore or improve movement and strength in people whose mobility has been impaired by injury or disease. It can include exercise, massage, water therapy, and assistive devices.

Porte-cochere A roofed structure that extends from a building's side or front entry over an adjacent driveway to protect and shelter persons getting in or out of vehicles.

Power-operated vehicles (POV) An electric-powered personal mobility vehicle often used instead of a wheelchair by nonambulatory individuals who lack the ability or have a limited ability to move on their own.

Programming The architect and sponsor define the goals, needs, and functions of the project; design expectations; available budget; pertinent building codes; and zoning regulations. The architect prepares a written statement setting forth design objectives, constraints, and criteria for a project, including special requirements and systems as well as site requirements.

Rehabilitation The combined and coordinated use of medical, social, educational, and vocational measures for training or retraining individuals disabled by disease or injury to the highest possible level of functional ability. Several different types of rehabilitation are distinguished: occupational, physical, speech, and others.

Residential care The provision of room, board, and personal care. Residential care falls between the nursing care delivered in skilled and intermediate care facilities and the assistance provided through social services. Broadly it is the provision of 24-hour supervision of individuals who, because of old age or impairments, need assistance with the activities of daily living.

Resident rights In certified nursing facilities, the rights of each resident are protected by law to safeguard and promote dignity, choice, and self-determination. The Omnibus Budget Reconciliation Act of 1987 requires each nursing facility "to care for its residents in such a manner and in such an environment as will promote maintenance or enhancement to the quality of life of each resident."

Respite care Temporary relief for a primary caregiver from the burden of caring for an individual who cannot be left alone because of mental or physical problems. This relief is provided in the home, a nursing home, or elsewhere in the community.

Schematic design The first phase of the design process, during which the architect consults with the owner to determine a project's requirements and prepares schematic studies consisting of drawings and other documents illustrating the scale and relationships of the project components for approval by the owner. The architect also submits to the owner a preliminary estimate of construction cost based on current area, volume, or other unit costs. By the end of this phase, architectural plans and specifications should be 15–20 percent complete. Those plans and specifications include a site plan, floor plans with identification of rooms, exterior elevations and cross-sections, and a calculation of gross floor area.

Section A type of drawing that cuts vertically through a building to show its interior and construction.

Senile dementia An outdated term once used to refer to any form of dementia that occurred in older people.

Senility The generalized characterization of progressive decline in mental functioning as a condition of the aging process. Within geriatric medicine, this term has limited meaning and is often substituted for the diagnosis of senile dementia and/or senile psychosis.

Senior housing developments Multiunit apartment buildings, condominiums, cooperatives, single-family home complexes, and mobile-home parks restricted by age. Not originally planned to include activities, supportive assistance, or personal/health care.

Shared occupancy A residential or health-care unit shared by more than one related or unrelated individual.

Sick-building syndrome According to the Environmental Protection Agency, the term "sick-building syndrome" (SBS) describes situations in which building occupants experience acute health and comfort symptoms that appear to be linked to time spent in a building but for which no specific illness or cause can be identified. The complaints may be localized in a particular room or zone or widespread throughout the building. See also building-related illness.

Site plan A drawing of a site's layout, including topography, vegetation, and groundwater.

Skilled care The provision of a higher level of care, such as injections, catheterizations, and dressing changes, by trained medical professionals.

Skilled nursing care Daily nursing and/or rehabilitative care that can be performed only by or under the supervision of skilled medical personnel.

Small house movement An increasingly popular movement to breakdown long-term care and other senior living facilities into smaller, house-scale semiautonomous units of 8–14 residents.

Special-care unit (SCU) A long-term care facility with environmental features and/or programs designed for people with dementia; these units may also provide care for persons with head injuries or serious illnesses. Also, a unit within a senior housing facility specially designed to meet the needs of residents suffering from Alzheimer's disease or other dementias.

Specialized nursing units Units in a healthcare setting that are organized around the delivery of care for a specific population, including those with dementia, younger adults, and those with physical disabilities.

Subacute care Short-term care provided by many long-term care facilities and hospitals. It includes rehabilitation services, specialized care for certain conditions and/or postsurgical care, and other services associated with the transition between the hospital and home. Residents on these units have often been hospitalized recently and typically have more complicated medical needs. The goal is to discharge residents to their homes or to a lower level of care. Also called transitional care or postacute care.

Sundowning The tendency for the behavioral symptoms of Alzheimer's disease to grow worse in the afternoon and evening. While the source of this term is unclear, writers have linked it to the historical term "sundowner," a person who hopes to obtain food and lodging after it is too late to perform work.

Tea kitchen/Pullman-style kitchen A small kitchen area equipped with a sink, refrigerator, and microwave.

Tuft bind Force required to pull a tuft from a carpet.

Tufted carpet Carpet manufactured by the insertion of tufts of yarn through a carpet-backing fabric, creating a pile surface of cut and/or loop ends.

Value engineering The act of seeking design options that achieve the desired goal at a lower cost. This is not the same as cost cutting, which involves making sacrifices to save money.

Wayfinding What people see, think about, and do to find their way from one place to another. Wayfinding systems include signs, arrows, other environmental cues, or person-to-person assistance.

Wellness A dynamic state of physical, mental, and social well-being; a way of life that equips the individual to realize the full potential of his or her capabilities and to overcome and compensate for a weakness; a lifestyle that recognizes the importance of nutrition, physical fitness, stress reduction, and self-responsibility.

Years to payback When choosing among building systems such as HVAC options with differing energy efficiencies, it is often valuable to calculate the years to payback; that is, if a more energy-efficient but more expensive system is chosen, how many years it will take for the savings in utility bills to make up for the additional first-cost investment.

Zoning The control by a municipality of the use of land and buildings.

BIBLIOGRAPHY AND REFERENCES

AARP. 1999. *National Survey of Mobile Home Owners*. Washington, D.C.: AARP. http://www.aarp.org/livable-communities/learn/housing/aarp-national-survey-of-mobile.html

Alzheimer's Association. 2010. *Alzheimer's Disease Facts and Figures*. Washington, D.C.: Alzheimer's Association.

American Institute of Architects. 1985. *A.I.A. Design for Aging: An Architect's Guide*. Washington, D.C.: AIA Press.

———. 2007. *Defining the Architect's Basic Services*. Washington, D.C.: AIA Press.

American Seniors Housing Association. 2010. *The State of Seniors Housing 2010*. Washington, D.C.: American Seniors Housing Association.

Barry, John R., and C. Ray Wilgrove, eds. 1977. *Let's Learn about Aging: A Book of Readings*. Cambridge, Mass.: Schenkman.

Baucom, Alfred H. 1996. *Hospitality Design for the Graying Generation*. New York: John Wiley & Sons.

Bednar, M. J. 1977. *Barrier-Free Environments*. Stroudsburg, Pa.: Dowden, Hutchinson, Ross.

Bonnema, Eric, Shanti Pless, and Ian Doebber. 2010. "Advanced Energy Design Guide for Small Hospitals and Healthcare Facilities." *FacilityCare* (March/April): 32–35. http://www.gghc.org/documents/misc/GreeningHealthcareMarchApril.pdf

Bonifazi, W. L. 1999. "Bathing the Alzheimer's Patient in Long-Term Care." *Contemporary Long-Term Care* (March).

Brawley, E. C. 1997. *Designing for Alzheimer's Disease*. New York: John Wiley & Sons.

Briller, S., and M. P. Calkins. 2000. "Conceptualizing Care Settings as Home, Resort, or Hospital." *Alzheimer's Care Quarterly* 1, no. 1: 17–23.

Burgio, L., K. Scilley, J. M. Hardin, C. Hsu, and J. Yancey. 1996. "Environmental 'White Noise': An Intervention for Verbally Agitated Nursing Home Residents." *Journals of Gerontology Series B: Psychological Sciences and Social Sciences* 51, no. 6: 64–73.

Byerts, Thomas O. 1979. "Toward a Better Range of Housing and Environmental Choices for the Elderly." In *Back to Basics: Food and Shelter for the Elderly*, edited by Patricia A. Wagner and John M. McRae. Gainesville: University Presses of Florida.

Carstens, Diane. 1985. *Site Planning and Designing for the Elderly: Issues, Guidelines, and Alternatives*. New York: Van Nostrand Reinhold.

Centers for Disease Control and Prevention. 2009. *Vital and Health Statistics: The National Nursing Home Survey: 2004 Overview*. Washington, D.C.: Centers for Disease Control and Prevention. Series 13, no. 167.

———. 2012, *Vital and Health Statistics: Summary Health Statistics for U.S. Adults: National Health Interview Survey, 2011*. Washington, D.C.: Centers for Disease Control and Prevention. Series 10, no. 256.

Cohen, Donna, and Carl Eisdorfer. 1986. *The Loss of Self: A Family Resource for the Care of Alzheimer's Disease and Related Disorders*. New York: W. W. Norton.

Council of American Building Officials. n.d. *American National Standard: Accessible and Usable Buildings and Facilities*, A117.1, Sect 4.22.

Crisp, B. 1998. *Human Spaces: Life Enhancing Designs for Healing, Working, and Living*. Gloucester, Mass.: Rockport.

Egan, M. David. 2007. *Architectural Acoustics*. Plantation, Fla.: J. Ross.

Fries, James F. 1980. "Aging, Natural Death, and the Compression of Morbidity." *New England Journal of Medicine* 303, no. 3 (July 17): 130–5.

Garg, A., and B. Owen. 1991. "Ergonomics." *AAOHN Journal* 35, no. 11: 1353–75.

Goldsmith, Selwyn. 1976. *Designing for the Disabled.* London: RIBA.

Hanser, S. B. 1996. "Music Therapy to Reduce Anxiety, Agitation, and Depression." *Nursing Home Medicine* 4, no. 10: 286–91.

Harkness, Sarah P., and James N. Groome, Jr. 1976. *Building without Barriers for the Disabled.* New York: Watson-Guptill.

Harvard University, Joint Center for Housing Studies. 2010. *The State of the Nation's Housing 2010.* http://www.jchs.harvard.edu/research/publications/state-nations-housing-2010.

Hiatt, Lorraine G. 1991. *Nursing Home Renovation Designed for Reform.* Boston: Butterworth Architecture.

Hoglund, J. D. 1985. *Housing for the Elderly: Privacy and Independence in Environments for the Aging.* New York: Van Nostrand Reinhold.

Howell, Sandra C. 1978. *Private Space: Habitability of Apartments for the Elderly.* Cambridge, Mass.: MIT Press.

_____. 1980. *Designing for Aging: Patterns of Use.* Cambridge, Mass.: MIT Press.

Joseph, Anjali, and Roger Ulrich. 2007. "Sound Control for Improved Outcomes in Healthcare Settings," Center for Health Design, Issue paper #4, January.

Keenan, Teresa. 2010. *Home and Community Preferences of the 45 + Population.* Washington, D.C.: AARP. http://assets.aarp.org/rgcenter/general/home-community-services-10.pdf

Kellert, Stephen, R., Judith Heerwagen, and Martin Mador, 2011. *Biophilic Design: The Theory, Science and Practice of Bringing Buildings to Life.* New York: John Wiley & Sons.

Koncelick, Joseph. 1976. *Designing the Open Nursing Home.* Stroudsburg, Pa.: Dowden, Hutchinson, Ross.

Lawton, M. Powell. 1980. *Environment and Aging.* Monterey, Calif.: Brooks/Cole.

_____. 1989. "Environmental Approaches to Research and Treatment of Alzheimer's Disease." In *Alzheimer's Disease Treatment and Family Stress: Direction for Research*, edited by B. D. Lebowita. Rockville, MD.: National Institute of Mental Health, U.S. Department of Health and Human Services, Public Health Service, pp. 340–62.

Lifchez, Raymond, and Barbara Wilson. 1979. *Designing for Independent Living: The Environment and Physically Disabled People.* New York: Whitney Library of Design.

Malkin, Jain. 1992. *Hospital Interior Architecture.* New York: Van Nostrand Reinhold.

Marberry, Sara O., ed. 1997. *Healthcare Design.* New York: John Wiley & Sons.

Moore, K. D., and M. Verhoef. 1999. "Special-Care Units as Places for Social Interaction: Evaluating an SCU's Social Affordance." *American Journal of Alzheimer's Disease* 14, no. 4: 217–29.

National Directory of Lifestyle Communities. N.d., https://www2.elpasotexas.gov/muni_clerk/agenda/01-08.../01080810G.pdf

National Hospice and Palliative Care Organization. 2010. *NHPCO Facts and Figures: Hospice Care in America.* 2010 edition. Alexandria, Va.: NHPCO.

National Institute on Adult Day Care. 1984. *Standards for Adult Day Care.* Washington, D.C.: National Institute on Adult Day Care.

Pile, John F. 1988. *Interior Design.* New York: Harry N. Abrams.

Pride Institute Journal of Long-Term Home Health Care. 1984. Vol. 3, no. 4. Special issue dedicated to Alzheimer's disease.

Proshansky, H., A. Fabian, and R. Kaminoff. 1995. "Place-Identity: Physical World Socialization of the Self." In *Giving Places Meaning*, edited by L. Groat. London: Academic Press.

Rashchko, Bettyann. 1982. *Housing Interiors for the Disabled and Elderly*. New York: Van Nostrand Reinhold.

Regnier, Victor, ed. 1979. *Planning for the Elderly*. Los Angeles: University of Southern California Press.

————. 1994. *Assisted Living Housing for the Elderly: Design Innovations from the United States and Europe*. New York: Van Nostrand Reinhold.

————. 2002. *Design for Assisted Living: Guidelines for Housing the Physically and Mentally Frail*. New York: John Wiley & Sons.

Regnier, Victor, Jennifer Hamiltoon, and Suzie Yatabe. 1991. *"Best Practices in Assisted Living: Innovations in Design, Management, and Financing*. Los Angeles: National Eldercare Institute on Housing and Supportive Services.

Regnier, Victor, and Jon Pyrnos. 1987. *Housing the Aged: Design Directives and Policy Considerations*. New York: Elsevier Science.

Reichman, William E., and Paul R. Katz, eds. 2009. *Psychiatry in Long-Term Care*. 2nd ed. New York: Oxford Univ. Press.

Rowe, John W., and Robert L. Kahn. 1998. *Successful Aging*. New York: Pantheon.

Scharlach, Andrew E, ed. 2009. "Creating Aging-Friendly Communities." *Generations* 33, no. 2: 5–11.

Schultz, D. J. 1987. "Special Design Considerations for Alzheimer's Facilities." *Contemporary Long-Term Care*, November.

Schwarz, Benyamin, and Ruth Brent. 1999. *Aging, Autonomy, and Architecture: Advances in Assisted Living*. Baltimore: Johns Hopkins University Press.

Sloane, P. D., V. Honn, S. Dwyer, J. Wieselquist, C. Cain, and S. Meyers. 1995. "Bathing the Alzheimer's Patient in Long-Term Care: Results and Recommendations from Three Studies." *American Journal of Alzheimer's Disease* 10, no. 4: 3–11.

Sloane, P. D., J. Rader, A. L. Barrick, B. Hoeffer, S. Dwyer, D. McKenzie, M. Lavelle, K. Buckwalter, L. Arrington, and T. Pruitt. 1995. "Bathing Persons with Dementia." *The Gerontologist* 35, no. 5: 672–78.

Suchman, Diane R. 2001. *Developing Active Adult Retirement Communities*. Washington, D.C.: Urban Land Institute.

United Nations, Department of Economic and Social Affairs, Population Division. 2009. "World Population To Exceed 9 Billion By 2050." Press release, March 11. http://www.un.org/esa/population/publications/wpp2008/pressrelease.pdf

U.S. Department of Housing and Urban Development. 1999. *Housing our Elders*. Washington, D.C.: U.S. Department of Housing and Urban Development. http://www.huduser.org/portal/publications/hsgspec/housec.html

Wayne, Karen. 2001. "Assisted Living Review: A New Era for Regulation." *Nursing Homes* (March): 64–66.

Webster, R., D. Thompson, G. Bowman, and T. Sutton. N.d. "Patients' and Nurses' Opinions about Bathing." *Nursing Times* 84, no. 37: 54–57.

Worpole, Ken. 2009. *The Modern Hospice Movement*. New York: Taylor & Francis.

Zeisel, John, Gayle Epp, and Stephen Demos. 1997. *Low-Rise Housing for Older People: Behavioral Criteria for Design*. Washington, D.C.: U.S. Department of Housing and Urban Development.

INDEX

access control, communicating systems, 237
accessibility
  aging process and, 5–6
  bathing equipment, 251–53
  building codes, 189–90
  community-based options, 15
  geriatric outpatient clinic, 22–23
  hearing loss, 262, 264
  senior living industry, 3–4
  site design/planning, 177, 179
Acoustical Society of America (ASA), 264
acoustics, 255–64
  codes, 262, 264
  considerations in, 255–57
  design guidelines, 258–62
    bathing areas, 260–61
    dining areas, 258, 260
    indoor pool spaces, 261, 264
    lobbies, 258
    mechanical, electrical, and plumbing
      (MEP) rooms, 261–62
    multipurpose spaces, auditoriums,
      theaters, spiritual areas, 260
  hearing loss, 255
  noise reduction coefficients, 257
  sound transmission class values, 257
active adult community (AAC), 119–23
  community center characteristics, 122
  described, 5
  finance, 122–23
  markets, 123
  ownership, 123
  program and design, 120–22
  residence characteristics, 122
  sponsors and settings, 119–20
  user's profile, 119
activity spaces. *See also* exercise areas; fitness
    rooms
  continuing-care retirement community
    (CCRC), 112
  lighting guidelines, 270
activity theory, social life, 10–11
adaptive reuse. *See also* renovation and
    restoration

existing structures, 143–45
  guidelines for, 305
  sustainability strategies, 204
adjacent land use, site planning, 171
adult day care/adult day health programs,
    24–33, 28
  defined, 4, 24–25
  food service equipment, 246
  historical perspective, 31
  program, 26–33, 356–57
  sponsors and settings, 25–26
  user's profile, 25
aesthetics
  construction process, 221
  structural systems, 209
affordability, interior design, 283–85.
    See also costs
age level
  active adult community (AAC), 120
  demography, future prospects, 125
aging process
  accessibility, 3–4
  design and, 5–12
  electrical systems, 216
  fire protection, 216
  HVAC systems, 215
  international perspective, 307–9
  plumbing systems, 215–16
  site design/planning, 177–79
  vision, 265–66
air-to-air heat pumps, HVAC systems, 224
alarms, fire, 230
alternative energy sources, sustainability
    strategies, 203
Alzheimer's care/dementia facility, 5,
    82–96. *See also* dementia
  design considerations, 90–95
  food service equipment, 248
  future prospects, 95–96
  garden, 88–89
  house model, 83–87
  independence, 94
  program and design, 83, 369–70
  residential quality, 95

sensory stimulation, 94–95
  support services, 89
  user's profile, 82–83
  wandering, 92
  wayfinding, 92–94, 287
Alzheimer's dementia. *See also* dementia
  adult day care/adult day health
    programs, 30
  China, 317
  long-term care/nursing home facility, 33
  sponsors and settings, 83
  statistics on, 82
*AMA Handbook Of Poisonous and Injurious
    Plants* (American Medical
    Association), 179
American Association of Housing and
    Services for the Aging (AAHSA),
    172
American Association of Retired People
    (AARP), 142
American Health Care Association
    (AHCA), 185
American Institute of Architects (AIA)
  code reference standards, 186
  licensing, 60
  project team selection and organization,
    152
  state building codes, 185
American Medical Association, 179
American National Standards Institute
    (ANSI)
  hearing loss, 264
  licensing, 60
  showers, 253
American Seniors Housing Association
    (ASHA), 325
American Society of Heating, Refrigerating,
    and Air-Conditioning Engineers
    (ASHRAE)
  codes, 216
  hearing loss, 264
Americans with Disabilities Act (ADA)
  accessibility, 189–90
  federal codes, 185

Americans with Disabilities Act (*cont.*)
  hearing loss, 262, 264
  licensing, 60
appearance. *See* aesthetics
appliances, long-term care/nursing home
    facility design programs, 54–55
approvals. *See* codes; public approvals
Asia. *See also* specific Asian countries
  aging, 308
  building codes, 314
  climate, 312–13
  high-rise construction, 310
asset leveraging, future prospects, 137
assisted-living residences
  central common areas, 76–79
  codes, 79–80
  continuing-care retirement community
      (CCRC), 115
  described, 5
  emergency call systems, 75
  finance and feasibility, 349
  food service equipment, 248
  future prospects, 80–82, 146–48
  gardens, 79
  HVAC systems, 75
  interior design finishes for, 285
  lighting guidelines, 275
  parking, 79
  personalization, 75
  postal service, 79
  program and design, 66, 75–79, 366–68
  renovation and restoration, 300
  resident units, 66–75
  sponsors and settings, 66
  storage, 75
  user's profile, 64–66
  wellness center, 78–79
audio systems, aging process, 216
audiovisuals, communicating systems
    (low-voltage), 239
auditoriums
  acoustical design guidelines, 260, 262, 263
  audiovisuals, communicating systems
      (low-voltage), 239
  continuing-care retirement community
      (CCRC), 112, 116, 117
autonomy, future prospects, 127

baby boom generation
  demography, 2–3
  future prospects, 130, 133
backflow prevention, fire protection system,
    219, 230–31
background music, audiovisuals, 239
bathing facilities
  acoustical design guidelines, 260–61
  Alzheimer's care/dementia facility, 85, 87
  assisted-living residences, 79
  equipment for, 249–53
  international perspective, 311–12
  lighting guidelines, 271, 272
  long-term care/nursing home facility
      design programs, 56
bathrooms
  Alzheimer's care/dementia facility, 85
  assisted-living residences, 70–72
  independent/residential living
      apartments, 100
  lighting guidelines, 276
  long-term care/nursing home facility
      design programs, 51–53
bedrooms
  assisted-living residences, 67–70
  independent/residential living
      apartments, 100
  lighting guidelines, 276
bidding controls, building codes, 190
biological aging. *See* Aging process
biophilia, interior design, 282–83
boardrooms, audiovisuals, communicating
      systems (low-voltage), 239
brand leveraging, future prospects, 137
budgets. *See also* costs; finance
  cost management, 335–36
  feasibility analysis, project process and
      management, 150
building codes, 183–92. *See also* codes;
      regulatory issues
  accessibility, 189–90
  energy and sustainability standards, 186
  enforcement, 190
  federal, 184–85
  fiscal and bidding controls, 190
  international perspective, 314
  land use policy, 190–91

  local, 186
  overview, 183–84
  reference standards, 186
  regulatory issues, 186–91
    building systems and construction
        practices, 188
    life safety, 187–88
    public policy, 188
    space standards, 188
  state, 185–86
  waivers, 191
building height
  MEP systems, 219–20
  structural systems, 207–8
building information modeling (BIM), 296
building management system (BMS), 222
building systems. *See also* mechanical,
      electrical, and plumbing (MEP)
      systems; specific building systems
  codes, 216–17
  program, 216, 217–18
  regulatory issues, 188
building types, 4–5
bulk delivery, food service equipment, 247
bumper guards, wall protection, 295
Business and Institutional Furniture
      Manufacturer's Association
      (BIFMA), 297–98

cable television, communicating systems
      (low-voltage), 238
Canada, country-specific issues, 323
capital structure, finance and feasibility,
      344–45
caregivers, Alzheimer's care/dementia
      facility, 91–92
Caribbean nations, country-specific issues,
      323–24
carpets, interior design, 290
casual living style, interior design,
      281–82
cataract vision, 9
ceiling and building height
  electrical systems, 220
  fire protection, 220
  HVAC systems, 219
  MEP systems, 219–20

plumbing systems, 219–20
structural systems, 207–8
ceiling fixtures, lighting guidelines, 275
ceiling-mounted lifts, 251
Centers for Disease Control (CDC), 194
Centers for Medicare and Medicaid Services
(CMS), 184–85
central common areas. *See also* lounge areas
Alzheimer's care/dementia facility, 88–89
assisted-living residences, 76–79
continuing-care retirement community
(CCRC), 112–15, 117–19
independent/residential living
apartments, 103–5
lighting design guidelines, 270–71
long-term care/nursing home facility
design programs, 57–59
ceramic flooring, interior design, 292
ceramic wall tile, interior design, 294
certificate of need
long-term care/nursing home facility, 47
project process and management, 158
state building codes, 185
certified nursing assistant (CNA), long-
term care/nursing home facility, 42
China
aging, 3, 308, 309–10
climate, 312
country-specific issues, 315–18
markets, 314
choice, future prospects, 127
Circadian lighting, 244
circulation
assisted-living residences, 76–79
gardens and landscaping, 180–81
geriatric outpatient clinic, 21–22
vehicular, site planning, 171–73
classrooms, audiovisuals, communicating
systems (low-voltage), 239
cleaning, operation and maintenance costs,
327–28
cleanliness, 333–34
client leadership, project process and
management problems, 162,
164–65
climate
international perspective, 312–13

site assessment, 176
closed circuit television (CCTV),
communicating systems (low-
voltage), 237
closets. *See* storage
closings, finance and feasibility, 348
cluster model, long-term care/nursing home
facility, housing models, 39–40
codes. *See also* building codes; regulatory
issues
acoustics, 262, 264
Alzheimer's care/dementia facility,
93–94, 95
assisted-living residences, 79–80
building systems, 216–17
changes in, structural systems, 206
electrical systems, 217
emergency response/nurse call, 236
fire protection, 216, 217
geriatric outpatient clinic, 18
HVAC systems, 216–17
lighting, light levels, reflectance values,
and glare, 267–68
long-term care/nursing home facility,
35–37, 48, 52, 55, 56, 59–60
plumbing systems, 217
structural systems, 205–6
sustainability strategies, 197
co-housing, independent/residential living
apartments, 107
cold cathode fluorescent lamps,
lighting, 269
college campuses, future prospects, 134–35
color theory, interior design, 286
combined structural systems, 213
common areas. *See* central common areas
communicating systems (low-voltage),
235–40
access control, 237
aging process and, 6–7
audiovisuals, 239
emergency response/nurse call, 236
future prospects, 240
Internet access, 238
movement alarms, 236–37
networks and intranets, 238
operations systems, 239–40

overview, 235
point-of-sale (POS) systems, 239
proliferation of, 235–36
telecommunications, 237–38
television, 238
visual monitoring, 237
wireless technology, 238–39
community
adjacent land use, site planning and, 171
Alzheimer's care/dementia facility, 90
continuing-care retirement community
(CCRC), 119
integration into, future prospects, 129
international perspective, 313
community-based options
assisted-living facilities, 80
described, 4
interior design, 283
program guidelines, 14–17
community center, active adult community
(AAC), 122
compact fluorescent lamps, lighting,
268–69
composite steel, structural systems, 211
computer-aided design, template
dimensions, 296
conceptual change, future prospects,
139–40
concrete, precase, structural systems, 211
concrete frame, structural systems, 211–12
concurrent/sequential decision making,
problem areas, 165
condominiums, active adult community
(AAC), 123
confidentiality, geriatric outpatient
clinic, 24
construction documents, project process
and management, 159–60
construction and FF&E installation teams,
selection of, 160–62
construction manager, role of, 161
construction practices, regulatory
issues, 188
construction process
aesthetics, 221
costs, 221
ease of, structural systems, 208

construction process (*cont.*)
ease of construction, 220–21
international perspective, 313–14
mechanical, electrical, and plumbing
(MEP) systems, 220–22
project process and management, 162
schedules, 208, 220
consumer expectation, future prospects,
126–29
continuing care at home (CCAH)
community-based options, 17
future prospects, 142
continuing-care retirement community
(CCRC), 107–19
assisted living residences, 115
described, 5
design development, project process and
management, 159
finance and feasibility, 117, 350
future prospects, 117–19, 127, 129, 134,
135, 137
India, 311
international perspective, 313
long-term care, 115–16
markets, 110–11
organization, 108
program and design, 108–10, 111–15,
375–83
sponsors and settings, 108
user's profile, 107–8
continuity theory, social life, 11–12
contracts
construction documents, project process
and management, 159–60
continuing-care retirement community
(CCRC), 117
future prospects, 127
control systems
HVAC systems, 222
mechanical systems and aging process, 7
program design, 221–22
cook-chill method, food service equipment,
247–48
corner guards, wall protection, 295
corridors, lighting design guidelines, 271,
273, 274
cosmetic renovation, 301

Costa Rica, American ex-patriots in, 324
cost management, 335–41
problem areas, 165–66
program development, 335–36
relative costs, 336, 337–41
value engineering and life cycle cost
analysis, 336, 341
costs. *See also* budgets; finance; operation
and maintenance
Alzheimer's care/dementia facility, 96
assisted-living residences, 80–82
building systems program, 217–18
carpets, 290
construction, building systems
installation, 221
electrical systems, 219
future prospects, 127, 130, 135–36,
141–48
HVAC systems, 220, 221
independent/residential living
apartments, 105
interrelationships among building
systems, 221
life cycle costs, structural systems, 208
long-term care/nursing home facility, 38,
59–60
operation and maintenance, 325–29
quality prioritization, problem areas,
165–66
staffing, future prospects, 137
state building codes, 186
structural systems, 208–9
sustainability, 195–96
utilities, program, 216
cottages
Alzheimer's care/dementia facility, 96, 97
continuing-care retirement community
(CCRC), 113
independent/residential living
apartments, 102
covenants, monitoring of, finance and
feasibility, 348–49
crash rails, wall protection, 295
crypton, upholstery, 296–97, 328
cultural diversity, future prospects, 126
Cultural Revolution (China), 316
culture change, future prospects, 139–40

daylighting. *See also* lighting
design, 269
long-term care/nursing home facility, 48
sustainability strategies, 202–3
debt, finance and feasibility, 344–45
dehumidification systems, HVAC
systems, 226
deinstitutionalization, long-term care/
nursing home facility, 35
delivery schedules
construction process, 220
structural systems, 208
dementia. *See also* Alzheimer's care/
dementia facility; Alzheimer's
dementia
adult day care/adult day health programs,
30, 32–33
assisted-living residences, 67
long-term care/nursing home facility, 47
demography
adult day care/adult day health programs,
31
aging process and, 6
China, 315–17
future prospects, 125–26
India, 318–19
international perspective, 307
Japan, 318
Latin America, 323
lifestyle changes, future prospects,
129–35
senior living industry, 2–3
sustainability, 193–95
Department of Housing and Urban
Development (HUD), 145,
147, 348
departments of health (DOH),
licensing, 60
design
aging process and, 5–12
Alzheimer's care/dementia facility, 90–95
gerontology and, 10–12
project process and management, 159
dining facilities
acoustical design guidelines, 258, 260
Alzheimer's care/dementia facility, 85–86
assisted-living residences, 77, 78

continuing-care retirement community
(CCRC), 112, 118
food service equipment, 246–49
hospice facilities, 63–64
lighting guidelines, 271
long-term care/nursing home facility,
housing models, 38–39, 43
long-term care/nursing home facility
design programs, 53–55
direct digital control (DDC), building
management system (BMS), 222
disengagement theory, social life, 10
diversity
demography, 3
future prospects, 126
site design/planning, 179–80
door security, communicating systems
(low-voltage), 237
downspouts and gutters, 230
dry fire protection systems, 231
duct work, HVAC systems, packaged
rooftop units, 223–24
durability, operation and maintenance
costs, 329

earthquake, 207
ease of construction
building systems installation, 220–21
structural systems, 208
economy. See also budgets; costs; finance;
operation and maintenance
China, 316–18
senior living industry, 1, 4
Eden Alternative, 140
efficiency, operation and maintenance,
329, 333
elder cottage housing opportunities
(ECHO), 143, 145
elderly, sustainability, 193–95
electrical systems, 231–33
aging process, 216
ceiling and building height, 220
codes, 217
emergency power, 232–33
metering, 232
space requirements, 219
switchgear, 232

transformers, 231–32
elopement prevention systems,
communicating systems (low-
voltage), 236–37
emergency call systems, assisted-living
residences, 75
emergency power systems, 232–33
endocrine system, 6–7
energy codes, building codes, 186
energy conservation
regulatory issues, 188
sustainability strategies, 196
energy efficiency, 216
energy management and control systems,
sustainability strategies, 202
energy recovery unit (ERU), exhaust,
ventilation, 228
enforcement, building codes, 190
entrances, vehicular circulation, site
planning, 171–73
environmental competence, social life, 12
Environmental Impact Statements, 191
environmentalism. See sustainability
environmental safety
regulatory issues, 187–88
vinyl wall coverings, 293
environments, non-institutional, future
prospects, 127–28
equipment, 245–53
bathing, 249–53
food service, 246–49
medical, 245
mobility devices, 246
universal design, 245–46
equity, finance and feasibility, 345
ethnic diversity, future prospects, 126
Europe
demography, 3
markets, 315, 324
exercise areas. See also activity spaces; fitness
rooms
landscaping, site planning, 175
lighting guidelines, 271, 272
exhaust
general ventilation, 228
kitchen/grease ducts, 228
laundry and lint traps, 228–29

existing structures, adaptive reuse, 136,
143–45

fabrics, operation and maintenance costs,
328
fabric wall coverings, interior design, 294
Fair Housing Amendments Act (FHAA),
federal codes, 185
falls
ADA, 190
bathing equipment, 251–53
detection of, 242
family, Alzheimer's care/dementia facility,
91–92
fan coil systems, HVAC systems, 226
feasibility. See finance and feasibility
federal building codes, 184–85
fencing, gardens and landscaping, 182
feng shui, 312
fileserver-based databases, 243
filtration systems, ventilation, 227–28
finance and feasibility, 343–50. See also
budgets; costs
active adult community (AAC), 122–23
Alzheimer's care/dementia facility, 95
assisted-living residences, 80–82
capital structure and sources, 344–45
closings, 348
continuing-care retirement community
(CCRC), 117
costs and covenants, monitoring of,
348–49
finance team formation, 345–46
geriatric outpatient clinic, 24
government approvals, 346
hospice facilities, 64
independent/residential living
apartments, 105
long-term care/nursing home facility,
59–60
market feasibility, 346
preliminary planning analysis, 344
project process and management, 150,
157, 158
steps in, 343–44
underwriting, 346–48
variations by setting, 349–50

finishes, interior design, 285–86, 287–89
fire protection, 230–31
   aging process, 216
   alarms, 230
   ceiling and building height, 220
   codes, 217
   dry systems, 231
   regulatory issues, 187
   space requirements, 219
   sprinkler systems, 230–31
   wet systems, 231
fire pumps, fire protection system, 230–31
first cost, construction, building systems
   installation, 221
fiscal controls, building codes, 190
fitness rooms. *See also* activity spaces;
   exercise areas
   continuing-care retirement community
     (CCRC), 112, 114–15
   future prospects, 133
   independent/residential living
     apartments, 104–5, 106
flexibility
   Alzheimer's care/dementia facility,
     90–91, 93
   HVAC systems, 220
   structural systems, 206–7
flooring
   interior design, 290–92
   wayfinding, interior design, 287
fossil fuels, sustainability strategies, 200
fresh air requirements, ventilation, 227
fuel cell systems, sustainability
   strategies, 203
furniture and furnishings
   gardens and landscaping, 175, 182
   interior design, 295–98
future prospects, 125–48
   Alzheimer's care/dementia facility, 95–96
   assisted-living residences, 80–82
   conceptual changes, 139–40
   consumer expectation, 126–29
   continuing-care retirement community
     (CCRC), 117–19
   costs, 141–48
   demography, 125–26
   historical perspective, 125

   independent/residential living
     apartments, 107
   lifestyle change, 129–35
   service partnerships, 135–38

gardens. *See also* landscaping; site design/
   planning
   Alzheimer's care/dementia facility, 88–89
   assisted-living residences, 79
   landscaping, site planning, 175,
     179–82
gates, gardens and landscaping, 182
geothermal heat pumps, HVAC systems,
   224–25
geothermal systems, sustainability
   strategies, 203
geriatric outpatient clinic
   described, 4
   program, 19–24, 353–55
   sponsors and settings, 18
   user's profile, 17–18
geriatrics, gerontology compared, 6
Gerontological Services, Inc., 193
gerontology
   design and, 10–12
   geriatrics compared, 6
glare, lighting, 267–68
glaucoma vision, 9
government approvals, finance and
   feasibility, 346
grab bars. *See also* handrails
   ADA, 189–90
   long-term care/nursing home facility,
     52–53
   universal design, 245
Green House Project
   food service equipment, 247
   future prospects, 139–40
gross area per bed guidelines, long-term
   care/nursing home facility, 358
group size, Alzheimer's care/dementia
   facility, 91
guaranteed minimum price, 161
gutters and downspouts, 230

halogen lamps, lighting, 269
handrails. *See also* grab bars

universal design, 245
   wall protection, 295
health codes, local building codes, 186
health status, future prospects, 125–26
hearing loss
   acoustics, 255
   aging process, 8–10
   codes, 262, 264
   noise, HVAC systems, 215
heat-detection systems, fire protection,
   216, 230
heating, ventilation, and air conditioning
   systems. *See* HVAC systems;
   ventilation
heat pumps, HVAC systems, 224–25
high-rise construction, Asia, 310–11
historic preservation, regulatory issues, 188
hospice facilities
   described, 5
   dining facilities, 63–64
   finance, 64
   historical perspective, 61
   long-term care/nursing home facility, 33
   neighborhood model, 64
   program and design, 62–64
   settings, 61–62
   sponsors, 61
   support spaces, 64
   user's profile, 60–61
hot water
   distribution of, plumbing systems, 229
   fossil fuels, sustainability strategies, 200
   plumbing systems, aging process, 215–16
   solar collection panels, 227
house model
   Alzheimer's care/dementia facility, 83–87
   long-term care/nursing home facility,
     38–44
housing, demography, 2–3
Housing Choice Voucher (Section 8), 145
hurricanes, structural systems, 207
HVAC systems. *See also* ventilation
   aging process, 215
   assisted-living residences, 75
   ceiling and building height, 219
   codes, 216–17
   components, 222–27

dehumidification systems, 226
fan coil systems, 226
flexibility, 220
generally, 222
geriatric outpatient clinic, 24
heat pumps, 224–25
packaged rooftop units, 223–24
packaged terminal air-conditioning
    units (PTAC), 222–23
program, 216
radiant heating/cooling, 227
solar collection panels, 227
space requirements, 218
sustainability, 195
sustainability strategies, 200–202
variable refrigerant volume (VRV)
    systems, 226
control systems, 222
costs, 220, 221
noise, 215, 256
ventilation, 227–29
    exhaust (general), 228
    exhaust (kitchen/grease ducts), 228
    exhaust (laundry and lint traps), 228–29
    filtration systems, 227–28
    fresh air requirements, 227
hybrid cluster model, geriatric outpatient
    clinic, 21

Illuminating Engineering Society of North
    America, 267
independence, Alzheimer's care/dementia
    facility, 94
independent/residential living apartments,
    96–107
    bathrooms, 100
    bedrooms, 100
    central common areas, 103–5
    described, 5
    finance and feasibility, 105, 349
    fitness rooms, 104–5, 106
    food service equipment, 248
    future prospects, 107
    interior design finishes, 286
    kitchens, 103
    laundry facilities, 103
    lighting guidelines, 276

living room, 100–102
    planning issues, 105
    program design, 98–99, 371–74
    renovation and restoration, 300–301
    sponsors and settings, 98
    support spaces, 105
    user's profile, 96, 98
India
    aging, 308, 309
    climate, 312–13
    continuing-care retirement community
        (CCRC), 311
    country-specific issues, 318–19, 322–23
indoor air quality
    elderly, sustainability and, 194, 204
    vinyl wall coverings, 293
indoor environments, sustainability
    strategies, 204
indoor pool spaces
    acoustical design guidelines, 261, 264
    lighting guidelines, 271, 273
information technology (IT) specialist, role
    of, 236
Institute of Transportation Engineers
    (ITE), 172
integrated scenario planning (ISP), major
    renovation, 301–5
interior design, 279–98
    color theory, 286
    design process, 279–85
        affordability, 283–85
        casual living style, 281–82
        centrality of, 279–80
        community-based, 283
        hospitality focus, 280–81
        outdoor areas, 282
        repositioning, 283
        sensory stimulation, 283
        wellness, 282–83
    finishes, 287–89
    flooring, 290–92
    furniture and furnishings, 295–98
    guidelines, 289–90
    wall coverings, 292–95
    wayfinding, 287
    windows and window treatments, 295
International Building Code (IBC)

lateral forces, 207
    state building codes, 185
International Mechanical Code (IMC),
    aging process, 216
international perspective, 307–24
    adult day care/adult day health
        programs, 31
    aging process, 307–9
    Americas, 323–24
    building codes, 314
    China, 315–18
    community, 313
    demography, 2–3, 307
    India, 318–19, 322–23
    Japan, 318
    markets, 314–15
    program and design, 310–13
    Thailand, 323
International Plumbing Code (IPC), aging
    process, 216
Internet
    communicating systems
        (low-voltage), 238
    continuing-care retirement community
        (CCRC), 117
    independent/residential living
        apartments, 104
    senior living industry, 1–2
    technology, 243
intranets, communicating systems
    (low-voltage), 238
irrigation (watering), gardens and
    landscaping, 182

Japan
    aging, 307, 309
    climate, 312
    country-specific issues, 318, 320–21
    markets, 314–15
    program and design, 310

kaigo hoken system (long-term care
    insurance, Japan), 309, 318
keys, communicating systems
    (low-voltage), 237
kitchen/grease ducts, exhaust
    ventilation, 228

kitchens
Alzheimer's care/dementia facility, 85–86, 90–91
assisted-living residences, 73–75
independent/residential living apartments, 103
long-term care/nursing home facility design programs, 53–55
universal design, 245–46
Korea, markets, 314
Kosher preparation, food service equipment, 248–49

labor costs
Asia, 310, 312
operation and maintenance, 325–26
lamping options, lighting, 268–69
landscaping, site planning, 173–75. *See also* gardens; site design/planning
lateral forces, structural systems, 207
Latin America, country-specific issues, 323–24
laundry and lint traps, exhaust ventilation, 228–29
laundry rooms
exhaust ventilation, 228–29
independent/residential living apartments, 103
long-term care/nursing home facility design programs, 55, 56
leadership, project process and management problems, 162, 164–65
Leadership in Energy and Environmental Design (LEED)
building systems, 216
standards, 186, 188
sustainability strategies, 196
learning. *See* libraries; lifelong learning
LED lighting, 269
libraries
assisted-living residences, 77–78
continuing-care retirement community (CCRC), 112
future prospects, 134–35
independent/residential living apartments, 104
lighting guidelines, 270–71

remote learning, 243
licensing
assisted-living residences, 66, 79–80
geriatric outpatient clinic, 18
long-term care/nursing home facility, 45, 47, 59–60
Lifecare Type A Contract, future prospects, 127
life cycle costs
construction, building systems installation, 221
mechanical, electrical, and plumbing (MEP) systems, 217–18
operation and maintenance costs, 327–29
structural systems, 208
sustainability, cost benefits, 195–96
value engineering and, cost management, 336, 341
life expectancy
aging process, 6
India, 319
lifelong learning, future prospects, 134–35. *See also* libraries
life safety
code reference standards, 186
regulatory issues, 187–88
state building codes, 185
lifestyle
active adult community (AAC), 120
future prospects, 129–35
lighting, 265–77. *See also* daylighting
Circadian lighting, 244
control systems, 222
daylighting and windows, 269
design guidelines, 269–76
common areas, 270–71
corridors, 271, 273, 274
generally, 269
emergency power, 232–33
lamping options, 268–69
light levels, reflectance values, and glare, 267–68
long-term care/nursing home facility, 48, 53, 55
overview, 265–66
recommendations for, 276–77

sustainability strategies, 202–3
wayfinding, interior design, 287
light levels
lighting, 267–68
site design/planning, 178–79
linear fluorescent lamps, lighting, 268
living rooms
Alzheimer's care/dementia facility, 86–87
assisted-living residences, 72
continuing-care retirement community (CCRC), 112
independent/residential living apartments, 100–102
lighting guidelines, 273–76
lobbies, acoustical design guidelines, 258
local building codes, 186
local construction industry
building systems installation, 220
structural systems, 208
long-span structures, structural systems, 212
long-term care/nursing home facility, 33–60
continuing-care retirement community (CCRC), 115–16
described, 5
design programs, 47–60
bathing areas, 56
bathrooms, 51–53
central common areas, 57–59
kitchens, 53–55
nurses station, 56
resident rooms, 47–51
support infrastructure, 59
support spaces, 55–56
finance and feasibility, 59–60, 349
food service equipment, 246–48
gross area per bed guidelines, 358
historical perspective, 34, 35
housing models, 38–44
interior design finishes for, 285
lighting guidelines, 273–74
program, 37–38, 359–65
renovation and restoration, 299
senior living industry, 1
short-term and long-term rehabilitation programs, 44–47
sponsors and settings, 34–37
user's profile, 33–34

lounge areas. *See also* central common areas
  lighting guidelines, 270
  long-term care/nursing home facility,
    housing models, 38–39
low-voltage electrical systems. *See*
  communicating systems
  (low-voltage)
luxury vinyl tile, interior design, 290–92

macular degeneration, 9
maintenance. *See* operation and
  maintenance
major renovation, 301–5
management systems, operations systems,
  239–40
markets
  active adult community (AAC), 123
  China, 315–18
  cleanliness, 333–34
  continuing-care retirement community
    (CCRC), 110–11
  Europe, 324
  feasibility study, 346
  future prospects, 126–29
  India, 319, 323
  international perspective, 314–15
  lifestyle changes, future prospects,
    129–35
  program, 13–14
  renovation and restoration, 299
  sustainability, 193–95
masonry bearing walls, structural systems,
  210–11
materials
  acoustical design guidelines, 258–60
  indoor air quality, 204
  operation and maintenance costs,
    327–29
  sustainability strategies, 203–4
mechanical, electrical, and plumbing
  (MEP) systems. *See also* building
  systems; HVAC systems; specific
  building systems
  ceiling and building height, 219–20
  communicating systems and aging
    process, 7
  construction process, 220–22

life cycle costs, 217–18
noise and vibration, 221, 256, 261–62
Medicaid
  affordability, 141
  assisted-living residences, 79, 136
  federal codes, 184–85
  public approvals, project process, 158
medical equipment. *See* equipment
medical products. *See* equipment
medical records management, operations
  systems, 240
Medicare
  federal codes, 184–85
  hospice facilities, 61, 64
  long-term care/nursing home facility,
    45, 47
  public approvals, project process, 158
memory-care residence. *See* Alzheimer's
  care/dementia facility
mercury, 269
metal studs, structural systems, 209–10
metering
  electrical systems, 232
  plumbing systems, 229–30
Mexico, American ex-patriots in, 324
minimum energy reporting value (MERV)
  rating, filtration systems,
  ventilation, 227–28
minorities, demography, 3
mixed meals, food service equipment, 247
mobility devices, 246
moderate renovation, 301
Montessori approach, Alzheimer's care/
  dementia facility, 96
movement alarms, communicating systems
  (low-voltage), 236–37
multipurpose spaces, acoustical design
  guidelines, 260
muscular system, mechanical systems and
  aging process, 7–8
music, communicating systems
  (low-voltage), 239

National Center for Assisted Living
  (NCAL), 66
National Electric Code (NEC), space
  requirements, 219

National Fire Protection Association
  (NFPA)
  code reference standards, 186
  codes, 217
  licensing, 60
  local building codes, 186
  state building codes, 185
National Hospice and Palliative Care
  Organization, 60
naturally occurring retirement community
  (NORC)
  community-based options, 15–16, 17
  independent/residential living
    apartments, 107
needs definition, strategic planning and,
  149–50
neighborhood model
  Alzheimer's care/dementia facility,
    83, 87
  assisted-living residences, 67, 76
  hospice facilities, 64
  independent/residential living
    apartments, 107
  long-term care/nursing home facility,
    housing models, 40–42
nervous system, communicating systems
  and aging process, 6–7
net-to-gross factors, 352
networks, communicating systems
  (low-voltage), 238
New York Times (newspaper), 316, 317
noise
  acoustics, 255–57
  HVAC systems, 215
  MEP systems, 221
noise reduction coefficients, 257
non-institutional environments, future
  prospects, 127–28
nonprofit structure, assisted-living
  residences, 66
nurses station, long-term care/nursing
  home facility design programs, 56
nursing home/long-term care facility. *See*
  long-term care/nursing home
  facility
nursing units, long-term care/nursing home
  facility, housing models, 38

occupancy, project process and management, 162
occupational therapy, adult day care/adult day health programs, 28
old-old category, 125
ongoing operation and maintenance costs, 327–28
operation and maintenance. *See also* cost management; costs
  cleanliness, 333–34
  communicating systems (low-voltage), 239–40
  costs, 326–29
  efficiency, 329, 333
  furniture and furnishings, 297
  overview, 325–26
  problem areas, 166–67
  site design/planning, 180
  vinyl tile, 292
  vinyl wall coverings, 293
orientation
  fossil fuels, sustainability strategies, 200
  international perspective, 312–13
  site assessment, 176
outdoor areas, interior design, 282. *See also* gardens; landscaping; site design/planning
outsourcing, future prospects, 137

packaged rooftop units, HVAC systems, 223–24
packaged terminal air-conditioning units (PTAC), HVAC systems, 222–23
paint, wall coverings, interior design, 293–94
palliative care, long-term care/nursing home facility, 33
pantry, long-term care/nursing home facility design programs, 55
parking
  assisted-living residences, 79
  site planning, 173
  sustainability strategies, 197
paths, landscaping, 175
patient/escort-centered model, geriatric outpatient clinic, 20
patterns, flexibility in, Alzheimer's care/dementia facility, 90–91

paved areas, landscaping, site planning, 175, 181
payment. *See* costs; finance
personal hygiene, adult day care/adult day health programs, 28. *See also* bathing facilities
personalization, assisted-living residences, 75
personal locator systems, 241–42
physical therapy, adult day care/adult day health programs, 28
planning failure, project process and management problems, 162
planters, gardens and landscaping, 181
plant selection, landscaping, 175
play areas, landscaping, 175
plumbing systems, 229–30
  aging process, 215–16
  ceiling and building height, 219–20
  codes, 217
  fixtures and fittings, 229
  hot water distribution, 229
  metering, 229–30
  rainwater, 230
  space requirements, 218
point-of-sale (POS) systems, communicating systems (low-voltage), 239
poisonous plants and insects, site design/planning, 178–79
pollutants, site assessment, 176
pool spaces
  indoor, acoustical design guidelines, 261, 264
  lighting guidelines, 271, 273
population statistics. *See* demography
porcelain flooring, interior design, 292
porcelain wall tile, interior design, 294
porches, gardens and landscaping, 180
postal service
  assisted-living residences, 79
  continuing-care retirement community (CCRC), 117
precase concrete, structural systems, 211
pre-engineered structures, structural systems, 212–13
privacy
  Alzheimer's care/dementia facility, 90

future prospects, 126–27
geriatric outpatient clinic, 24
long-term care/nursing home facility, 50
private payor sources, future prospects, 136
products. *See* equipment
profit structure, assisted-living residences, 66
program, 13–123
  active adult community (AAC), 119–23
  adult day care, 24–33, 356–57
  aging process and, 5–12
  Alzheimer's care/dementia facility, 82–96, 369–70
  assisted living residences, 64–82, 366–68
  building systems, 216, 217–18
  community-based options, 14–17
  continuing-care retirement community (CCRC), 108–10, 111–15, 375–83
  control systems, 221–22
  furniture and furnishings specifications, 296–97
  geriatric outpatient clinic, 17–24, 353–55
  hospice facilities, 60–64
  independent/residential living apartments, 96–107, 371–74
  international perspective, 310–13
  long-term care/nursing home facility, 33–60, 359–65
  markets, 13–14
  operation and maintenance costs, 329, 333
  project process and management, 153–54
  space guidelines, 14
  structural systems, 205
Program for All-Inclusive Care for the Elderly (PACE), 16, 17, 32
project process and management, 149–67
  approvals and financing, 157, 158
  construction, 162
  construction and FF&E installation teams and purchasing, 159–62
  construction documents, 159–60
  design development, 159

feasibility analysis, 150
occupancy, 162
overview, 149
problems in, 162–67
program, 153–54
project team selection and organization,
  150–53
schematic design, 155–57
strategic planning/needs definition,
  149–50
project team
project process and management,
  150–53
selection and organization problems,
  163–64
public approvals
problem areas, 165
project process and management,
  157, 158
public housing, future prospects, 145–48
public institutions, assisted-living
  residences, 66
public payor sources, future prospects, 136
public policy, regulatory issues, 188
public toilet, long-term care/nursing home
  facility design programs, 55
purchasing, construction and FF&E
  installation teams and, project
  process and management, 159–62

quality prioritization
cleanliness, 333–34
problem areas, 165–66

radiant heating/cooling, 227
rainwater, plumbing systems, 230
ramps, ADA, 190
recycling, elderly, sustainability and,
  193–95
reference standards, building codes, 186
reflectance values, lighting, 267–68
Regenerative Community concept, 140
regional-based design, interior design, 283
regulatory issues, 186–91. See also building
  codes; codes
building systems and construction
  practices, 188

government approvals, finance and
  feasibility, 346
life safety, 187–88
public policy, 188
space standards, 188
rehabilitation services
adult day care/adult day health
  programs, 28
long-term care/nursing home facility, 33,
  44–47
relative costs, cost management, 336,
  337–41
remote biometric monitoring systems, 241
renovation and restoration, 299–305. See
  also adaptive reuse
assisted-living residences, 300
cosmetic, 301
independent/residential living
  apartments, 300–301
long-term care facilities, 299
major, 301–5
moderate, 301
need for, 299
rentals, active adult community
  (AAC), 123
replacement costs, operation and
  maintenance, 329
repositioning, interior design, 283
request for proposal (RFP), 152
request for qualification (RFQ), 152
residence characteristics, active adult
  community (AAC), 122
resident-directed care concept, 140
resident-free/individualized care
  concept, 140
residential quality
Alzheimer's care/dementia facility, 95
continuing-care retirement community
  (CCRC), 111–12
resident rooms
Alzheimer's care/dementia facility,
  83–85
assisted-living residences, 66–75
hospice facilities, 62–63
independent/residential living
  apartments, 98–100
lighting guidelines, 273–76

long-term care/nursing home facility
  design programs, 47–51
resident voice systems, communicating
  systems (low-voltage), 238
respiratory disease, elderly, sustainability
  and, 193–95
restoration. See adaptive reuse; renovation
  and restoration
retirement options, senior living industry, 1
reverberation, acoustics, 256–57
rhythms, flexibility in, Alzheimer's care/
  dementia facility, 90–91

Scandinavia, aging, 307
schedules
construction process, 220
structural systems, 208
schematic design
defined, 154
project process and management,
  155–57
seasonal affective disorder, Circadian
  lighting, 244
seating, gardens and landscaping, 175, 182
Section 8 Housing Choice Voucher, 145
security
communicating systems
  (low-voltage), 237
future prospects, 129
site assessment, 177
seismic activity, structural systems, 207
senior living industry
accessibility, 3–4
building types, 4–5
demography, 2–3
historical perspective, 1–2
options in, 4–5
sensory stimulation
aging process, 8–10
Alzheimer's care/dementia facility, 94–95
interior design, 283
sequential/concurrent decision making,
  problem areas, 165
service-enriched housing, future prospects,
  146–47
service partnerships, future prospects,
  135–38

sheet vinyl, interior design, 290–92
showers, bathing equipment, 251–53
sightlines, site design/planning, 178
signage
    Alzheimer's care/dementia facility, 93–94
    gardens and landscaping, 182
site design/planning, 169–82. *See also* gardens; landscaping
    accessibility, 179
    active adult community (AAC), 120–21
    adjacent land use relationships, 171
    aging process, 177–79
    diversity, 179–80
    guidelines for, 180–82
    landscaping, 173–75
    maintenance, 180
    overview, 176
    parking facilities, 173
    site assessment, 176–77
    size factors, 169–70
    structural systems, 207
    sustainability strategies, 197–98
    user's perspective, 177
    vehicular circulation, 171–73
size factors. *See* space requirements
small house movement
    food service equipment, 247
    future prospects, 139–40
smell, aging process, 8–10
smoke-detection systems, fire protection, 216, 230
social life, gerontology, 10–12
soils
    site assessment, 176
    structural systems, 207
solar collection panels, HVAC systems, 227
solar orientation
    international perspective, 312–13
    site assessment, 176
    sustainability strategies, 200
solar power, sustainability strategies, 203
sound transmission class values, 257
space requirements
    active adult community (AAC), 122
    assisted-living residences, 67, 76–79
    continuing-care retirement community (CCRC), 118–19

electrical systems, 219
fire protection, 219
HVAC systems, 218
international perspective, 310
long-term care/nursing home facility, 48, 53, 56
plumbing systems, 218
program, 14
regulatory issues, 188
site planning, 169–70
unit types, 351
spas. *See* bathing facilities
special care units (SCU)
    Alzheimer's care/dementia facility, 82–83 (*See also* Alzheimer's care/dementia facility)
    food service equipment, 248
special technologies. *See* technology; specific technological applications
speech therapy, adult day care/adult day health programs, 28
sprinkler systems, fire protection, 216, 230–31. *See also* fire protection
staff/administration-centered model, geriatric outpatient clinic, 20–21
staff and staffing
    efficiency in, problem areas, 165–66
    future prospects, 137
    international perspective, 312
    operations systems, communicating systems (low-voltage), 239–40
    vehicular circulation, site planning, 171–73
staff toilet, long-term care/nursing home facility design programs, 55
staff voice systems, communicating systems (low-voltage), 238
state building codes, 185–86
State of Seniors Housing 2010 survey, 325
steel frame and concrete plank, structural systems, 211
stone flooring, interior design, 292
storage
    Alzheimer's care/dementia facility, 84, 85
    assisted-living residences, 75
    international perspective, 310

strategic planning, needs definition and, project process and management, 149–50
structural systems, 205–13
    aesthetics, 209
    ceiling and building height, 207–8
    codes, 205–6
    costs, 208–9
    ease of construction, 208
    flexibility, 206–7
    lateral forces, 207
    life cycle costs, 208
    local construction industry, 208
    program, 205
    schedules, 208
    soil conditions, 207
    types of, 209–13
        combined systems, 213
        composite steel, 211
        concrete frame, 211–12
        long-span structures, 212
        masonry bearing walls, 210–11
        metal studs, 209–10
        precase concrete, 211
        pre-engineered structures, 212–13
        steel frame and concrete plank, 211
        wood frame, 209
subsidized housing, future prospects, 141, 145–46
support spaces
    Alzheimer's care/dementia facility, 89
    hospice facilities, 64
    independent/residential living apartments, 105
    long-term care/nursing home facility design programs, 55–56, 59
sustainability, 193–204
    building codes and standards, 186
    cost benefits, 195–96
    furniture and furnishings, 297–98
    future prospects, 137
    markets, 193–95
    regulatory issues, 188
    strategies for, 196–204
        adaptive reuse, 204
        alternative energy sources, 203
        fossil fuel use, 200

HVAC systems, 200–202
indoor environmental, 204
lighting and daylighting, 202–3
materials and waste management, 203–4
site factors, 197–98
water conservation, 198–200
switchgear, electrical systems, 232

taste, aging process, 8–10
tax credits, public housing, future prospects, 147–48
Tax Equity and Fiscal Responsibility Act of 1982, 61
technology, 241–44. *See also* communicating systems (low-voltage)
Circadian lighting, 244
community-based options, 16
fall detection, 242
Internet, 243
personal locator systems, 241–42
remote biometric monitoring systems, 241
remote learning, 243
telemedicine, 242–43
virtual reality therapy, 243
telecommunications, communicating systems (low-voltage), 237–38
telemedicine, 242–43
television, communicating systems (low-voltage), 238
temperature controls
communicating systems and aging process, 6–7
geriatric outpatient clinic, 24
Thailand
climate, 313
country-specific issues, 323
theaters. *See* auditoriums
timekeeping systems, operations systems, communicating systems (low-voltage), 240
toilets, geriatric outpatient clinic, 22–23
topography, site assessment, 176
touch, aging process, 8–10

traffic, vehicular circulation, site planning, 171–73
transformers, electrical systems, 231–32
transportation
community-based options, 15
sustainability strategies, 197
tubs, bathing equipment, 249–51

Underwriters Laboratories (UL)
code reference standards, 186
emergency response/nurse call, 236
underwriting, finance and feasibility, 346–48
United Kingdom, aging, 307
United States Census Bureau
aging process and, 6
future prospects, 125–26
senior living industry, 2–3
United States Green Building Council (USGBC), 196
universal design, equipment, 245–46
upholstery
furniture and furnishings, 296
operation and maintenance costs, 328
urban models
continuing-care retirement community (CCRC), 119
future prospects, 129
useful life, operation and maintenance costs, 329, 330–32
utility rooms, long-term care/nursing home facility design programs, 55–56
utility services, site assessment, 176

value, future prospects, 127, 130
value engineering, life cycle cost analysis and, cost management, 336, 341
variable air volume (VAV) box, HVAC systems, packaged rooftop units, 223–24
variable refrigerant volume (VRV) systems, HVAC systems, 226
vatsu (India), 313
vehicular circulation, site planning, 171–73
ventilation, 227–29. *See also* HVAC systems
codes, 216

exhaust
general, 228
kitchen/grease ducts, 228
laundry and lint traps, 228–29
filtration systems, 227–28
fresh air requirements, 227
vibration, MEP systems, 221
views, site assessment, 176
Villages Movement, 16, 17
vinyl wall coverings, interior design, 292–93
virtual reality therapy, 243
vision
ADA, 190
aging process, 8–10
lighting, 265–66
visual cues, wayfinding, interior design, 287
visual monitoring, communicating systems (low-voltage), 237

waivers, building codes, 191
walks, landscaping, site planning, 175
wall coverings, interior design, 292–95
wall protection, 295
wander alert systems, communicating systems (low-voltage), 236–37
wandering, Alzheimer's care/dementia facility, 92
waste management, sustainability strategies, 203–4
water conservation, sustainability strategies, 198–200
watering (irrigation), gardens and landscaping, 182
water source heat pumps (WSHP), HVAC systems, 224–25
wayfinding
Alzheimer's care/dementia facility, 92–94
geriatric outpatient clinic, 24
interior design, 287
Web portals, technology, 243
wellness
future prospects, 133
interior design, 282–83
wellness center, assisted-living residences, 78–79
wet fire protection systems, 231

INDEX

wheelchairs
  ADA, 190
  aging process and, 5
  gardens and landscaping, 180
  long-term care/nursing home facility, 34
windows
  daylighting, 269
  interior design, 295

wind power systems, sustainability
    strategies, 203
winds, structural systems, 207
wireless technology, communicating
    systems (low-voltage), 238–39
wood flooring, interior design, 292
wood frame, structural systems, 209

wood trim, wall coverings, interior design,
    294–95

years to payback, sustainability, cost
    benefits, 195–96

zoning, sustainability strategies, 197

BUILDING TYPE BASICS FOR SENIOR LIVING:

1. Program (predesign)
What are the principal programming requirements (space types and areas)?
Any special regulatory or jurisdictional concerns?
13–124, 351–83

2. Project process and management
What are the key components of the design and construction process?
Who is to be included on the project team?
149–67

3. Unique design concerns
What distinctive design determinants must be met? Any special circulation requirements?
125–48

4. Site planning/parking/landscaping
What considerations determine external access and parking? Landscaping?
169–82

5. Codes/ADA
Which building codes and regulations apply, and what are the main applicable provisions?
(Examples: egress; electrical; plumbing; ADA; seismic; asbestos; terrorism and other hazards)
183–92

6. Energy/environmental challenges
What techniques in service of energy conservation and environmental sustainability can be employed?
193–204

7. Structure system
What classes of structural systems are appropriate?
205–14

8. Mechanical systems
What are appropriate systems for heating, ventilating, and air-conditioning (HVAC) and plumbing?
Vertical transportation? Fire and smoke protection? What factors affect preliminary selection?
215–31

9. Electrical/communications
What are appropriate systems for electrical service and voice and data communications?
What factors affect preliminary selection?
231–40

10. Special equipment
What special equipment is required, and what are its space requirements? Is security a factor?
241–54